From Compositors to Collectors

PRINT NETWORKS

Previous titles in the series

This series publishes papers given at the annual Print Networks
Conference on the History of the British Book Trade

From Compositors to Collectors
ESSAYS ON BOOK-TRADE HISTORY

Edited by

John Hinks &
Matthew Day

OAK KNOLL PRESS
THE BRITISH LIBRARY
2012

First edition 2012

Oak Knoll Press
310 Delaware Street
New Castle, DE 19720
www.oakknoll.com
and
The British Library
96 Euston Road
London NW1 2DB
www.bl.uk/publishing

ISBN 978-1-58456-301-3 (Oak Knoll)
ISBN 978-0-7123-5872-9 (British Library)

∞ Printed in the United States of America on acid-free paper
meeting the requirements of ANSI/NISO Z39.48–1992
(Permanence of Paper)

Cataloguing-in-Publication Data
A CIP Record for this book is available
from both the Library of Congress
and The British Library

Contents

PART II: TO COLLECTORS

Introduction

MATTHEW DAY

At a time when the book as material object appears to be heading for obsolescence with purchases of electronic books matching and exceeding those of paper copies and the ever-increasing availability of texts through the Internet transforming notions of collection, it might seem perverse to publish a compilation of essays which focuses on the production, circulation and collection of texts and book-trade history. However, it is precisely at such moments of cultural transition that the need to understand more fully the practices of the past becomes crucial for, as Robert Darnton recently observed, 'to foresee the future ... [we should] look into the past'.[1] Investigating the activities of earlier ages both preserves their memory and facilitates a better comprehension of our own generation's transitions. No doubt, one driver for the rapid development of academic interest in book history is the realization that the material form of the text and the attendant practices of production, circulation and consumption are (at the very least) being challenged, even if they are not yet completely outmoded.

Studies in the history of the book have produced much good work on many aspects of textual culture ranging from detailed bibliographic studies, through investigations of manuscript and print culture, to censorship and the use and abuse of books. Particularly rich veins of study have been those on the book as material object – including such issues as paratextuality and the multi-agency nature of textual production – and on libraries and collections – whether they are considerations of the theory and nature of collections and collecting, overarching histories of libraries, or more detailed investigations elucidating the nature and history of particular collections.[2] Given such riches, what can this collection hope to add? The answer, we believe, is quite a lot.

---

[1] Robert Darnton, *The Case for Books Past, Present and Future* (New York, 2009), p. 43.
[2] Compare, for example, Alberto Manguel, *The Library at Night* (New Haven, 2006) with *The Cambridge History of Libraries in Britain and Ireland*, ed. by Peter Hoare et. al. 3 vols (Cambridge, 2006) and *Libraries within the Library: the Origins of the British Library's Printed Collections*, ed. by Giles Mandelbrote and Barry Taylor (London, 2009).

The papers that follow are a selection of those given at a series of *Print Networks* conferences between 2006 and 2009. They are brought together to shed light on the book trade's impact on three main aspects of textuality: creation, circulation and reception. By juxtaposing essays that consider these features, this volume seeks both to illuminate the book trade's involvement with them on a case by case basis and to offer an overview of the diverse functions and roles of the trade itself. Each essay therefore makes a valid contribution to knowledge in its own right and in relation to its own particular time period and geographical location. Yet, it is also to some extent representative of facets of the book trade. Thus, Mariko Nagase highlights the role of compositors in book production while Maureen Bell reminds us of the overlap of manuscript and print culture. At the other end of this book's time-frame, Rachel Bower focuses on one contemporary work, but her discussion of the packaging and presentation of texts is pertinent to publications from all periods. Her essay considers new writing but a number of the contributions comment on the way in which texts were repackaged and reinvented in different formats or in new collections. They are testimony to the importance of editors and publishers in the creation of texts, but these are only some of the agents involved in book creation and circulation that this volume considers. Designers and illustrators, binders and printers, the Catholic Church, Parliament and the United States Armed Services all had an impact on textual production and distribution. Moreover, while many books were new, others were old and, as the chapters by William Noblett, Lindsay Levy and Joseph Marshall make clear, were valuable for being so. Their essays bring to the fore the trade in second-hand and antiquarian books and, in addition to providing new information about those markets, offer insights into the competitive and compulsive nature of collecting. The private holdings of West, Scott and Cassidy can be contrasted with those collections intended to be more widely available such as the Linen Hall Library or those discussed by Keith Manley in his examination of twopenny libraries. Taken together, then, these essays disclose the multiple personnel and practices of the book trade.

It is worth examining in more detail the ways in which these essays speak to each other. This volume is divided into two sections, reflecting something of the traditional split between textual creation on the one hand and circulation and reception on the other. Convenient as this separation is, these essays disclose that it is an artificial divide. The

Print Networks series grew out of an interest in British book-trade history, and a number of recent histories of the book have been drawn up on national lines. By contrast, essays in this collection remind us that the book trade is not a national enterprise. Stephen W. Brown's paper on Smellie's *Philosophy of Natural History* and Jim Cheshire's on Tennyson's works reveal how texts first published in Britain crossed to America, while Helen Smith's discussion of the United States Armed Services Editions exemplifies their world-wide spread, including use by British armed forces. The global nature of modern textual production is clear in Rachel Bower's paper while the international nature of collecting, both ancient and modern, is evident in the papers of Daniel Starza Smith, Lindsay Levy and Joseph Marshall. These papers show that textual production, dissemination and circulation have traversed international boundaries for centuries.

Both parts of this collection also attest to the financial issues of the book trade. Papers such as those of Day, Hillyard, Cheshire, Allen and Bower show how commercial considerations had a significant impact on the contents, cost, format and form of books. Nor is this only an issue for publishers and financial backers of textual production. As the case of Fadia Faqir's *My Name is Salma* reveals, being deemed commercially unsuccessful can have an enormous impact on literary intentions and Faqir's experience, as an author keen to make her way, can be contrasted insightfully with Cheshire's analysis of Tennyson's experience at the hands of American publishers and indeed of his British ones. Commercial considerations also lay at the heart of the issues discussed by Keith Manley while William Noblett's and Lindsay Levy's chapters highlight the very real financial impact of bibliomania. Helen Smith's essay shows how even those items distributed to readers at no cost could attract value and how monetary considerations were only one of the motives that drove both the production and collection of texts. Indeed, it is the tension between financial and commercial and other factors such as authorial ambitions and vanity, editorial and publishing principles, and collectors' perceptions of their status, aims and aspirations that bring out the complexity of book history and its inherent tensions.

Nor is the question of collections merely restricted to the reception side of the hermeneutic circle. Many of those involved in textual production, whether authors, editors, printers or publishers, were themselves collectors who used their acquisitions to influence their textual creations. Whether authors such as Scott, gaining inspiration from the contents of his library, editors such as John Nichols, bringing together texts in new combinations, or publishers seeking to repackage texts for new markets, those involved in textual production were acquirers of texts just as much as purchasers and readers. However, many collectors, such as Titus Wheatcroft, were themselves authors or had their notion of an earlier author's *oeuvre* shaped by their own ability to gather texts. This was true both in the seventeenth and twentieth centuries irrespective of location.

There are, then, a number of common features which emerge from these papers which reach across the divide of production and reception. Yet, the essays also provide fruitful comparison within each section. Part I focuses on textual production and many of the essays serve as a reminder of the complex and problematic nature of notions of authorial intention. They highlight not only the multiple agency nature of book production but also the impact on a text that the ideas and wishes of agents, editors, printers and publishers have on it as it goes through the metamorphosis engendered by the processes of publication. Notions of authorship, these papers remind us, need to move away from concepts of single author functionality and intention towards ideas of partnership, teamwork or, if those terms suggest too comfortable a relationship, of rivalry. The pragmatics of textual production evident in the work of Jim Cheshire, Catherine Delafield and Rob Allen suggest that we should think of textual creation less as a smooth transition of authorial intention into published form and more as a struggle for dominance between the competing aspirations of the different agents involved in the process of production. Frequently, these participants had different agendas and, as Rachel Bower's paper makes manifest, authorial intention and commercial success have not always been easy bedfellows. On the other hand, it would be erroneous to oversimplify the issue, and to suggest that authors were uninterested in commercial success, or that publishers cared nothing for literary integrity or merit. As Stephen W. Brown's discussion of William Smellie's *Philosophy of Natural History* and Jim Cheshire's investigation of Tennyson's works demonstrate, authorial intention and commercial interests could dovetail effectively.

Cheshire's paper discloses, as do a number of others, the importance of format, form and extra-textual features to our understanding of book history. Gérard Genette's conceptualization of such paratextual features informs Rob Allen's analysis of Dickens's self-representation but is also pertinent to Rachel Bower's discussion of the packaging of Fadia Faqir's *My Name is Salma*.[3] The two papers provide contrasting examples of the control of this aspect of textual production. Allen shows that Dickens exerted a considerable degree of influence over this aspect of the text while Bower suggests that Faqir's ability to control the presentation of her work is minimal. Further aspects of the nature and use of paratextual features emerge from my own discussion of eighteenth-century editors' use of prefatory material to shape and comment on the text to which it was attached and to critique competitors' publications. Together, the essays in the first part of this volume help to exemplify and modify Genette's analysis by extending consideration of the purpose and use of the paratext.

While Part I focuses on the process of textual production, Part II considers the nature of collecting. Again continuities and differences across the period are evident. One of the things that emerges as consistent from these papers is the compulsive and sometimes competitive nature of an individual's collecting habits. Daniel Starza Smith's essay on Conway's seventeenth-century bibliophilia, William Noblett's analysis of James West's eighteenth-century mania, Joseph Marshall's record of Thomas Cassidy's hoarding and Helen Smith's discussion of the collecting habits of USA military personnel in the twentieth century all demonstrate its addictive and compulsive nature. Although the time periods in which these 'hunter-gatherers' lived and the book-trade environment in which they functioned were very different, it is clear that each was driven by a strong passion. By contrast, the papers of Brian Hillyard and Keith Manley highlight more formal, less personal collections and in doing so establish the very great differences in eighteenth- and twentieth-century attitudes towards libraries and librarianship, attitudes which seem very different again in the twenty-first century.

If the temporal aspect of these essays facilitates comparisons and contrasts, another function is to bring to light little-known libraries. The papers of Joseph Marshall and Helen Smith do just this and show not only the different reasons that libraries – both as collections of books owned by individuals and as larger accumulations held in

---

[3] G. Genette, *Paratexts: Thresholds of Interpretation*, trans. by J. E. Lewin (Cambridge, 1997).

buildings by institutions – come into being but also how they do so. The purposes of libraries are investigated in many essays. While some served the needs of individuals – whether to satisfy their reading habits or satiate their thirst for collection *per se* – others served communities. In some cases, indeed, individual collections, such as those of Cassidy and West, ultimately formed the basis of, or contributed significantly to, institutional holdings. Such additions to major holdings were no doubt welcome, but these libraries differed greatly from the more purposeful and targeted collections of the Linen Hall Library or twopenny libraries discussed by Arndt and Manley respectively. One of the things, then, that these papers make manifest is the diverse nature of libraries themselves and the ways that they come into being.

Although many libraries are collections of texts, not all collections of texts are libraries, as Stephen W. Brown's paper on songbooks demonstrates. His paper focuses instead on the way texts could be accumulated and recast to create new entities – in this case the song-book. The philosophy of these eighteenth-century publishers had something in common with that of the Council of Books in Wartime discussed by Helen Smith, bringing together a diverse range of texts with the intention of making them available to particular groups. The scale and motivations of the publishers and the Council may have been different but their role in the initial constitution of a collection was similar. Moreover, as both papers demonstrate, collecting texts helped to preserve them, though in different ways. In the case of the song-books, bringing texts into print may have prevented the loss that might have ensued if they had remained only in the oral tradition; in the case of the Armed Services Editions, by withdrawing texts from the ravages of war and the field of conflict, Armed Services personnel preserved what had only ever been intended as ephemeral.

Libraries and collectors – whether individual or institutional – accumulate their material through interactions with the book trade. These essays show just how multifaceted, diverse and complex are the relationships between the book trade, libraries and collectors. Keith Manley, Daniel Starza Smith and Helen Smith all demonstrate the impact of government on collections. Whether through regulation or commissioning, governments affected both the book trade and the way texts circulated. Iain Beavan's discussion of Fraser and Brian Hillyard's account of Ruddiman demonstrate too the very active involvement in the trade that librarians of earlier epochs could undertake, while many other papers explore the diverse ways in which book collectors acquired their texts from auctioneers, booksellers and agents.

The essays in this collection, therefore, seek to shed light on the ways in which the book trade intervenes in and shapes the production of texts and impacts on their circulation, consumption and collection. They focus on individual stories but the insights they offer extend beyond the particular to the general. Their methodological divergence is testimony to the eclectic nature and strength of book history, which is a broad church. Ultimately, these essays remind us that textual production, dissemination and consumption are not separate activities but complementary and deeply integrated. They highlight too that readers' experiences of texts are shaped not only by authorial intention and reader attitude but by the very varied and complex interventions of a diverse and multi-agency trade. What is true of a period when texts had a predominantly physical form is no less true now that we are in a digital age.

Contributors

ROB ALLEN is a lecturer in the English Department at the University of Amsterdam (UvA) and PhD Fellow in the UvA's Research Institute of Culture and History. His PhD project, on paratext and Victorian serial fiction, is due to be completed in December 2011.

SARAH CRIDER ARNDT is a Long Room Hub scholar in the Texts, Contexts, and Cultures programme based at Trinity College Dublin where she is currently working with Professor David Dickson towards completion of her PhD on a comparative analysis of the print cultures of provincial print centres in the Atlantic world.

IAIN BEAVAN retired in 2009 from Aberdeen University as Emeritus Keeper of Rare Books. He is currently an Honorary Research Fellow in Historic Collections at the same institution, where he is working with colleagues on the history and evolution of the University's library and archive collections.

MAUREEN BELL is Honorary Reader in English Literature at the University of Birmingham and Director of the British Book Trade Index (www.bbti.bham.ac.uk). Her *Catalogue of the Library of Titus Wheatcroft of Ashover* was published in December 2008 by Derbyshire Record Society.

RACHEL BOWER is currently undertaking doctoral research at the University of Cambridge. This research focuses on epistolarity and encounter in the late twentieth and early twenty-first century novel. Her wider research includes work on Arab anglophone writing, postcolonial institutions and the archive, and the impact of historical and political contexts on material texts. She is a co-convener of the 'Postcolonial Institutions' group at the Centre for Research in the Arts, Humanities and Social Sciences (CRASSH) in Cambridge, and also a member of the Centre for Material Texts at the University of Cambridge.

STEPHEN W. BROWN is Professor of English and 3M Fellow at Trent University in Canada. He is co-editor of volume two of the *Edinburgh History of the Book in Scotland, 1707-1800*.

JIM CHESHIRE is a Senior Lecturer at the University of Lincoln. He was editor of, and contributor to, *Tennyson Transformed: Alfred Lord Tennyson and Visual Culture* (Lund Humphries, 2009). He is currently working on a monograph about Tennyson's relationship with the publishing industry and co-writing a book about the stained glass of Lincoln Cathedral.

DANIEL COOK completed his PhD at the University of Cambridge with a thesis on the reception of Thomas Chatterton. Since then he has held an AHRC Research Fellowship on the *Cambridge Edition of the Works of Jonathan Swift* and a Leverhulme Early Career Research Fellowship at the University of Bristol, as well as a library fellowship at Harvard. He has published widely on eighteenth-century literature and biography and has edited such books as *The Lives of Jonathan Swift*, 3 vols (Routledge, 2011).

MATTHEW DAY is Head of English at Newman University College. He has research interests in print culture and early modern travel, and their intersection. He has published on censorship, paratexuality and the reception of early modern travel narratives in the eighteenth century. He was co-editor of *Periodicals and Publishers*.

CATHERINE DELAFIELD has previously taught at the University of Leicester and is the author of *Women's Diaries as Narrative in the Nineteenth-Century Novel* (Ashgate, 2009). She is currently researching the serialization of the novel in the Victorian periodical and has articles forthcoming on woman's life writing in the nineteenth century.

BRIAN HILLYARD is Rare Book Collections Manager at the National Library of Scotland. His research into Thomas Ruddiman dates back to the late 1980s when he was working on chapters for *The Encouragement of Learning*, a book of essays published in 1989 to celebrate the 300th anniversary of the formal opening of the Advocates Library.

JOHN HINKS is an Honorary Fellow at the Centre for Urban History, University of Leicester, and an Honorary Research Fellow in English at the University of Birmingham, where he edits the British Book Trade Index website (www.bbti.bham.ac.uk) and contributes to MA teaching at the Shakespeare Institute. He is Chairman of the Printing Historical Society.

LINDSAY LEVY is the Rare Books Cataloguer of the Advocates Library at Edinburgh. She has been cataloguing Sir Walter Scott's library at Abbotsford for the past eight years and is currently working on a doctoral thesis at the University of Glasgow on Scott as a book collector.

KEITH A. MANLEY was formerly editor of *Library History* and co-edited (with Giles Mandelbrote) volume two of the *Cambridge History of Libraries in Britain and Ireland* (2006). He was previously a librarian at the Institute of Historical Research, University of London, is co-convenor of the Seminar in the History of Libraries held at the University of London's Institute of English Studies, and is currently cataloguing the library of Agatha Christie for the National Trust.

JOSEPH MARSHALL is Rare Books Librarian at the University of Edinburgh. He formerly worked at the National Library of Scotland where he was Senior Curator of the Rare Books Collection.

MARIKO NAGASE is a PhD student at the Shakespeare Institute, the University of Birmingham. Her research investigates the formation process of play editing for publication and the elevation of the status of drama to literature in seventeenth-century England.

WILLIAM NOBLETT is an Under-Librarian at Cambridge University Library where he is Head of the Official Publications and Inter-Library Loans Departments. Educated at the Universities of Cambridge and Sheffield, his research interests are firmly based in the eighteenth century. He is currently working on Benjamin White and Samuel Paterson.

HELEN SMITH is a lecturer in English and Related Literature at the University of York. She has published on the early modern book trades and the material text and recently edited a collection on *Renaissance Paratexts* (Cambridge University Press, 2011). A monograph on women and book production in early modern England is forthcoming.

DANIEL STARZA SMITH completed his PhD, 'John Donne and the Conway Papers', at University College London in 2011, funded by the AHRC. His research focuses on the circulation of early seventeenth-century literature in manuscript and he has published on John Donne junior and on the history of the Conway Papers.

PART 1
From Compositors

The Publication of The Mayor of Quinborough (1661) and the Printer's Identity

MARIKO NAGASE

Thomas Middleton's *The Mayor of Quinborough* (1661) is a record of theatrical revisions that the play had undergone and, at the same time, of editorial procedures for producing the play as drama for the use of a reading public.[1] The quarto version (Q) of *The Mayor of Quinborough* preserves a variant reading of a play *Hengist, King of Kent, or the Mayor of Queenborough*, which was probably written between 1616 and 1620, the text of which is extant in two manuscripts – the Portland Manuscript (P) and the Lambard Manuscript (L).[2] The quarto text (Q) was published by Henry Herringman with no printer's name in 1661.[3] The printer has not yet been identified. The existence of both manuscript and print versions of *The Mayor of Quinborough* permits comparison of the texts before and after the theatrical revisions and literary editing for publication, and gives us a glimpse of textual editing as a play was transmitted from the theatre to the reader's mind. I contextualise this transition within the social framework of the contemporary English book trade investigating the networks of the stationers who made it possible for the

I am grateful to Yoshida Scholarship Foundation and the Overseas Research Students Award Scheme for their kind support for my research in England.

[1]   Thomas Middleton, *The Mayor of Quinborough* (London, 1661).

[2]   The Portland Manuscript (P) is owned by the University of Nottingham's Hallward Library (MS Pw V20) and is available as Thomas Middleton, *Hengist, King of Kent, or the Mayor of Queenborough*, ed. by Grace Ioppolo, Malone Society Reprints (Oxford, 2003). The Folger Shakespeare Library possesses the Lambard Manuscript (L) (MS J.b.6), whose text is represented in Thomas Middleton, *Hengist, King of Kent; or the Mayor of Queenborough*, ed. by R. C. Bald (New York, 1938). The Lambard manuscript was the text used for Thomas Middleton, *Hengist, King of Kent; or, The Mayor of Queenborough*, ed. by Grace Ioppolo, in *Thomas Middleton: The Collected Works*, ed. by Gary Taylor and others (Oxford, 2007). Further references to the two manuscripts will be made by their initials, 'P' and 'L'.

[3]   For a modern edition of the 1661 text, see Thomas Middleton, *The Mayor of Queenborough; or, Hengist, King of Kent*, ed. by Howard Marchitello (New York, 2004).

play to survive in print.[4] Although previous studies have not attempted to identify the printer of *The Mayor of Quinborough*, doing so is indispensable for discovering the division of the editorial work between the editor and the printer. By examining the stationers' networks this paper attempts to identify the printer of the play and to explore the editorial and compositorial practice of his printing house.

The earliest reference to the title of the play was made by Sir George Buc, Master of the Revels, in one of his cancelled playlists which includes plays composed between 1615 and 1620.[5] He names the play '[Th]e Maior of Quinborough' with a later inserted alternative title 'or Hengist K. of Kent' instead of the other way around as it appears in the title-page of P. What is intriguing about his naming of the play is that it is much the same as the title of the quarto version.[6] Among the plays detailed in the same slip with '[Th]e Maior of Quinborough' are 'The Tragedy of Jeronimo', which is probably Thomas Kyd's *The Spanish Tragedy* (c. 1589), and 'The Tragedy of Ham[let?]' (1601?)[7], both staged in Elizabethan times, years before Buc began his career as Master of the Revels.[8] Inclusion of some older plays with '[Th]e Maior of Quinborough' in the same list suggests that the plays were being considered for a court performance, and it seems unlikely that Buc had just licensed *Hengist* for the stage when he

---

[4]   Historical and sociological approaches to the transition from script to print have been embraced recently by David M. Bergeron, *Textual Patronage in English Drama, 1570-1640* (Aldershot, 2006); Adrian Johns, *The Nature of the Book: Print and Knowledge in the Making* (Chicago, 1998); Sonia Massai, *Shakespeare and the Rise of the Editor* (Cambridge, 2007); Andrew Murphy, *Shakespeare in Print: A History and Chronology of Shakespeare Publishing* (Cambridge, 2003); Julie Stone Peters, *Theatre of the Book, 1480-1880: Print, Text, and Performance in Europe* (Oxford, 2000); Michael Seanger, *The Commodification of Textual Engagements in the English Renaissance* (Aldershot, 2006).

[5]   For Sir George Buc, see Richard Dutton, *Mastering the Revels: The Regulation and Censorship of English Renaissance Drama* (Iowa City, 1991); Mark Eccles, 'Sir George Buc, Master of the Revels' in *Thomas Lodge and Other Elizabethans*, ed. by Charles J. Sisson (Cambridge, MA; 1933), pp. 409-507. The cancelled play-lists are Revels' Office waste. All four lists have been cancelled by cross lines or vertical or horizontal strokes. They were inserted to make corrections in Buc's *History of the Life and Reign of Richard III* dated 1619. For the lists, see Frank Marcham, *The King's Office of the Revels, 1610-1622* (London, 1925); E. K. Chambers, 'The King's Office of the Revels, 1610-1622, by Frank Marcham', *Review of English Studies*, 1 (1925), 479-84; Bald, *Hengist*, p. xiii.

[6]   Marcham, *King's Office*, pp. 10-11.

[7]   E. K. Chambers, *The Elizabethan Stage*, 4 vols (Oxford, 1923; repr. 1967), III, 395-97, 486-87.

[8]   Marcham, *King's Office*, pp. 10-11; Chambers, 'The King's Office', p. 481.

included it under the alternative title since the play had already undergone public performance before it was nominated for court performance.[9] If the play '[Th]e Maior of Quinborough' was added after it had been publicly staged, it is highly possible that the play had already undergone theatrical revision and been given the new title by 1619-1620 when the list was made.

The two manuscripts of the play are probably in different hands, but were evidently transcribed from the same theatrical script and share a general similarity of script.[10] They preserve theatrical notes referring to minor actors' real names, one of which is 'Brigs Robrt St Blackson' appearing six lines ahead of a dumb show in P.[11] The two scribes of P and L also faithfully copied down the sound directions such as 'Showte' and 'Musique / Musick' in the left margin where the company's book-keeper would have added them in the playbook for staging.[12] Theatrical annotators often inserted real names of the players in the margin pointing to their entrance or the speech headings of their roles, and stage directions for offstage sound in the left-hand margin of playbooks specifying its timing.[13] If either of the manuscripts was the playbook, those theatrical annotations would appear in a different hand from that of the rest of the text, but none of the stage directions was a later addition and all of them were copied down consistently in the same scribal hand as that of the rest of each manuscript.

The texts of P and L largely correspond with each other, both including two sections marked by vertical lines in 3. 1. and 5. 2.[14] That vertical lines were conventionally used to mark the text for deletion is attested by those left in many extant manuscript plays.[15] Most of the

---

[9]   That Buc had the plays in the lists under consideration for court performance has also been pointed out by Chambers, '*The King's Office*', p. 484.

[10]   Bald's view that P is 'a transcript by the same hand as that of *L*, and has many features in common with it' (*Hengist*, p. xxvi) is rejected by Peter Beal, *Index of English Literary Manuscripts*, 5 vols (London, 1980-93), I, pt. 2, 345. Ioppolo supports Beal in *Hengist* (2003), p. ix.

[11]   Ioppolo, *Hengist* (2003), p. 18.

[12]   Bald, *Hengist*, pp. xxix-xxx.

[13]   William B. Long, 'Stage Directions: A Misinterpreted Factor in Determining Textual Provenance', TEXT, 2 (1985), 121-37 (p. 126).

[14]   Bald, *Hengist*, pp. 38-39, 95-96; Ioppolo, *Hengist* (2003), pp. 30, 79-80.

[15]   In some manuscript plays such as *The Book of Sir Thomas More*, *Edmond Ironside, or War Hath Made All Friends*, and *The Launching of the Mary*, many lines marked by vertical strokes are crossed off. In *The Poor Man's Comfort* which is extant both in

play manuscripts which preserve the vertical strokes marking the text for deletion are judged to have been playbooks or books that had been designed to meet the needs of the stage, whether or not they were actually performed.[16] The absence of the passages marked by vertical strokes in Q *The Mayor of Quinborough* indicates that the marked passages were eventually cut from a later version of the play in accordance with the implicit instruction given by the vertical lines and that Q derives from the revised version. In addition, the correspondence of the two vertical lines between P and L suggests that the lines were also transcribed from their copy-text, which is undoubtedly a playbook; therefore, it seems safe to conclude that the passages marked by the vertical lines were cut in theatrical revision. The omission of the two passages in Q indicates that a playbook behind the copy-text of Q derives from the same antecedent as the manuscripts.

Whilst the traces of some theatrical revisions of the play are detected in the text of the dialogue, such as the 175 lines in the manuscripts not present in Q, and the 25 lines added to Q, those of editorial procedures are found in stage directions. Q omits two songs and twenty stage directions for music and noises out of the twenty-four standing in the manuscripts. Fourteen stage directions which describe the visual performance on the stage were introduced into Q.[17] Songs were usually kept separate from a playbook since they were used by musicians on stage. Printed plays often contain only headings for songs in the text and the actual songs printed at their back pages.[18] The absence of the two songs from Q *The Mayor of Quinborough* can be

---

manuscript and in print, like *Hengist*, two lines in a passage marked by a vertical stroke in the manuscript are omitted from the 1655 printed edition. See *The Book of Sir Thomas More*, ed. by W. W. Greg, Malone Society Reprints (Oxford, 1911; repr. 1961); *Edmond Ironside, or War Hath Made All Friends*, ed. by W. W. Greg, Malone Society Reprints (Oxford, 1928); Walter Mountfort, *The Launching of the Mary*, ed. by W. W. Greg, Malone Society Reprints (Oxford, 1933); Robert Daborne, *The Poor Man's Comfort*, ed. by Kenneth Palmer, Malone Society Reprints (Oxford, 1955), p. 27; Robert Daborne, *The Poor-Mans Comfort* (London, 1655), sig. C3ᵛ.

[16] For the lists of manuscript plays classified according to their purposes, see W. W. Greg, *Dramatic Documents from the Elizabethan Playhouses: Stage Plots, Actors' Parts, Prompt Books* (Oxford, 1931; repr. 1969), pp. 191, 237-369.

[17] Bald, *Hengist*, pp. xxix-xxxi.

[18] Tiffany Stern's analysis of lost songs of the early editions clarifies the theatrical function of moveable sheets of songs. Tiffany Stern, 'Re-patching the Play,' in *From Script to Stage in Early Modern England*, ed. by Peter Holland and Stephen Orgel (New York, 2004), pp. 151-77 (pp. 157-58).

attributed to the fact that they had been on other sheets of paper and lost by the time the printer's copy of the play was prepared. Since many of the stage directions for music and properties added by the book-keeper for theatrical use are found in the left margins of extant manuscript playbooks, a paucity of those in printed plays has been occasionally regarded as an indication that their copy-texts descended from authorial foul papers which did not receive theatrical annotations.[19] However, considering the signs of theatrical revision presented by the quarto text, the hypothesis about foul papers cannot be applied to the case of Q *The Mayor of Quinborough*. In fact, in conventional textual practice there was a tendency to eliminate theatricality from stage directions when reproducing a literary dramatic text.[20] Therefore, the elimination of the twenty stage directions for offstage sound effects may well be attributed to editorial intervention.

The fourteen stage directions incorporated by the editor in Q are later documents of the actions and the dramatic effects rather than the actual theatrical notes. They assist a reader who has not seen a performance in visualising the stage. Most of the directions which appear only in the quarto, explain the actions on the stage, which are difficult for a reader to know instantly from the text. At 1.2, Constantius kisses Castiza immediately after his line: 'I will do that for joy I never did / Nor ever will again'.[21] In the manuscripts, which have no direction disclosing Constantius's action, a reader cannot recognise that this has occurred until Vortiger's remark: 'This way of kissing' which appears four lines after the actual action. The direction appearing at the same time as his action in the quarto, 'As he kisses her, Enter Vortiger and

---

[19] William Shakespeare, *Measure for Measure*, ed. by J. W. Lever (London, 1965; repr. 2008), p. xxiv.

[20] Scholars have concurred that Ralph Crane removed theatrical directions for music and noises in transcribing his copy-text of F *2 Henry IV* to reproduce a more literary kind of text. See Eleanor Prosser, *Shakespeare's Anonymous Editors: Scribe and Compositor in the Folio Text of 2 Henry IV* (Stanford, 1981), pp. 19-50; John Jowett, 'Cuts and Casting: Author and Book-Keeper in the Folio Text of "2 Henry IV"', *AUMLA*, 72 (1989), 275-95 (p. 283); Gary Taylor, ''Swounds Revisited: Theatrical, Editorial, and Literary Expurgation', in *Shakespeare Reshaped, 1606-1623*, ed. by Gary Taylor and John Jowett (Oxford, 1993), pp. 51-106 (pp. 65-69). I am grateful to Professor John Jowett for drawing my attention to conventional textual practice of eliminating theatricality from literary dramatic texts.

[21] Middleton, *Mayor of Quinborough*, sig. B4ᵛ. For act and scene divisions and line numbers of the quarto, I follow Marchitello's edition. See note 3 above.

Gentlemen', helps a reader who has not seen a performance to understand the context, by reproducing his speechless action in the text.[22] Compared with the bare entry in the counterparts of the manuscripts, 'Enter Vort: & Gentle:', the first half of Q's direction which describes Constantius's action is judged to have been added later.[23] Although Bald suggests that some of the stage directions which describe the stage action in Q go back to the authorial manuscript, there is no reasonable explanation found for their absence in the manuscripts which descend from a playbook perhaps at one remove from the author's first draft.[24] Another sign indicating the editorial process involved in preparing the quarto text is a modification made to the point of timing where the entry directions appear. Many such directions are anticipated by several lines in the manuscripts except for those appearing at the beginning of the acts and scenes. The discrepancy was resolved in the quarto, and all the directions appear with the proper timing. The adjustments to the timing of the entry directions suggest that the text was edited for reading before publication. It is when a play is conveyed only through the text that the stage directions have to be adjusted at the appropriate timing.

Whilst the nature of Q's copy-text is revealed by the textual variance between the manuscripts and Q, when and by whom the text was edited remain a mystery. The circumstances of the publication of Q *The Mayor of Quinborough* offer clues to resolving this. The play was entered in the Stationers' Register with forty-seven other plays of the King's Men's repertoire by Humphrey Robinson and Humphrey Moseley on 4 September 1646. The Lord Chamberlain's list shows that the play remained in the company's repertoire in 1641.[25] The players did not sell the play even when they joined the King's Army on the outbreak of the Civil War in August 1642, since they believed they would win back their right to tread the stage under the protection of the King again.[26] However, the protracted theatre closure plunged the players into financial difficulties and the demolition of the Globe

---

[22] Ibid.

[23] Bald, *Hengist*, p. 20; Ioppolo, *Hengist* (2003), p. 15.

[24] Bald, *Hengist*, pp. xxx-xxxiv.

[25] E. K. Chambers, 'Plays of the King's Men in 1641', in *Collections*, I, pts. 4-5, Malone Society Reprints (Oxford, 1911), pp. 398-99.

[26] Leslie Hotson, *The Commonwealth and Restoration Stage* (Cambridge, MA; 1928), p. 8.

theatre in 1644, coupled with the disastrous defeat of the royalist forces at Naseby on 14 June 1645, deprived them of their vague hope of reopening the theatres. In March 1646, three months after the King signed an act 'for the putting downe of stage-playes', the King's Men presented to the Lords a petition for the payment of 'the arrears of salary which had been owing to them, before the wars, from King Charles'.[27] It was in this series of adverse circumstances that the King's Men decided to sell copies of their plays. In the light of the players' desperate situation, most of the copies sold to the stationers were probably theatrical scripts at hand. Robinson and Moseley only procured the right to a copy of *The Mayor of Quinborough* and never published it. The play was published after Moseley's death by Henry Herringman, a bookseller in the Lower Walk of the New Exchange. Moseley died on 31 January 1661, and on 13 February, Herringman entered *The Mayor of Quinborough* in the Stationers' Register.[28] There is no record showing that the ownership of the right to the copy was transferred from Moseley's successors to Herringman. There are two possible explanations for the double entries of *The Mayor of Quinborough* by Moseley and Herringman. One is that they acquired different copies and Herringman entered his in the Stationers' Register without knowing Moseley's entry. The other is that Moseley's copy was informally passed to Herringman. It is odd, however, that Humphrey Robinson and Anne Moseley described Francis Kirkman's legitimate competition for publishing *The Beggars Bush* as piracy in the title-page of their own 1661 quarto of the play while they overlooked Herringman's edition of *The Mayor of Quinborough*.[29]

A parallel case to *The Mayor of Quinborough* is found in the publication of Thomas Killigrew's *The Princess* in 1664. This play was also included in the forty-eight plays entered by Robinson and Moseley in 1646, but again Herringman re-entered the play with another eight plays of Killigrew's in 1663 without any reference to assignment of the

---

[27] Hotson, *Commonwealth and Restoration Stage*, pp. 19-20; *Mercurius civicus*, 3 December 1645, p. 158.

[28] Henry R. Plomer, *A Dictionary of the Booksellers and Printers Who were at Work in England, Scotland and Ireland from 1641 to 1667* (London, 1907), pp. 132-33; *A Transcript of the Registers of the Worshipful Company of Stationers: from 1640 – 1708 A.D.*, ed. by G. E. Briscoe Eyre, 3 vols (London, 1913; New York,1950), I, 245, II, 288.

[29] Francis Beaumont and John Fletcher, *The Beggars Bush* (London, 1661); Bald, *Hengist*, p. xv.

copy from Robinson and Moseley to Herringman.[30] The entry itself was undoubtedly made for the collected works of Killigrew published by Herringman in 1664. The absence of the entry which shows the assignment of the copy of *The Princess* raises a possibility of its informal transfer from Robinson and Moseley to Herringman. This is supported, if indirectly, by two pieces of evidence which are found in Killigrew's collected works.[31] In fact, besides the nine plays entered by Herringman in 1663, the collected works includes two other plays not entered by Herringman. It was Andrew Crooke who entered *The Prisoners* on 2 April 1640 and *Claricilla* on 4 August 1640 and published them in 1641 in one volume as '*The Prisoners and Claracilla. Two Tragae-Comedies*'.[32] These two plays appear in the 1664 collection published by Herringman with imprints which show Crooke's name as publisher. The imprints read, 'Printed by *J. M.* for *Andrew Crook*, at the Sign of the *Green Dragon* in St *Pauls Church-yard.* 1663.', yet in the 1664 reissue, Crooke's name was replaced by Herringman's.[33] W. W. Greg includes, among alternative explanations for the appearance and removal of Crooke's name, a possibility that the printer simply overlooked the publisher's name in the first issue. Yet the printer duly replaced the name of Thomas Cotes who printed the 1641 collection for Andrew Crooke with his own initials 'J. M.'. Furthermore, as Greg suggests, the separate signatures of *Claricilla* and *The Prisoners* in the 1664 collection seem to indicate that the inclusion of the two plays was an afterthought. Besides, it seems unlikely that in John Macocke's press where Herringman's name had previously been included in the imprints of the title-page for the whole collection and of the separate title-pages for all the nine plays, the compositor failed to replace Crooke's name while replacing the printer's name. What the presence of Crooke's name in the imprints of the two plays suggests is that Herringman and Crooke had planned to publish Killigrew's collection jointly. Greg convincingly concludes that 'some sort of joint publication was at first contemplated and that it was only after a portion of

[30]   *Transcript,* ed. by Briscoe Eyre, II, p. 331.
[31]   Thomas Killigrew, *Comedies, and Tragedies* (London, 1664).
[32]   *A Transcript of the Registers of the Company of Stationers of London; 1554-1640 A.D.,* ed. by Edward Arber, 5 vols (London, 1875-1894), IV, 478, 491; Thomas Killigrew, *The Prisoners and Claracilla* (London, 1641); W. W. Greg, *A Bibliography of the English Drama to the Restoration,* 4 vols (London, 1939-59), III, 1084-85.
[33]   Killigrew, *Comedies, and Tragedies,* sigs a1^r, f4^r; Greg, *Bibliography,* II, 748-49.

the edition had been issued that Herringman acquired Crooke's interest', hence the removal of the latter's name from the reissue.[34] Taking into consideration the facts and circumstantial evidence mentioned above, the absence of the record to show the assignment of the copies of the two plays indicates that Crooke's rights to the copies were privately transferred to Herringman. As far as the publication of the collected works of Killigrew is concerned, Herringman acquired the rights to the copies of the three plays, which had belonged to Moseley and Crooke without making formal entries in the Stationers' Register.

Moseley and Herringman seem to have worked more closely together soon after the latter took over the shop of John Holden in the New Exchange in 1653.[35] William Miller discovered that 'Roger Boyle's romance, *Parthenissa*, published in 1655, bears identically printed title-pages with variant imprints, one carrying Herringman's name, the other, Moseley's'.[36] This romance had been entered in the Stationers' Register by Herringman alone in 1653. Herringman participated in Moseley and Thomas Dring's joint publication in 1657, 1658, and 1660.[37] Although it was only during Moseley's last years that Herringman started his business association with him, they seem to have become close friends. Herringman's name is mentioned in

---

[34] Greg, *Bibliography*, III, 1086.

[35] Plomer, *Dictionary*, pp, 96-97, 100. Holden and Moseley were business associates. Their names appeared together as booksellers on the tile page of John Quarles's *Gods Love and Mans Unworthiness* in 1651. They jointly entered a copy of 'Cassandra, the whole ten bookes' on 7 January 1651/2 for the first time. The book was duly published in 1652, but its title page bears Moseley's name only. Reversely, a copy of *Cleopatra* was entered by Moseley alone on 3 January 1651/2, but he published the book in partnership with Holden in 1652. When Holden died in 1652, Moseley was assigned the full right to the copies of *Cassandra* and *Cleopatra* from Holden's widow, Susanna. John Quarles, *Gods Love and Mans Unworthiness* (London, 1651); *Transcript*, ed. by Briscoe Eyre, I, 387-88, 402; Gaultier de Coste La Calprenède, *Cassandra* (London, 1652); Gaultier de Coste La Calprenède, *Cleopatra* (London, 1652). William Miller's study suggests that Moseley was interested in Herringman because he succeeded Holden. William Miller, 'Henry Herringman, Restoration Bookseller-Publisher,' *Proceedings of the Bibliographical Society of America*, 42 (1948), 292-306 (pp. 299-300).

[36] Miller, 'Henry Herringman', p. 300.

[37] The works were: the first and second volumes of Honoré d' Urfé, *Astrea* (London, 1657); Olaus Magnus, *A Compendious History of the Goths, Swedes, & Vandals and Other Northern Nations* (London, 1658); the third volume of Honoré d' Urfé, *Astrea* (London, 1658); Monsieur de Vaumorière, *The Grand Scipio* (London, 1660).

Moseley's will and he left the younger bookseller 'Twenty shillings For a Ring'.[38] That Herringman enjoyed the fullest confidence of Moseley and his successors is indicated by his purchase of Moseley's 'most vendible copyrights – the poems of Cowley, Waller, Denham, Crashaw, Donne, and Suckling, and certain plays of Davenant and Jonson' in 1664 and 1667.[39] In the light of the above, the copy of *The Mayor of Quinborough* was probably informally passed from the Moseleys to Herringman, and it was most likely a playbook which was in use until the theatres were closed in 1642. If this was the case, the literary editing of the play described above would have been conducted after the copy fell into Herringman's hands. Nevertheless, the extent of the editor's work and that of the printer remains to be accounted for until the printer has been identified and his conventional practice investigated.

In the quarto text, the beginning of each scene and the 'Drammatis Personae' are ornamented by a row of florets (Figure 1). Each row did not exist as a block but was composed of individual florets.

Fig. 1 Sig. A3[r] of *The Mayor of Quinborough*, showing the row of florets, reproduced by permission of the Bodleian Library, University of Oxford

It is clear from the photographic image that each floret does not stand in a straight line. Some of them protrude slightly upward and others downward. Each floret is between 4.5 and 5 mm in length and 3 mm in width. Each has a crown with a wick and a stem of 3 mm in length with a round head and a flat base of 1 mm in width. Each floret has an arc at both sides of a stem. The top end of each arc forms a lozenge-shaped leaf, and its bottom end a foot with turned-up toes. On the waist of each arc is a loop. Florets of exactly the same shape appear in more than eighteen books printed between 1659 and 1668 by John

---

[38]   John Curtis Reed, 'Humphrey Moseley, Publisher', *Proceedings and Papers* [Oxford Bibliographical Society] 5 vols (Oxford, 1928), II, pt. 2, 57-142 (p. 141).

[39]   Miller, 'Henry Herringman', p. 300; *Transcript,* ed. by Briscoe Eyre, II, 341, 380-81.

Macocke. Other contemporary printers seldom used the same type of ornamental device except Macocke's regular business partners such as John Streater and James Flesher. Rows of florets of the same type as those of Macocke's printings appear in two books, *A Letter Sent from General Monck* and *A Letter from a Captain of the Army*, both of which were printed by John Streater and John Macocke in collaboration in 1659.[40] They also appear at the beginning of Chapter 10 of *Orbis miraculum* printed in 1659, whose imprint carries Streater's name alone as its printer, and in *De laudibus legum Angliae* printed by Streater and Elizabeth Flesher, widow of James Flesher, and Henry Twyford in 1672.[41] James Flesher also used a row of the same florets in the first page of Richard Allestree's *A Sermon Preached before the King* in 1667.[42] The conventional practice of borrowing and lending ornamental stocks among early modern printers and the existence of duplicate castings and copies have often made it difficult to identify the owner of an ornament.[43] However, that the same ornamental device is concentrated in books printed by Macocke, and that its occurrence is also confined within books printed by those related to Macocke, indicate that in all probability John Macocke was the owner of the device. The occurrence of Macocke's device in books printed by others helps us trace the relationships between the printers and to detect silent shared printing of Macocke.

Macocke was appointed printer to the Parliament with John Streater in 1660, and to the House of Lords with Francis Tyton. By 1668, he ran one of the largest printing houses in London, holding three presses, three apprentices and ten workmen.[44] He was also one of the most frequent business associates of Henry Herringman. In the STC, there are more than twenty records of Macocke's name as printer for Herringman. Among them are Thomas Killigrew's *Comedies, and Tragedies* (1664) (Figure 2), Ferdinand Mendez Pinto, *The Voyages and Adventures of Ferdinand Mendez Pinto* (1663) (Figure 3), John Den-

---

[40] George Monck Albemarle, *A Letter Sent from General Monck* (London, 1659); *A Letter from a Captain of the Army* (London, 1659).

[41] Samuel Lee, *Orbis miraculum, or The Temple of Solomon* (London, 1659); John Fortescue, *De laudibus legum Angliae* (London, 1672).

[42] Richard Allestree, *A Sermon Preached before the King* (London, 1667).

[43] Adrian Weiss, 'Bibliographical Methods for Identifying Unknown Printers in Elizabethan/Jacobean Books', *Studies in Bibliography*, 44 (1991), 183-228 (p. 191).

[44] Plomer, *Dictionary*, p. 121.

ham's *Poems and Translations with The Sophy* (1668) (Figures 4 and 5), John Dryden's adaptation of *The Tempest* (1676) and the second edition of the Beaumont and Fletcher folio (1679).[45] The conjunction of Macocke's device appearing in *The Mayor of Quinborough* and Herringman's name as its publisher considerably narrows down possible printers to one, John Macocke.

Fig. 2 Preface of Killigrew's *Comedies, and Tragedies*, sig. A0[r], printed by Macocke in 1664, reproduced by permission of Special Collections, Cadbury Research Library, University of Birmingham

Fig. 3 Ferdinand Mendez Pinto, *The Voyages and Adventures of Ferdinand Mendez Pinto* printed by Macocke in 1663, sig. A2[v], reproduced by permission of the Bodleian Library, University of Oxford

---

[45]   For Killigrew's collection, see note 31 above. Ferdinand Mendez Pinto, *The Voyages and Adventures of Ferdinand Mendez Pinto* (London, 1663); John Denham, *Poems and Translations with The Sophy* (London, 1668); John Dryden, *The Tempest, or The Enchanted Island* (London, 1676); Francis Beaumont and John Fletcher, *Fifty Comedies and Tragedies* (London, 1679).

Fig. 4 The Dedicatory Epistle of John Denham's *Poems and Translations with The Sophy*, sig. A2ʳ, printed by Macocke in 1668, reproduced by permission of Special Collections, Cadbury Research Library, University of Birmingham

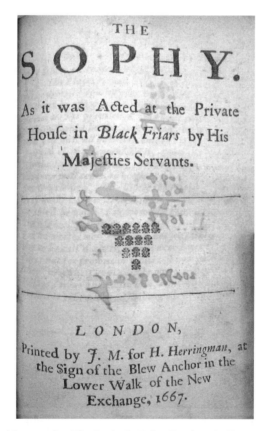

Fig. 5 Separate title-page for *The Sophy* in John Denham's *Poems and Translations with The Sophy*, sig. Aa1ʳ, printed by Macocke, reproduced by permission of Special Collections, Cadbury Research Library, University of Birmingham

In order to confirm whether the play was printed by Macocke or not, I have examined five original copies of Q and other texts printed by Macocke for identical damaged types.[46] As far as I could distinguish, at least five distinctly damaged types are recurrent in the five copies of Q *The Mayor of Quinborough*. A damaged Roman uppercase 'A' appears as the first letter for 'Act' at each heading of 1.1, 2.1, 3.1, 3.3, 4.1, 5.2 (Figures 6 and 7).[47] An italic uppercase 'E' whose two horizontal bars are distorted by pressure is found at two places for 'Enter'.[48] An italic capital 'K' for 'Kent' with a fracture in the middle of the upper diagonal line appears twice.[49] An italic lowercase 'st' ligature with a crack in its long 's' occurs twice and an italic lowercase 'v' for three speech prefixes for Vortiger has a chink close to the root of its right-hand diagonal line.[50] Among these five, I have only found one

Fig. 6 Damaged type 'A' in the heading of 1.1 in *The Mayor of Quinborough*, sig. A3ʳ, reproduced by permission of the Bodleian Library, University of Oxford

Fig. 7 Close up of damaged type 'A' of *Fig. 6*, reproduced by permission of the Bodleian Library, University of Oxford

---

[46] The copies are Special Collections, Cadbury Research Library, University of Birmingham (Selbourne Collection PR 2714.M29), Bodleian Library, University of Oxford (Douce M 673 and Mal. 245(9)), and British Library (162.k.11 and 644.f.10).

[47] Middleton, *Mayor of Quinborough*, sigs A3ʳ, C1ᵛ, D3ʳ, E3ᵛ, F4ʳ, I4ʳ.

[48] It occurs at sigs C2ᵛ, E3ᵛ.

[49] Sigs H1ᵛ, I3ʳ.

[50] The 'st' ligature occurs at sigs G1ʳ and K1ᵛ; the lowercase 'v' appears at sigs B4ʳ, D3ʳ and H1ᵛ.

outside of *The Mayor of Quinborough*. The identical damaged Roman uppercase 'A' reappears once only in each of two books which carry Macocke's name or initials as their printer. One of them is Denham's *Poems and Translations with The Sophy*. The damaged type 'A' appears in an essay entitled 'The Destruction of Troy', which has an individual title-page with the imprint showing Macocke's initials as its printer and the year 1667, one year earlier than the publication of the whole volume.[51] The damaged 'A' is found in the head title prefaced to the main text (Figures 8 and 9).[52] The title reads 'The Destruction of Troy, An Essay on the Second BOOK of *Virgil's Æneis*'. The type is 5 mm in both length and width. Types of the same size and shape were used to set the headings of acts and scenes and an advertisement of the title-page of *The Mayor of Quinborough*. They also appear in headings, some of the head titles and occasionally separate title-pages for individual plays in the Killigrew collection. In the running titles of Ferdinand Mendez Pinto's *The Voyages and Adventures* the same fount is also used. From their limited uses it is inferred that the number of the same fount kept by Macocke was small. This is probably one of the reasons that the damaged type 'A' was not thrown away for six years and reappeared in 1667. The damaged type 'A' suffers a fracture in its left leg at 1mm above the foot. The abrasion of the surface of the type occurring in the 1667 text clearly shows that it had been in use during the past six years, but I have been unable to find the identical type in other publications printed after 1661 and before 1667.

Fig. 8 Damaged type 'A' in the head title of 'Destruction of Troy' in John Denham's *Poems and Translations with The Sophy*, sig. C8ʳ, printed by Macocke in 1667, reproduced by permission of Special Collections, Cadbury Research Library, University of Birmingham

---

[51] See *Fig. 5* above.
[52] Denham, *Poems*, sig. C8ʳ.

When two images of the damaged type 'A' are juxtaposed (Figure 10) both the legs and feet of the one from the 1667 text look thicker, but this was caused by the ink's having blotted. A closer look reveals that the lines of the type are blurred by ink. Besides the fracture on the left leg, there are four other correspondences between the two images. The outer line of the left leg close to its root slightly falls inward probably because of some pressure. As a result, the inner side of the same part blisters. A chink at the left end of the bridge also corresponds in the two images. Its surrounding area has been abraded and the cleft has become wider in the 1667 text. The fractured area on the left leg has been buckled under the upward pressure. These correspondences of damage in the same fount 'A' across the two books printed at an interval of six years appear sufficient to confirm that the two letters are printed from the identical damaged type.

Fig. 9 Damaged type 'A' of Denham's *Poems and Translations with The Sophy*, British Library, C.131.b.17 (1), C8^r, reproduced by permission of the British Library

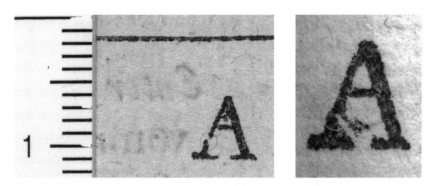

Fig. 10 Damaged type 'A' of *The Mayor of Quinborough* from *Fig. 6* and that of Denham's *Poems* from *Fig. 8*

The other book which carries the damaged type 'A' is William Hicks's *ΑΠΟΚΑ΄ΛΥΨΙΣ ΑΠΟΚΑ΄ΛΥΨΕΩΣ, or, The Revelation Revealed*, first published two years earlier than *The Mayor of Quinborough* (Figure 11).[53] Its imprint reads '*LONDON*, Printed by *J. Macock*, for *Daniel White*, and sold at his Shop at the Seven Stars in Sᵗ *Pauls* Churchyard, 1659'. The damaged type is used to set the first 'A' of a running title 'A Catalogue of divers Questions' at d3ᵛ, which is followed by 'In this Treatise Discussed' set in the facing page. Close examination of the type from an original copy of *The Revelation Revealed* at the British Library has led me to the conclusion that its damaged type 'A' was also set from the type identical with the one used both in *The Mayor of Quinborough* and in *Poems and Translations with The Sophy*. The damaged type 'A' in *The Revelation Revealed* is of the same size as the recurrent damaged type in the other two books.

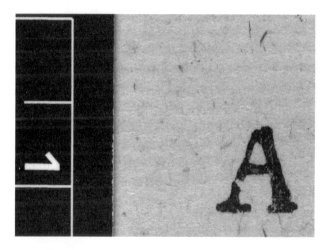

Fig. 11 Damaged type 'A' from William Hicks, *ΑΠΟΚΑ΄ΛΥΨΙΣ ΑΠΟΚΑ΄ΛΥΨΕΩΣ or The Revelation Revealed*, sig. d3ᵛ, printed by Macocke in 1659, reproduced by permission of the British Library

Its left leg is fractured at 1 mm above the foot, and the distance between the upper end of the fracture and the root of the leg is a little longer than 3 mm. The lower part of the fractured leg has been buckled under the upward pressure. These physical characteristics correspond

[53]   William Hicks, ΑΠΟΚΑ΄ΛΥΨΙΣ ΑΠΟΚΑ΄ΛΥΨΕΩΣ, or, The Revelation Revealed (London, 1659).

with those of the damaged 'A' in the other two books, but the distance between the upper end of the fracture and its junction with the bridge in the type of *The Revelation Revealed* is obviously shorter than that of the other 'A's. This has been caused by over-inking of the typeface which has made the bridge twice as thick as the others. The thickness of the right diagonal stroke of the damaged type 'A' used in *The Mayor of Quinborough* is about 0.6 mm, whereas that of *The Revelation Revealed* swells from 0.7 mm to 0.9 mm and reaches almost 1 mm at the junction with the foot. That the thickness varies in size from place to place in the right diagonal stroke and that its outline is uneven indicate that the ink oozed from the typeface. It is the oozing ink which makes the letter look thicker. If the blotted parts are discounted, the type is exactly the same size and shape as that in *The Mayor of Quinborough* and *Poems and Translations with The Sophy*, and also has a fracture on the same spot. It can be concluded that the damaged uppercase 'A' which occurs in Hicks's *The Revelation Revealed* was printed from the identical type as that used for printing *The Mayor of Quinborough* and *Poems and Translations with The Sophy*. The occurrence of the identical damaged type across the two books printed by Macocke clearly demonstrates that the type was owned by the printer at least between 1659 and 1667. The fact that the identical damaged type is recurrent in *The Mayor of Quinborough* confirms the theory that the play was printed by John Macocke, which has been proposed by the occurrence in the play of the same ornaments as Macocke regularly used in 1660s and of the name of Henry Herringman, one of the most frequent business associates of Macocke as its publisher.

In addition to these facts pointing to Macocke as the printer of Q *The Mayor of Quinborough*, another piece of evidence supports the view that the quarto edition of the play was produced at Macocke's press. I have examined the paper used in the British Library's two copies of Q *The Mayor of Quinborough* and twelve printings produced at Macocke's press between 1659 and 1662.[54] The paper used to print the quarto

---

[54] The twelve printings are following: William Hicks, *ΑΠΟΚΑ΄ΛΥΨΙΣ ΑΠΟΚΑ΄ΛΥΨΕΩΣ, or, The Revelation Revealed* (London, 1659; British Library [BL] shelfmark 4453.g.9); *Hē Katēchēsis Tēs Christianikēs Thrēskeias Syntomōtera* (London, 1660; BL shelfmark RB.23.a.8593); *A Declaration* (London, 1660; BL shelfmark cup 21.g.43/22); *Mercurius publicus* (London, 1661; BL shelfmark G.3810); Cicero, *Marci Tullii Ciceronis epistolarum* (London, 1661; BL shelfmark RB.23.a.33890); Abraham Cowley, *A Proposition for the Advancement of Learning* (London, 1661; Petyt Library);

shares common features with that found in four other printings produced by Macocke in 1661. All the leaves of paper in the two copies of the play have nine chain lines running at intervals of about 21 mm across the longer sides of a leaf. The distance from both the edges of the shorter sides of a leaf to the terminal chain lines is about half an interval of each chain line. Each sheet has a watermark of a pair of capital letters 'PH' in the middle of the longer edge at the side of the fold. They stand parallel to the chain lines with their heads pointing to the fore-edge and their feet close to the binding. 'P' is woven between the fourth and fifth chains and 'H' between the fifth and sixth from the top. The same watermark as that in *The Mayor of Quinborough* is found in the paper of the copies of Abraham Cowley's *A Proposition for the Advancement of Learning* (Figure 12), its reissue, *A Proposition for the Advancement of Experimental Philosophy*, John Meriton's *Curse not the King* and Fabian Philipps's *Ligeancia lugens*.[55] The first three books were printed by John Macocke for Henry Herringman in 1661, and the same paper was used from beginning to end. Cowley's two editions are in octavo, and the paper is folded in half between the two letters. Each of the letters appears upside down on the top corner of a leaf. Philipps's *Ligeancia lugens* was printed by Macocke for Andrew Crooke in the same year, and the same watermark 'PH' appears only on signatures C2^{r-v} in the book. The rest of the leaves in the book bear different watermarks of complicated pictures. Judging from the fact that paper with different watermarks is used throughout the book except for signatures C2^{r-v}, the leaf is probably a cancel. The paper used for the cancel leaf was obviously picked up from remnants of a set of paper supplied for Macocke's press to print other books including the above-mentioned three titles published by Herringman, one of which is The Mayor of Quinborough.[56]

Abraham Cowley, *A Proposition for the Advancement of Experimental Philosophy* (London, 1661; BL shelfmark 536.d.19/4); John Gauden, *A Pillar of Gratitude* (London, 1661; BL shelfmark 4105.h.5); John Meriton, *Curse Not the King* (London,1661; BL shelfmark 226.g.8); Fabian Philipps, *Ligeancia lugens; or Loyaltie Lamenting* (London, 1661; BL shelfmark 1379.c.8); Francis Fullwood, *The Grand Case of the Present Ministry* (London, 1662; BL shelfmarks 847.a.30 and 4106.a.19). I am grateful to Dr Hugh Adlington for his kind advice on the potentialities of paper identification.

[55] For locations of the copies consulted, see note 54 above.

[56] The two editions of Cowley's *A Proposition for the Advancement of Learning* are counted as one title.

Fig. 12 Watermarks 'H' and 'P' from Abraham Cowley, *A Proposition for the Advancement of Learning* printed by Macocke and published by Herringman in 1661, sig. A2ʳ (left), and sig. C7ʳ (right), reproduced by permission of the Petyt Library, Skipton Town Council

Allan Stevenson's study of the paper sequences in early printed books demonstrates that a printer in general preferred to use up his first supply of the running paper during a run before proceeding to use the next stock.[57] In fact, Cowley's *A Proposition for the Advancement of Learning* and Meriton's *Curse not the King* were entered in the Stationers' Register by Herringman on 13 February 1661, the same day as *The Mayor of Quinborough*, and all three books were printed on the same paper and published in 1661.[58] Considered on the basis of Stevenson's theory, these facts indicate that Herringman's copies of the three books were brought to Macocke's press at one time and printed in sequence. Since the same paper is localised within the books published by Herringman in 1661, it was probably Herringman who bought a sufficient set of the same paper for his publications and commissioned Macocke to undertake the printing of them.[59] Thus, the fact that the paper used to print Q *The Mayor of Quinborough* was the same as other printings of Macocke's in 1661 supports the earlier conclusion that Macocke is the printer of Q *The Mayor of Quinborough*.

Having established the printer's identity in this way enables us to consider his compositorial practice by comparing it with the extant

---

[57] Allan Stevenson, *The Problem of the Missale Speciale* (London, 1967), pp. 71-99.

[58] *Transcript*, ed. by Briscoe Eyre, II, 288.

[59] For a possible paper supplier, see Philip Gaskell, *A New Introduction to Bibliography* (Oxford, 1972), p. 142; John Bidwell, 'The Study of Paper as Evidence, Artefact, and Commodity', in *The Book Encompassed: Studies in Twentieth-Century Bibliography*, ed. by Peter Davison (Cambridge, 1992), pp. 69-82 (pp. 78-80).

manuscript printer's copy for eleven editions of William Lilly's *Merlini Anglici ephemeris* printed at Macocke's press from 1667 to 1677.[60] The copy was prepared by the author who left editorial directions for Macocke in printing the text. Comparison between the printer's copy and its printed text reveals the extent to which the author-editor was responsible for the editing of the text, and what alteration was made to the text at the discretion of the printer. If the patterns of the compositorial practices of Macocke's press are explained, they will give a clue to the extent of compositorial interference in editing Q *The Mayor of Quinborough*, and consequently to the nature of the copy-text of the quarto.

The manuscript of Lilly's work is written throughout in the same hand with a mixture of italics and secretary. Minor corrections were made throughout the text in the same author's hand, but he drew bolder lines to delete and rewrite. Different hands appear across the manuscript sheets, frequently using blacker ink to mark the beginning of a new page. They inserted a square bracket before each word which starts a new page, and put its page signature alongside in the left margin. The hands which are responsible for marking the page breaks are considered to be compositors' at Macocke's press. Basically, one compositor marked throughout one edition. In order to understand how the author-editor and the printer divided their editorial work in publication of Lilly's almanacs, I compared manuscript and print versions and investigated who took decisions about the following four compositorial issues: spelling; typeface; punctuation; and layout of the text.

Spelling

The author's spellings are standardised by compositors. Redundant letters of authorial spellings in the manuscript are removed in the printed editions. Where Lilly preferred to use 'wee', 'putt', 'penn', 'vppon', 'selfe' and 'harmfull' in his manuscript, the print counterparts present 'we', 'put', 'pen', 'upon', 'self' and 'harmful.' Contractions such as 'o^r', 'wth' and 'p[ro]duced' are expanded into 'our', 'with' and 'produced'.[61]

---

[60]   The manuscript is Oxford, Bodleian Library, MS Ashmole 241, fols 61^r-189^v.
[61]   MS Ashmole 241, fols 94^v-107^r, *passim*; Lilly, *Merlini, passim*.

Typeface

The choice of typeface appears to have been mostly trusted to compositors but where the author intended particular letters to be printed in italics, compositors followed his direction. For the 1670 edition, Lilly presented Latin quotations and prophesies coupled with proper nouns in distinct italics, and for the 1674 edition, he underlined the words he wanted to have printed in italics.

Punctuation

In most cases compositors followed the authorial punctuation. They occasionally added commas to make the text more readable and replaced dashes with colons.

Layout of the text

Compositors faithfully followed the divisions of paragraphs in the manuscript in the printed editions. Lilly frequently gave instructions for the layout of the figures. On folio 73^r of the manuscript copy for the 1668 edition, the author left a direction for a compositor. It reads 'hear place the figure of the Suns ingress with [a mark signifying another figure].' A similar direction appears at folios 74^r, 77^v, 82^v and 83^v. In a copy for the 1669 edition, Lilly wrote 'Mr Macock, if you find matter inough besides the figure, set it above' (Figure 13).[62]

One direction left on fol. 99^v suggests that Lilly was using the figures to fill in blank space to make his book look fuller. He wrote, 'Mr Macock, if you haue matter sufficient, you may leaue out what is marked to the end of this side – and this figure also'. Immediately after the author's epistle of his copy for the 1670 edition, Lilly asked Macocke to print an advertisement in the same edition. He stated, 'I desire you to print in this Advertisement as gracefully as you can it beeing for a widdow, besides the Elixar is of admirable Vertue' (fol. 95^v). Macocke printed the advertisement at the final page of the 1670 edition.

---

[62]   MS Ashmole 241, fol. 82^v.

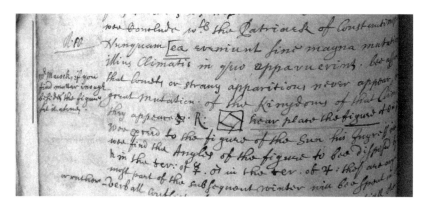

Fig. 13 Printer's copy of William Lilly's *Merlini Anglici ephemeris* for the 1669 edition, Bodleian Library, MS Ashmole 241, fol. 82ᵛ, reproduced by permission of the Bodleian Library, University of Oxford

It is clear from the printer's copy for Lilly's almanacs that the compositors at Macocke's press followed the author's editorial directions as much as possible. The printer's copy conveys the author's editorial intention, but we cannot hear the printer's voice. On the whole, what the compositors altered in their manuscript copy of their own accord was restricted to spellings. In the light of the compositorial convention at Macocke's press, the spellings standardisation in *The Mayor of Quinborough* is probably attributable to the compositors, but ascribing responsibility for the verse relineation to them questionable.[63] In Lilly's almanacs, the paragraphs are set as they appear in the copy prepared by the author. If the copy-text of Q *The Mayor of Quinborough* was prepared by the editor who was concerned as much about the layout of the text as Lilly, the verse might well have been relineated by the editor and the compositors would have followed their copy. However, the setting of the layout of Lilly's text cannot be directly applied to that of *The Mayor of Quinborough* because the relineation of the verse is a different kind of editorial practice from the dividing of the paragraphs. The issue of the verse relineation will need to be considered in a broader framework of early modern dramatic publication. What can be inferred about the divisions of the editorial work in *The Mayor of Quinborough* from the

---

[63] The verse relineation in Q has been conjecturally attributed to compositorial intervention by Ioppolo. See Grace Ioppolo, 'Revision, Manuscript Transmission and Scribal Practice in Middleton's *Hengist, King of Kent, or The Mayor of Quinborough*,' *Critical Survey*, 7.3 (1995), 319-31 (p. 322).

compositorial convention at Macocke's press revealed by the printing of Lilly's almanacs is that all the textual alterations had been made by the time the printer's copy was prepared and that the appearance of the text, such as the spelling and the typeface except the relineation of the verse, was decided by the compositors at the press.

Starting from the observations of the textual variance between the manuscript and printed versions, this essay has explored the editorial circumstances in which *The Mayor of Quinborough* reached print. In the attempt to investigate the extent of the textual editing of the play before and after it was sent to the press, non-textual pieces of evidence such as the ornamental device, the recurrent damaged type, the paper and the Stationers' Register's entries have led me through the networks of the stationers to the identity of the play's printer. The recurrent occurrence of the florets of exactly the same size and pattern across John Macocke's printings and *The Mayor of Quinborough* has pointed to a possible relation between the printer and the play. This has been strengthened by the fact that Macocke was one of the most frequent business associates of Herringman, the play's publisher. Bearing in mind the possibility that Macocke is the printer of the quarto, I have searched *The Mayor of Quinborough* and Macocke's printings for recurrent damaged types. The prime determinant in identifying the printer is only one broken type 'A', which occurs six times in Q *The Mayor of Quinborough* and once in each of the two printings of Macocke's, *Poems and Translations with The Sophy* and *The Revelation Revealed*. That the same paper used in *The Mayor of Quinborough* was also found in another two titles printed by Macocke for Herringman has supported the view that Macocke printed the play. The identification of the printer has enabled consideration of the conventional practice of the compositors at Macocke's press. The survival of the voluminous manuscript printer's copy of Lilly's *Merlini Anglici ephemeris* from Macocke's press has enabled comparison of it with the printed versions. The information derived from this comparison about the compositors' conventional practice at Macocke's press has provided an indicator of the extent of compositorial intervention in Q *The Mayor of Quinborough*. The clues to the central issues of the printing and publishing of that text have been provided by material aspects of the book such as the ornamental device, the recurrent damaged type, the paper and the Stationers' Register's entries. As if they were the footprints of the book-producers, the material pieces of evidence have indicated the paths they followed.

'Generally very tedious, often trifling': Promoting Eighteenth-Century Travel Collections

MATTHEW DAY

The admission, in the 'Preface' to *A New General Collection of Voyages and Travels* (1745), which was probably written by John Green, that 'the Adventures of Travellers are generally very tedious, often trifling' is somewhat surprising given its location at the front of a new, four-volume collection of voyage narratives.[1] The apparently self-defeating remark, however, turns out to be a rhetorical trope. Green claimed that travel accounts 'admit of large Retrenchments; [...] as several Travellers visiting the same Parts must necessarily repeat the same Things'. He suggested therefore that 'a vast deal of superfluous Matter [could] be expunged, and consequently Room made for introducing many more [narratives] than could possibly be brought into the same Compass'.[2] Asserting that judicious editing could reduce tedium and increase space for new material, the author turned a vice into a virtue and in critiquing earlier publications, promoted his own. This practice of overtly discrediting the work of others in order to justify the existence of one's own or assert its particular merits, is one which has now largely lapsed. Yet it demonstrates what Bourdieu, in his observations on the development of a field of cultural production, has termed 'the struggle between the established figures [of a field] and the young challengers'.[3] Bourdieu focuses his analysis on the nineteenth century and on the genres of poetry, drama and the novel. Yet, as I shall show, such behaviour was also an important feature of eighteenth-century voyage collections. It merits attention not only because of the light it sheds on historical publishing practices but also because it can help us chart the link between the development of a genre or field of cultural

---

[1] [John Green], *A New General Collection of Voyages and Travels*, 4 vols (London, 1745), I, p. vii.

[2] Ibid.

[3] Pierre Bourdieu, 'The Field of Cultural Production, or: The Economic World Reversed', trans. by Richard Nice, in *The Field of Cultural Production: Essays on Art and Literature*, ed. by Randal Johnson (Cambridge, 1993), pp. 29-73, (p. 60).

production, such as collections of travel narratives, and the justifications editors made as they sought to position their work in a potentially lucrative trade.[4] Taken together, they demonstrate Bourdieu's
assertion that 'the literary or artistic field is a [...] *field of struggles*
tending to transform [...] this field'.[5]

Travel writing was one of the most popular genres of the eighteenth
century. It was notoriously wide ranging and included both fictional
works and factual accounts of real journeys. The latter increased in
number significantly for several reasons including the promotion of
voyages of exploration and discovery, the rise of the Grand Tour,
developments in trade and commerce, increased colonisation, war and
buccaneering. Though often published as individual works, such
narratives also found their way into collections. Indeed, there was 'a
whole publishing industry of collections of voyages, multi-volume
editions to go on the library shelves of Georgian houses'.[6] Between
1695 and 1830, eighty-five distinct collections were published, averag-
ing between fifteen and twenty volumes each.[7] Amongst such a
plethora of publications, new entrants fought hard to justify their
existence and, in addition to puffing their own works, discredited those
of rivals whose authority they sought to overthrow.

Although an increasing amount is known about the practices for
book promotion in the eighteenth century, including the use of
advertising, book reviews, puffing, trade cards, and the mechanisms
and sales practices of the book trade, relatively little attention has been
paid to the practice of discrediting the work of rivals as a marketing
strategy.[8] Yet this seems to have been common. Moreover, although

---

[4]   For the lucrative nature of travel collections as a genre see Shef Rogers, 'Enlarging
the Prospects of Happiness: Travel Reading and Travel Writing' in *The Cambridge
History of the Book in Britain*, ed. by Michael F. Suarez, SJ and Michael L. Turner
(Cambridge, 2009), V, 781-90 (p. 786).

[5]   Bourdieu, 'Field of Cultural Production', p. 30.

[6]   Philip Edwards, *The Story of the Voyage: Sea Narratives in Eighteenth Century
England* (Cambridge, 1994), p. 3.

[7]   Rogers, 'Enlarging the Prospects', V, 781. See also G. R. Crone and R. A. Skelton's
survey which gives a useful overview of travel collections over a slightly longer period:
'English Voyage Collections, 1625–1846', in *Richard Hakluyt and His Successors*, ed. by
E. Lynam (London, 1946), pp. 63–140.

[8]   For a general overview see James Raven, *The Business of Books* (New Haven, 2007);
for discussion of the eighteenth-century book trade see *Books and their Readers in
Eighteenth-Century England* (Leicester, 1982) and *Books and their Readers in Eighteenth-*

the prefatory matter may not be an obvious location for promotional material, particularly when a volume was paid for by subscription, it is nevertheless true that editors' use of this paratextual space shows an acute awareness of their publications' relationship to the market. Usually, as we shall see, this involved denigrating rival works that had already been published but the second edition of John Harris's *Navigantium atque itinerantium bibliotheca* (1744) sought to spike the guns of later writers. Opining, 'such as are possessed of this Work, need never find themselves obliged to purchase another Collection falling within the same Space of Time', he implied that his collection would never become obsolete.[9] Not surprisingly, this view was not shared by later compilers. Nevertheless, the competitive nature of the trade in travel collections that it reveals confirms Bourdieu's observation that the struggle was both with contemporaries and those from whom one was separated in respect of time.[10] This confrontation was carried out with varying degrees of brazenness. John Campbell, the actual editor of Harris's second edition, certainly was not atypical in his willingness to criticize earlier works which he described as 'heavy and tiresome' or not fit for purpose. However, he was being rather disingenuous when he claimed: 'I would not have the Reader imagine, that I am giving him a bad Opinion of other Peoples Books, that I may recommend my own.'[11] Of course he was doing precisely what he denied and he differed from other compilers only in being more apologetic about it. As they made a case for their own particular take on what a travel collection should comprise, his rivals did not hesitate to disparage the contents, methodology and editorial practices of each others' collections.

Century England: New Essays (London, 2001) both ed. by Isabel Rivers; for reviews see Antonia Fraser, 'Book Reviewing' in *Cambridge History of the Book in Britain*, V, 631-48; for puffing, see Raven, *Business of Books*, pp. 282-93 and also O. M. Brack, Jr, 'Tobias Smollett Puffs his Histories' in *Writers, Books and Trade: An Eighteenth Century English Miscellany for William B. Todd*, ed. by O. M. Brack Jr. (New York, 1994), pp. 267-88; for trade cards, see Phillippa Plock, 'Advertising Books in Eighteenth-Century Paris: Evidence from Waddesdon Manor's Trade Card Collection', in *Books for Sale: The Advertising and Promotion of Print since the Fifteenth Century*, ed. by Robin Myers, Michael Harris and Giles Mandelbrote (London, 2009), pp. 87-107.
[9]   John Harris, *Navigantium atque itinerantium bibliotheca*, 2nd edn, 2 vols (London, 1744), I, sig. c2^v.
[10]   Bourdieu, 'Field of Cultural Production', p. 60.
[11]   Harris, *Navigantium* (1744), II, sig. 5B1^v.

At the start of the eighteenth century books of voyages were influenced by those of earlier centuries, particularly Richard Hakluyt's *Principal Navigations* (1589, 1598-1600) and Samuel Purchas's *Purchas his Pilgrimes* (1625).[12] Despite some overlap in content, these eclectic editions differed significantly in their approach. Hakluyt tended to provide full texts of narratives, copies of documents and accounts of sea-battles as well as voyages and travels, and arranged all this by geographical region, each in a broadly chronological sequence. He provided no illustrations and included just one map in each edition. Purchas more frequently excerpted sections from narratives or summarised them, was less methodical in his arrangement and did provide maps and a few illustrations. Developments in the book trade during the eighteenth century such as the cheaper production of images and publication in separates, as well as changes in navigational achievements, such as an increased number of circumnavigations, as well as the discovery of new geographical areas, inevitably impacted on the nature of travel collections but these extraneous factors were supplemented by what might be thought of as intrinsic, ideological differences about the most appropriate content, method and editorial practice suited to the genre. It was these aspects in particular that drew the ire of editors.

Complaints about the content of travel collections varied as the eighteenth century progressed. The attitude of each editor was shaped, of course, by their own particular desires as each sought to assert their own judgement and promote their publication. The issue of content went to the heart of disagreements about the nature of voyage collections. Editors made three types of complaint: that earlier works included irrelevant information and texts; omitted whole geographical regions and were therefore incomplete; and/or that they contained obsolete material, being insufficiently modern. In each case the criticism served as prelude to a puff for the edition in hand and an attempt to assert cultural hegemony.

Throughout the genre many editions, such as that published by John and Awnsham Churchill as *A Collection of Voyages and Travels*

---

[12]   Richard Hakluyt, *The Principall Navigations, Voyages and Discoveries of the English Nation* (London, 1589); 2nd edn as *The Principal Navigations, Voyages, Traffiques and Discoveries of the English Nation* (London, 1598-1600); Samuel Purchas, *Purchas his Pilgrimes*, 4 vols (London, 1625).

(1704), stressed that the purpose of such collections was to provide both enjoyment and utility. Consequently, they criticized earlier editions which they felt infringed this principle.[13] Thus, 'The Catalogue and Character of most Books of Travels' included in the 'Introductory Discourse' of the Churchills's collection lamented the 'great mass of useless matter, which swells our *English Hackluyt* and *Purchas*'.[14] In relation to Hakluyt's work, the anonymous author specifically objected to

> so many warlike exploits not at all pertinent to his undertaking, and such a multitude of articles, charters, privileges, letters, relations, and other things little to the purpose of travels and discoveries.

Purchas was condemned because he imitated Hakluyt too much 'swelling his work into five volumes in *Folio*'.[15] Perhaps in the light of this criticism the Churchills's collection focussed on voyages, rather than battles, and narratives rather than documents. Their compilation (which went through four editions) was in competition with the first edition of John Harris's *Navigantium atque itinerantium bibliotheca* (1705) which, by contrast, included accounts of the 'most remarkable accidents at sea and several of our considerable engagements' as well as documents such as papal bulls and letters patent.[16] The competing works made manifest two very different notions of what a voyage collection should be.

As the Churchills had done, editions throughout the century claimed to combine utility and pleasure, but their attitude toward these two aspects differed. Some editors, like Thomas Osborne in his *A Collection of Voyages and Travels*, supplied a range of geographical information because 'collections of this kind, heretofore published,' had been 'all or most of them blamed for the want' of it.[17] This desire to provide things that were useful was shared by John Meares who hoped that his *Voyages Made in the Years 1788 & 1789 from China to the North-West Coast of America* would contain 'instructions which future

---

[13] John and Awnsham Churchill, *A Collection of Voyages and Travels*, 4 vols (London, 1704), I, sig. a1ᵛ.
[14] Churchill, *Collection of Voyages and Travels* (1704), I, sig. k4ᵛ.
[15] Churchill, *Collection of Voyages and Travels* (1704), I, sig. m3ᵛ.
[16] Harris, *Navigantium* (1705), I, title-page.
[17] Thomas Osborne, *A Collection of Voyages and Travels*, 2 vols (London, 1745), I, sig. B1ʳ.

navigators may not disdain to consider'.[18] However, there was also an increasing emphasis on the entertainment to be derived from these works, perhaps a response to a growing reading public. These types of collections showed a very different attitude towards geographical and navigational content. Tobias Smollett lambasted earlier 'voluminous collections' because they were

> generally so stuffed with dry descriptions of bearings and distances, tides and currents, variations of the compass, leeway, wind and weather, sounding, anchoring, and other terms of navigation, that none but meer pilots, or seafaring people can read them without disgust.[19]

Showing a somewhat condescending attitude towards 'meer pilots', Smollett sought to prioritise the pleasure of readers over those whose skills had made the journeys possible: in effect he esteemed leisure over industry. A similar prioritisation, though giving greater credit to those involved in undertaking the journeys, was evident in 1774, where David Henry thought that such navigational data, 'though of infinite concern to future navigators, and without which the Voyages themselves would be useless, yet are of no moment to the generality of readers'.[20] These collections from the later eighteenth century were more concerned with providing entertainment for their readers than precise navigational information. They bear witness to Bourdieu's claim that those involved in literary production take part in a 'struggle to impose the legitimate definition' of it.[21]

It was not just in terms of what they included that voyage collections played out this confrontation. If early editions had been deemed to include irrelevant things, as the number of available texts multiplied, then later ones had to deal with the problem of having too much material. This led to a new criticism: that earlier editions were incomplete and inadequate. Thus, the second edition of John Harris's *Navigantium atque itinerantium bibliotheca* (1744) claimed that this

---

[18] John Callander, *Terra Australis Cognita* (Edinburgh, 1766), sig. A2ᵛ; John Meares, *Voyages Made in the Years 1788 & 1789 from China to the North-West Coast of America* (London, 1790), p. vii.
[19] [Tobias Smollett], *A Compendium of Authentic and Entertaining Voyages, Digested in a Chronological Series*, 7 vols (London, 1756), I, sig. A2ᵛ.
[20] David Henry, *An Historical Account of All Voyages Round the World*, 4 vols (London, 1774), I, sig. A4ᵛ.
[21] Bourdieu, 'Field of Cultural Production', p. 46.

work was 'much more perfect in its kind than the Scheme of any Collection of Voyages hitherto offered to the Publick' because whereas they 'relate[d] only to a few Countries', this would 'comprehend all'.[22] Despite this mid-century claim, fifty years later William Henry Portlock asserted that earlier editions were 'naturally confined to some PARTICULAR parts of the World' whereas in his own work the reader would find 'the most important Voyages to ALL the different parts of the World'.[23]

Such general assertions about earlier collections ran along side more specific disputes and we can trace the development of this debate through a series of editors' comments. They exemplify very clearly Bourdieu's observation that late entrants to a field of cultural production must establish a new position at the vanguard of the genre, displacing the whole series of earlier authors.[24] The first edition of John Harris's *Navigantium atque itinerantium bibliotheca* (1705) was condemned for its sins of omission. The 'Preface' to the 1745 *New General Collection of Voyages and Travels* published by Thomas Astley and probably edited by John Green, claimed that Harris's work lacked 'a great number of the most valuable Relations to be found in Hakluyt and Purchas [...] as well as many of those published since they wrote'.[25] Inevitably, Green claimed his own collection solved this problem but it too was subsequently attacked. The anonymously edited *A New and Complete Collection of Voyages and Travels* (1760), though it praised Green's edition for its sections on Africa and Asia, claimed it was deficient in relation to Europe. Unusually, the editors proposed a happy compromise suggesting their volume on Europe should be added to Green's which, 'would complete th[at] work, and render both more valuable'.[26] John Pinkerton, however, was much more aggressive. Engaging in an *ad hominem* attack on Green, whose 'judgement and taste' were 'by no means equal to his erudition', Pinkerton asserted that Green's edition suffered such a 'decline of estimation, that

---

[22]   Harris, *Navigantium* (1744), I, sig. a4ᵛ.
[23]   William Henry Portlock, *A New, Complete and Universal Collection of Authentic and Entertaining Voyages and Travels to All Parts of the World* (London, 1794), 'Preface', no page numbers.
[24]   Bourdieu, 'Field of Cultural Production', p. 60.
[25]   [Green], *New General Collection*, I, p. vi.
[26]   Anonymous, *A New and Complete Collection of Voyages and Travels* (London, 1760), 'Preface', no page numbers.

it stopped at the fourth volume'.[27] Wanting no part of such failure, Pinkerton implied that his collection should supersede Green's, and boasted that his was 'the most complete collection of voyages and travels ever laid before the Public in any age or country'.[28] His implication that earlier editions were inadequate, found explicit expression in Cavendish Pelham's 1810 compilation, *The World: or the Present State of the Universe being a General and Complete Collection of Modern Voyages*. Intimating a never to be achieved utopia, he belittled almost all previous collections when he claimed:

> A Collection of Voyages and Travels is rendered the more interesting and valuable, when its sources are from modern information. [...] the nearer such information approaches the present period, so much the nearer to perfection will our collection arrive than any similar productions which have preceded it.[29]

With an ever-increasing number of voyage accounts to select from, assertions of newness and modernity were an easy way to claim not only a niche in the market but also to be at its forefront. As they made such declarations, compilers spoke in terms both of completeness and currency as they sought to establish their works as the true exemplars of both taste and value, discrediting all that had gone before.

That currency, in particular, was a means of expressing authority within the field is demonstrated by the frequency with which the word 'New' appears in the titles of eighteenth-century collections. Editions could be new either because they had come to the market for the first time in the current format or because they contained previously unpublished narratives; on either ground they could be challenged. As early as 1704, John and Awnsham Churchill's collection dismissed Captain William Hacke's small compilation of four narratives published in 1699 which claimed to be *A Collection of Original Voyages* as having 'very little new in them, the three first being in other Collections, and the last being a very indifferent piece'.[30] More commonly,

---

[27] John Pinkerton, *A General Collection of the Best and Most Interesting Voyages and Travels in All Parts of the World*, 17 vols (London, 1808), I, sig. a1r; sig. a1v.

[28] Pinkerton, *General Collection*, I, sig. a3v.

[29] Cavendish Pelham, *The World: or, the Present State of the Universe being a General and Complete Collection of Modern Voyages*, 2 vols (London, 1810), I, 2.

[30] Churchill, *Collection of Voyages and Travels* (1704), I, sig. n1r. Hacke's edition was William Hacke, *A Collection of Original Voyages* (London, 1699).

the ready supply of genuinely new material gave editors the chance to condemn earlier collections as out of date. The anonymous editor of a compilation published by John Knox in 1767 claimed that the only three former editions of any note – those of Purchas, the Churchills and Harris – were all old fashioned and 'purchased rather from motives of curiosity than pleasure, rather by the antiquary than the modern reader'.[31] As William Mavor neatly put it in 1801,

> there is no general collection that is not become obsolete by time, or imperfect by subsequent discoveries [...]. Much, therefore, that has been accumulated by former assiduity, will be deservedly rejected by modern taste and learning.[32]

For Mavor, not only did these older collections contain information that was rather *passé*, but they also failed to meet modern standards of good judgement, knowledge and taste. Like those before him, Mavor aspired to be an arbiter of fashion and to put himself in the vanguard of voyage collection publishing.

This constant supply of new material, however, itself brought challenges if a collection was not to become impossibly expensive or unwieldy. Consequently, boasting about the number of works one had synthesised into a more manageable collection was another, different means of establishing the cultural capital of one's publication. Thus, the 1705 edition of *Navigantium atque itinerantium bibliotheca* reduced 'Four Hundred of the most Authentick Writers', into just two volumes while the second edition claimed the reader was 'enabled to make as ready a Use of upwards of *Six hundred Volumes*, the substance of which are included in these two'.[33] This was not just a question of quantity for there was an economic consideration as well. That such compression constituted value for money was most clearly articulated by Pinkerton at the start of the nineteenth century when he claimed to include 'the only travels worth preservation, in the former large collections in the English language, by Churchill, Green, Harris, the Harleian' in addition to 'many volumes of high price' now republished

---

[31]   Anonymous, *A New Collection of Voyages, Discoveries and Travels*, 7 vols (London, 1767), I, sig. A2ᵛ.

[32]   William Mavor, *Historical Account of the Most Celebrated Voyages, Travels and Discoveries from the Time of Columbus to the Present Period*, 25 vols (London, 1796-1801), I, sig. A4ᵛ.

[33]   Harris, *Navigantium* (1705), I, title-page; *Navigantium* (1744), II, sig. a4ʳ.

in their entirety. He confidently asserted, 'the purchaser of this work could not procure the same collection, in the originals, for less than three or four hundred pounds'.[34] While Pinkerton expressed the financial value of his collection in absolute terms, George Anderson claimed that by publishing his work in separates and thereby spreading the cost over a longer period, his publication would enable a wider readership of some particularly significant voyages: 'the Price of THIS WORK is rendered so moderate and easy, the WHOLE of CAP[t] COOK's VOYAGES &c. will be more universally read.'[35] All of these editions criticized earlier ones. They implied that their predecessors contained material which could be jettisoned without loss at the same time as suggesting that the material which merited reproduction could be provided more cheaply.

Yet, abridgement was a highly contentious issue for each editor inevitably cut to reflect their own tastes. Despite differences of opinion, however, as Carol Urness has noted, there seems to have been widespread condemnation of Samuel Purchas's practice. John Green's judgement was that the seventeenth-century editor's interventions had 'render[ed] his Work in great Measure useless'. Green also condemned Harris's first edition, and sought to 'restore all the Authors castrated in Harris'.[36] Repeatedly, those who aspired to digest – that is re-tell in their own words – rather than abridge volumes, claimed that earlier attempts were inadequate. Thus, the 'Preface' to Knox's edition dismissed abridgements on a number of counts – that they seldom went through more than one edition, were largely forgotten, were compiled with little judgement and printed with little care. The edition claimed that the poor quality of such productions derived from the fact that they were published by those whose aspirations were 'merely lucrative'; the editions, therefore, were appropriate only for 'the vulgar'.[37] In this move Knox's edition sought to distinguish itself from those that it positioned at the lower end of the market, thereby demonstrating the truth of Bourdieu's claims that those who operate at the bourgeois end of the market are in confrontation with those

---

[34]   Pinkerton, *General Collection*, I, sig. a2[v].
[35]   George Anderson, *A New, Authentic and Complete Collection of Voyages Round the World, Undertaken and Performed by Royal Authority* (London, 1784), title-page.
[36]   Carol Urness, 'Purchas as Editor', in *The Purchas Handbook*, ed. by L. E. Pennington, 2 vols (London, 1997), I, 121-44, (p. 122).
[37]   Anonymous, *New Collection* (1767), I, sigs A2[v]-A3[r].

positioned at the lower end, who they actively seek to prevent from moving up the hierarchy.[38] Such struggles were defined not only in terms of printing quality but also in terms of taste: abridgements were only fit for 'the vulgar'.

Abridgement was just one of a number of editorial practices to be disputed. Debates raged around whether narratives, if not included in their entirety, should be abridged or 'digested'. If digested, editors argued about whether they should use the first or third person.[39] The value of editorial comments was also debated, as were the merits of including illustrations, while the most heated discussion was reserved for arguments about editorial method, including the sequencing of narratives and the location of circumnavigations. Once again, developments in the genre were accompanied by a belittling of what had gone before and a desire to establish hegemony over other works in the field.

Voyage collections presented a particular challenge to editors because they had to find the best means of presenting events which might have occurred simultaneously but in different geographical regions. Editors mused over whether they should prioritise location, bringing together all the narratives pertaining to one area and ordering them in chronological sequence; or whether they should prioritise time, putting together all the narratives of a particular period, whichever part of the world they took place in. Editors also had to deal with the problem of circumnavigations which took many years to complete and which related to many geographical areas. As the eighteenth-century progressed, and the number of such voyages increased, so the problem became more severe. Whatever method of organization was used, compilers critiqued earlier arrangements defending their own method, which was inevitably presented as better than any previous attempts.

Editors were extremely critical of those collections which they deemed lacked coherence. Purchas again received particular condemnation. John Harris's second edition described *Purchas his Pilgrimes* as 'a very trifling and insignificant Collection: His Manner, for I cannot call

---

[38]   Bourdieu, 'Field of Cultural Production', p. 46.
[39]   See John Hawkesworth, *An Account of the Voyages undertaken by the Order of His Present Majesty for Making Discoveries in the Southern Hemisphere*, 3rd edn, 4 vols (London, 1785), I, sig. a1ʳ.

it Method, is irregular and confused, his Judgement weak and pedan-
tick'.[40] John Green also attacked the work but supplemented it with an
attack on Harris's first edition, observing that both of them made
'strange Havock with the Books' they edited and then juxtaposed in
such 'an abrupt and unconnected Manner'.[41] Perhaps somewhat
surprisingly, the second edition of Harris's collection also disparaged
the first for its method. Of course, such a policy was a means to signify
the perfection of the second edition in which the duplication evident
in the first was now avoided since its 'Two Volumes have been reduced
into their natural Order, and all the Parts so disposed, as to bring them
into their proper Places'.[42] Yet, despite the second edition's claims for
its careful arrangement, at the start of the nineteenth century James
Burney dismissed early voyage collections *en masse*, because he
claimed, 'Carefulness of arrangement [wa]s seldom to be found' in
them.[43] He then complained about the large number of works in the
genre which he thought sufficient 'to form a considerable library' but
which lacked 'any general arrangement'. He asserted that, along with
the length of some modern narratives, this lack of coherent structure
meant such publications acted only as 'vexatious obstructions to the
acquisition of knowledge in maritime geography'.[44] Inevitably, this
gripe justified his organization of a collection which aimed to provide
both method and compression.

The importance of method to editors of voyage collections should
not be understated and it is worth exploring some of their different
solutions to the problem. A number of publications gave extended
justifications for their own practice and prolonged critiques of that of
others. These commentaries provide further insights into the ways
editors positioned their works in the market. Thus, John Green
claimed to

> have deviated from the common Method of collecting, and instead of giv-
> ing each Author entire in the Order he was published, [had] separated his
> Journal and Adventures from his Remarks on Countries.[45]

---

[40]   Harris, *Navigantium* (1744), I, sig. B1[v].
[41]   [Green], *New General Collection*, I, p. vii.
[42]   Harris, *Navigantium* (1744), I, sig. c2[v].
[43]   James Burney, *A Chronological History of the Discoveries on the South Sea or Pacific Ocean*, 5 vols (1803-17), I (1803), sig. b1[r].
[44]   Burney, *Chronological History*, I, sig. b2[r].
[45]   [Green], *New General Collection*, I, p. vii.

However, Green's work was condemned by Pinkerton for its 'needless repetition' and deemed naïve for its assumption that

> voyages into distant countries, performed by distant persons, and even at distant ages, could form the subject of a history, which implies a continuous and well digested narrative of successive events in chronological order.[46]

This problem of how to weld into a smooth sequence a series of temporally and geographically disparate works troubled eighteenth-century compilers considerably. The second edition of Harris's collection dedicated nearly two folio pages to a discussion of method before concluding,

> the Design of this Undertaking is much more perfect in its kind than the Scheme of any Collection of Voyages hitherto offered to the Publick; for whereas They [...] are not disposed according to any regular Method, Ours will comprehend all and in an Order which gives them a perfect Connection.[47]

Harris's second edition, then, was claiming comprehensiveness and a smooth connection between voyages. Despite this claim, twelve years later Smollett complained about the inadequacies of earlier compilations critiquing them as impenetrable and intimidating to readers. In his *Compendium of Authentic and Entertaining Voyages* (1756), he offered another new methodology:

> we have deviated from the plan which has been followed by all other compilers of Voyages; instead of beginning with the circum-navigators, and classing together the different Voyages which have been made to the same countries; we have set out with the Discoveries of Columbus, and introduced every subsequent Voyage in chronological order, so as to form, as it were, The Annals of Navigation.[48]

He claimed thereby to 'give a new entertainment, and avoid the fatiguing sameness of immediate repetition'. Some eleven years later again, the anonymous *A New Collection of Voyages, Discoveries and Travels* (1767) published by Knox (and only a year after a second edition of Smollett's compilation), plagiarised the former *verbatim* in

---

[46] Pinkerton, *General Collection*, I, sigs a1ʳ⁻ᵛ.
[47] Harris, *Navigantium* (1744), I, sig. a4ᵛ.
[48] [Smollett], *Compendium*, I, sig. A3ʳ.

its criticism of earlier collections.[49] Now, however, Knox's work proffered yet another new method. Though it followed the pattern which Smollett rejected by combining together 'the different accounts of each country into one view, though they may have been made at very distant periods' it separated out 'Voyages' which 'visited the coasts only' and 'Travels' which ventured into the interior of countries.[50] This method, the editor inevitably claimed, would make the collection 'more authentic and useful than any hitherto published'.[51] This, however, did not prevent John Hamilton Moore in the 'Preface' to his *A New and Complete Collection of Voyages and Travels* from 'censur[ing]' earlier compilers even though he claimed it would be 'tedious to the reader and very disagreeable' to himself to do so.[52] He complained of the size of their works, their concern with trivia, their price and their method. Like Knox he separated 'Voyages' from 'Travels' and felt sure that readers would be fully satisfied with the efforts he had taken to 'entertain and please them [...] as no work of this kind [wa]s so well calculated for the purpose'.[53] Like so many other editions which belittled other publications, Moore's positioned itself as the best in its field.

Criticisms of editorial method were not, however, restricted to sequencing or structure. Writing style came in for severe scrutiny. Purchas again found himself scorned by eighteenth-century compilers. The Churchills's collection complained that he was 'Excessive[ly] full of his own Notions, and of mean quibbling [sic] and playing upon Words'.[54] The second edition of Harris's compilation stated the need to revise the first 'with Regard to Matter and Style'; John Green, moaned that the Churchills's publication brought together texts 'without Judgement or Care' and that the translations from foreign accounts were 'religiously scrupulous to retain all Superfluities both in the Matter and Stile'.[55] Smollett aimed to improve earlier collections

---

[49] Compare [Smollett], *Compendium*, I, sigs A2^r-A3^r with Anonymous, *New Collection*, I, sigs A3^{r-v}.

[50] Anonymous, *New Collection*, I, sigs A4^{r-v}.

[51] Ibid., I, sig. A3^v.

[52] John Hamilton Moore, *A New and Complete Collection of Voyages and Travels*, 2 vols (London, [1778]), I, no page numbers.

[53] Moore, *New and Complete Collection*, II, sig. T2^v.

[54] Churchill, *Collection of Voyages and Travels* (1704), I, sig. m4^v.

[55] [Green], *New General Collection*, I, p. v.

by promising to 'polish the stile, strengthen the connexion of incidents, and animate the narration'.[56] However, the anonymous *A New and Complete Collection of Voyages and Travels* (1760) could still claim that many voyage collections were 'written in so careless a manner, with regard to style and method, that few will take the trouble of perusing them'.[57]

If editors' style was one subject for complaint, the accretions with which they surrounded texts were another. Harris's second edition complained of the 'frequent Censures, long Disputes, and tedious Digressions' evident in collections that preceded it.[58] Green berated Harris's first edition for 'adding Fancies of his own, which alter the Sense' and was in turn chastised by Pinkerton who raged at Green's habit of providing an introduction to texts and then commenting on them.[59] This practice, claimed Pinkerton, resulted in 'solemn discussions of mere trifles', 'notes replete with learned contradictions' and 'minute and microscopic balancing of one straw against another' which 'disgust[ed] the most patient reader'.[60] Given the efforts that editors took to compile their collections and the attention they paid to editorial decisions, the key selling point of *The World Display'd* (1759), which had an introduction by Samuel Johnson, is perhaps ironic. It lacked any discussion of editorial method or critique of earlier collections. Such a policy made sense when it claimed prominently on its title-page that it published its narratives with 'the Conjectures and Interpolations of several vain Editors and Translators [...] expunged'.[61]

This survey of eighteenth-century travel collections demonstrates how development of a genre was accompanied by a willingness to criticise publicly earlier works in the field as new entrants sought to find their niche in the market. I want to suggest that such conduct was an essential part of the eighteenth-century book trade's promotional strategies and should be considered alongside puffing as an important means of positioning texts within a genre. The practice of discrediting earlier travel collections was as wide ranging as the genre itself and all

---

[56]   [Smollett], *Compendium*, I, sigs A2^v-A3^r.

[57]   Anonymous, *New and Complete Collection of Voyages*, 'Preface', no page numbers.

[58]   Harris, *Navigantium* (1744), II, sig. 5B1^v.

[59]   [Green], *New General Collection*, I, p. vi.

[60]   Pinkerton, *General Collection*, I, sigs a1^v-a2^r; I, sig. a1^v.

[61]   Anonymous, *The World Display'd or, A Curious Collection of Voyages and Travels*, 12 vols (London, 1759), I, title-page.

aspects of compilations were open to criticism. This included the contents – which were appraised for their completeness, relevance and currency – and the methodology – assessed for the coherence it brought to a collection, the treatment of texts it entailed, and the ease with which readers could extract from it both pleasure and instruction. Other editorial factors such as style and editorial commentary were also evaluated. These critiques exemplified the truth of Bourdieu's claim that those entering a field of cultural production needed to assert their authority. They would seek to position themselves at the forefront of the field, while those at the top end of the market would seek to keep down those they wanted to position at the lower end. At the conclusion of his essay on the field of cultural production, surveying novels, poetry and drama, Bourdieu wondered about the extent to which those who were involved in it were aware of the struggle in which they were engaged and of the nature of it as a game.[62] The criticisms of earlier publications suggest that editors of eighteenth-century travel collections were very much aware of the struggle but the vehemence with which they engaged in them suggests they thought it was rather more important than a game.

---

[62] Bourdieu, 'Field of Cultural Production', p. 73.

Labor ipse voluptas:
John Nichols's Swiftiana

DANIEL COOK

So, – to John Nichols in the Shades, ten out of ten for persistence.[1]

Jonathan Swift's corpus has long benefited from the industrious hands of skilful textual scholars who were also enthusiastic collectors of manuscripts and Swiftiana. Sir Harold Williams and Herbert Davis, in particular, gathered a substantial amount of new materials for their mid-twentieth century editions of Swift's poems and prose respectively. To date, James Woolley, John Irwin Fischer and Stephen Karian have uncovered thousands of new texts under the auspices of *The Swift Poems Project*, an electronic catalogue of all known poems by, or related to, Swift and his circle through to the early nineteenth century. Inevitably, the wide dispersion of Swift materials in both print and manuscript throughout the world means that new items, often of dubious attribution, will continue to appear. Certain items remain elusive largely because they remain hidden within the holdings of others, or because they were at some point wrongly or tentatively catalogued. Some works cannot be definitively attributed to Swift as they were collaborative ventures in effect. Another problem concerns transmission more starkly. Swift's friends and relatives were notoriously careless in their handling of his materials, often out of indifference or with intent to polish up the vagaries of the canon as they perceived it. Scores of contemporary collections were reprints of other, poorly or lightly edited works deriving largely from Faulkner's Dublin editions that first appeared in 1735. Devious editors, such as Edmund Curll and Jonathan Smedley, further compromised the stability of the canon with plagiarisms and forged literary and critical works.

The eighteenth-century printer and anecdotist John Nichols deserves to be ranked alongside the most diligent of scholarly hunter-

---

[1]   D. Woolley, 'The Canon of Swift's Prose Pamphleteering, 1710-1714, and *The New Way of Selling Places at Court*', *Swift Studies*, 3 (1988), 96-117 (p. 117).

gatherers, even if his exploits remain largely unexplored.[2] Among
other pursuits, mainly antiquarian and topographical, Nichols was an
avid collector of English and Irish manuscripts and printed materials,
particularly those of Steele, King, Hogarth, and Swift.[3] In fact, he
earned a reputation amongst his peers for being too avid a collector. In
the *Catalogue of Five Hundred Celebrated Authors of Great Britain, Now
Living* (1788) the entry for Nichols reads: 'His characteristic qualities
are industry without taste, and the faculty of collecting a vast quantity
of materials without discrimination.'[4] Harold Williams writes: 'Nichols, an untiring worker, was by no means a careful editor, but he
brought genuine enthusiasm to his self-appointed task of presenting a
complete collection of Swift's writings.'[5] Untiring indeed: Nichols
authored more than forty books and edited in excess of one hundred
and fifty volumes of the writings of others.

Yet if his editing has been largely unexamined, Nichols's large
published collections of anecdotes have always been indispensable to
historians, bibliographers and biographers – and, indeed, noted contemporary scholars, such as Edmond Malone and George Steevens,
owned copies.[6] Nichols published much of what he recovered from
libraries and correspondence, and so here I am interested in the
relationship between printed and unprinted collections. In particular, I
wish to demonstrate that, *contra* Williams, Nichols wilfully published
his collections as *incomplete*, insisting on many occasions in his
prefaces, headnotes and footnotes that he would be obliged to readers
to supply newly recovered or forgotten materials. Here I perceive a
difference between Nichols and Swift's foremost twentieth-century

---

[2]   See M. Maner, '"The Last of the Learned Printers": John Nichols and the Bowyer-
Nichols Press', *English Studies*, 65:1 (1984), 11-22; James M. Kuist, *The Works of John
Nichols: An Introduction* (New York, 1986), passim. A detailed account of Nichols's
involvement with Samuel Johnson's *Works of the English Poets* can be found in *The
Lives of the Most Eminent English Poets*, ed. by Roger Lonsdale, 4 vols (Oxford, 2006), I,
53-72.
[3]   See *Minor Lives: A Collection of Biographies by John Nichols*, ed. by Edward L. Hart
(Cambridge, MA, 1971), pp. xviii-xxxii.
[4]   Marshall, *Catalogue of Five Hundred Celebrated Authors of Great Britain, Now
Living* (London, 1788), no page numbers.
[5]   *The Poems of Jonathan Swift*, ed. by H. Williams, 2nd edn, 3 vols (Oxford, 1958), III,
p. xl.
[6]   Malone bought Steevens's copy of Nichols's *Bibliographical Anecdotes of William
Bowyer* for £1 17s. 0d. See Thomas King, *Bibliotheca Steevensiana* (London, 1800), p. 117.

editors, Davis and Williams, and indeed David Woolley, all of whom were also enthusiastic and prodigious collectors. Nichols, I am arguing, knowingly distinguished between the duties of editors and collectors in his contextual scholarship. Other Swift scholars in the eighteenth century, including Thomas Sheridan the Younger and Deane Swift, set themselves in opposition to Nichols, choosing to constrict rather than to expand the corpus. Of course, collecting and editing are not mutually exclusive activities – quite the contrary – but nonetheless one can collect without editing just as one can edit without collecting. There are also different types of collectors. One might collect only folios, or first editions, or only rare and unusual editions, or works from a specific period or in a certain genre, or the works (and indeed artefacts) of a single author, or an author's circle: such collections rely on choices being made. Or, at the other end of the spectrum, a scholar might enjoy collecting for its own sake.

To put this into more abstract terms, a collector (of the Nichols variety, at least) gathers materials without discrimination; an editor, a canon-maker, usually seeks to sanitise the author's corpus for public consumption and to remove misattributed and inauthentic pieces and non-authoritative emendations. Yet, whereas modern Swift scholars have focused in considerable detail on the latter, on editing practices, I am interested in exploring the former, the theory and practice of collecting Swiftiana.[7] My attention is not on the *completeness* of editing

---

[7] For detailed discussions of Nichols's editing see D. Woolley, 'A Dialogue upon *Dunkirk* (1712), and Swift's "7 penny Papers"', J. I. Fischer, 'Swift's Early Odes, Dan Jackson's Nose, and "The Character of Sir Robert Walpole": Some Documentary Problems', and J. Woolley, 'The Canon of Swift's Poems: The Case of "An Apology to the Lady Carteret"', in *Reading Swift: Papers from The Second Münster Symposium on Jonathan Swift*, ed. by Richard H. Rodino and Hermann J. Real, with the assistance of Helgard Stöver-Leidig (Munich, 1993), pp. 215-23, pp. 225-43, and pp. 245-64; M. Maner, 'An Eighteenth-Century Editor at Work: John Nichols and Jonathan Swift', *Papers of the Bibliographical Society of America*, 70 (1976), 481-99. For authoritative accounts of Nichols's dealings with the book trade see A. H. Smith, 'John Nichols, Printer and Publisher', *The Library*, 5th series, 18:3 (1963), 169-90; R. Myers, 'John Nichols (1745-1826), Chronicler of the Book Trade', in *Development of the English Book Trade, 1700-1899*, ed. by Robin Myers and Michael Harris (Oxford, 1981), pp. 1-35; J. Pooley, 'The Papers of the Nichols Family and Business: New Discoveries and the Work of the Nichols Archive Project', *The Library*, 7th series, 2:1 (2001), 10-52. I owe many thanks to Mr. Pooley for supplying me with some unpublished correspondence from his own *ongoing* collection, the Nichols Archive Project based at Leicester: < http://www.le.ac.uk/elh/resources/nichols/index.html >.

but on the *process* of collecting. Harold Love put it well, if provocatively, in his 1968 lecture to the Monash University Library. Nichols, he suggested, came close to the modern concept of the 'research edition', an 'edition which exists for the use of the scholar and literary middleman rather than for the public at large'.[8] By implication such editions play a part in a larger hub of scholarly activity and, as such, are permitted to be work-in-progress. At issue here is the critical value of Nichols's contribution to Swift studies. Historically, Nichols's role as an editor has been overshadowed by others, most notably Walter Scott, who, much to Nichols's chagrin, profited greatly from his work.[9] At the same time, Nichols's role is often unclear. In the course of this essay I will subjoin local debates about Nichols's involvement with the 1789 *Miscellaneous Pieces*, printed by his friend Charles Dilly, and touch upon issues and problems associated with his attributions, albeit tangentially. My intention throughout is to provide a salutary reminder that collecting, not unlike printing or writing, is by its very nature a communal activity in which individuals play their part, until said individuals die or otherwise cease to engage in the activity of collecting, and thence their materials (whether original copies or copies of copies) are bequeathed or broken up. At this point the process may begin anew.

Swift & Swiftiana

For more than forty years Nichols laboured over Swiftiana in libraries. In the then relatively new British Museum Library, which opened its doors to the public in the late 1750s, he collated and deciphered the heavily degraded manuscripts of the letters that are still collectively and controversially known as *The Journal to Stella* (his coinage). Nichols also made good use of the Lambeth Palace Library. Here he found authoritative copies of a number of new or previously corrupted items, including 'Horace, Book II, Ode I', 'Horace, Book I, Ep. V',

---

[8] H. Love, *Swift and His Publishers: A Talk Delivered to Friends of the Monash University Library on November 11, 1968, with a Short-Title Catalogue of Early Editions of Swift and Swiftiana in the Monash University Library* (Clayton, Vic., 1969), p. 7.

[9] J. Nichols, *Illustrations of the Literary History of the Eighteenth Century*, 8 vols (London, 1817-58), v, 397 n. See also G. Falle, 'Sir Walter Scott as Editor of Dryden and Swift', *University of Toronto Quarterly*, 36 (1966-7), 161-80 and L. H. Potter, 'The Text of Scott's Edition of Swift', *Studies in Bibliography*, 22 (1969), 240-55.

'The Present State of Wit' and 'Peace and Dunkirk', among others. He even found (and printed) annotations by Archbishop Tenison contained in the folio editions held at Lambeth.

Nichols also frequented bookshops and sale auctions and thereby built up a network of friendships with other collectors. As a literary executor he inherited unique manuscript holdings from his master (and later partner in business) the printer William Bowyer, and from George Hardinge and Samuel Pegge. Bowyer, a friend of Swift's Dublin printer George Faulkner, started to gather copyrights of pieces by Swift and his countrymen as far back as 1729. (Faulkner would send Bowyer printings as soon as they were ready; Irish publications were not automatically protected in England). When Bowyer died in 1777 Nichols became proprietor of one of the largest printing houses in London. He also soon became sole printer of arguably the most influential periodical in the country, the *Gentleman's Magazine*. Even before he finally gained complete control of the periodical in 1792, after the death of Edmund Cave's son-in-law David Henry, Nichols had been using the *Gentleman's Magazine* to solicit aid for his project from its vast, anonymous readership.[10] This garnered a sizable mass of materials, some of which proved useful, though much of it lacked authority. John Loveday ("Scrutator") was a particularly keen respondent to Nichols's queries, often tediously and sometimes in error.

By his own claim Nichols had sought out Swiftiana since 1762, when, aged 17, he worked as a 'humble Assistant' to William Bowyer on seeing the thirteenth and fourteenth volumes of John Hawkesworth's large edition of Swift's works through the press. At this time Nichols (in his words) 'first acquired an inclination for becoming a Commentator, which I afterwards freely indulged, on the Works'.[11] While Nichols can be credited with recovering a not unsubstantial amount of works back to Swift's canon, he attributed an equal number of works to Swift that have been authoritatively denounced over the years, such as 'Helter Skelter' and the epigram 'Behold! A Proof of Irish Sense!'.[12] His textual scholarship was inconsistent, to say the least, but nonetheless Nichols superintended many key editions of

---

[10] See, for example, *Gentleman's Magazine*, 47 (1777), 159-60, 217-18, 260-1, 419-21, 531-2; 48 (1778), 521-3.

[11] Nichols, *Illustrations*, V, 391.

[12] See J. Woolley, 'Canon', 247-8; *Poems*, ed. by Williams, passim.

Swift through the press. In the 1770s, he added substantial supplementary volumes to the canon, and in 1801 he produced in nineteen volumes what could be termed the Nichols's edition of Swift, though it is in fact a dense variorum of accreted scholarship. He expanded the works further still in 1803 and even more emphatically in 1808. As his correspondence with his son John Bowyer Nichols shows, he was still gathering materials and sources as late as 1825, a matter of months before his death. He was driven by the impulse of collecting – at once seeking to finish the edition but fully aware that this could never be achieved. Alexander Chalmers misconstrued this conundrum in his 'Memoir of John Nichols' for the *Gentleman's Magazine* in December 1826, in which he wrote: 'The public is indebted to Mr. Nichols for the very complete state in which [Swift's] works are now formed.'[13] This places undue emphasis on the completeness of scholarship. To put it another way, the process was interrupted. A few months before he died Nichols was still augmenting his findings. In the January 1826 issue of the *Gentleman's Magazine*, under the pseudonym "M. Green" (his second wife's maiden name), Nichols provided a letter from Swift to Dr. Henry Jenny of Armagh dated 1732, thereby supplementing the publication in the 1808 *Works* of a similar letter to the same correspondent communicated by Lord Cremorne to Edmond Malone and thence to Nichols.[14]

Friends and Enemies

During his long career in the book trade Nichols benefited greatly from friendships with Malone, Chalmers, Isaac Reed, Jeremiah Markland, John Duncombe, Richard Gough, Thomas Percy, and other scholars, and also printers, especially his master, Bowyer. Nichols also developed a strong working relationship with the librarian of the Lambeth Palace Library, the antiquary Andrew Coltée Ducarel; and Thomas Astle supplied Nichols with further materials, as he warmly noted in the eighteenth volume of the 1801 *Works of Swift*.[15] Nichols

---

[13] A. Chalmers, 'Memoir of John Nichols', *Gentleman's Magazine*, 96:2 (1826), 489-504 (p. 490) and *Imperial Magazine*, 9:99 (1827), 214. This was reprinted as *Memoir of John Nichols* (London, 1827).

[14] *Gentleman's Magazine*, 96:1 (1826), 3.

[15] *The Works of the Rev. Jonathan Swift, D.D.*, 19 vols (London, 1801), XVIII, 218-19 n.

frequently acknowledged his gratitude to the somewhat reclusive Isaac Reed, the owner of a volume of tracts which formerly belonged to Charles Ford, a contemporary of the Dean. In a footnote to the 1803 *Works* Nichols listed articles contained therein, 'which Mr. Ford attests to be "all writ by Dr. Swift, now Dean of St. Patrick"'.[16] Here Nichols listed ten tracts, only four of which had appeared in the large Hawkesworth edition of the mid-century. 'The Importance of the Guardian Consider'd', in particular, was a text that long eluded Nichols. He had, in his words, 'in vain advertized for a copy of it, in most of the public papers, for many months'.[17] It eventually appeared in his 1779 *Supplement to the Works of Swift*, thanks to Reed. To give a further example of the tangible benefits of Nichols's working relationship with Reed: in annotating Swift's response to John Macky's characterisations of prominent contemporaries that were attached to the posthumously printed *Memoirs of the Secret Services of J. Macky* (1733) Nichols stated that he made use of notes taken from 'a copy formerly belonging to John Putland, esq., a near relation to the dean, who took them from Swift's own handwriting'.[18] Isaac Reed's heavily annotated copy of Macky, now in the British Library, contains the same notes from the Putland copy.[19] Presumably Reed showed the notes to Nichols or, if Nichols somehow obtained them from the private library at the Deanery, supplied them to Reed. In the second volume of the 1801 edition of Swift, Nichols noted in the 'Preface' to *A Tale of a Tub* that, 'The following Historical Particulars were originally communicated to Mr. Nichols in 1777 by the Rev. Samuel Salter, D. D. then master of the Charter-house.'[20] To be precise, the poet and artist Susanna Duncombe had put Nichols in contact with Salter in November 1777. Evidently, Nichols pounced on leads quickly and with relish. He also maintained ties with collectors far from the London book trade. Among his correspondents were men such as Dr. Bewick of Lucan in Ireland. On Nichols's behalf Malone had written

---

[16] *The Works of the Rev. Jonathan Swift, D.D.*, 24 vols (London, 1803), IV, 226.

[17] *A Supplement to Dr. Swift's Works*, 3 vols (London, 1779), II, 69. Unless otherwise stated I quote from this three-volume *Supplement* (small octavo).

[18] *Works* (1801), XVIII, 218 n.

[19] British Library shelfmark, General Reference Collection G.15289. See also H. Williams, *Dean Swift's Library, with a Facsimile of the Original Sale Catalogue and Some Account of Two Manuscript Lists of His Books* (Cambridge, 1932), pp. 63-4.

[20] *Works* (1801), II, p. iii.

to other contacts in that kingdom; the 1801 *Works* was dedicated to the
Irish aristocrat Francis Rawdon-Hastings, the second earl of Moira.

There were also misconnections, indeed quibbles, among collectors,
particularly those who did not value Nichols's indiscriminate approach
to the gathering of materials. An ideological tension existed between
tireless collectors such as Nichols and so-called men of taste, such as
Deane Swift (Swift's junior cousin) and Thomas Sheridan the Younger,
both of whom collected only what they valued and pointedly disre-
garded anything they did not. Sheridan, who produced a new edition
of Swift's works in 1784, wrote to William Strahan on 5 June that
year, perhaps with Nichols in mind: 'I have long beheld with indignation the shameful manner in which the Works of Dr. Swift have been
published, which are now swelled to the enormous bulk of XXV
volumes.'[21] This letter, incidentally, can be found in Nichols's *Illustrations of the Literary History of the Eighteenth Century*; Nichols collected
and published a large body of materials without discrimination,
however badly it might reflect on his character. As a caveat, he
proceeded with tact when he felt others might be embarrassed by the
materials in his holdings; a number of indiscreet letters or parts of
letters did not make their way into the compendious *Literary Anecdotes
of the Eighteenth Century* or *Illustrations*.[22] Above all, Nichols's catch-
all method is surely preferable to that of Deane Swift's. Once a text
appeared in print Swift's cousin would destroy the manuscripts – an
attitude anathema to most book collectors, even though it was not an
uncommon printing practice in the period. Deane Swift wrote:

> I think it would be the best way to burn all manuscripts after a book is
> once printed, if it were for no other reason than because every edition of
> a book, after the first, (unless it be corrected by the author) is, generally
> speaking, worse than the former.[23]

Again, our source is Nichols's *Illustrations*. Nichols might collect
everything, but his presentation of materials allowed his subjects to
shame themselves. Indeed, he made pointed use of Patrick Delany's
admonishment of the cousin. Not only did Delany claim that he 'knew
Dr. Swift fifty times better than you' he insisted that 'there are few

---

[21] Quoted in Nichols, *Illustrations*, V, 394.
[22] Nichols replaced Deane Swift's phrase 'infamous, lying scoundrel' with a polite
dash, for example.
[23] Quoted in Nichols, *Illustrations*, V, 376.

things [Swift] ever wrote that he did not wish to be published one time or other'.[24]

Not only did Deane Swift destroy manuscripts, he pointedly refused to read and thence to preserve texts not to his taste. In a letter dated 7 June 1778 he observed that 'five or six and forty years ago' his mother-in-law, Mrs. Whiteway, showed him her cousin's [i.e. Jonathan Swift's] 'Ode to King William', apparently in printed form, but that, owing to its 'Pindarique way' he was unable to drudge through more than 'fifty or sixty lines of it'.[25] Deane Swift duly omitted it from the 1765 volume of the *Works*. At the reference supplied by Nichols to Johnson's *Works of the English Poets* a footnote flatly states that the piece 'cannot now be recovered'.[26] In 1780, however, Nichols printed an 'Ode to King William' in his *Select Collection of Poems* – itself presented as a supplement to Johnson's *Works* – with this footnote:

> With much pleasure I here present to the publick an Ode which had been long sought after without success. That it is Swift's, I have not the least doubt [...] He refers to it in the second stanza of his 'Ode to the Athenian Society' [...] See the "English Poets", vol. xxxix, p. 10; and "The Gentleman's Journal", July, 1692, p. 13.[27]

The precision of the citations notwithstanding the triumphalism of the collector is misjudged here: the poem does not match Deane Swift's description. After all, it is not in Pindarics, nor does it run to the fifty or sixty lines that turned the cousin's stomach so. Samuel Fairbrother, who had access to George Faulkner's unpublished manuscripts, seems to have found the right piece and printed an incomplete version in the fourth volume of his *Miscellanies* in 1735.[28] Hindered by the destroyer of manuscripts, Nichols was led astray.

---

[24] Nichols, *Illustrations*, v, 393. Deane Swift conceded Delany's point about his greater intimacy with Swift, see Nichols, *Illustrations*, v, 376-7.

[25] Quoted in Nichols, *Illustrations*, v, 382.

[26] S. Johnson, *The Works of the English Poets. With Prefaces, Biographical and Critical*, 68 vols (London, 1779-81), XXXIX, 10 n.

[27] *A Select Collection of Poems* ed. by J. Nichols, 8 vols (London, 1780-82), IV, 303.

[28] *Vol. IV of the Miscellanies Begun by Jonathan Swift, D.D. and Alexander Pope, Esq.*, 4 vols (London, 1735), IV: *Poems*, p. 1. The ode was published in Dublin in late 1690 or 1691, according to James Woolley, 'Swift's First Published Poem: *Ode. To the King*', in *Reading Swift: Papers from The Fourth Münster Symposium on Jonathan Swift*, ed. by Hermann J. Real and Helgard Stöver-Leidig (Munich, 2003), pp. 265-83.

Sometimes Nichols acted naïvely. In April 1790, he attended the auction of Nathaniel Chauncy's vast collections inherited in 1777 from his brother, Dr. Charles Chauncy, a physician and preeminent collector of literary manuscripts. Nichols was particularly keen on Hibbert's copy of *A Tale of a Tub*, which had annotations by Charles Chauncy and, so Chauncy guessed, by Lady Betty Germain, an art collector with whom Swift shared many heated debates up until 1737.[29] In a handwritten letter composed years later, on 14 January 1825, Nichols informed Jeremiah Markland about this copy:

> I bought it in 1790, but I soon found it was of little or no use to me, and I had more than 13 years before seen a similar copy which had belonged to the Duke of Buckingham, from which I had extracted all that related to Thomas Swift, and printed it in 1779 in my Supplement to Swift's Works, and it was copied and prefixed to the Tale of a Tub, in my regular editions of Swift's works in 1801 and 1808.[30]

He continues: 'What is supposed to be T. Swift's writing, may or may not be his, but it is taken from the printed key to the Tale of a Tub'. Much of the information here is highly revealing of Nichols's habits of collecting, and also his naïvety. He was right to question the value of the annotations in this copy in shedding light on Thomas Swift, a cousin of the poet, but he was too hesitant in denouncing the 'printed key to the Tale of a Tub'. This source – an unauthorised edition of *A Tale of a Tub* with 'Considerable Additions, &c explanatory Notes, never before printed' (1720) – was a gross if ingenious forgery from the printing presses of Thomas Johnson in The Hague that extended the unofficial 'key' produced by the piratical bookseller Edmund Curll.[31] Its authenticity was immediately and authoritatively denounced by Justus van Effen in his 1721 translation of *Tale*. Nevertheless, Nichols frequently relied on the dubious text throughout his work on Swift; it is a mark of his desire to collect and print everything to-hand without critical discrimination. Perhaps, as his contemporaries did, it is fair to

---

[29] "Lot 2408", *A Catalogue of the Elegant and Valuable Libraries of Charles Chauncy* [...] *and of his Brother, Nathaniel Chauncy* (London, 1790), p. 86. See also Nichols, *Illustrations*, VIII, 603-4.

[30] The letter is located in the Cambridge University Library with Williams 270, a copy of the fifth edition of *A Tale of a Tub* printed in London by John Nutt in 1810.

[31] See *A Tale of a Tub and Other Works*, ed. by Marcus Walsh (Cambridge, 2010), pp. lxxxvi-lxxxvii.

judge Nichols as a passable textual scholar at best, but as an excellent discoverer of texts, one to whom Swift scholars remain indebted.[32]

Supplements

Broadly speaking everyone agreed that John Hawkesworth's collected edition proved inadequate.[33] Deane Swift, for one, damned it as 'the vilest that ever was yet published'.[34] Certainly, it was far from complete, and Nichols worked diligently to augment the collection, initially with one volume in 1775 (i.e. volume seventeen of the *Works*) as planned, though this eventually became three supplementary volumes in various formats by 1779. Nichols's 'Advertisement' to the 1775 volume traced the complicated publication history of this edition of Swift's *Works*: the first twelve volumes were arranged by Hawkesworth (in 1755), a further two were taken from Faulkner (in 1764), two more were added by Deane Swift (in 1765), three volumes of literary correspondence were edited by Hawkesworth and the Reverend Thomas Birch in 1766, and Deane Swift supplied three more in 1767. 'In this state was the collection', wrote Nichols,

> when in the latter end of 1774, the present Editor, having occasion to peruse with attention the fifteenth and sixteenth volumes, was induced to read, in a regular series, the whole of Dr. *Swift's* Correspondence. In this pursuit, he could not but be astonished to perceive that many pieces, which the Dean acknowledges as his own, were not to be found in the most expensive editions of his Works [...] To remedy that inconvenience, is the design of this volume; consisting of materials, which, if not entirely new to the world, are such in the editions just mentioned.[35]

Here Nichols proffered the creed of an indiscriminate collector as opposed to that of an editor: make materials widely available, regardless of quality. Thereby he fell into an awkward concession that soon proved false: that it was to be merely a small, supplementary volume. To continue:

---

[32] See *Gentleman's Magazine*, 47 (1777), 381.
[33] *The Works of Jonathan Swift, D.D., Dean of St. Patrick's, Dublin*, 12 vols (London, 1755).
[34] Quoted in Nichols, *Illustrations*, V, 376.
[35] *The Works of Dr. Jonathan Swift* (1775), XVII, pp. v-vi.

> If the irregular position of the whole be objected, let it be remembered,
> that the present publication is no more than a single volume [...] Many of
> [the pieces] are admirable; some of them indifferent; and some, perhaps,
> rather below mediocrity.

Soon enough Nichols would be far less coy about unloading his mass
of recovered materials onto readers but, for now, he buried his missive
at the back of the book. Under the second part of Nichols's index, as a
footnote situated below the entry entitled SWIFTIANA, signed "N",
the text *in toto* reads: 'The Editor of the present volume hath endeav-
oured, as far as he was able, to recover what he could trace out to be
the Dean's; and he flatters himself his search hath not been wholly
unsuccessful.'[36] Not unsuccessful, indeed, and not yet finished.

In the 'Advertisement' to the first volume of the 1779 *Supplement* to
the *Works* – an expanded version of the 1776 *Supplement* – Nichols
continued to seek the approval of the men of taste who might object to
the perils of unfiltered editing:

> It may perhaps be objected against some of the articles [...] that they are
> too trifling, and were never intended by the Author for the eye of the
> publick. But it was thought it would be an agreeable entertainment to the
> Curious, to see how oddly a man of his great wit and humour could now
> and then descend to amuse himself with his particular Friends. "His *baga-
> telles*", lord *Chesterfield* tells us, "are much more valuable than other peo-
> ple's".[37]

There was a strategic double-play here: Nichols was fully aware of the
criticism that might be levelled at his baggy collection – that the pieces
were insignificant, that Swift did not wish to see certain works published – but instead he found the pieces to be of 'Curious', if not
literary, value and chose to make the private public. Outwardly
conceding authority to the critical reader, the collector gained a
foothold in the editing process.

In the prefatory note to the 'Biographical Anecdotes of Dean Swift:
in addition to the Life by Dr. Hawkesworth' in the first volume of the
1779 *Supplement* Nichols wrote:

---

[36]   *Works* (1775), XVII, 677n.
[37]   *Supplement* (1779), I, p. xi.

The papers, whence most of the following articles are extracted, were put into the hands of the Editor by a Friend, who had accidently met with them without knowing by whom they were written; but are certainly the productions of a person well informed, and probably an intimate of the Dean's.[38]

The materials collected by Nichols include an interleaved copy of Hawkesworth's 'Life of Swift' with numerous corrections made in July 1765. He continued,

As the facts contained in them are curious and have every internal mark of authenticity to recommend them, the Editor would have thought himself culpable in with-holding from the reader what he believes will afford both entertainment and information.[39]

In corresponding page-per-page endnotes within the edition, Nichols reproduced the annotations from this interleaved edition intermixed with his own notes, as well as some from Reed, information extracted from letters received from Deane Swift and others, and extensive quotes from 'J.S.', whom, for the first time, Nichols identified as Patrick Delany. Indeed, in his work on *The Journal to Stella*, most notably, Nichols printed small excerpts on facing pages, thereby placing emphasis on the judgment of the readers rather than dictating to them.

The small octavo *Supplement* reprinted in three volumes in 1779 was an expanded version of the *ad hoc* volumes of 1775, 1776 and 1779. I do not want to belabour the differences and corrections of these different versions here, but I do want to outline the rhetorical emphasis placed on the process of collecting and editing. The 'Advertisement' to the first volume was largely the same but had an additional footnote. Acknowledging new materials received from George Faulkner, specifically the 'Additional Letters' he had publicly sought, Nichols wrote: 'On this article, the Editor still solicits the assistance of the curious'.[40] Elsewhere in the edition he admitted, 'with regret he owns, there are *still* some pieces by the Dean, which have eluded his most diligent researches'.[41] As we have seen, however, the process of

---

[38] *Supplement* (1779), I, p. xvii.
[39] Ibid.
[40] *Supplement*, (1779) I, p. xi.
[41] Ibid., I, p. xii. Also, *Supplement* (1776), large octavo, I, p. x.

collecting outweighed the finality of owning. It was a race one could not – and should not – finish, even if the end was perpetually in sight.

In the section of the large octavo *Supplement* entitled 'Omissions and Principal Corrections in Volume XVIII', Nichols had, by 1779, introduced a significant footnote:

> That part of the *Journal to Stella*, which was published by Dr. *Hawkesworth*, appearing abundantly *more published* than the other given to the world by Mr. *Deane Swift*; it was natural to imagine that some alteration had been made. On examining, I find that in the originals, now in *The British Museum*, besides a few corrections which appear to have been by the Dean at the time of writing them, there are some *obliterations*, and many whole sentences omitted.[42]

Here we see a different facet of Nichols's work-in-progress approach to collecting and publishing: his hunch, which proved correct, took him back to the original manuscripts and thereby he redacted Deane Swift's gross textual liberties. Collecting did not merely entail the pursuit of materials; it demanded sifting. A commentator for *The Monthly Review* in 1779 nonetheless treated Nichols as an indiscriminate collector and thence a poor editor:

> Many things are admitted into this Supplement which add little to its value, and reflect no honour on Dean Swift. Though we approve of the industry of the ingenious Editor, and heartily recommend this work to the curious reader, yet, the impartiality of criticism obliges us, though reluctantly, to acknowledge, that Mr. Nichols employed his time to a purpose unworthy of his abilities, when he searched the *British Museum* for some originals to complete his useless list of omissions and corrections.[43]

He continues: 'The *Journal to Stella*, in the state in which it was first written, deserved all that correction and alteration which the Editor complains of. It was not fit to appear before the public eye in its original form'. Here it is Nichols's critical taste, rather than his collecting, that is under scrutiny. Perhaps even his friend George Faulkner hinted at the potential dangers of the indiscriminate approach favoured by Nichols when he berated vulturine collectors: 'I

---

[42] *Supplement* (1779), large octavo, II, 225, emphasis retained. This also appears in the second volume of the small octavo *Supplement* as 'Omissions and Principal Corrections in Volume XIX' (p. 237 ff).

[43] *The Monthly Review*, 61 (1779), 356-65 (p. 364).

know many people have laid themselves out to collect the most Grub-street trash that would disgrace the poorest and meanest of presses.'[44]

Yet, Nichols's tireless research and the gathering of materials shed stark light on the poor editing practices of those men enlisted to produce the authoritative works of Swift: John Hawkesworth, an erstwhile member of Swift's circle, and Deane Swift, a relative. Their editions were far from complete; the texts were messy and heavily corrupted; and they continued to rely on works that had been identi-fied as authored by Pope, Arbuthnot, Gay and others. A new edition was sorely needed; as a dedicated collector of and expert on Swift manuscripts, Nichols was among the most qualified for a role which he was keen to undertake. Copyright problems intervened, however. As he wrote, somewhat acerbically, in his *Illustrations of the Literary History of the Eighteenth Century*:

> A material obstacle in respect to the then existing state of Literary Prop-erty, as far as it related to Copyright (a right still held sacred by every re-spectable Bookseller), prevented *my* undertaking at that period a regular Edition of Swift [...]. Of the Twenty-five Volumes *Five* only were my ex-clusive property and an *eighth* share of *Six* others, which had been pur-chased by Mr. Bowyer and myself [...]. Any proposal for an amalgamation was constantly opposed by some of the other proprietors, particularly Mr. Bathurst, who possessed an exclusive right to *Six* of the Volumes.[45]

Curiously the problems were soon overcome as the conglomeration of the twenty-five or so booksellers accepted the proposal of another of Swift's friends, or rather a son of a friend, Thomas Sheridan the Younger, to produce a new edition in 1784. Like Nichols, Sheridan knew the canon existed in a state of disrepute, but he felt it needed pruning rather than augmenting: 'The first thing to be done in this edition, was, to disembroil these works from the chaos in which they have hitherto appeared'.[46] Swift's twentieth-century editor Sir Harold Williams savages Sheridan's neglect of Nichols's research: 'the larger omissions noted by Nichols are ignored'. 'No conscientious attempt is made to mend the text, which remains substantially that of Hawkesworth', he continues. 'Indeed, the editor's carelessness is

---

[44] Quoted in J. Nichols, *Literary Anecdotes of the Eighteenth Century*, 9 vols (London, 1812-15), III, 207-8.
[45] Nichols, *Illustrations*, V, 394, emphasis retained.
[46] *The Works of the Rev. Dr. Jonathan Swift*, 17 vols (London, 1784), II, [p. vi].

incredible'.[47] Sheridan died in 1788 but, nonetheless, some years had passed before Nichols was finally able to bring out his own authoritative edition in 1801. Ever diligent in his collecting, he expanded it further in 1803 and in 1808, before Walter Scott augmented it further still in 1814.[48] Indirectly it became, after Scott's intervention, the base text for most subsequent editions of Swift until the mid-twentieth century.

Nichols also contributed to editions in the interim, though the extent to which he did so has caused some debate among critics. The 1789 *Miscellaneous Pieces, in Prose and Verse* is, as John Irwin Fischer rightly puts it, 'something of a mystery book'.[49] Teerink and Scouten and George P. Mayhew suggest that John Nichols had edited this book, but Fischer disagrees.[50] After all, the book 'can scarcely be said to be edited at all', he asserts.[51] Martin Maner finds the evidence 'inconclusive' as the volume exhibits elements of Nichols's work and yet 'lacks the abundant annotation which is the surest sign of Nichols's care'.[52] I am of the opinion that Nichols was very much involved but chose to downplay his role in the light of Sheridan's heavy-handed treatment of his painstaking research in the mid-1780s. Further, as Fischer also observes, Nichols and the printer of the volume, Charles Dilly, frequently collaborated:

> On this occasion, Nichols seems to have licensed Dilly to levy a donation for this volume from material that, for the most part, Nichols had previously published and [Thomas] Sheridan had not. For example, the 'List of Desiderata in Swift's Works' among the preliminary pages of this volume is mostly reset from Nichols's 1779 *Supplement* to Hawkesworth's edition of Swift's *Works*.[53]

Fischer claims, 'It is easy to spot one point in this volume at which Nichols's materials begin [...]. Page 215 of the book, sig. P4r, begins

---

[47] *Jonathan Swift: The Journal to Stella*, ed. by H. Williams, 2 vols (Oxford, 1948), I, p. li.
[48] *The Works of Jonathan Swift*, ed. by Walter Scott, 19 vols (Edinburgh, 1814).
[49] Fischer, 'Swift's Early Odes', p. 231.
[50] H. Teerink, *A Bibliography of the Writings of Jonathan Swift*, 2nd edn, rev. and corr. by A. H. Scouten (Philadelphia, 1963), p. 158; G. Mayhew, *Rage or Raillery: The Swift Manuscripts at the Huntington Library* (San Marino, CA, 1967), p. 9.
[51] Fischer, 'Swift's Early Odes', p. 231.
[52] Maner, 'Eighteenth-Century Editor at Work', 494-5.
[53] Fischer, 'Swift's Early Odes', p. 232.

that section that contains Swift's three previously unpublished early odes.'[54] The leaves containing 'Three Original Poems, by Dr. Swift' are marked out by a small ornament at the bottom of page 214, in distinction from the miscellaneous poems that precede it, and at the bottom of page 238, sig. Q7^v, after Swift's last ode. Nichols's presence here, as throughout eighteenth-century Swift scholarship, is pronounced if fragmentary.

Fischer's rejection of Nichols as the editor of *Miscellaneous Pieces* is focused on the role of the editor.[55] In the purview of collector-editors such as Nichols we ought to treat the book as a mishmash of Nichols's and Sheridan's labour on Swift. Whereas collected works tend to have an authoritative editor, or a clearly labelled team of sub-editors, the art of collecting is often an enterprise undertaken for its own sake. As Fischer notes, Nichols, after the fact, claimed that from 1785 to 1801, 'not wishing to trouble the publick with any more *last words* of Dr. Swift, I contented myself with noting in the margin of my own books such particulars as occurred, relative to the Dean or to his Writings'.[56] Whereas Fischer takes this at face value, I would suggest that such a man as Nichols, in whom the impulse of collecting was so strong, favoured the role of hunter-gatherer over editor here.

Desiderata

My final section looks at Nichols's use of a frequently adapted 'List of Desiderata' more closely, a technique reprised in his other books, and thereby traces more minutely his open-ended approach to the collecting and editing of Swift.[57] The list first appears in the front matter of the 1776 *Supplement* but the impulse towards announcing desiderata can be glimpsed throughout the previous editions.[58] For instance, in a

---

[54] Ibid.

[55] Ibid., p. 235.

[56] Nichols, *Illustrations*, V, 396.

[57] See, for example, *The Progresses, and Public Processions, of Queen Elizabeth*, 2 vols (London, 1788), I, p. xxxii.

[58] It is worth pointing out that the large octavo and small octavo editions of the *Supplement to the Works of Swift* (both published in 1779) are markedly different, especially with regards to the lists of 'Desiderata'. The list in the small octavo version is much closer to the 1801 list. Whereas the large octavo has nine items these have fourteen, of which three items are different. A one-volume quarto edition of *Supplement* was also published in 1779. Its list is similar to that in the small octavo, with pages renumbered.

small footnote in the 1775 volume of the *Works*, Nichols declared his long-standing desire to print *A New Journey to Paris* 'if a copy of it could have been met with'.[59] It duly appeared in the 1776 *Supplement*. In that volume Nichols decided to print a most wanted list of fourteen missing works by Swift. The list yielded results very quickly. In the 1776 version of the 'Desiderata', for instance, Nichols listed what seemed to him to be an elusive item, 'Peace and Dunkirk', and, soon enough, he gleefully announced the acquisition of it in the *Gentleman's Magazine* for June 1777.[60] In the September issue he went into more detail, declaring that he had found a copy of this poem on a folio half sheet in the Lambeth Palace Library, along with a copy ('perhaps the only one existing', he wrote) of 'Toland's Invitation to Dismal', a work recovered in Deane Swift's *Essay upon the Life, Writings, and Character, of Dr. Jonathan Swift* (1755).[61] 'Peace and Dunkirk' had appeared in print, it is important to note, as a broadside in 1712. Even if Swift himself declared to Ford in 1733 that he could not remember the poem, Nichols was determined to find an autograph version.[62]

By 1779 Nichols had found several pieces mentioned in his original 1776 list and had gathered 'Biographical Anecdotes' from John Lyon's annotations in a copy of Hawkesworth's 'Life of Swift'. Yet Nichols was far from satiated and, at his request, Malone sent Lord Charlemont an abbreviated list of desiderata in April 1779.[63] Nichols also sent a copy of the 1779 *Supplement* to Deane Swift, who died in 1783, and in the meantime could not, or would not, offer any help. Nichols wrote as well to his heir, Theophilus Swift, asking for assistance, but the younger Swift replied that the edition was 'in a manner' finished by his father, and that it would be easy for him to 'complete any deficiencies under which it may at present labour'. Indeed, the younger Swift felt the canon was finally settled: 'I am *confident* that so *perfect* and *accurate* an Edition will never be given of Swift as it is now in my power to offer to the world.' The young editor claimed to follow the model Bishop Hurd established in his work on Warburton: a complete edition that is in fact a selection. Such a selection would contain only pieces 'worthy [of] the pen of Swift; weeded and purged of such tracts,

---

59   *Works* (1775), XVII, 610 n.
60   *Gentleman's Magazine*, 47 (1777), 261.
61   *Gentleman's Magazine*, 47 (1777), 419.
62   See *Poems*, ed. by Williams, I, 167 ff.
63   Maner, 'Eighteenth-Century Editor at Work', p. 492.

&c. as discredit him'.[64] For Theophilus Swift, somewhat paradoxically, collecting Swift's works entailed the contraction rather than the expansion of volumes.

In the 1801, 1803 and 1808 editions Nichols inserted a much altered list of 'Desiderata', though items he had sought earlier continued to elude him, namely 'A Ballad (full of Puns) on the Westminster Election, 1710', 'Dunkirk still in the Hands of the French', 'A Hue and Cry after Dismal', 'It's Out at Last', and 'A Dialogue upon Dunkirk'. Some of these items finally resurfaced well into the twentieth century; others are still to be found. Purchased at auction by Bernard Quaritch Ltd, 'A Hue and Cry after Dismal' was republished *circa* 1938 and 'It's Out at Last' appeared in *The Athenaeum* on 8 November 1902.[65]

The 'Desiderata' allowed Nichols to recover items piece by piece with the help of attentive readers, but, perhaps out of impatience, or propelled by the collector's desire, Nichols sought to recover a number of the most wanted items by himself. As David Woolley has demonstrated, Nichols was the first editor to investigate thoroughly the problem of identifying all of the seven 'penny Papers', largely by combing through John Morphew's advertisements headed "Just publish'd" in the folio numbers of *The Examiner* of late June and July, 1712.[66] In doing so he recovered texts of two of the seven papers: 'A Letter from the Pretender' (not advertised) and 'Peace and Dunkirk', which appeared in the 1776 and 1779 supplementary volumes respectively.[67] Debate still lingers over the identity of the seventh paper. Frank H. Ellis has put forward 'The Description of Dunkirk' as his candidate while David Woolley offers an altogether more convincing case for 'A Dialogue upon Dunkirk'.[68] Woolley's item, it must be noted, is to be found among Nichols's list.

Conclusion

Nichols's attributions were frequently misjudged, and his annotations and sources often lacked credibility, especially when taken from the

---

[64] Quoted in Nichols, *Illustrations*, V, 389-90.

[65] See D. Woolley, '*Dialogue*', p. 216.

[66] '*Dialogue*', passim; see also his article '"The Author of the Examiner" and the Whiggish Answer-Jobbers of 1711-12', *Swift Studies*, 5 (1990), 91-111.

[67] *Supplement* (1776), I, 196-8; *Supplement* (1779), III, 199-200.

[68] See D. Woolley, '*Dialogue*', p. 217.

anonymous contributors to the *Gentleman's Magazine*. Unlike Deane Swift – the destroyer of manuscripts – Nichols had been an indefatigable and even obsessive collector of books and manuscripts pertaining to Swift and his circle since the age of 17. In an unpublished letter, dated March 1808, Nichols's compositor Henry Dench gave his master a first-hand account of the infamous fire that tore through their printing premises a month earlier. He had the *History of Surrey* and Swift's *Works* in his frames at the time. Fire, indifference, lost and mythical manuscripts, Swift's blundering friends and relatives – nothing could hinder the progress of John Nichols the collector. *Labor ipse voluptas*, his personal motto, captures it best: work is itself a pleasure.

Pirates, Editors, and Readers: How Distribution Rewrote William Smellie's Philosophy of Natural History

STEPHEN W. BROWN

An unfortunate first edition

In February 1781, the London-based Scottish publisher John Murray complained to one of his Edinburgh colleagues, William Smellie, about the latter's failure to send him a copy of his translation of Buffon's *Histoire Naturelle*, for which Murray had promised to secure a London bookseller. Murray wrote:

> I also desire to have a copy of *Buffon* sent to me by coach. Of this desire though often repeated you take no notice: and I can plainly perceive will see me d'ed before you gratify me in this particular. Do you imagine then that my bookseller will treat for your book without *seeing* it? Or do you apprehend what is practised in Scotland, that the work will be pirated here and detain the copy I wrote for on that account. How immensely contemptible is that conduct[1]

Yet Murray's derisive observation about the Scottish refusal to respect the London interpretation of copyright, however justified in many instances during the period, was misplaced here – Smellie's problem was pathological disorganization and a busy social life, not fear of literary piracy, and Murray would still be requesting the Buffon translation twenty-one months later, in November of the following year.[2] In fact, five years would pass before Smellie would see a London imprint for his translation of Buffon's *Histoire Naturelle*, an instance of prompt efficiency when compared to his next literary venture, *The Philosophy of Natural History*.

Smellie did not so much translate Buffon as rewrite the French original, essentially re-conceiving it in English with ample commentary and notes.[3] The resulting text was widely read and praised throughout

---

[1] Edinburgh, National Library of Scotland, John Murray Archives, MS 41903.
[2] Edinburgh, National Library of Scotland, John Murray Archives, MS 41904.
[3] The translation is examined by Aaron Garrett, see 'Introduction' in George Louis

Britain and America. Smellie had first been drawn to the emerging discipline of natural history as a student at Edinburgh University in the late 1750s and early 1760s, where he was particularly influenced by Professors John Hope and John Gregory. After leaving his studies, Smellie became Edinburgh's primary academic printer, specializing in medical and scientific work with official responsibility – in partnership with John Balfour – for printing all the University's theses, until his death in 1795. He was also an influential journalist and editor, through which activities he first came together with Charles Elliot, as two of four partners who initiated the seminal and politically controversial *Edinburgh Magazine and Review* in 1773.[4] Shortly after this, Smellie began to print some of Elliot's most valuable titles and brought other successful literary properties to Elliot, including the first two volumes of the *Thesaurus Medicus* (a compilation of all the Edinburgh medical theses) and James Gregory's *Conspectus medicinae theoreticae*. After the success of Smellie's translation of Buffon, Elliot, who had become one of Europe's most important publishers of medicine and science, agreed in 1787 to pay Smellie one thousand pounds for the first volume of an original philosophy of natural history. Elliot must have anticipated a significant readership for him to have committed so large a sum in securing Smellie, a supposition that we shall see confirmed in Elliot's correspondence with several European clients.[5] Although the potential

---

Leclerc, Comte de Buffon, *Natural History, General and Particular*, trans. by William Smellie, 8 vols (Edinburgh, 1780 and 9 vols London, 1785; repr. Bristol, 2000), I, pp. v-xvii.

[4]   The contract in manuscript with contextual correspondence is in Edinburgh, National Museum of Scotland Library, Manuscript Papers of William Smellie, Book Trade Documents. On the *Edinburgh Magazine and Review*, see Stephen W. Brown, 'William Smellie and Natural History: Dissent and Dissemination', in *Science and Medicine in the Scottish Enlightenment*, ed. by Charles W. J. Withers and Paul Wood (East Linton, 2002), pp. 198-201 and William Zachs, *Without Regard to Good Manners: A Biography of Gilbert Stuart, 1743-1786* (Edinburgh, 1992), pp. 63-95.

[5]   The circumstances surrounding Elliot's advance to Smellie and the subsequent dispute with Elliot's estate over the balance owing in 1790 have been the cause for some controversy and misunderstanding. However, the Trustees' Minute Book in the John Murray Archives carefully and indisputably clarifies the matter. See the entries for 30 January 1790, 1 March 1790, 1 September 1790, 30 November 1790, and 3 January 1791. I am grateful to Dr Warren McDougall for originally having drawn my attention to these materials. See also the most recent discussion of Elliot and Smellie's *Philosophy* in Richard Sher's *The Enlightenment and the Book: Scottish Authors & Their*

market for the *Philosophy* had already been explored through a proposal for the work circulated in 1786, Elliot could not have foreseen the extraordinarily complicated literary fate that the book-trade gods had decreed for Smellie's *opus*. [6] The text was 'forthcoming' and 'in the Press' for years, finally appearing in 1790 after Elliot's premature death; the second volume was completed posthumously by Smellie's son and published almost a decade later in 1799.[7] Although the volume commissioned by Elliot languished in Britain despite a favourable critical reception, it was republished internationally in Germany, Denmark and Greece, as well as the more usual sites of Ireland and America, becoming in the latter the single most reprinted work on natural history for nearly fifty years, and thriving, in particular, as a textbook at Harvard.[8] William Smellie's *Philosophy of Natural History* demonstrates the dramatic unpredictability of literary properties. As the text was pirated and edited and rewritten, it enriched others as it never did the owners of its copyright until, by 1872, in its ultimate edition, it had been gutted of all that originally distinguished it. Yet it remained 'Smellie's *Philosophy*' to the generations of Americans who studied it – including Ralph Waldo Emerson, Henry David Thoreau, and William James – despite its having been divested of property, originality, and personality, the hallmarks of ownership in those eighteenth-century copyright decisions that mattered so much to men like John Murray.

Publishers in Eighteenth-Century Britain, Ireland & America (Chicago, 2006), pp. 228-9.

[6] The detailed four-page proposal was sewn into the blue wrappers of the August 1786 issue of the *Scots Magazine*. See Stephen W. Brown 'Wrapping the News: *The Historical Register* and the Use of Blue Paper Cover Wrappers on Eighteenth-Century Scottish Magazines', *Journal of the Edinburgh Bibliographical Society*, 1 (2006), 49-70.

[7] The earliest advertisement for Smellie's *Philosophy of Natural History* was in the *Edinburgh Evening Courant* on 6 March 1788, where Elliot offered the *Prospectus gratis* while the work 'will be published in a few months [at] 21 shillings in boards'. When the text finally appeared on18 February 1790, early reviewers all remarked upon the extraordinary delay in its publication; on 5 April 1790, the *Caledonian Mercury* opened a two-column, front-page review by observing that 'this work so long promised has at last made its appearance, and it is believed the expectations of the Public will not be disappointed'. See also, William Smellie, *The Philosophy of Natural History*, 2 vols (Edinburgh, 1790-1799; repr. Bristol, 2001), I, pp. v-xxxiii.

[8] Three translations appeared in Germany (1791), in Denmark (1796), and in Greece (1846). The last of these is based on John Ware's edition of Smellie's *The Philosophy of Natural History*, (Boston, 1824).

Elliot considered the copyright for Smellie's work one of his hot properties in 1788. He taunted a bookseller at Versailles by telling him that

> it would have been much to your Interest and advantage had you acted &
> paid me like a man of business; I am to publish Dr Cullens treatise on the
> Materia Medica 2 vols 4o, Smellies Philosophy of Natural History one vol
> 4o, the New Edinburgh Dispensatory with the London Pharmacopoea
> 1788 included, these works will all be published in the course of the Au-
> tumn, & I am certain will have a great Demand in France.[9]

Earlier that year, on 28 February, he had written to a colleague in Rotterdam, promoting Smellie in the same breath as Dr Cullen and insisting that the 'Ph. Of History [was] in the Press', though it was not.[10] Smellie's own surviving manuscripts for the *Philosophy* indicate that he was still organizing the structure for the volume and had very little writing in hand.[11] Much of his time was taken up with printing jobs for William Creech and Elliot, and with his work as an executive officer of the struggling Society of Antiquaries of Scotland. His publisher proved patient and understanding, even settling £350 of promised copyright money in an account for Smellie and observing to a Danish correspondent in October 1788 that 'a man in the Trade' as Smellie was, would have 'a great deal to mind and cannot be expected [to] write fast'.[12] Still, throughout the publishing high seasons of 1788 and 1789, the *Philosophy of Natural History* was advertised in the Edinburgh newspapers as about to appear – one such advert in the *Caledonian*

---

[9]   Edinburgh, National Library of Scotland, John Murray Archives, Elliot Letter Books, volume 8, letter 4214. See also letters 4215 and 4216.

[10]   Edinburgh, National Library of Scotland, John Murray Archives, Elliot Letter Books, volume 8, letter 4154.

[11]   The manuscript suggests that Smellie had written nothing more than the introductory material and that the rest of the work existed only as rough notes and jottings (Edinburgh, National Museum of Scotland Library, William Smellie Manuscript Papers, Manuscript Works: Natural History (1780-1800)).

[12]   See Elliot's ledger entries for 6 March 1788 and 5 April 1788, Edinburgh, National Library of Scotland, John Murray Archives, Ledger 4. Charles Elliot to Dr. Engelhart, 10 October 1788: 'Smellie's Book is very much retarded & I do not even think he will be ready in the Spring--it comes hard upon a man in Trade who has a great deal to mind and cannot be expected he can write fast.' (Edinburgh, National Library of Scotland, John Murray Archives, Elliot Letter Books, volume 8, letter 4231). Among the things distracting Smellie in 1788 was an attempt on his part to form a consortium to publish a Whig newspaper in Edinburgh to be called the *Scottish Chronicle*.

Mercury on 3 March 1788 promised that it 'will be published in a few months'. The same announcement ran at least four more times in March and April in both the *Mercury* and the *Edinburgh Evening Courant* though it was not until April 1790 that the volume finally came out in Edinburgh and London bookshops. It was well received and positively reviewed. The *Caledonian Mercury* for 5 April 1790 printed a two-column review with a lengthy excerpt announcing that

> the work, so long promised, has at last made its appearance; and it is believed, the expectations of the Public will not be disappointed. The Learned Reader will find much useful information, the Superficial receive high entertainment – even the Ladies, such is its perspicuity, may peruse this Treatise with real advantage and pleasure.[13]

Critical accounts elsewhere were even more positive, despite a considerable controversy over Smellie's critique of Linnaeus on the sexuality of plants.[14] However, Elliot was now deceased and there was no one to follow up quickly on the publication's initial momentum; any chances of a second edition in octavo or even a commitment to the second quarto volume were thus lost. On 15 January 1791, the Edinburgh solicitor Adam Bruce placed an advertisement in the *Caledonian Mercury* on behalf of Charles Elliot's estate, announcing an auction for

---

[13] *Caledonian Mercury*, 5 April 1790, p. 1. Smellie always thought of his audience in an inclusive manner, and his announced intention to give public lectures on Natural History under the auspices of the Society of Antiquaries of Scotland in 1780 was a chief impetus in awakening the ire of the University of Edinburgh, especially that of its Principal, William Robertson. Such a public venue would have been open to women. For one example of Smellie's opinion that women should be allowed access to the Society's museum, see his correspondence with James Cumming, Secretary of the Antiquaries (Edinburgh, University of Edinburgh Special Collections, Letter & Notes to James Cumming, 1781-85. La. ll.82).

[14] William Creech, who had published Smellie's translation of Buffon and was Smellie's acrimonious, sometime business partner, employed the Edinburgh science hack-writer and eventually Professor of Natural History at St. Andrews University, John Rotheram, to produce a pamphlet attacking Smellie's reluctance to accept Linnaeus's position on the sexuality of plants. The pamphlet – which sold at one shilling compared with the two or three shillings usually charged for a work of this sort – was titled, *The Sexes of Plants Vindicated In a Letter to Mr. William Smellie, Member of the Antiquarian and Royal Societies of Edinburgh --- containing a Refutation of his Arguments against the Sexuality of Plants and Remarks on certain Passages of his Philosophy of Natural History*. Creech ran substantial advertisements for the pamphlet in Edinburgh's newspapers from late March and throughout April 1790.

the copyright to the first volume of the *Philosophy*. Smellie spent the final few years of his life negotiating unsuccessfully and eventually simply pleading with various publishers to purchase the rights to his second volume. The few who bothered to reply were all dismissive, and some openly rude.[15] Smellie thus went from being a hot property in 1788 to a literary *persona non grata* by 1791. Had Elliot misjudged the author, the book, and its market? He certainly could not have foreseen the political troubles of the 1790s, which disrupted the book trade as they did the whole social order in Britain, making political titles more desirable than scientific ones, and, by 1801, William Paley's *Natural Theology* had made any popular entertainment of Smellie's more radical intuitions about evolution untenable.[16] Nor could Elliot exercise any influence from the grave over Smellie's diminished personal credibility in Edinburgh, where his Whig sentiments and financial irresponsibility increasingly isolated him. Still, if his market disappeared in Britain and with it Smellie's reputation, the case was quite different abroad where unauthorized publication paved the way for an unexpected readership.

Eventual American acclaim

The first unauthorized publication of the *Philosophy* appeared in Dublin in late-April 1790, with a two-volume octavo edition printed by William Porter for a consortium of booksellers headed by Chamberlaine and Rice. It was followed by two American editions, both single-volume octavos: one was published by Robert Campbell at Philadelphia in 1791 – Campbell specialized in medical and scientific works and boasted a stock of more than 1900 items in 1796, including Smellie's translation of Buffon; the other was printed in Dover, New Hampshire, almost two decades later in 1808 by the partnership of Thomas & Tappin and Samuel Brigg, who sold it at their shops in Portsmouth and Dover respectively and advertised it for sale by

---

[15] See Robert Faulder's reply declining Smellie's request that he print a second edition in which he dismisses the *Philosophy* as a work no longer in vogue (Edinburgh, National Museum of Scotland Library, William Smellie Manuscript Papers, General Correspondence).

[16] For a succinct historical discussion of the influence of Paley's text, see William Paley, *Natural Theology*, ed. by Matthew D. Eddy and David Knight (Oxford, 2006), pp. ix-xxix.

booksellers in Worcester, Boston, and Troy, New York. Unlike the first (1790), the second volume of the *Philosophy* (1799) was never pirated nor was it used in any way to supplement the many editions of the first volume that eventually appeared in edited form in America. Its emphasis on human and animal psychology – including an impressive examination of sleep and dreams – took volume two of the *Philosophy* beyond the early nineteenth century's popular purview of natural history.[17] Of the three unauthorized English-language editions of Smellie's 1790 first volume, Campbell's is the intriguing one, its publication launching the *Philosophy*'s extraordinary American career. The edition also announced Campbell's career as a publisher; for whatever reason Campbell chose Smellie's text as his first significant independent venture.[18]

Campbell employed an editor to prepare Smellie's text, a curious decision since it delayed publication of the book until 1791 and incurred an unnecessary additional expense. The editor was Benjamin Smith Barton, who had strong links with Edinburgh and was a corresponding member of the Society of Antiquaries of Scotland, through which he had met William Smellie in 1787, while Barton was a medical student. He was also a specialist in American botany, a colleague and disciple of Dr Benjamin Rush, and a Professor of Natural History at the University of Pennsylvania. As well, Barton must have had some prior dealings with Charles Elliot who, in the *Edinburgh Evening Courant* for 28 March 1788, had advertised the '*Florula Pennsylvania or Outlines of Botanical History of Pennsylvania* [...] *with Remarks on the Oeconomical and Medical Uses of Plants* by Benjamin Smith Barton' as one of his forthcoming titles. In editing the *Philosophy of Natural History* for Campbell, Barton appended twenty-eight discursive notes which included references to some thirty literary sources beyond those mentioned in Smellie's own extensive citations. He added material on tulips drawn from his time in Holland, enriched the text's references to the distinctions between animal and vegetable, and predictably brought more American botany into Smellie's work, remarking at one point 'how a similar notion [to Smellie's] very

[17] The first four chapters are a sort of hotchpotch, collected together by Alexander from his father's notes and not especially novel. Chapter Five is, however, quite forward looking. See, in particular, 'Of Sleep and Dreaming,' and 'Of the Language of Beasts', (Smellie, *Philosophy*, II, 361-67 and II, 413-43.

[18] Sher, *Enlightenment and the Book*, p. 562.

generally prevails in these United States'.[19] Campbell sold the volume for two dollars. The 1808 Dover edition, however, returned to the original of 1790 for its copy text.

After 1808, Smellie's *Philosophy* seemed headed for the same oblivion in America that had swallowed it whole in Britain, until 1823, when George Emerson the educator, botanist, and cousin of Ralph Waldo Emerson, asked Dr John Ware to prepare a textbook on natural history for the schools and colleges of Massachusetts. Ware was a Harvard medical professor, an activist in the Unitarian community, and the son of Dr Henry Ware, the Hollis Professor of Divinity at Harvard, whose preaching had led to the formal separation of the Unitarians from the Congregationalists.[20] Together with the Emersons, the Wares were one of the leading intellectual families in Massachusetts, and John would go on to write and edit a number of important books, including the very popular American edition of William Paley's *Natural Theology*.[21] There is nothing extant to tell us why Ware selected Smellie's work as his best option for a textbook on natural history. We know that Emerson required a book that would be suitable for young women as well as young men, because he was headmaster of a distinguished academy for girls, and, as a member of Harvard's teaching staff, Ware no doubt foresaw the usefulness (and commercial possibilities) of a volume that could serve colleges, senior schools and academies equally well. Smellie had written his *Philosophy* with the intention of making it accessible to a popular as much as a learned readership, a democratic impulse that he brought to all his journalism and one that had determined the founding principles of his

---

[19]   William Smellie, *The Philosophy of Natural History*, ed. by Benjamin Smith Barton (Philadelphia, 1791), p. 97.

[20]   John Ware's efforts as an editor included fifteen volumes of *New England Journal of Medicine, Surgery and Collateral Branches of Science* (January 1812-October 1826); the first volume, with Walter Channing, of *New England Medical Review and Journal* (1827); and the first three volumes of *Boston Journal of Philosophy and the Arts, Intended to Exhibit a view of the Progress of Discovery in Natural Philosophy, Mechanics, Chemistry, Geology and Mineralogy, Geography, Natural History, Comparative Anatomy and Physiology* (1823-26).

[21]   William Paley, *Natural Theology: or Evidences of the Existence and Attributes of the Deity, Collected from the Appearances of Nature*, ed. by John Ware (Boston, 1850). Ware's edition was reprinted thirteen times between 1851 and 1872. The 1850 text ran to 344 pages and included 29 plates; this was expanded in 1854 to 420 pages with the plates unaltered.

Society of Antiquaries of Scotland, creating an historic distinction between it and Edinburgh's co-nascent Royal Society.[22] Throughout his career, he was sensitive to female readers and to the education of women, something that became a hallmark of his *Philosophy* and was noted by its first reviewers in Edinburgh.[23] Smellie's style also had the advantage of lacking the obscurities of his rivals, a feature of academic writing which he openly criticized to the detriment of his reputation among some in the university community;[24] his was the prose style of a public intellectual whose literary work as a journalist and editor had always been inclusive, something apparent from his earliest efforts with the first edition of the *Encyclopaedia Britannica* and Dr William Buchan's *Domestic Medicine.*[25]

In the advertisement to his first edition of Smellie's *Philosophy*, Ware indicated that in editing the text he 'shall appear to have taken no greater liberties than were necessary to fit it for the purpose for which it is principally intended – the instruction of the young'.[26] That principal intent led Ware to drop seven full chapters from Smellie's original, and to rewrite substantial sections, a strategy well-illustrated

---

[22] For a discussion of Smellie's democratic impulses, see Brown, 'William Smellie and Natural History: Dissent and Dissemination', in *Science and Medicine*, ed. by Withers and Wood, pp. 201-3.

[23] Smellie's regard for women as intellectual equals is nowhere more evident than in his relationship with Maria Riddell. He arranged for Peter Hill to publish her *Voyages to the Madeira and Leeward Caribbean Islands*, and did the printing himself. See his correspondence with Riddell in Robert Kerr, *Memoirs of the Life, Writings, and Correspondence of William Smellie*, 2 vols (Edinburgh 1811; repr. Bristol, 1996),II, 353-92.

[24] In his 'Life of John Gregory MD,' Smellie called upon academic writers to 'communicate [...] with perspicuity, and in a language as void of technical terms as the nature of the subject will permit', *Literary and Characteristical Lives of J. Gregory, M.D., Henry Home, Lord Kames, David Hume, and Adam Smith, LL.D.*, (Edinburgh, 1800; repr. Bristol, 1997), p. 25. No doubt the accessibility of Smellie's own style is what led John Ware to choose the *Philosophy of Natural History* as the ideal textbook for academies and colleges.

[25] Smellie was fundamental in establishing the success of both these ventures as the editor of their first editions (the *Britannica* in 1768-71 and *Medicine* in 1769) but reaped none of the riches that accrued to their publishers from subsequent editions. See Richard Sher, 'William Buchan's *Domestic Medicine*: Laying Book History Open', in *Human Face of the Book Trade*, ed. by Peter Isaac and Barry McKay (New Castle, Delaware, 2001), pp. 45-64.

[26] John Ware, 'Advertisement Respecting this Edition', in *The Philosophy of Natural History by William Smellie*, ed. by. John Ware (Boston, 1824), p. vi. All further references are to this edition unless otherwise indicated by date.

in the chapter on 'Respiration'. Smellie's opening two chapters on the physiology of plants and animals were replaced by Ware's own introductory three-chapter treatment of the same topic, but one incorporating recent developments in the field. Smellie's controversial ninth, tenth, and eleventh chapters, dealing respectively with sexuality in animals and plants, puberty, and love were deleted in their entirety, as were his eighteenth and nineteenth chapters which hinted at evolution while exploring the dispositions of animals and especially 'the Principle of Imitation in animals [as] the nearest approach to reasoning and language' (1790, p. 469). The removal of sexual materials fitted with Ware's scheme to make the book suitable for young readers; however his dropping of Smellie's discussion of animal imitation as a form of reasoning and similar editorial decisions throughout the text shared another single-minded purpose: to suppress Smellie's inclination to see a close connection between animal and human physiology and behaviour. [27] In fact, as Ware edited and eventually rewrote Smellie's work during the subsequent five decades, he moved the *Philosophy* away from its intuitive appreciation of the evolutionary patterns in nature to an explicitly creationist position, acknowledging in the process of suppressing it, what was progressive and even revolutionary in Smellie's anticipation of Darwin, and thus revealing the essential conservatism of this aspect of Harvard's science curriculum. [28] Ware was always scrupulous in distinguishing between his text and Smellie's, however, and in each of his various editions, he placed single inverted commas around his own passages. Along with a nine-page 'Analytical Table of Contents', Ware also provided a five-page 'Explanation of Terms', both appearing at the back of the book in every American edition. Perhaps the most telling of Ware's substantive changes came when he rewrote Smellie's final five paragraphs which contemplated the organic interdependence of the natural world and speculated about the likeness of man and the 'orang-outang', building on the observations of Lord Monboddo while anticipating Darwin and the bioethics

---

[27] Ware's attitude toward sex education is best expressed in his influential and popular, *Hints to Young Men on the True Relation of the Sexes. Prepared at the Request of a Committee, and Published under Their Direction* (Boston, 1850; revised, 1879).

[28] See Joseph Ewan's discussion of the curriculum in 'Smellie's *Philosophy of Natural History*, Harvard's Biology Classes and Biocaenosis', *Taxon*, 31 (1962), 462-66; and, especially, Edward J. Larson, *Evolution: The Remarkable History of a Scientific Theory* (New York, 2004), pp. 42-6.

of ecosystems.[29] Smellie wrote in the first of those five visionary paragraphs that

> in descending the scale of animation, the next step, it is humiliating to remark, is very short. Man, in his lowest condition, is evidently linked, both in the form of his body and the capacity of his mind, to the large and small orang-outangs [...] From the orang-outangs and apes to the baboons, the interval is hardly perceptible [...] The monkeys [...] terminate this partial chain of imitative animals, which have such a detestable resemblance to the human frame and manners. (1790, p. 523).

Ware replaced this paragraph with the following:

> In descending the scale of animation, the next step brings us to the monkey tribe. Man, in many particulars, undoubtedly resembles the animals of this tribe [...] [but] notwithstanding the attempts of some philosophers to confound their own species with monkeys, it requires only a small share of knowledge of the anatomical structure of animals, and the general principles of natural history, to convince any one of the folly and absurdity of such speculations. (1824, p. 309).

Ware's desire to eliminate from Smellie's *Philosophy* all of the 'modern' tendencies of its reliance on scientific observation would eventually lead him to re-conceive the text entirely in creationist terms, but that radical rewriting of Smellie was some twenty-odd editions away.

Ware's first edition of the *Philosophy* was printed by the University Press at Cambridge, Massachusetts for Cummings, Hilliard and Company of Boston in 1824. The moment was propitious. Thomas Nuttall had just arrived at Harvard and was establishing his course in natural history. On the advice of Benjamin Smith Barton, whom he knew from his time in Philadelphia and who had edited the first American edition of the *Philosophy* for Robert Campbell in 1791, Nuttall decided to make Smellie's the text for his class, not simply on the authority of Barton's recommendation, but equally because of the volume's timely appearance that year in Boston's bookshops. That coincidence helped promote the use of Ware's *Smellie* in schools across the state. By all accounts it proved a popular instructional text; Nuttall's course acquired the nickname 'Smellie' among his students and, in 1829, the junior class at Harvard is reported to have petitioned

---

[29] Ewan, 'Smellie's *Philosophy of Natural History*', p. 466.

to have the *Philosophy of Natural History* made 'a substitute for Gries-
bach's Greek Testament'.[30]

By 1829, Ware's *The Philosophy of Natural History by William
Smellie* was in its third edition, the second having appeared in 1827,
both with runs of a thousand, selling at $1.80 a copy.[31] These two
editions each incorporated minor, largely stylistic, alterations to the
1824 original, reducing the text from 336 pages in 1824, to 322 in 1827,
and then increasing it to 327 in 1829.[32] Ware steadily decreased his own
use of adjectives in the edition, especially the word 'great' for which he
had shown a propensity in the sections of the 1824 volume which he
had rewritten. He also began to use the phrase 'kind of animal'
consistently in the place of Smellie's original 'sort of animal.' Stylistic
rewrites were usually in the following vein. In the third chapter of his
introduction to the 1824 edition, Ware had written: 'The third tribe of
this order possess the characteristics of carnivorous animals in the
highest degree' (p. 40). In 1829, this became: 'The animals of the third
tribe possess the characteristics of this order in the highest degree' (p.
39). The volume's tenure in Harvard's natural history classes continued, and after its introduction by Nuttall, it was used successively by
Professors Thaddeus Harris and Asa Gray in the 1830s and 1840s.
Although Ware's edition had diluted the intellectual vigour and
originality of Smellie's 1790 text, this watered-down version was
apparently preferable as a teaching aid; Gray, for instance, remarked
that the text in this state provided him with the opportunity to 'give
plenty of illustrations, explanations, and ideas not in the book, which
pleases and interests [my students]'.[33]

The 1829 edition was followed by two more in 1832 and 1834, both
still announcing themselves as 'from the University Press at Cam-

---

[30] Jeannette E. Graustein, *Thomas Nuttall, Naturalist: Explorations in America, 1808-
1841* (Cambridge, Mass., 1967), pp. 224-5. Nuttall produced his own botany text (*An
Introduction to Systematic and Physiological Botany* (1827); revised second edition
(1830)), but continued to use Smellie's *Philosophy* to introduce students to general
issues in natural history.

[31] Ware's edition of *The Philosophy* was issued in such great numbers that copies of
most editions are still readily available. I have been able to locate and examine each
edition already listed in such sources as the *National Union Catalogue*, and have
discovered and examined four previously unrecorded printings (see Appendix).

[32] The differences in page lengths among these three editions are due entirely to
Ware's pruning of his own style as he tries to emulate Smellie's succinctness.

[33] Ewan, 'Smellie's *Philosophy of Natural History*', pp. 464-5.

bridge', after which a stereotype of the text was first printed at the Boston Type and Stereotype Foundry and published by Hilliard, Gray and Company. Ware had retained the copyright for the first five editions, but it was now registered in the Clerk's Office of the District Court of Massachusetts in the name of the current publishers, Hilliard and Gray. The copyright in turn passed to Samuel G. Simpkins in 1841, W. J. Reynolds in 1843, and finally Brown, Taggard and Chase in 1858, who then commissioned the last major rewriting of the volume by John Ware in 1860, and continued to hold the rights through several changes in partnership within the firm, until the final edition of the *Philosophy* in 1872. These were all Boston publishing companies with extensive textbook catalogues, with Brown and Taggard particularly notable for this speciality.

In 1841, John Ware was contracted by Samuel Simpkins to produce a pamphlet entitled *Questions to Smellie's Philosophy of Natural History*, which was registered with the Clerk's Office in Massachusetts that year and sold separately from the *Philosophy*. A headnote addressed 'To the Teacher' suggests that the publication was originally intended only for the instructors using Ware's edition of Smellie's *Philosophy* and not all of those purchasing the book. The whole is thirty-two pages in length, comprising hundreds of questions organized by chapter and section. W. J. Reynolds acquired this teacher's guide along with the copyright to Ware's edition in 1843, and the questions thereafter become a part of the text, beginning with the edition of 1844. However, a separate issue of the questions was printed in 1843, intended as a supplement to Reynolds's first edition of the title that year, with pagination running from page 313 through 344, so that the questions might be bound in between the final page of the text proper of the *Philosophy* (p. 312) and the 'Analytical Table of Contents' and the 'Explanation of Terms,' which thus became a sort of appendix. Subsequently, Reynolds always made the *Questions* available as a separate title with its own imprint, as well as printing them in the text, a practice that ceased when the copyright changed hands after 1855.[34]

After 1844, with the addition of the study questions, Ware's edition of Smellie's *Philosophy* ran to 360 pages, and Reynolds published a total

---

[34] All editions through 1855 included a separate title-page for the 'Questions,' acknowledging the Simpkins copyright. Beginning with Brown, Taggard & Chase in 1858, the 'Questions' were simply printed as an 'Appendix' to the main text.

of ten editions under their imprint before the copyright was registered by Brown, Taggard and Chase in 1855. They published the twenty-third edition that year, bringing to twenty-five the number of American editions of the *Philosophy of Natural History*, volume one, since its first cross-Atlantic appearance in the Benjamin Smith Barton version, commissioned by Robert Campbell in 1791. Subsequent editions appeared under Brown and Taggard's textbook imprint in 1855 and 1858, but the publication in 1859 of Charles Darwin's *Origin of the Species by Natural Selection* changed the market for natural history and began to threaten the way natural history was taught in schools and colleges. In response, John Ware completely reworked his edition of Smellie's *Philosophy* altering it so radically that the new text was no longer described on its title-page – as it had been for thirty-six years and twenty-seven editions – as *The Philosophy of Natural History by William Smellie with an Introduction and Various Additions and Alterations by John Ware, MD*; it now became *The Philosophy of Natural History by John Ware, MD, Prepared on the Plan, and Retaining Portions, of the Work of William Smellie*. For the first time, Ware included illustrations with the text, some forty-nine figures in all, but it is the philosophical repositioning of the argument that so radically alters this edition.[35] Here, Ware retained only thirty-nine pages from Smellie's 1790 original, amounting to two innocuous chapters dealing respectively with the 'Habitations' and 'Artifices' of animals. In his new concluding chapter, Ware was insistent upon treating mankind as a special case, separate from the general plan of nature, which he now constantly referred to as a 'Kingdom'. He argued that because 'a spiritual is now induced upon the vital' in man, there 'is not a difference of degree but of kind' between human and animal (p. 413). Natural history became for Ware an opportunity to present an argument from design for the existence of God. William Smellie's *Philosophy* was thus made over into a version of William Paley's *Theology*. Notably, in 1850, John Ware had edited a school text version of Paley's *Natural Theology* for the Boston publishers Gould, Kendall and Lincoln. That book would have fourteen editions through 1872

---

[35] Ware here emulated his edition of Paley' *Natural Theology*, which used all of Paxton's plates. In fact, from this point on, Ware's edition of Smellie's *Philosophy* looks and reads very like his version of Paley's *Natural Theology*.

and its influence on Ware's ultimately creationist re-visioning of Smellie's *Philosophy* is everywhere apparent.

Ware's new version of the *Philosophy* was as popular as the earlier editions, running through the press eight times between 1860 and 1872, and remaining on the lists of texts used in Harvard classes. Thus, the total number of American editions of Smellie's *Philosophy* published between 1791 and 1872 stands at thirty-five. By contrast, there were four editions in England after the initial Edinburgh edition of 1790, one from the firm of Scott, Webster, and Geary of London in 1837, and a subsequent three under the imprint of William Milner of Halifax in 1844, 1845, and 1850.[36] All four were duodecimos, whereas all but one of the American editions were octavos (see Appendix). The 1837 imprint of the Scott, Webster, and Geary reads 'Sixth edition,' and the text follows that of Hilliard, Gray, and Company's fifth American edition of 1834 – their last before the text was stereotyped in 1835 – with one exception: the 'Analytical Table of Contents' was relocated to the front of the English edition, although the 'Explanation of Terms' was retained at the back of the book. Milner's three editions all followed Scott, Webster, and Geary's text in every point, including the relocation of the contents pages. The only change was Milner's choice of engraving for his title-pages.[37] Other than a modern Greek translation of Ware's 1840 edition of Smellie's *Philosophy* which appeared at Constantinople in 1846, the publishing history of the *Philosophy of Natural History* after 1800 is thus almost entirely an American affair, including a version for the blind, printed as a quarto with embossed roman type by S. G. Howe at Boston in 1845 for the Perkins Institute for the Blind. The copy text, predictably, was taken from John Ware's 1824 edition.

---

[36] Milner's edition is sometimes misidentified as Halifax, Nova Scotia in Canada (see Sher, *Enlightenment and the Book*, pp. 90-1). Milner also published duodecimo editions of William Paley's *Natural Theology* in 1844 and 1858.

[37] Scott, Webster, and Geary embellished Ware's edition of Smellie's *Philosophy* with two engravings: one, a frontispiece illustration of a tiger hunt in a jungle setting; the other, on the title-page, portraying two hounds chasing a fox in the English country-side. Milner kept the tiger-hunt frontispiece, but made his title-page all the more Romantic by replacing the fox hunt with the exotic depiction of a feral man being led captive by an armoured knight on horseback. None of the engravings, of course, in any way relates to the text that follows. After all, the English editions were trade books intended for the general market, and not the formal textbooks published in America.

A coda on readers of the *Philosophy of Natural History*

Charles Elliot's fine quarto of the first volume of William Smellie's *Philosophy of Natural History* probably never recouped the publisher's investment. Circumstances of all sorts conspired against it in Edinburgh. However, through an unauthorized Irish printing and the efforts of two keen American academic editors, the work had a second life in the United States, not as Elliot had published it, nor as Smellie had conceived it, but as the product of readership. The *Philosophy* was resurrected from its premature literary grave first by the astute Benjamin Barton Smith, who gave it an American slant in 1791, and later by Dr. John Ware in 1824. In fact, Ware continued to be Smellie's most obsessed reader, coming back to the text many times, and ultimately rewriting the *Philosophy* to reflect his own personality. The marginalia in surviving copies of Smellie's *Philosophy*, beginning with the 1790 quarto through its several unauthorized printings and into its many editions as a school text, indicate how passionately the book was valued by some, and disdained by others.

Smellie presented a signed copy to Captain Cochrane of *HMS Hind*, when the latter agreed to accept Smellie's son John as a lieutenant. Cochrane would later become an Admiral, a Knight of the Bath, and the naval hero of the war of 1812, who oversaw the siege of New Orleans and planned the burning of Washington. After his role in the extraordinary British victory at Alexandria, Cochrane, while still in Egypt, presented his copy to a young Samuel Briggs, who was to become Britain's power broker in the Levant for nearly fifty years.[38] William Bartram, whose *Travels Through North & South Carolina, Georgia, East & West Florida* (1791) repositioned natural history for a Romantic readership, owned a copy of the 1791 text, edited by his close friend and mentor Benjamin Smith Barton.[39] Darwin read the 1790 Edinburgh quarto carefully and his copy survives with more than twenty annotations in his hand.[40] However, not all Smellie's readers

---

[38] For some insight into Briggs and the Levant see, Frederick Stanley Rodkey, 'The Attempts of Briggs and Company to Guide British Policy in the Levant in the Interest of Mehemet Ali Pasha, 1821-41', *The Journal of Modern History*, 5 (1933), 324-51.

[39] His copy is at the Library Company of Philadelphia (shelfmark, W22.254 [Bartram]).

[40] The copy of the 1790 Edinburgh edition was a gift to Darwin from Josiah Wedgwood and is now part of the special collection of Charles Darwin's manuscripts and related materials, Cambridge University Library, no shelfmark.

were famous men. The 1837 London edition was presented, for instance, to exceptional scholars at Edinburgh's Merchiston Castle Academy annually, at least until the mid-1850s, gilt-edged and finely bound in tooled leather covers, bearing an image of the school's historic building.[41] Among the thousands of American students who read Ware's version of the *Philosophy* in academies and colleges throughout the nineteenth century were many adolescent girls whose readership fulfilled Smellie's own plan for his book to be accessible to the young and especially to women. However, one such female reader's annotations were less critically insightful than those of Barton, Ware, and Darwin. In 1855, she filled the margins of her copy with original poetry, all addressed to 'Lizzie,' her Sapphic classmate, thus undermining in her own way John Ware's attempt to take sex, puberty, and love out of Smellie's *Philosophy*.[42]

If the fate of Smellie's *Philosophy of Natural History* does nothing else, it draws the attention of book historians to the crucial role of readers in determining one vital line of book distribution. At the right historic moment of need or controversy, the professional reader as editor can redirect a book in a way that would never have been anticipated by a business-minded publisher, no matter how closely they had taken the pulse of their market. The professional reader can also transcend all the legal definitions of literary property by re-originating a text as their own conception and bringing to it a personality that its author would never recognize. Such was the fate of William Smellie's *Philosophy of Natural History*.

---

[41] I have seen three copies of these Merchiston Castle Scholar's Prize volumes, two at the National Library of Scotland and one in a private collection.

[42] The copy is part of a private collection.

Appendix

Editions of Smellie's *Philosophy of Natural History* edited by Dr. John Ware

(All texts printed and published in Boston, Massachusetts, unless otherwise indicated.)

Date/Format	Publisher	Printer
1824/8o	Cummings, Hilliard & Co.	University Press: Hilliard & Metcalf
1827/8o	Hilliard, Gray, Little & Wilkins	University Press: Hilliard & Metcalf
1829/8o	Hilliard, Gray, Little & Wilkins	University Press: Hilliard & Metcalf
1832/8o	Hilliard, Gray & Co.	Manson, Emerson & Grant
1834/8o	Hilliard, Gray & Co.	Manson, Emerson & Grant
1835/8o	Hilliard, Gray & Co.	Boston Type and Stereotype Foundry
1836/8o	Hilliard, Gray & Co.	Boston Type and Stereotype Foundry
1837/12o***	Scott, Webster & Geary	Alfred Sweeting, London
1838/8o	Hilliard, Gray & Co.	Boston Type and Stereotype Foundry
1839/8o	Hilliard, Gray & Co.	Boston Type and Stereotype Foundry
1840/8o	Hilliard, Gray & Co.	Boston Type and Stereotype Foundry
1841/8o*	Samuel G. Simpkins*	Boston Type and Stereotype Foundry
1843/8o**	W. J. Reynolds**	Boston Type and Stereotype Foundry

Date/Format	Publisher	Printer
1844/8o	W. J. Reynolds	Boston Type and Stereotype Foundry
1844/12o	William Milner	William Milner: Halifax, England
1845/8o	W. J. Reynolds	Boston Type and Stereotype Foundry
1845/12o	William Milner	William Milner: Halifax, England
1845/4o	Perkins Institute for the Blind	S. G. Howe
1846/8o	W. J. Reynolds	Boston Type and Stereotype Foundry
1847/8o	W. J. Reynolds	Boston Type and Stereotype Foundry
1848/8o	W. J. Reynolds	Boston Type and Stereotype Foundry
1850/8o	W. J. Reynolds	Boston Type and Stereotype Foundry
1850/12o	William Milner	William Milner: Halifax, England
1851/8o	W. J. Reynolds	Boston Type and Stereotype Foundry
1852/8o	W. J. Reynolds	Boston Type and Stereotype Foundry
1853/8o	W. J. Reynolds	Boston Type and Stereotype Foundry
1854/8o	W. J. Reynolds	Boston Type and Stereotype Foundry
1855/8o***	W. J. Reynolds	Boston Type and Stereotype Foundry
1858/8o	Brown, Taggard & Chase	H. O. Houghton
1860/8o	Brown & Taggard	H. O. Houghton
1863/8o	Taggard & Thompson	H. O. Houghton
1864/8o***	Taggard & Thompson	H. O. Houghton
1866/8o***	Taggard & Thompson	H. O. Houghton

Date/Format	Publisher	Printer
1867/8o***	Taggard & Thompson	H. O. Houghton
1868/8o	Taggard & Thompson	H. O. Houghton
1870/8o	Thompson, Bigelow & Brown	H. O. Houghton
1872/8o	Thompson, Bigelow & Brown	H. O. Houghton

* First Printing of Questions to Smellie's 'Philosophy of Natural History' by Simpkins.

** First printing of Questions by Reynolds, available as a separate title from Reynolds through 1855. Both publishers used the Boston Type and Stereotype Foundry.

*** Previously unrecorded editions.

Thomas Ruddiman: Librarian, Publisher, Printer and Collector

BRIAN HILLYARD

Thomas Ruddiman (1674-1757) would deserve to be recorded in history even if his only work had been what he did as (successively) 'Bibliothecar's servant', Under-Keeper ('Hypobibliothecarius'), and finally Keeper ('Bibliothecarius') of the Library of the Faculty of Advocates in Edinburgh from May 1702 to his retirement in January 1752.[1] It was that, primarily, which gave him his status, defined who he was. His bookplate styled him as 'Fac.[ultatis] Jurid.[icae] Edinb.[urgensis] Bibliothecarius', and the invitation to his funeral sent out by his son-in-law James Steuart referred to him as 'Mr. Thomas Ruddiman, late Keeper of the Advocates Library'.[2] The development of the library owed much to his work over nearly fifty years, especially since he began there only twenty years after the first books had been acquired in 1682.

As well as being responsible for the Advocates Library, Ruddiman was himself a collector.[3] Very little has been written about his library of

---

[1]   For monographs on Ruddiman see George Chalmers, *The Life of Thomas Ruddiman, A.M. The Keeper, for almost Fifty Years, of the Library belonging to the Faculty of Advocates at Edinburgh* (London, 1794; facsimile reprint, Garland, 1974), and Douglas Duncan, *Thomas Ruddiman: A Study in Scottish Scholarship of the Early Eighteenth Century* (Edinburgh, 1965). For his work in the Advocates Library see also Brian Hillyard, 'The Formation of the Library, 1682-1728', in *For the Encouragement of Learning: Scotland's National Library 1689-1989*, ed. by Patrick Cadell and Ann Matheson (Edinburgh, 1989), pp. 23-66, and Brian Hillyard, 'Thomas Ruddiman and the Advocates Library, 1728-1752', *Library History*, 8:6 (1991), 157-70.
[2]   ESTC N471336, unique copy at Edinburgh, National Library of Scotland [hereafter NLS] shelfmark 5.2483(4). 'Mr.' i.e. 'Magister' referred to his status as a university graduate.
[3]   It has not been possible, here, to follow up the question of tension between purchases for Ruddiman's own collection and the Advocates Library. In 1738, when there was a possibility of buying some pamphlets on Scottish history that were not already in the Advocates Library, Ruddiman advised the Curators that 'tho many of them [sc. Scottish authors] considered singly were of small Worth, yet a great Collection of them together in one Library made them on that Account of considerable Value' (see Hillyard, 'Thomas Ruddiman', pp. 161-62), but he may not have attached importance to making a comprehensive collection of, for example, editions of

which he was evidently proud.[4] An advertisement that followed his death stated it was 'the earnest wish of the worthy proprietor, that these books, which he had collected with so much care and expense, might not be dispersed'.[5] However, nobody came forward to buy the collection as a single entity, and it duly went to auction at the beginning

Fig. 1 Bookplate of Thomas Ruddiman (author's collection)

---

works by George Buchanan such as his own and so he may not have felt any conflict of interests.

[4]   There are three surviving manuscript catalogues of Ruddiman's library (NLS MSS. 764-66), the first two entirely in his own hand. They provide good examples of how Ruddiman documented meticulously his possessions and their worth: he valued his library at £200 in 1735, £300 in 1746, and £400 in 1750 (figures from NLS MS 762, fols 1^r, 15^v, 20^v).

[5]   Anonymous, *To Be Sold: A Part of the Library, Belonging to the Deceased Mr Thomas Ruddiman* ([Edinburgh, 1757]); unique copy at NLS, shelfmark L.C.1957(034), not recorded in ESTC. I cannot find evidence for Chalmers's claim (*Life*, p. 286) that 'Though [Ruddiman] had once designed to bequeath [his library] to the Faculty of Advocates, his generosity was, in the end, overruled by his justice'.

of February 1758 and is now quite widely dispersed.[6] Rather than a book-collector's library, his was a scholar's working collection evidenced, for example, by the large number of editions of George Buchanan needed for his editing of Buchanan's works.[7] Yet, Ruddiman also had an appreciation of collecting as this note on an edition of Horace's *Epistles* (Paris, 1553) demonstrates: 'This given to Dr James Douglas of London, who made it his Business to collect all the Editions of Horace, that he could come at. Besides this I gave him other two, which he had not.'[8] The Scots-born, London anatomist James Douglas was a noted collector, and it would be interesting to know more about their acquaintance.[9] The assiduous nature of Ruddiman's own collecting is evident from *Bibliotheca Romana*, a classified catalogue of only part of his library, on Latin language and literature.[10] The third section ('classis tertia') arranges grammars alphabetically by author, but there is also a special listing, 'grammaticae Latinae a Scotis scriptae, secundum temporis quo quisque scripserit ordinem dispositae' (i.e. Latin grammars written by Scots, arranged chronologically in the order in which they were written), that includes Ruddiman himself, here described as 'Keeper of the Advocate's [sic] Library, and sometime Schoolmaster at Laurence Kirk in the Mearns'.[11] This historical approach to enumerative bibliography ties in well with the evidence from Joseph Ames's *Typographical Antiquities*. Ames's 'Appendix Relating to Printing in Scotland' drew on an account of the *Breviarium Aberdonense* (Edinburgh, 1510) sent to him by Charles Mackey, an Edinburgh professor, based on an

---

[6]   A. Kincaid and A. Donaldson, *A Catalogue of a Rare and Valuable Collection of Books: Being the Whole Library of the Late Mr. Thomas Ruddiman* (Edinburgh, 1758). ESTC N47126 records the Newberry Library, Chicago, as sole location, but there is also a copy in the Signet Library, Edinburgh, of which NLS holds a microfilm, shelfmark Mf.17(15). Many – if not all – of the books Ruddiman owned carry his easily recognisable bookplate (*Fig. 1*).

[7]   Chalmers, *Life*, p. 282, writes: 'rather a selection of the most valuable editions, than a collection of rare classics'.

[8]   NLS, MS 764, fol. 43ʳ. See also Chalmers, *Life*, p. 283.

[9]   He published a catalogue of his Horace collection: *Catalogus editionum Quinti Horatii Flacci ab ann. 1476. ad ann. 1739. quae in bibliotheca Jacobi Douglas [...] adservantur* (London, 1739).

[10] Thomas Ruddiman, *Bibliotheca Romana* (Edinburgh, 1757). The copy at NLS, shelfmark RB.s.330, is a presentation copy to Ruddiman's secretary William Preston.

[11] Ruddiman, *Bibliotheca Romana*, pp. 61-63.

examination of the first volume. Ames continued, 'I have had a further account of the second part of this book, from my worthy friend Mr. Professor Ruddiman himself, no small encourager of this undertaking, by his many searches for me at Edinburgh, and elsewhere.'[12] Ruddiman's manuscript catalogues and *Bibliotheca Romana* would repay further detailed study as a bibliographically reliable record of books Ruddiman owned and for the occasional comments he makes about printers or authorship.[13]

Following his studies at King's College, Aberdeen, graduating MA in 1694, Ruddiman spent five years as a schoolmaster at Laurencekirk.[14] He was a highly accomplished Latinist, and this and his teaching background are fundamental to an understanding of his later career. In 1700, as a result of meeting Archibald Pitcairne, he came to Edinburgh, where, after beginning his official employment in the Advocates Library as 'Bibliothecar's servant' in May 1702, he seems to have been always on the look-out for making extra money.[15] Chalmers drew attention to the list of pupils he taught, beginning in March 1705, and the list of lodgers he took in from early 1706.[16] He also states that Ruddiman, turned 'auctioneer', in 1707, and 'naturally dealt in school-books, when he instructed scholars'.[17] Ruddiman's pocket-book provides no evidence of his setting up an auction but

---

[12] Joseph Ames, *Typographical Antiquities* (London, 1749), pp. 573-96 (p. 574).

[13] For example, MS 764, fol. 12^v has a note on E1.4 'Rudimenta Grammatices in gratiam Juventutis Scoticae conscripta - - - Edinb. 1680' in which Ruddiman records that according to what he was told by the author's great-grandson, Andrew Simson, Minister of Douglas, this grammar was written by Andrew Symson, schoolmaster at Dunbar, and that Lipenius refers to a very old edition of 1587: 'Antiquissimam vero horum Rudimentorum Editionem Anno 1587 meminit Lipenius in Biblioth. Philosopica [sic] p. ' (no page reference is given). In *Bibliotheca Romana*, p. 61, Ruddiman has the same details about Andrew Symson (again naming his great-grandson as his source), and states that the first edition of *Rudimenta grammatices* was Edinburgh, 1587. He then lists as contained in his library ('in hac bibliotheca'), Edinburgh editions of 1612, 1639, 1660, 1680 and 1709. None of these editions, except for that of 1709, can be located today. Ruddiman's reference to a 1587 edition, however, is puzzling. M. Lipenius, *Bibliotheca realis philosophica* (Frankfurt, 1682), p. 789, actually refers to 'Grammaticae Rudimenta in gratiam Juventutis Scoticae. Edinb. 8 [i.e. octavo]. 1580.', an edition known from other evidence to have been printed by Plantin for Henry Charteris.

[14] Chalmers, *Life*, pp. 12-25.

[15] Ibid., pp. 31-38.

[16] Ibid., pp. 38-39.

[17] Ibid., p. 41.

there is a note, 19 October 1703, of his buying three works 'for Mr Robert Spence Schoolmaster at Brechin'.[18] This Robert Spence appears, with other schoolmasters, in later lists of people to whom Ruddiman supplied books (below, p. 102). A note on 10 June 1706 also indicates Spence owed him for the binding of a book.[19] Ruddiman's work at the Advocates Library made him well placed to perform or arrange such services.

Some of his other 'extra-curricular' money-making activities in these early years – such as transcribing manuscripts for which the pocket-book records him as being paid by the University of Glasgow – probably stemmed from his work in the Library.[20] That would certainly have strengthened – if it did not initiate – his association with Robert Freebairn. Freebairn sold books to the Advocates Library at least as early as 1703, and was an important supplier: in the period 1702–09 about two thirds of all the money spent buying books went to him.[21] However, Freebairn was also a printer. According to the *History of the Art of Printing* (1713)

> In 1706, Mr. John Spotiswood Advocate, and Professor of the Law, brought Home a neat little House for printing his Law Books: But in a little time after, dispos'd of it to Mr. Robert Freebairn Bookseller, who has very much enlarg'd the same, and done several large Works in it, at Edinburgh.[22]

Spottiswood must have passed the press on quite quickly because under 22 October 1706 Ruddiman's pocket-book records that Freebairn took on Walter Ruddiman – Thomas's younger brother – as apprentice in the printing trade.[23]

Bearing in mind this close association, Freebairn's output, especially the advocates' theses and other legal works, is interesting:

1706 *The History of the Picts*;

1707 *A Letter from the Most Renouned Pastors and Professors of the Church and University of Geneva; to the University of Oxford,*

---

[18]   Ruddiman's pocket-book is now NLS, MS 5047, which has been used, and foliated, from both ends. For these purchases see (from the front) fol. 11^r.
[19]   NLS, MS 5047, (from the front) fol. 11^v.
[20]   NLS, MS 5047, (from the back) fol. 10^r.
[21]   Hillyard, 'Formation', p. 45.
[22]   Jean de la Caille, *The History of the Art of Printing* (Edinburgh, 1713), pp. 18-19.
[23]   NLS, MS 5047, (from the back) fol. 4^v.

in both Latin and English editions; John Spottiswood, *An Introduction to the Knowledge of the Stile of Writs, Simple and Compound, Made Use of in Scotland*; Volusenus, *De animi tranquillitate*; and eight advocates' theses;

1708 Thomas Craufurd, *Notes and Observations on Mr George Buchanan's History of Scotland*, and a reprint of Spottiswood's *Introduction*;

1709 Ruddiman's own edition of Arthur Johnston's poetical Latin version of the Song of Solomon, *Cantici Solomonis paraphrasis poetica*; three advocates' theses and a medical book (not a university thesis);

1710 *Virgil's Aeneis* (printed with Andrew Symson); three advocates' theses;

1711 Patrick Abercromby, *The Martial Atchievements of the Scots Nation*, 2 vols (1711–15); George Mackenzie, *An Idea of the Modern Eloquence of the Bar*; Jonathan Swift, *The Conduct of the Allies*; three advocates' theses;

1712 twenty-one items, including six advocates' theses.

The pocket-book records three sums owed to Ruddiman by Freeebairn on 22 November 1706: for £3, £10 and £17 Scots – but we do not know for certain what these debts were for, though the original of the *History of the Picts* was a manuscript in the Advocates Library, and correcting the text of Volusenus was something that as a Latin scholar Ruddiman was well suited to.[24] He was also paid £60 Scots by Spottiswood for helping him with the editing of his grandfather's *Practicks*, and £100 Scots by Andrew Symson for compiling the glossary to his edition of Virgil's *Aeneid*.[25] After 1710 when the Copyright Act was passed, Ruddiman asked the University of St Andrews to appoint him as their agent in demanding books from Stationers' Hall. Ruddiman was indeed given a commission to do this, but it did not last more than a couple of years. Nor did he continue to carry this out for the Advocates Library, but the job was given to

---

[24] NLS, MS 5047, (from the back) fol. 12. The writer of the 'advertisement' in *History of the Picts* refers to 'the original Manuscript in the Lawyers Library in Edinburgh', and says 'I have taken care to compare it [i.e. the history] exactly with the Original'.

[25] NLS, MS 5047, (from the back) fol. 12ᵛ, (from the front) fols 22ᵛ, 23ᵛ; Robert Spottiswood, *Practicks of the Law of Scotland* (Edinburgh, 1706); Virgil, *Aeneis*, trans. by Gawin Douglas (Edinburgh, 1710).

Edinburgh booksellers, first George Stewart and then John Paton, who also acted as agent for St Andrews.[26] The evidence of imprints suggests that both Stewart and Paton were closely associated with Ruddiman in publishing and bookselling from 1722 until 1748 (Stewart) and 1755 (Paton).[27] It would have been natural for Ruddiman to have steered this work in their direction.

The printing of advocates' theses by Freebairn merits some attention. *Table 1* details (where known) the printers of all the theses for intrants (new advocates) 1693-1757.[28] In the period before 1716 (when his name dropped out from imprints) Freebairn gradually cornered the market, and it is a fair guess that his success in doing this owed something to his association with Spottiswood and Ruddiman, especially perhaps Ruddiman. On 19 November 1698,

> It was enacted and appointed that the Curators of the Library, the Clerk and Library keeper be the only revisers and censures of all theses to be printed and distributed by the candidats [sic] and that the said censures take particular notice and care that no error or incongruity either in the style or matter of the theses be alloued to be printed as they shall be ansu-erable to the Faculty.[29]

Ruddiman was well qualified to check the style, i.e. the Latinity, and although strictly speaking the regulations did not allow him to do this, seeing as in many other ways he behaved like a Keeper, he probably did.[30] On 9 December 1710 the Faculty recommended all intrants 'to

[26] Philip Ardagh, 'St Andrews University Library and the Copyright Acts', *Edinburgh Bibliographical Society Transactions*, 3:3 (1956), 179-211 (pp. 185-87); Hillyard, 'Formation', pp. 48-51.

[27] On the basis of ESTC, there are seven publications linking Stewart to Ruddiman, and eleven linking Paton to Ruddiman. ESTC T166185, 'printed for George Stewart', without name of printer, may also have been printed by Ruddiman, to judge from the border on the title-page.

[28] Figures in the printer columns are derived from the British Library's ESTC OPAC (accessed 21 March 2010), with additions from NLS, MS 763 (for 1713-15), Edinburgh University Library OPAC (for 1722), and Paxton House Library (for 1735, 1751, 1755-56). The figures for 1728 and 1751 each include a thesis with the imprint date of that year but presented at the beginning of the following year. Figures in the 'Total no. of intrants' column have been calculated from *The Minute Book of the Faculty of Advocates*, ed. by John MacPherson Pinkerton and others (Edinburgh, 1976–).

[29] *Minute Book*, I, 190.

[30] Hillyard, 'Formation', pp. 42-43.

Table 1 **Printers of theses of new advocates 1693-1757**

Year	Total no. of intrants	J. Reid	Heirs & successors of A. Anderson	G. Mosman	J. Watson	G. Jeffrey & J. Reid jr	A. Symson	R. Freebairn	T. Ruddiman	T. W. & T. Ruddimans	T. & W. Ruddimans	Hamilton, Balfour & Neill	W. Ruddiman & socii
1693	2	1	1										
1694	10		3	7									
1695	5	1	4										
1696	13		10	2	1								
1697	7		3	2	3								
1698	14		9	1	2								
1699	6		5		3								
1700	8		7		2								
1701	14	1	9		3	1	2						
1702	9		2	1									
1703	10		3	1	1			3					
1704	10		5	1				2					
1705	10		7					5					
1706	6		1					3					
1707	13		4		1			8					
1708	8		7										
1709	3				1			3					
1710	11		4		2			3					
1711	7		4					3					
1712	11		1		1			6					
1713	7				1			2					
1714	10		1					8					
1715	6							3					
1716	10								2				
1717	12								11				
1718	8								8				
1719	4								4				

1720	7									4				
1721	4													
1722	11									2				
1723	11									2				
1724	9									1				
1725	9									1				
1726	5									2				
1727	8									1				
1728	12									3				
1729	7													
1730	11									1				
1731	7									1				
1732	3									1				
1733	5									1				
1734	10									6				
1735	7									3				
1736	7									4				
1737	6									5				
1738	6									6				
1739	3									3				
1740	1									1				
1741	3									3				
1742	2									1	1			
1743	13										13			
1744	5										3			
1745	1										1			
1746	1										1			
1747														
1748	6											6		
1749	2											2		
1750														
1751	9											9		
1752	7											2		
1753	3											3		
1754	10											7		
1755	9											8	1	
1756	4											5		
1757	6													4

pay Mr. Thomas Rudiman underkeeper of their library each of them a guinea before they pass their private trial and that in place of the two crowns and a half [i.e. 12s. 6d.] formerly paid to him by intrants'.[31] The thesis was the public trial, but this payment before the private trial might still cover the correcting of the thesis.[32] When Ruddiman had this close relationship with all intrants, what could be more natural than that he recommended Freebairn as printer? We should remember, too, that his brother Walter was apprenticed to Freebairn.

On 11 August 1711 Robert Freebairn was appointed Printer to the Queen for Scotland and the extra demands that this would have made on his printing business may explain why it was soon after this that Ruddiman decided to set up his own printing house. He was also, of course, able to utilise the experience of his brother Walter, and he paid him an 'Allowance of eight Pounds Sterl. per annum for his Assistance in managing the house' from 'Martinmass [i.e. 11 November] 1712 to Whitsunday 1719'.[33] So Walter was the manager but, as the documents themselves convey very clearly, Thomas was in the driving seat.

Ruddiman ran a substantial printing business: more substantial, I think, than has been appreciated but assembling the evidence for the output of the Ruddiman press is not easy. David Foxon used Ruddiman's ledger when researching *English Verse 1701–1750*, but did not succeed in identifying all the poems mentioned in it because some seem not to have survived.[34] In addition, much of the printing was of legal works – petitions, memorials, answers, etc. – and until the vast collections of such papers in the Advocates Library and the Signet Library have been fully catalogued, it will be difficult to locate these

---

[31] *Minute Book*, I, 289.

[32] See also *Minute Book*, I, 286-87, for the Faculty Minutes for 15 July 1710 (this was when there was a possibility of Ruddiman's leaving to become rector of the Grammar School in Dundee) recording agreement to pay him an annual pension of £363 6s. 8d. to include all fees and emoluments formerly payable to him except 'the small gratifications in use to be paid him by intrants'. Chalmers (*Life*, p. 36) states that Ruddiman received 'an honorary present from every student, when he was about to be admitted an advocate, for correcting his thesis', for which he cites the pocket-book. The pocket-book does have references to money from intrants, but nothing this specific.

[33] Edinburgh, NLS, MS 763, fol. 131ᵛ. NLS, MS 763 is Ruddiman's printing ledger 15 November 1712 to 23 April 1715. Following the weekly accounts there are a number of statements of clearances.

[34] D. F. Foxon, *English Verse, 1701-1750: A Catalogue of Separately Printed Poems with Notes on Contemporary Collected Editions*, 2 vols (London, 1975). The value of this ledger was also noted by Robert Hay Carnie and Ronald Paterson Doig, 'Scottish Printers and Booksellers 1668-1775: A Supplement', *Studies in Bibliography*, 12 (1959), 131-59 (p. 132).

items, if indeed they survive. The week ending 31 July 1714 indicates the extent of the problem: Ruddiman printed fifty legal papers that week whereas the British Library's ESTC OPAC (accessed 19 March 2010) shows only twenty-eight such legal papers printed in Scotland during the whole of 1714.[35] Legal papers tend not to have imprints, but, on the evidence of the other publications in the ledger that have been located so far, nothing disproves the view that before 1716 no publication printed by Ruddiman appeared with Ruddiman's imprint: it was all 'printed by Robert Freebairn' (or words to that effect). This must have been a special arrangement between Ruddiman and Freebairn. In 1714 it applied, for example, even to the printing of the first edition of Ruddiman's famous *Rudiments*, which was 'Printed by Mr. Robert Freebairn, Printer to the King's Most Excellent Majesty'.[36]

Turning to books printed in 1716 and after, when they did have Ruddiman imprints, and assessing his output without the help of a printing-house ledger, there are several problems of evidence.[37] One is how few surviving copies (if any) there are of some books with a Ruddiman imprint. As private libraries and local studies libraries in Scotland go through the process of reporting their holdings to ESTC, new works are likely to emerge. For example, recent years have brought to light an edition of Tony Aston's *The Medley Songs* 'printed for the author, by Mr. Thomas Ruddiman, 1726' and the cataloguing of Paxton House Library has uncovered some hitherto unrecorded advocates' theses printed by Ruddiman.[38] Another problem is that of books in which Ruddiman is not named as printer. For *English Verse 1701-1750* David Foxon identified a number of false 'London' imprints

---

[35] Searches were carried out in ESTC for title words 'petition', 'answers', 'information', 'memorial', 'reply/ies', and 'duplies'. No attempt has been made yet to match the entries in Ruddiman's ledger to those in ESTC.

[36] Thomas Ruddiman, *The Rudiments of the Latin Tongue* (Edinburgh, 1714), later entitled *Ruddiman's Rudiments* and published well into the nineteenth century.

[37] There are a number of different imprints (which will not normally be distinguished from one another in what follows): 1716- in aedibus Tho. Ruddimanni / printed by Mr. Thomas Ruddiman; 1728- printed by Mr. Thomas and Walter Ruddimans (but theses and other Latin books remain 'in aedibus Tho. Ruddimanni' until 1732); 1740- apud Tho. Wal. & Tho. Ruddimannos / T. W. and T. Ruddimans; 1742- theses 'apud T. W. & T. Ruddimannos'; 1745- W. & T. Ruddimans; 1748- T. & W. Ruddimans.

[38] Tony Aston, *The Medley Songs* (Edinburgh, 1726), now ESTC T225925. The unique Paxton House theses will be included in ESTC in due course.

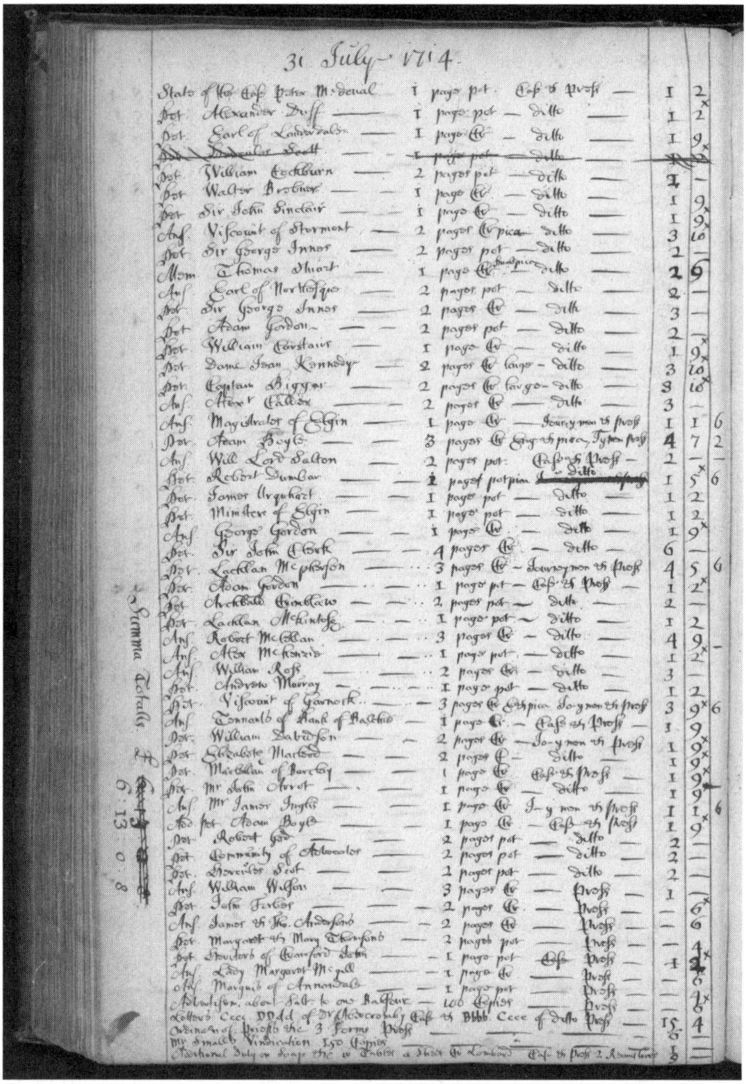
31 July 1714

Fig. 2 Page of Ruddiman's ledger for week ending 31 July 1714 listing the 50 legal papers printed by Ruddiman for that week (NLS, MS 763, fol. 90v). Reproduced by permission of the Trustees of the National Library of Scotland

some with an Edinburgh origin which he often attributed to Ruddiman on the evidence of their ornaments.[39] A considerable

[39] Foxon's working papers on Edinburgh piracies are now NLS, MS Acc.10079.

amount of prose publications can also be attributed to Ruddiman on the same basis. Some can be identified initially by using Ruddiman's advertisements such as that for 'Books printed and sold by Mr. Thomas and Walter Ruddimans' at the end of their 1733 edition of selections from Ovid.[40] It lists two works by James Dundass, *A View of the Elections of Bishops in the Primitive Church* and *A Supplement to the View of the Elections of Bishops in the Primitive Church*.[41] Comparison of the headpieces (Figures 3a and 3b) confirms the evidence of the advertisement, and the *Supplement*'s illustrated initial T is also found in *The History of the Church under the Old Testament* which was an explicit Ruddiman imprint of the same year, 1730.[42]

In addition to the 1733 advertisement, two others exist which merit careful study.[43] Where copies of the books listed survive and contain no name of printer, the attribution to Ruddiman can be checked by comparison with books known to be his. Other books pose more of a problem. The 1727 advertisement includes reference to 'A new Vocabulary Latin and English, for the use of Schools; to which is added a Collection of the most common Adjectives and Verbs. By *John Forrest*, A.M.'. This appears to refer to the missing sixth or seventh edition of what had been published as *A New Vocabulary, English and Latin*, fourth edition, 1717, and fifth edition in 1720; the next surviving edition is the eighth of 1749.[44] None of those editions mentions John Forrest, even in the prefatory material. However, 'A New Vocabulary, English and Latine. 3d. edition. Edinburgh, 1713' is included in a list of 'Books printed and to be sold by Mr. Robert

---

[40] Ovid, *Decerpta ex P. Ovidii Nasonis Metamorphoseon libris, notis anglicis illustrata* (Edinburgh, 1733), pp. [175-76].

[41] James Dundass, *A View of the Elections of Bishops in the Primitive Church* (Edinburgh: Thomas Ruddiman, 1728); James Dundass, *A Supplement to the View of the Elections of Bishops in the Primitive Church* (Edinburgh: [s.n.], 1730).

[42] Robert Millar, *The History of the Church under the Old Testament* (Edinburgh: Thomas and Walter Ruddimans, 1730).

[43] The advertisements are at the end of Sallust, *C. Crispi Sallustii Belli Catilinarii & Jugurthini historiae* (Edinburgh, 1727), pp. [141-42], and Anonymous, *A Short and Easy Vocabulary, Latin and English* (Edinburgh, 1735), pp. [82-83].

[44] *A New Vocabulary, English and Latin, for the Use of Schools*, 4th edn (Edinburgh: printed by Mr. James McEuen, 1717); *A New Vocabulary English & Latin, for the Use of Schools*, 5th edn (Edinburgh: printed by Mr. James McEuen, 1720); *A New Vocabulary English & Latin, for the Use of Schools*, 8th edn (Edinburgh: printed by T. and W. Ruddimans, 1749).

Freebairn Book-seller, in the Parliament-Closs, Edinburgh.' printed at the end of William King's *A Discourse Concerning the Inventions of Men*, and that does seem to be the immediate predecessor of *A New*

Figs 3a and 3b Comparison of headpieces in James Dundass, *A View of the Elections of Bishops in the Primitive Church*, and James Dundass, *A Supplement to the View of the Elections of Bishops in the Primitive Church* as confirmation of Ruddiman's printing of the *Supplement* (National Library of Scotland, shelfmarks H.38.c.11 and H.38.c.12). Reproduced by permission of the Trustees of the National Library of Scotland

Vocabulary Latin and English.[45] This 1713 book can also be traced in Ruddiman's ledger, which records his payments for twenty-two reams of paper 'for printing Mr Forrest's Vocabulary' and for the press-work signature by signature from December 1712 to May 1713.[46] Infuriatingly, Forrest's book does not survive.

To return to the advocates' theses (*Table 1*), 125 of these are known to survive (ESTC file as accessed, augmented by holdings of Paxton House Library) for the years 1716-54 and none of them is recorded as printed by anybody other than Ruddiman. From the Faculty minutes it is possible to make up a list of a total of 245 theses presented in these years, and it looks to be a fairly safe conclusion that Ruddiman printed them all, though copies of only about fifty per cent of them have been located so far.

How significant as printing jobs were these theses? They may have been normally only twelve pages in length (one and a half sheets of quarto), but in February 1754 George Wallace received a bill from Walter Ruddiman of £2 3s. 5d., for 164 copies of his thesis on common paper and thirty-six on fine paper.[47] There is no reason to think these numbers exceptional, and Warren McDougall has noted that there are several references to law theses in quantities of 200 in Patrick Neill's printing ledger, 1764-67.[48] Just over ten years before Walter Ruddiman billed George Wallace for his thesis, Thomas Ruddiman had billed James Erskine £2 12s. 6d., 'for printing his Theses & furnishing paper both for the fine & the common copies'.[49] When Erskine's thesis was the normal twelve pages, why did it cost more than Wallace's?[50] It seems unlikely that Wallace had provided the paper (two kinds) and paid less for that reason, and it is more probable that Erskine had more than 200 copies printed. Ruddiman's ledger shows that he usually charged 10s. 6d. for composing and printing 250 copies of theses, as in

---

[45] William King, *A Discourse Concerning the Inventions of Men in the Worship of God* (Edinburgh, 1713).

[46] NLS, MS 763, fols 3^v, 5^v-26^v.

[47] See John W. Cairns, 'Advocates' Hats, Roman Law and Admission to the Scots Bar, 1580-1812', *The Journal of Legal History*, 20 (1999), 24-61 (p. 30), citing Edinburgh, Edinburgh University Library, MS La.II.694.2.1-5.

[48] Warren McDougall, 'Gavin Hamilton, John Balfour and Patrick Neill: A Study of Publishing in Edinburgh in the 18th Century' (unpublished Ph.D. thesis, University of Edinburgh, 1974), p. 200.

[49] NLS, MS 5100, fol. 226^r.

[50] Erskine's thesis survives: ESTC T154332, copy in Advocates Library.

the entry for James Holborne's thesis (1714).[51] This was the same for all other theses included in the ledger except for Alexander Cuming's (1714) for which the charge was 14s. 0d.[52] However, Cuming's thesis took two sheets and was charged pro rata at the same rate. It looks therefore as though printing at least 250 copies was the norm in the 1710s, that this lasted until the 1740s and that the printing of advocates' theses was a good source of work.[53]

The profitability of the thesis business may have motivated Ruddiman to seek appointment as printer to the University of Edinburgh in 1728 (below, p. 102) as this enabled him to add the printing of university dissertations (mainly but not exclusively medical) to the printing of advocates' theses. The earliest printed by Ruddiman was in 1726 and the next was printed in 1730. Table 2 shows that Ruddiman printed them all until 1739 and thereafter had a reasonable share of the market until challenged by Hamilton, Balfour

Table 2 Printers of University of Edinburgh dissertations 1726-55

Year	T. Ruddiman	T.W. & T. Ruddimans	W. & T. Ruddimans	T. & W. Ruddimans	A. Alison	W. Cheyne	No printer named	R. Fleming	Sands, Murray & Cochran	R. Foulis	Neill	Hamilton, Balfour &
1726	1											

---

[51]   NLS, MS 763, fol. 66ᵛ. The entry for James Holbourne's has 1½ sheets, case & press, 250 copies, £0 10s. 6d.; that for George Gordon's (fol. 56ᵛ, 1713) was 1½ sheets, £0 7s. 6d. for case, and £0 3s. 0d. for press, 250 coarse, 32 fine (if this means, as it seems to, 282 in total, Gordon got a better deal).

[52]   NLS, MS 763, fol. 67ᵛ.

[53]   Why so many copies? One might guess that intrants gave them to their fellow-advocates. There may be some confirmation of this from a pamphlet volume in Paxton House Library that includes two theses of 1754, seven of 1755, and five of 1756. Sir Patrick Home of Billie (1728-1808), for whom Paxton House was built in 1758, was admitted advocate in 1755.

1727										
1728										
1729										
1730	1									
1731	5									
1732	4									
1733	1									
1734	3									
1735	2									
1736	1									
1737	1									
1738	2									
1739	1						3			
1740	1			1						
1741										
1742	3	2			2		2			
1743		1								
1744		3			2					
1745			1		1			1		
1746						1	4			
1747							1	1		
1748				2		2	3		1	
1749				7			3		1	
1750				8				1		3
1751				4						7
1752							1			6
1753				2			3			10
1754				1		2		2		10
1755								1		15

& Neill (Hamilton & Balfour were in fact appointed Printers to the University in May 1754).[54] University dissertations were as good as, if not better than, advocates' theses as a source of work for printers.

---

[54] This information is derived from the Edinburgh University Library OPAC and the British Library's ESTC OPAC (both accessed 26 March 2010). Neill was dropped from the Hamilton, Balfour & Neill imprint in the course of 1754. For 1742 two dissertations with the joint imprint of Alison and Fleming have been entered under both their names.

University Regulations of 1812 stated 'the printer to the University should, upon certain conditions have the sole privilege of printing the Inaugural Dissertations of candidates for that degree' and set out rules concerning paper, type, and costs.[55] Print runs of up to 300 were detailed, and university dissertations were longer than legal theses, some reaching fifty pages (although later they were in octavo, before 1750 the normal format was quarto).[56]

Having looked at Ruddiman's printing activities, we now need to consider his publishing and bookselling. The first books with the Ruddiman imprint belong to 1716 when he brought out the second edition of his *Rudiments* 'Edinburgh: printed, and sold by the author, and the booksellers there': this is perhaps the first book for which he is clearly the publisher.[57] However, there is some evidence that he published the 1709 edition of Johnston's paraphrase of the Song of Solomon.[58] Although the imprint reads 'apud Robertum Freebairn', Ruddiman owed Freebairn £36 12s. 0d. Scots 'For paper to print the Cantica, which he [i.e. Freebairn] paid to Mr Watkins', £24 Scots 'For printing', £6 Scots 'For stitching 200 in blue paper', and then £2 Scots 'For stitching another 100 I having furnished the blue paper and thread'.[59] Ruddiman also seems to have been selling it. A small itemized receipt for money paid to him 7 March 1710 by James Haldane includes seven copies of 'Arth. John', probably the *Cantica*.[60] James Haldane is not a recorded bookseller: in fact the name is found elsewhere in the pocket-book as one of Ruddiman's lodgers from July 1709.[61]

Ruddiman's inventories of his own worth also give a very clear idea of his publishing activities. The 'Inventory of the Goods and Effects belonging to Mr Thomas Ruddiman, as drawn up and valuyed in a Writ under his Hand 6 October 1735, & subscribed by him 18 May 1736', (Figure 4) values his private library at £200.[62] However, the

---

[55]   *Last edition. Regulations, &c, with Respect to Printing Inaugural Dissertations, &c.* ([Edinburgh], 1818.) The text is dated 10 May 1812. Copy at NLS shelfmark 5.4412(25).

[56]   The table of costs (*Regulations*, p. 5) sets out costs per sheet (16 pages, i.e. in octavo) for 100, 150, 200, 250 and 300 copies.

[57]   Thomas Ruddiman, *The Rudiments of the Latin Tongue* (Edinburgh, 1716).

[58]   Arthur Johnston, *Cantici Solomonis paraphrasis poetica* (Edinburgh, 1709).

[59]   NLS, MS 5047, (from the front) fol. 22^r.

[60]   NLS, MS 5047 (from the front) fol. 20^v.

[61]   NLS, MS 5047 (from the back) fol. 5^v.

[62]   NLS, MS 762, fol. 1^r.

third item down is the largest sum and the one that interests us now: £527 4s. 9½d. for 'Copies of Books printed for sd Tho. Ruddiman'. This figure is more than double the combined value of the printing and dwelling houses. There are similar inventories for other years.[63]

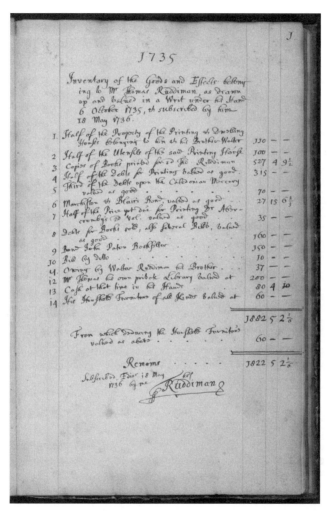

Fig. 4 Inventory of Thomas Ruddiman's 'Goods and Effects', 1735, valuing his library at £200 (NLS, MS 762, fol. 1ʳ). Reproduced by permission of the Trustees of the National Library of Scotland

---

[63] 1736 (fol. 5), 1739 (fol. 9), 1746 (fol. 15), and 1750 (fol. 20). There are statements that no inventories were drawn up for 1737-38 (fols 6-7), 1740-45 (fol. 14ᵛ), and 1747-49 (fol. 18ᵛ).

Particularly interesting are the lists of people owing Ruddiman money, sometimes 'for books sold'; and the lists of books in stock. Mostly people are specified, for example, in the list covering books sold 1 January to 20 May 1736, as booksellers, usually in Edinburgh or Glasgow.[64] At the head of this list 'Mr Robert Spence Master of the High School Edinburgh' is presumably the same person as 'Mr Robert Spence Schoolmaster at Brechin' for whom he bought three books in October 1703 (above, p. 87). There are no details of what books were sold to the booksellers listed, but some of the sums are significant: the highest is £9 12s. 1d. owed by the Edinburgh bookseller John Paton. For 1739 we have a different kind of list showing what the books were that Ruddiman sold: 'List of School Authors and others printed for and sold by Mr Thomas Ruddiman, presently in his Possession with the Values he has thought fit to put upon them, this day of October 1739.'[65] This list (Figure 5 shows the beginning of it) specifies where the books are stored, and gives numbers of copies for books in sheets and for books bound. Lists of this kind survive also for 1746 and 1750.[66] They reveal the size and complexity of his business, and also – as suggested by the phrase 'School Authors and others' in the heading – his fundamental interest in providing textbooks.[67]

The lists contain many other points of interest. Ruddiman's stock included bound copies in reasonable numbers: the 1739 list records 135 bound copies of his edition of selections from Ovid's *Metamorphoses* priced at 6½d.[68] The source of some of the books in his stock is also interesting. In the 1739 list there is a separate entry at the end for 1272

---

[64]   NLS, MS 762, fol. 4^v.

[65]   NLS, MS 762, fols 12^v-13^v.

[66]   NLS, MS 762, fols 17^v-18^r, 21^r.

[67]   In 1728 James Davidson, a bookseller in Edinburgh, and Ruddiman pointed out to Edinburgh Town Council that 'whereas the far greater part of the books taught in our schools and colledges are imported from forraign places into this country to the great discouragement of their own manufactorys', this could be prevented by appointing them printers to the University of Edinburgh, which the Town Council duly did. (See, Edinburgh, Edinburgh City Archives, SL1/1/51). Archie Turnbull, 'Academiae Typographus', *University of Edinburgh Gazette*, 25 (October 1959), 34-42, is probably right to see some patriotic motives here, but Ruddiman would also have seen the financial advantage of benefiting from the 'drawback', or rebate, on the duty levied on paper that was given to the six University Presses of the United Kingdom for books printed in Latin, Greek, Oriental or Northern languages.

[68]   NLS, MS 762, fol. 13^r.

copies of 'Horatii opera, printed by the late Ja. Watson, & purchased by the sd Mr Tho. Ruddiman at an auction for --- £5 15s 0d'.[69]

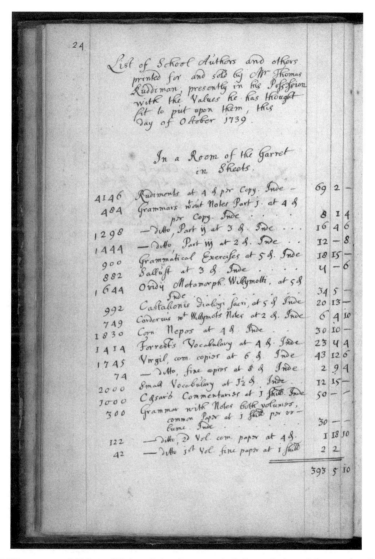

Fig. 5 First part of 'List of School Authors and Others Printed for and Sold by Mr Thomas Ruddiman' drawn up by Ruddiman in 1739 (NLS, MS 762, fol. 12ᵛ). Reproduced by permission of the Trustees of the National Library of Scotland

---

[69]   Ibid., fol. 13ᵛ.

In later lists the Horace is included as one of Ruddiman's publications.[70] There are other examples where he seems to have taken over stock: the 1739 list records multiple copies of 'Cornelius Nepos', a total of 1858 in sheets at 4d., and ninety-eight bound at 5d.[71] In 1744 the Ruddimans printed Nepos with Robert Arrol's literal English translation, but in 1739 the only earlier Edinburgh-printed edition this could be is Freebairn's 1714 edition.[72] The printing of this work is detailed in Ruddiman's ledger which has an entry for the week ending 29 May 1714: 'For gathering 1st Alphab. of Dr Abercrombie's book & all Cornelius Nepos, of which there are 5014 copies': it is not clear if 5014 refers to both books or just to Nepos, but even if to both, most of them must have been Nepos.[73] It seems possible then that nearly 2000 copies were still for sale twenty-five years later. That only one copy has survived is testament yet again to the poor survival rate for textbooks.

So MS 762 lists books in stock and also lists booksellers and others owing money for books, but has no details of the titles and quantities distributed to individual booksellers. Fortunately the Advocates Library's records preserved as part of the Faculty's Records (on deposit in NLS) include some of Ruddiman's personal memoranda – itself an example of his not keeping separate his business interests from his professional job. This provides us with details of some individual accounts. As an example, consider the account with John Paton:[74]

1727

21 January	26 Corderius Qres	00	9	0
28 January	52 Rudiments Qres	1	5	0
	26 Grammatical Exercises Qres		14	1
	26 Ovid. Metamorph. Qres		14	1
13 February	12 Grammars without Notes pt 1st bd		8	0
28 February	6 Ditto bd		4	0
14 June	6 Ditto bd		4	0
30 June	26 Grammatical Exer. Qres		14	1
	26 Corderius Qres		9	0

[70] Ibid., fol. 17ᵛ (1746, recording 1092 copies).
[71] Ibid., fols 12ᵛ-13ʳ, 13ᵛ.
[72] Cornelius Nepos, *Cornelii Nepotis excellentium imperatorum vitae* (Edinburgh, 1714), recorded by ESTC (T166526) as Liverpool University Library only.
[73] NLS, MS 762, fol. 81ᵛ.
[74] NLS, Faculty Records 339.e(i), Bundle 1.

7 July	12 Grammars without notes pt 1st bd		8	0
	6 Gramm. Exercises bd		5	0
	26 Rudiments Qres		12	6
11 July	26 Ovid. Meta. Qres		14	1
9 August	26 Paterson's Qres		5	0
	26 Forest's Vocab Qres		12	6
10 August	6 Grammars without Notes bd pt 1st		4	0
	52 Rudiments Qres	1	5	0
30 September	26 Grammatical Exer. Qres		14	1
3 October	6 Grammars without Notes bd		4	0
23 October	52 Rudiments Qres	1	5	0
6 November	26 Corderius Qres		9	0
9 November	6 Grammars without Notes pt 1st bd		4	0
10 November	6 ditto bd		4	0
16 November	2 copies of Sallust bd		[no price]	
22 November	26 Forest's vocab. Qres		12	6
11 December	12 Paterson's Vocab. bd		4	0

There are similar accounts with other booksellers, and for a later period there is a 'Memorandum of what Books are given out since March 5th 1728', which lists chronologically the various consignments that Ruddiman sent out, with names of booksellers, titles and quantities, but no prices.[75] Taken all together, these documents enable us to build up a detailed picture of the distribution of Ruddiman's publications.

After all this discussion about schoolbooks, it is important not to forget the amount of routine legal work that the Ruddimans probably took on in addition to the advocates' theses. There is no reason to think that the printing of session papers as documented in the 1712-15 ledger did not continue. The Faculty Minutes for 27 July 1723 record:

> A Petition being given in by Walter Ruddiman, Printer in Edinburgh, humbly craving that the Faculty would give Order to their Treasurer for paying him a small accompt due for Printing the Case of Mr. Patrick Haldane before the House of Lords, the Faculty appointed the Treasurer to make payment of the same.[76]

As it happens, this *Case* survives, and carries Ruddiman's ornaments.[77]

[75]   NLS, Faculty Records 339.e(i), Bundle 1.

[76]   *Minute Book*, II, 67.

[77]   Patrick Haldene, *The Case of Mr Patrick Haldene, Advocate* ([Edinburgh], 1723).

This was not usual (proceedings were in the House of Lords), but it does seem likely that they printed many more ordinary legal papers.

Nor should we forget that having printed the *Caledonian Mercury* from January 1724, the Ruddimans owned it from March 1729. In due course, like some other newspaper proprietors, they went into paper-making too: in 1742 Walter Ruddiman, in partnership with Robert Fleming of the *Edinburgh Evening Courant* and the Edinburgh bookseller John Aiken, set up Springfield Mill at Polton in Midlothian.[78]

We may conclude with a further example of how Thomas Ruddiman merged his professional and business activities in his printing for the Faculty. No catalogue of the Advocates Library had been printed since 1692, and one of Ruddiman's achievements was the first volume of the new catalogue which was 'Printed by Thomas, Walter, and Thomas Ruddiman'. The imprint date is 1742, but this title-page was not printed until 1772, and the process from when printing started, probably in 1734, to the 1750s was fraught with problems, including financial wrangling.[79] The Faculty Minutes for 21 February 1751 record:

> Mr. Gilbert Elliot one of the Curators of the Library laid before the Faculty ane Accompt of one hundred and five pounds nine shillings one penny halfpenny Sterling money yet due by the said Faculty to Mr Thomas and Walter Ruddimans for printing the first part, or Alphabetical Catalogue, of the Faculty's Library, as by a Contract entered into be Act of Faculty betwixt the then Curators & Messrs Ruddimans in the year 1733 together with the interest charged thereupon since the finishing said first part, in terms of said Contract; and inform'd the Faculty in name of the Curators, that they had strictly examined the said Accompt, and had made considerable defalcations from the Interest as it was at first charg'd, in regard that the said Messrs Ruddimans had fail'd in the performance of their part, in so far as the Execution of the work had been postpon'd for many years after the time stipulated, during which time they had in their hands thirty four pounds ten shillings Sterling of the Faculty's money, ...[80]

---

[78] See Alistair G. Thomson, *The Paper Industry in Scotland 1590-1861* (Edinburgh, 1974), p. 98; Robert Waterston, 'Further Notes on Early Paper Making near Edinburgh', *Book of the Old Edinburgh Club*, 27 (1949), 40-59 (pp. 55-56).
[79] See Hillyard, 'Thomas Ruddiman', pp. 168-69.
[80] *Minute Book*, III, 3-4.

Even if there were anywhere at the present day a librarian of Ruddiman's status who was also the owner of a printing firm, it seems unlikely that the line between the librarian's professional and private interests would be crossed to the same extent as it was in Ruddiman's case.

This brief survey has paid little attention to Ruddiman's work as an author of Latin grammars and other school books, and of other books, or as an editor of texts, but even without taking those into account, his achievements as librarian, collector, printer and publisher are impressive. Throughout his long life he displayed an enormous capacity for hard work, but, equally important, he was able to draw on great scholarly abilities. James Boswell referred to him as 'that excellent man and eminent scholar, by whose labours a knowledge of the Latin language will be preserved in Scotland, if it shall be preserved at all.'[81] Perhaps we may allow Samuel Johnson the last word: on receiving a copy of Boswell's thesis (Boswell was admitted advocate in 1766), he wrote to him with corrections that were needed to the Latin – the kind of corrections that Ruddiman would have made to advocates' theses while he was alive – ending with the words 'Ruddiman is dead'.[82]

---

[81] James Boswell, *The Journal of a Tour to the Hebrides* (London, 1785), p. 74 (21 August 1773).
[82] James Boswell, *The Life of Samuel Johnson*, 2 vols (London, 1791), I, 281-82. I take Johnson's point to be that after Ruddiman's death there was nobody capable of correcting to a high standard the Latin of advocates' theses.

The Poet and his Publishers: Shaping Tennyson's Public Image

Jim Cheshire

In 1862 Julia Margaret Cameron described hearing her friend Alfred Tennyson bemoan the contemporary thirst for celebrity ephemera:

> He said he believed every crime and every vice in the world were connected with the passion for autographs and anecdotes and records, — that the desiring anecdotes and acquaintance with the lives of great men was treating them like pigs to be ripped open for the public; that he knew he himself should be ripped open like a pig; that he thanked God Almighty with his whole heart and soul that he knew nothing, and that the world knew nothing, of Shakespeare but his writings.[1]

This was in 1862, when Tennyson was approaching the height of his popularity. Three years before his publisher had sold 10,000 copies of *Idylls of the King* in six weeks and two years later Moxon & Co. sold 17,000 copies of *Enoch Arden* on the day of publication.[2] Earlier poems continued to sell well: Moxon and Co.'s book list in August 1864 stated that *Poems* (of 1842) was in its sixteenth edition, *The Princess* was in its twelfth edition, *Maud and Other Poems* was in its sixth edition and *In Memoriam* was in its fifteenth edition.[3] Despite the overwhelming public interest, this was a troubling period for Tennyson: a series of arguments with his publisher culminated in a rift in 1869 and the end of a professional relationship that had lasted for thirty-seven years. At the root of this argument was a conflict over the shape that Tennyson's popularity took: an image was forming in the public mind not just of the poetry but of the poet. The public perception of Tennyson was clearly influenced by his literary output but his cultural presence overflowed the boundaries of literary culture. Although Tennyson complained about autograph hunters he was actively involved in the creation of his public image: he sat for numerous portraits and was

---

[1] *Illustrated London News*, 15 October 1892, p. 492.
[2] J. S. Hagen, *Tennyson and His Publishers* (London, 1979), pp. 110, 112.
[3] 'A list of books published by Edward Moxon & Co., Dover St.' (London, August 1864), p. 1.

very sensitive about how he was perceived. The real issue was not the fact he was famous but what form this fame took and who had the power to shape it. This essay will argue that the Moxon firm was a powerful influence on the construction of Tennyson's public image but that commercial pressures created a conflict between how the publisher presented the poet and how Tennyson wanted to be seen. This conflict emerged over the material form of Moxon's books. Tennyson approved of the small, plain, green books normally published by Moxon: they had good type, wide margins and no illustrative material to distract the reader. From 1857 the Moxon firm published a series of illustrated editions: the physical form and marketing of these books linked Tennyson's poetry to a new kind of reader. Gift books were commercial, potentially effeminate and decidedly middle-brow, three ideas that were not in sympathy with how Tennyson wanted to be seen.[4] These books promoted Tennyson's image in one very literal sense: they were important vehicles for the circulation of his portrait. Moxon published no portraits of the poet prior to the first gift book of 1857 but they featured in most of the illustrated books after this date. The nature of these images, their commercial background and, at times, surprising sources proved to be an interesting battleground between publisher and poet: Tennyson's public image became contested ground.

Rather than concentrate on illustrations, this essay will consider what might now be described as 'paratext' following Genette's ruminations on the subject. Genette sees paratext as the area through which the author is presented to the reader 'what enables a text to become a book and be offered as such to its readers and, more generally, to the public'.[5] Paratext is a 'zone' of 'transaction' an area where negotiations are made between author and reader.[6] Despite being implicitly condoned by the author, paratext is largely generated by the publisher and in Tennyson's case this led to arguments rooted in the differing motives and expectations of publisher and poet. In this context it is perhaps not surprising that the paratext to Moxon's illustrated editions

---

[4]   For a discussion of these aspects of the gift book see Lorraine Koositra, 'Poetry in the Victorian Marketplace: The Illustrated *Princess* as Christmas Gift Book', *Victorian Poetry*, 45 (2007), 49-76.

[5]   G. Genette, *Paratexts: Thresholds of Interpretation*, trans. J. E. Lewin (Cambridge, 1997), p. 1.

[6]   Ibid., p. 2.

contains signs of the conflict that broke out between Tennyson and his publisher.

In the mid 1850s a flurry of activity suggested that portraitists now saw Tennyson as an opportunity. Between 1855 and 1857 two sculptural portrait busts (by William Brodie and Thomas Woolner), one sculptural medallion (by Woolner), one painted portrait (by G. F. Watts) and at least one photograph (by Mayall) were created.[7] Edward Moxon was interested in this activity – he considered commissioning Woolner's bust – but his main project at this time was an illustrated edition of Tennyson's poetry.[8] He saw this as a way of profiting from the poet's fame and he confidently offered Tennyson £2000 out of the anticipated profits. The 'Moxon Tennyson' has since become one of the most famous illustrated books of the Victorian period but for the purposes of this essay its significance lies not in its Pre-Raphaelite woodcuts but because it marks the start of Moxon's promotion of the poet's image. Moxon decided to use an engraving of Woolner's medallion of 1856 (Figure 1). The medallion format had several advantages. Firstly, as John Lord has pointed out, 'its connotations of heroism had a cachet and its allusions to antique cameos, coinage and commemorative roundels gave it a cultural significance.'[9] Secondly, the classical allusion helped to position the frontispiece not so much as a likeness but as an idealized image: this was not the poet as he looked in 1857 (he had a prominent beard by this stage for a start) but a vision of the creator of the poetry in the volume, which had been first published as a collection in 1842. Thirdly, relief sculpture inevitably transfers better to a two-dimensional format than sculpture in the round and so Woolner's medallion was a better choice than his more famous bust.

---

[7] The most complete list of Tennyson's portraits can be found in R. Ormond, *Early Victorian Portraits* (London, 1973) pp. 446-58. Woolner's portraits are discussed in Leonée Ormond, *Tennyson and Thomas Woolner* (Lincoln, 1981). The Mayall photograph had been taken by 1855 when Emily Tennyson showed it to friends, see James Hoge, *Lady Tennyson's Journal* (Charlottesville, 1981), p. 55. It was subsequently published in the first issue of a short-lived periodical *The National Magazine*, November 1856, p. 1.

[8] R. Ormond, *Early Victorian Portraits*, p. 451; for the 'Moxon Tennyson' see Julia Thomas, '"Always Another Poem": Victorian Illustrations of Tennyson', in *Tennyson Transformed, Alfred Lord Tennyson and Visual Culture*, ed. by Jim Cheshire (London, 2009), pp. 20-31.

[9] John Lord, 'Greatness Confirmed: The Sculpted Portraits of Tennyson', in *Tennyson Transformed*, ed. by Cheshire, pp. 68-75 (p. 70).

There was a range of ways in which Tennyson's portrait could be experienced at this date and it is worth considering why its position as a frontispiece to a volume of poetry was particularly significant. Woolner's bust of the poet and two photographic portraits of Tennyson were on display at the Manchester Art Treasures Exhibition; an engraving of the bust was then published and a photograph of it exhibited. Within a couple of years further photographs of Tennyson had been issued as *carte-de-visites*.[10] The experience of these portraits would have been quite specific to the physical and spatial contexts in which they were experienced and it is worthwhile considering these in

Fig. 1 The frontispiece to *Poems by Alfred Lord Tennyson* (the 'Moxon' Tennyson), 1857. Engraved after a sculptural medallion of 1856 by Thomas Woolner, reproduced by permission of the Tennyson Research Centre. Photograph by Andy Weekes

[10]   *Tennyson Transformed*, ed. by Cheshire, catalogue nos. 76, 81, 87, pp. 137, 140, 145; the other photograph in the Manchester Exhibition was by Mayall (see note 7 above); Woolner's bust was engraved in *Illustrated London News*, 21 November 1857, p. 520 and a photograph of it exhibited at the Photographic Society Exhibition of 1859 see *The Times*, 10 January 1859, p. 8.

relation to the portrait as frontispiece. Despite illustrations later in the book, a frontispiece, typically opposite the title-page, has little to compete with visually, especially when compared to an artwork in a large exhibition, or a *carte-de-visite*, which would typically be placed in an album with many similar images. Secondly, the image is not there as an artwork (as in an exhibition) or as a celebrity image (as in a *carte-de-visite*). The frontispiece presents an invitation to attach the semantics of the literary text to the image of the poet: it asks the reader to connect the poems and the image before them. The experience of a frontispiece portrait is unlikely to be a chance encounter. Few people would have gone to the Manchester Art Treasures Exhibition specifically to see Tennyson's portraits but most readers would have made a conscious decision to read Tennyson's poetry: in an important sense they would have encountered the portrait deliberately, even if looking at the frontispiece was not the primary purpose of opening the book. A similar point could be raised in relation to engravings in periodicals: for most readers seeing Tennyson's portrait would have been a matter of chance. The frontispiece portrait in a poetry gift book might be viewed repeatedly as a result of the nature of poetry: repeated readings of a poem could mean repeated encounters with Tennyson's portrait.

Edward Moxon's foray into illustrated editions was cut short by his death in June 1858. The 'Moxon Tennyson' had been an economic failure and left the firm with financial problems; the remaining copies had to be sold on to Routledge, who then marketed the edition more successfully at a lower price. Edward Moxon's other project, an illustrated edition of *The Princess*, seems to have met the same fate.[11] After Moxon's death, Tennyson's relationship with his publishers suffered, especially when they tried to recoup the costs of the 'Moxon Tennyson' from him. After Edward Moxon's death the firm was managed by Bradbury and Evans who had previously acted as printers for Moxon, this situation was far from ideal and Tennyson was considering transfer-

---

[11]   Koositra, 'Poetry in the Victorian Marketplace', p. 49 shows that the illustrated *Princess* was a critical success and implies that it was a commercial success for Moxon, dubious in the context of its resale: it was listed as sold by Routledge 'reduced to 10s. 6d.' (from 16s.), in 1861. See Anon., *The English Catalogue of Books for 1861* (London, 1862), p. 61. Anon., *The English Catalogue of Books for 1865* (London, 1866), p. 54 lists an 1865 reissue of the Illustrated *Princess* again by Routledge although the title-page of the book still lists Moxon as publisher.

ring his business to another publishing house.[12] Tennyson's motivation for staying with the firm was his loyalty to Emma Moxon and her children as he knew how heavily they relied on the sales of his books. In 1864 Emma Moxon appointed a new manager, James Bertrand Payne. Under Payne's management in just five years the firm was in ruins. Emma Moxon eventually came to see Payne's actions as fraudulent resulting in a trial, which she won on appeal.[13] Payne's career, although disastrous in a commercial sense, is of great interest historically because of his overtly commercial approach and the way that he asserted his identity as publisher.

Payne's first project immediately marked a change of direction. *A Selection from the Works of Alfred Tennyson* (Figure 2) was published in January 1865 but was much more than a selected edition of Tennyson: it was the start of a whole series of selections from different poets under the title 'Moxon's Miniature Poets'. This catchy label implied a popular audience and promoted the Moxon firm's reputation as the pre-eminent specialist publisher of poetry. Payne enlisted the services of a number of literary men to make and edit selections. William Michael Rossetti was prominent among these and described his involvement:

> My work consisted in selecting for reproduction editions of the various authors not including any copyright matter (unless indeed it was copyright of the Moxon firm); arranging the contents according to my best discretion; and writing for each volume a condensed account of the poet.[14]

Volumes of the poetry of Wordsworth, Browning, Praed and others were issued each following a similar physical format: the cover, spine, vignettes and format of preliminary pages all followed the same pattern.

---

[12] Hagen, *Tennyson and His Publishers*, p. 107.

[13] Payne's son wrote a brief memoir of his father as an introduction to a reprint of one of his father's articles, see J. B. de V. Payen-Payne 'Introduction' to 'Jersey' reprinted in the *The Jersey Society in London Occasional Publications No. VI*. London, 1927, pp. 1-13. A copy can be found at London, British Library, shelfmark A.C.8141. Information on the trial can be found in the judgement and *The Times*'s report: Moxon v Payne, Incorporated Council of Law Reporting: Chancery Appeal [1872.M.37] - (1873) L.R. Ch.App.881 (available at < http://www.Lexixnexis.com >); *The Times*, 13 June 1873, p. 12.

[14] William Michael Rossetti, *Some Reminiscences of William Michael Rossetti*, 2 vols (London, 1906), II, 406.

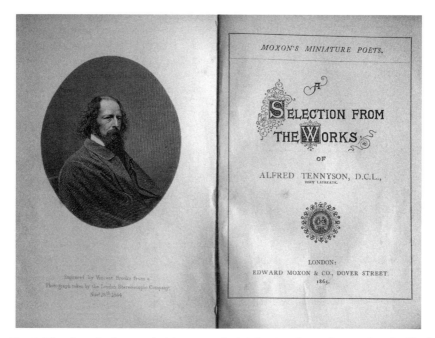

Fig. 2 The frontispiece and title-page of *A Selection from the Works of Alfred Tennyson*, 1865. Frontispiece engraved after a photograph by the London Stereoscopic Company. Reproduced by permission of the Tennyson Research Centre

Payne saw the series as substantially his creation, territory marked by the insertion of a phrase on the reverse of the title-page: 'The Series Projected and Superintended by' followed by his monogram 'JBP' (Figure 3). He subsequently marked all his editions in a similar way.

It later emerged during the trial that this ownership was financial too, the *Times* reporting that:

> Payne obtained very considerable portions of the assets of the firm, such as original drawings and shares of copyrights, among which was a half-share of the copy-right of the series called *Moxon's Popular* [sic] *Poets*, the conception of which series he said was entirely due to himself.[15]

Tennyson's idea about a selected edition of his poetry was very different. He wanted to issue a cheap edition aimed at the working-class reader: Hallam Tennyson took pains to make this clear in his

---

[15] *The Times*, 13 June 1873, p. 12.

Fig. 3 James Bertrand Payne's monogram, printed on the reverse side of the title-page in all illustrated editions published by Moxon and Co. from 1864. Reproduced by permission of the Tennyson Research Centre

Memoir where he printed Tennyson's 'Preface' dedicated to the 'Working Men of England'.[16] The 'Preface' was not printed in Payne's series, which Hallam Tennyson failed to mention. Charles Tennyson's biography of his grandfather was more candid, explicitly linking Tennyson's working-class edition with Payne's project, suggesting: 'he was persuaded, against his will, to issue the volume in a more ornamental style than his severe taste generally admitted.'[17] Payne's *Selection* was not the serious book that Tennyson envisaged. John Leighton's cover was a busy design dominated by nationalistic iconography: a border formed by wreaths of oak leaves punctuated with Gothic derived ornament enclosed a diaper of *fleur-de-lys* with the standard 'E M & Co.' monogram in the centre.[18] The spine highlighted the series over the poet:

[16]   Hallam Tennyson, *Alfred Lord Tennyson a Memoir*, 2 vols (London, 1898), II, 19.
[17]   Charles Tennyson, *Alfred Tennyson* (London, 1968), p. 376. Charles Tennyson also states (p. 354) that the volume was published as eight sixpenny parts but it is unclear if they were ever published as such.
[18]   John Leighton was a widely respected book designer see, E. M. B. King, 'Leighton,

'MOXON'S MINIATURE POETS' on a ground of gold appeared at the top, *'SELECTIONS FROM TENNYSON'* followed about half way down. Even the main body of the book was contaminated by ornament: a vignette preceded most of poems and a red border enclosed all the poetry: there was not a single page left untainted by the more decorative approach of the series. All these features pointed away from an honest working-class edition and towards a flashy gift book. In fact, the descriptor 'miniature' gave away the status of the book because it was actually slightly larger than the normal Moxon editions. This was, in reality, a miniature *gift book*, only diminutive when compared to Moxon's other illustrated editions.

Payne's advertisements for the series underlined this fact: he reprinted a passage from the *Fortnightly Review*, which, from Tennyson's perspective, made all the wrong connections: 'A series with which thousands of drawing-room tables are already familiar, and which deserves its success: daintier 'gift books' cannot be mentioned.' [19] The volume was linked with commerce ('gift-book') and twice with a female readership ('drawing-room' and 'dainty') clearly associating Tennyson's poetry with a middlebrow, female readership. Tennyson's portrait, used as the frontispiece, was the only illustration. It is a dense engraving taken from a photograph but retains formality through the severe and thoughtful expression of the poet and the demarcation of the image from the page through the oval shape formed by the dark background: it is presented as if the image had been mounted and framed. Payne's marketing of the series shows that he saw the inclusion of a portrait as an important selling point: the Moxon book list for October 1866 detailed ten volumes from the series each time mentioning the inclusion of a portrait and in four instances making clear that the portrait was 'new' or had been commissioned specifically for the series. [20]

Tennyson's portrait in Payne's series was glossed by the text: 'Engraved by Vincent Brooks from a Photograph taken by the London Stereoscopic Company. Novr 28th 1864.' In sending Tennyson into the photographic studio Payne was obtaining his own images of the poet but

---

John [Luke Limner] (1822-1912)' *Oxford Dictionary of National Biography* < http:// www.oxforddnb.com > [accessed 21 June 2011].

[19] 'A list of books published by Edward Moxon & Co., Dover St.' (London, October 1866), p. 7.

[20] 'A list of books', (October 1866), pp. 7-9.

Fig. 4 Frontispiece to *Enoch Arden* illustrated by Arthur Hughes, 1865, engraved after a sculptural medallion by Thomas Woolner of 1864. Reproduced by permission of the Tennyson Research Centre

his plans involved more than just the frontispiece for his *Selection*. With Tennyson he sent the sculptor Thomas Woolner, whose diary reads: 'Went with A.T. to Stereoscopic Co.: - to pose him for photographs - '.[21] On 2 December Payne dined with Woolner and on 3 and 4 December Woolner recorded communicating with Payne about 'new med. of A.T.'.[22] On 6 December Payne sent over the photographs of Tennyson and from 8 to 19 December Woolner was at work on his third medallion of the poet. This project turned out to be a well-planned exercise in the commercial exploitation of Tennyson's image. The vehicle for this project was Payne's next Christmas gift book, *Enoch Arden*, illustrated by Arthur Hughes and published in December 1865.[23] An engraving of Woolner's medallion formed the frontispiece (Figure 4) but that was only part of the idea. The first item in Payne's new booklist announced:

[21]   Leeds, Henry Moore Institute, MS 'Thomas Woolner's Diary for 1864' (16/1990) fol. 96. This is the entry for 29 November but both references clearly describe the same occasion.

[22]   MS 'Thomas Woolner's Diary for 1864' (16/1990), fol. 97.

[23]   Alfred Tennyson, *Enoch Arden* (London, 1866), the edition was released in December 1865 but forward dated to 1866.

Messrs. Edward Moxon & Co. Have the pleasure to announce that they have just published a medallion portrait of Alfred Tennyson, Esq. D.C.L, Poet Laureate, Executed by Thomas Woolner, Sculptor, an engraving of which is the frontispiece to this volume.[24]

A paragraph went on to suggest that the medallion would 'form a peculiarly elegant and appropriate Christmas and New Years' Gift'. The medallion (Figure 5) could be purchased in a number of formats: 'Plain or Bronzed, without Frame, 30s.; Framed for Drawing-Room or Library, 63s.; Oxidized Silver, by Elkington, 94s. 6d.; and Bronze, 84s.'[25]

The first thing to notice in this enterprise is the linguistic slippage in the use of the word 'publish'. When the advert announced that a medallion had been 'published' the most obvious response is to think that

Fig. 5 Bronzed electrotype after Thomas Woolner's sculptural medallion. Reproduced by permission of the Tennyson Research Centre. Photograph by Andy Weekes

---

[24] 'A list of books published by Edward Moxon & Co., Dover St.' (London, December, 1865), p. 2.
[25] The Usher Gallery holds two versions: one in marble and one in the 'Bronze' version: it is not cast bronze but a bronzed electrotype.

this referred to the frontispiece. When it becomes evident that this is not the case, then it is clear that 'publish' is used not in the ordinary sense of issuing books but in the more general sense of 'to make public' and more specifically 'to make generally accessible or available for acceptance or use (a work of art, information etc.)'.[26] This usage, however, belies the commercial motive, which was complex. Firstly, this was a collaboration between Payne and Woolner. The latter noted in his diary while making the medallion: 'Called to see Payne promised to run the risk of A.T. Med: - I to have £50 or guins: first profits, and afterwards to share equally.'[27] Woolner was prepared to share the financial risk of the project: he would work for free on the assumption that he would make his sculptor's fee from the initial profits of the medallion and then go on to share further profits with Payne. Secondly, we might question the relative importance of the gift book and the medallion. The frontispiece clearly added to the attraction of the gift book and, rather neatly, Payne did not have to pay Woolner a fee for the new medallion. The medallion venture gained a great deal from the book, the frontispiece was in effect a high quality advertisement delivered to an ideal audience. Given that the book was published at one guinea it is quite possible that Payne hoped to make as much money from the medallion as the book. Payne's book list for October 1866 listed the medallion again but this time no unframed medallions were offered and the two remaining categories had increased considerably in price: 'Framed for Drawing-Room or Library' now cost five guineas (up from three guineas) 'Bronze and Oxidized Silver, by Elkington' were now offered at the price of ten guineas (as against the original price of four-and-a-half and four guineas). Although it is unclear what the profits were, the most obvious conclusion to draw from this is that sales had been good and that Payne and Woolner had determined to sell the remaining casts for a high price. What is clear is that it was not Tennyson but Woolner and Payne who stood to profit from this venture.

Even before the illustrated *Enoch Arden* was published, Payne was planning a far more ambitious project: a lavish edition of *Idylls of the King* illustrated by the French artist Gustave Doré.[28] This was issued in

---

[26] 'publish, v.' *OED Online* < http://dictionary.oed.com > [accessed 14 December 2009].
[27] MS 'Thomas Woolner's Diary for 1864' (16/1990), fol. 101.
[28] Alfred Tennyson, *Elaine*, illustrated by Gustave Doré (London, 1867); Alfred Tennyson, *Guinevere*, illustrated by Gustave Doré (London, 1867); Alfred Tennyson,

successive years as a series of Christmas gift books: *Elaine* for Christmas 1866, *Guinevere* and *Vivien* for Christmas 1867, and *Enid* for Christmas 1868. These editions had no independent frontispieces: instead, one of the main illustrative plates was printed opposite the title-page, oddly in the first three books this disrupted the sequence of the illustrations both in terms of the narrative and list of illustrations. In 1868, a collected edition of all four illustrated *Idylls* was issued with a new frontispiece, specially commissioned from Doré. This image further developed the relationship between the poet and his publisher and introduced two bizarre but interesting twists to the story.

Fig. 6 Frontispiece to the collected edition of the illustrated *Idylls of the King* published by Moxon and Co. in 1868, engraved after a design of Gustave Doré. Reproduced by permission of the Tennyson Research Centre. Photograph by Andy Weekes

---

Vivien, illustrated by Gustave Doré (London, 1867); Alfred Tennyson, *Enid*, illustrated by Gustave Doré (London, 1868). *Elaine* and *Enid* were forward dated, the former released late in 1866, and dated 1867 and the latter released in late 1867, and dated 1868. I have argued elsewhere that this edition was the cause of the rift between publisher and poet. See J. Cheshire, 'The Fall of the House of Moxon: James Bertrand Payne and the Illustrated *Idylls of the King*' forthcoming *Victorian Poetry* 50:2, Summer 2012.

Doré's frontispiece (Figure 6) to the collected edition is an early example of the depiction of an author surrounded by his fictional creations.[29] Moxon's habit of portraying Tennyson's head in a sculptural medallion was preserved but with an odd development. Initially the image appears to be from the same source as that in the illustrated *Enoch Arden*: an engraving of Woolner's medallion. Closer inspection reveals a different source. This portrait was derived from Mayall's 1864 photograph of Tennyson (Figure 7), which became the poet's favourite photograph of himself.

Fig. 7 J. E. Mayall, *Alfred Tennyson* albumen print from wet collodian negative, *c.* 1864. Reproduced by permission of the Tennyson Research Centre. Photograph by Andy Weekes

---

[29]   I would like to thank Leonée Ormond for pointing out the significance of this aspect of the frontispiece.

Interestingly, this image never had been a sculptural medallion but in the Doré frontispiece was represented as such. This could be explained in terms of Doré conforming to what had almost become a convention: sculpture and sculptural imagery had dominated Tennyson's portraits since the later 1850s. The other problem for Doré was the combination of Arthurian fictional characters with a living poet and here the sculptural medallion was useful: an idealized image with physical boundaries was easy to separate from the fictional characters. This is not an image of Tennyson surrounded by his characters but an image of Tennyson's *portrait* surrounded by his characters. The separation of the portrait from the characters is emphasised by Doré's design: a cherub sits on top of the medallion and two characters bear its weight further down. Doré shows five identifiable figures, Geraint and Enid (the only couple who survive the *Idylls* intact), Merlin and his nemesis Vivian and finally King Arthur, who sits below Tennyson just right of centre, his hands on the hilt of his sword, which presents an obvious cruciform shape. With this figure rests the most surprising twist: King Arthur was modelled from a portrait of James Bertrand Payne (Figure 8). Payne's son later made this sound like Doré's decision but his version of his father's career sets out

Fig. 8 James Bertrand Payne in *c.* 1867 reproduced by permission of the British Library

to minimize Payne's ambitions.[30] Payne's portrait was recognized: Alexander Macmillan seems to have pointed it out to Emily Tennyson who responded in a measured way:

> I am not sure I would have recognized the king. The lifted brows make the expression different. I think I might have said 'how like' rather than 'it is he', so I hope the ridicule that might have come to him had the likeness been more exact may be avoided.[31]

It is doubtful whether Emily Tennyson or her husband were really concerned about how much ridicule landed on Payne: the problem for them was that their publisher's face had been used to represent King Arthur, the model of morality and virtue in the *Idylls of the King* and the character that Tennyson had related to the deceased Prince Albert.[32] The danger here was making the whole poem seem ridiculous and at the very least it highlighted Tennyson's lack of control over his own books. Payne's inclusion of his own portrait is a telling piece of publishing iconography: it represents the publisher as the author's lieutenant and insists that he is recognized as such. In another sense (and one less comforting to Payne) it shows the publisher as one of Tennyson's creations and in a way he was: he was a figure of little significance until he became manager of the Moxon firm and Tennyson's status gave Payne his power in the literary world. A few months after the frontispiece was published Tennyson wrote a vicious epigram that represented Payne not as one of his own characters but as one of Shakespeare's:

> Ancient Pistol, peacock Payne,
> Brute in manner, rogue in grain,
> How you squeezed me, peacock Payne!
> Scared was I and out I ran
> And found by Paul's an honest man.
> Peace be with you, peacock Payne,
> I have left you, you remain

---

[30]   Payen-Payne 'Introduction', p. 13.

[31]   London, British Library, Additional MS 54986, fol. 211.

[32]   In 1862 Tennyson added a 'Dedication' to *Idylls of the King* in memory of Prince Albert which commenced: 'These to His Memory -- since he held them dear, / Perchance as finding there unconsciously / Some image of himself.' See A. Tennyson, *The Poems of Tennyson*, ed. by Christopher Ricks, 2nd edn, 3 vols (London, 1987), III, 263.

Ancient Pistol, sealskin Payne.[33]

A couple of months earlier Tennyson had noticed that the *Daily Telegraph* had praised Payne's activities, stating that 'the Moxon connection [...] has closed in a blaze of glory'. Tennyson wrote furiously to his friend Frederick Locker: 'Won't you store this from the Daily Telegraph among your curiosities? Fancy 'Antient Pistol F.R.S.L, Editor of the Idylls,' closing in a blaze of glory, sealskin jacket and all, in a Bude light!!!'[34] Tennyson's anger was caused by the fact that Payne's claims had been accepted by the *Daily Telegraph*. The real power, however, lay with Tennyson as his stark line 'I have left you' made clear. This was very real power: within a few years Payne was ruined and it took him until 1892 to clear his debts.[35] Payne, however, was not yet finished and two very significant publications followed that were to cause the Poet Laureate further anxiety over his status.

In 1869 Tennyson discovered that a concordance to his poetry had been published by Moxon and Co. with Payne's sanction.[36] He was furious for several reasons. Firstly, the volume included 'The Window', a poem that Tennyson had become dissatisfied with and sought to suppress. Secondly, he thought that the publication would seem arrogant, or as Emily Tennyson described it: 'It seems to him that the world must think it an assumption to have one [a concordance] published during his lifetime'.[37] The concordance included a portrait of Tennyson that he found particularly offensive (Figure 9). He ended an indignant letter to the author Daniel Brightwell:

> as to the fac-simile or fac-dissimile - the caricature at the beginning of your book, it is equally disgraceful to publisher and engraver, and will I am afraid annoy my good honest friend Jeffrey seeing it is as like me as I am to - Ancient Pistol.[38]

---

[33]   A. Tennyson, *The Poems of Tennyson*, ed. by Christopher Ricks, 2nd edn, 3 vols (London, 1987), III, 11.

[34]   *The Letters of Alfred Lord Tennyson*, ed. by Cecil Lang and Edgar Shannon, 3 vols (Oxford, 1982-90), II, 513. Payne was described as 'editor' and 'F.R.S.L' in a review of *Elaine*, see Anon., 'Doré's Elaine' *Art Journal*, New Series 6 (1867), pp 51-2.

[35]   *Pall Mall Gazette*, 8 December 1892, p. 6.

[36]   D. Baron Brightwell, *A Concordance to the Entire Works of Alfred Tennyson* (London, 1869).

[37]   Hoge, *Lady Tennyson's Journal*, p. 297.

[38]   *Letters*, II, 534.

Vincent Brooks Day & Son, Lith.

ℐ. Tennyson

Facsimiled from a Photograph by W. Jeffrey Esq. of Gt. Russell St.

Fig. 9 Frontispiece to Brightwell's *Concordance*, lithograph after a photograph by William Jeffrey, *c.* 1869. Reproduced by permission of the Tennyson Research Centre

Emily Tennyson expressed her own dismay in terms of a convenient racial stereotype: 'The portrait is very like an Irish Beggar.'[39] These vehement responses raise some interesting issues. This is the first portrait that departed decisively from the formal images used previously. It lacked the visual emphasis on the poet's forehead preventing it from being a reflection on the imaginative power of the author. Instead, Tennyson was shown full length, facing right and looking at the reader with a strange sideways glance. Odd details, such as the prominent creases in Tennyson's frock coat took on inappropriate prominence. All these features added up to an image which could not function effectively as an idealized portrait, as the words 'caricature' and 'beggar' both suggest. Tennyson, keenly aware of the effect that Brightwell's *Concordance* could have on his public image, wrote to Alexander Strahan, his new publisher, on 5 October 1869:

> A question arises whether it would be worth while to state publicly that the Book is published altogether without my sanction. In fact I think it makes me ridiculous - if it be not understood that it is Moxon and Co.'s doing and that I am thoroughly against it.[40]

Tennyson was right, as a sneering review a few days later in *The Athenaeum* underlined:

> An elaborate concordance of the Laureate's poetry in 477 large octavo pages of closely-printed type, set in double columns! No such piece of methodical madness was ever before perpetrated in [not on!] behalf of a living author.

They went on to explain:

> In other words, when Messrs. Moxon and Co. made arrangements for the manufacture of this big index they were publishers of the works which it illustrates; but shortly after they had undertaken to produce what ill-natured folk will perhaps stigmatize as a piece of commercial adulation, they ceased to be closely connected with the writer whom they delighted to honour, or to be beneficially interested in the compositions which it was their purpose to render still more popular.[41]

---

[39] Ibid., II, 533.
[40] *Letters*, II, 534.
[41] *Athenaeum*, 9 October 1869, pp. 462-63.

This review is quite explicit in both its mockery of Payne and the academic pretensions and commercial motives of the publication, as the phrases 'big index' and 'commercial adulation' make very clear. The reviewer acknowledged Tennyson's own lack of responsibility but this did little to protect his authorial status in the broader sense: it still raised questions about inappropriate commercial exploitation of his poetry.

Payne was almost certainly involved in one last edition of Tennyson's poetry, a book which arguably had an enormous impact on Tennyson's reputation but which has failed to generate academic interest. Harper and Brothers *Poetical Works of Alfred Tennyson* was published in New York in 1870; it was cheap and seems to have sold in huge numbers.[42] An advertisement of *c.* 1870 stated: 'Poetical Works of Alfred Tennyson, Poet Laureate. With numerous illustrations and Three Characteristic Portraits. Thirty-fifth Thousand. 8vo, Paper, 50 cents; Cloth $1 00'.[43] The reviews that Harper and Brothers chose to print with the advertisement stressed the value: 'A marvel of cheapness. - *The Christian Era*' and

> The whole get-up and style of this edition are admirable, and we are sure it will be a welcome addition to every book-case, large or small. But the marvelous [*sic*] thing about it is the price, which is only *one dollar* for the handsome cloth binding. - *Tribune* (Wilmington, Del.)

Tennyson complained repeatedly about American editions but through an agreement with a Boston publishing firm he managed to profit considerably from the publication of his poetry in America, even in the absence of any protection from copyright law. The 1842 poems were published in America by W. D. Ticknor. By 1868, the firm (now Ticknor and Fields) advertised nine 'complete' editions and a number of separately published poems.[44] Tennyson had written to confirm that he considered them his chosen American publisher and

---

[42] Alfred Tennyson, *The Poetical Works of Alfred Tennyson* (New York, 1870).

[43] 'Harper and Brothers' List of New Books' (*c.* 1870), p. 4. Copy bound into a paperback edition of Harper's *Poetical Works of Alfred Tennyson* (New York, 1870), Lincoln, Tennyson Research Centre, 3615.

[44] Advertisement in *The Poetical Works of Alfred Tennyson* (Boston, 1868) published by Ticknor and Fields, copy in Tennyson Research Centre, 3610. For a discussion of the business of Ticknor and Fields see Michael Winship, *American Literary Publishing in the Mid-Nineteenth Century* (Cambridge, 1995).

they printed his endorsement on the reverse of the title-page: 'It is my wish that with Messrs. Ticknor and Fields alone the right of publishing my books in America should rest.' Payne had already disrupted this agreement by offering Cassell, Petter, and Galpin the exclusive right to publish the first volume of the illustrated edition of *Idylls of the King* an agreement, which, in a letter to the publisher of 28 October 1866, the poet grudgingly acknowledged.[45] Payne seems to have objected to the arrangement with Ticknor and Fields as he was admonished by Tennyson for his behaviour towards the Boston publisher in 1866.[46]

Several circumstances link this edition with Payne. Firstly Tennyson wrote angrily to James Knowles in January 1870 'Have you heard of Payne's last American dodge?' and later referred to 'the dishonourable conduct of Harper and Co. with regard to my work'.[47] Secondly Harper's *Poetical Works* included a substantial amount of material that was not widely available, material to which Payne had access. It included images taken from a variety of illustrated editions including four from Doré's *Idylls of the King* and sixteen from the 'Moxon Tennyson'. An even more direct connection can be made via one of the portraits, which is the frontispiece to Brightwell's *Concordance* that both Emily and Alfred Tennyson had found so objectionable. It was not just the images but the poetry included that suggested an intimate relationship with the Moxon firm: Harper's *Poetical Works* shows an inside knowledge of Tennyson's corpus, printing many poems not currently available in any quantity and many that Tennyson did not want reprinted. It included the *Poems* of 1830, the *Poems* of 1832 that were omitted from *Poems* of 1842, poems that had been sent to periodicals and early poems such as 'Timbuctoo'. The book was remarkably current, *The Holy Grail and Other Poems* had been published in December 1869 with a short explanatory preface setting out the order in which the new Arthurian poems should be combined with the existing poems.[48] This prefatory information was incorporated on the contents page of Harper's *Poetical Works* which printed the entire sequence in the correct order. Harper's printing was almost simultaneous with the first printing of the entire *Idylls* sequence in England,

---

[45] *Letters*, III, 464.

[46] Ibid., II, 428.

[47] Ibid., II, 539 and note.

[48] Alfred Tennyson, *The Holy Grail and Other Poems* (London, 1870).

which occurred with Strahan's *'Miniature Edition'* also released in December 1869.[49] In 1871 'The Window' was added to Harper's *Poetical Works*, giving Tennyson further cause for complaint. In fact, the volume could be interpreted as a calculated attempt to annoy Tennyson and it was certainly in direct competition with his endorsed publisher whose editions suffered by comparison.

The 'complete editions' published by Ticknor and Fields in the late 1860s were inferior in almost every way: they had less poetry (only four *Idylls*, no *Window*, no early poems), they were more expensive and they were much more limited in terms of illustrations: their 'Farringford Edition' ($3 to $5) had one portrait and three steel plates and the cheapest version of their 'Illustrated Farringford Edition' cost $10. Their only advantage was Tennyson's endorsement and this cannot have done Tennyson's image much good as he was recommending inferior, expensive editions to the American public. Harper and Brothers had enormous power within the American literary world, their periodical *Harper's New Monthly Magazine* had an impressive circulation of 200,000 and they shamelessly used their power to promote their edition over that of their rivals (by now Fields, Osgood, and Co.):

> We greatly prefer such a complete edition of Tennyson's poems as is afforded by *The Poetical Works of Alfred Tennyson* (Harper and Brothers), to any special work like the *Holy Grail and other Poems* (Fields, Osgood, and Co.). It is not merely that the reader gets more for his money - poetry is not to be measured by the line or the page.

The 'editorial' continued:

> This complete edition of Tennyson, in fair, readable print, on good paper, with illustrations, all of which are creditable, and some of which are admirable, and furnished, in paper covers at fifty cents, bound for one dollar, is a remarkable specimen of what the modern art of book-making can accomplish, and leaves no reader any excuse for being without the works of one who is, take him for all in all, the greatest of living poets.[50]

In fact, Harper's *Poetical Works* could be seen as a product of rivalry in the periodical market. In 1868 Tennyson had published three poems,

[49]   *The Works of Alfred Tennyson*, 10 vols (London, 1870).
[50]   *Harper's New Monthly Magazine*, March 1870, pp. 610-11.

'The Victim', '1856-1866' and 'Lucretius' in two American periodicals: the *Atlantic Monthly* and *Every Saturday*. Both periodicals were owned by Ticknor and Fields who were consciously trying to compete with *Harper's Monthly* by offering exclusive new poetry by Tennyson.[51] All these poems were reprinted in Harper's *Complete Edition* suggesting that this was a calculated effort to nullify any threat posed by their rivals.[52]

Harper and Brothers had produced an attractive, cheap, comprehensive and affordable edition of Tennyson's poetry but without the poet's permission. This edition was insulting to Tennyson both materially and symbolically: it rendered the editions of his endorsed publishers obsolete and his commercial rivals had managed to present themselves as the benefactor of the less wealthy reading public. Here lay the most bitter irony: Harper and Brothers' *Poetical Works* was freely available to Americans but not the 'Working Men of England' because Tennyson and his publisher were actively prosecuting any British booksellers who imported American editions.[53] So far from facilitating a working man's edition Tennyson found himself blocking one: he had been forced to switch sides in order to protect his income.

Tennyson had been 'ripped open' but not quite in the way he expected. It was not autograph hunters who were responsible for challenging his status but the commercial pressures of the Victorian book trade that the Moxon firm tried, but failed, to profit from. Tennyson wanted to minimize the presence of the publisher within his books but Payne saw his role differently. The status that Payne claimed for himself might have been pompous and presumptuous but his attitude to some extent reflected the changes in the Victorian book trade. By the mid nineteenth century few publishers would have been content to issue small, plain editions for an author of Tennyson's status: there was simply too much potential to profit from his popularity in other ways. Producing gift books and alternative editions gave publishers significant new areas of responsibility such as commissioning artwork, making selections and creating serials. With this in mind it was inevitable that the publisher's role in mediating between author

---

[51] For a discussion of this issue see K. Ledbetter, *Tennyson and Victorian Periodicals* (Aldershot, 2007) pp. 180-87.

[52] 'Lucretius' and 'The Victim' were also reprinted in *The Holy Grail and Other Poems.*

[53] Hagen, *Tennyson and his Publishers*, p. 131.

and audience would become more and not less conspicuous. Whether Tennyson liked it or not he was writing for a mass audience and his publisher had a crucial role to play in how he was perceived by his readers.

Text in Context: The Law and the Lady and The Graphic

Catherine Delafield

In 1871, Wilkie Collins contributed his novella *Miss or Mrs?* to the Christmas number of *The Graphic*, an illustrated weekly newspaper. This was followed from 26 September 1874 to 13 March 1875 by the serialization in twenty five parts of a major novel, *The Law and the Lady*, which *The Graphic* disowned as unfit for its readers in a column of text immediately adjacent to the final instalment. This essay discusses the consumption of the weekly illustrated newspaper to examine the experience of serial print for the audience of *The Graphic* and to investigate the editor's accusation that Collins's novel was unsuitable for that audience. An examination of the text of the novel in context demonstrates an uneasy interface between the actions of Valeria Macallan, heroine and narrator of *The Law and the Lady*, and the newspaper's representation of the 'lady' in picture, poem and advertisement. It also demonstrates ways in which a text might be visually exploited; in this case to reinforce propriety whilst attracting popular attention.

Well before 13 March 1875, the editor of *The Graphic*, Arthur Locker, had amended the end of the eighteenth instalment of the novel, claiming that Collins had depicted in it the attempted violation of Valeria Macallan by the disabled villain Miserrimus Dexter.[1] A clause in Collins's contract, however, forbade the alteration of any part of the serial and Locker was forced to print a retraction along with the actual proof version on 30 January 1875. In private, Collins described Locker's interference as a 'little explosion of spite' and this became a more open conflict two months later on the publication of the last instalment of *The Law and the Lady*.[2] Locker maintained the terms of

---

[1] See *The Graphic*, 23 January 1875 and 30 January 1875. When she puts her hand on his shoulder out of pity, Dexter clasps Valeria around the waist and covers her hand in kisses. Although Valeria describes this as an 'outrage' at the beginning of the next chapter (*The Graphic*, 30 January 1875, p. 107), she has voluntarily visited Dexter alone as a means of obtaining information relevant to her investigation.

[2] W. Collins, *The Public Face of Wilkie Collins: The Collected Letters*, ed. by W. M. Baker and others, 4 vols (London, 2005), III, 78.

the contract by allowing the rest of the novel to appear as written but in the column adjacent to its final paragraph a denial of responsibility was printed.

The novel's final instalment itself included a newspaper article entitled 'Strange Doings' presented as if it were a report in *The Graphic*. The novel ended just over halfway down the middle column of text with Valeria's final words to the reader: 'pray think kindly of Eustace for my sake' and 'THE END' followed by a perfunctorily ornamented textual dividing line (Figure 1).

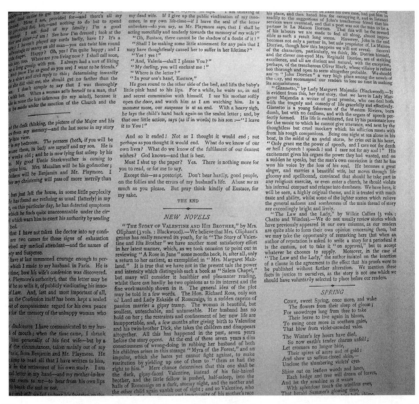

Fig. 1 The final column of the serialization of the *The Law and the Lady*, and '*NEW NOVELS*' in *The Graphic*, 13 March 1875, p. 251

This column then continued with the customary review of '*NEW NOVELS*', including Margaret Oliphant's *The Story of Valentine and his Brother*. The reviewer praised Oliphant's 'most satisfactory effort in her latest manner' which was 'healthier and pleasanter' than the earlier

Salem Chapel.[3] The reviewer also commended the 'taste and ability' of Lady Margaret Majendie's novel *Giannetto* which plainly reworked the legend of Faust but was nonetheless claimed to be 'highly original'.[4] The material of the column came to an end immediately parallel with the final line of *The Law and the Lady* but then continued with a coda from the editor who observed: 'We do not usually review stories which have previously appeared in our own columns, as our readers are quite able to form their own opinion concerning them.' He thus puts his remarks into the context of a review which was at once slightly divorced from the novel text but yet suggested that the appearance of the serial in *The Graphic* had hitherto been tantamount to approval in the manner of the Oliphant and Majendie commendations. Locker offered an excuse for his reverse commendation of *The Law and the Lady* based on the moral responsibility of authorship by observing that 'when an author of reputation is asked to write a story for a periodical it is the custom, not to take it "on approval" but to accept whatever he chooses to supply'. He then, however, found it necessary to comment on the commercial arrangement with Collins in mitigation for the appearance of the text which he was now seeking to undermine and disown. A legally binding 'agreement' had determined that Collins's 'proofs were to be published without further alteration.' Locker concluded in pious indignation: 'We mention these facts in justice to ourselves, as the story is not one which we should have voluntarily selected to place before our readers.'[5]

Interactions between the serial and the periodical, novel and illustrations, chapter and comment column were part of the original textual experience for readers of most of Collins's novels in their first published format.[6] The reader's experience of the serial as a text took

---

[3]   *The Graphic*, 13 March 1875, p. 251.

[4]   Lady Margaret Majendie (née Lindsay) (1850-1912) was the second daughter of the 25th Earl of Crawford and had married Lewis Ashurst Majendie of Hedingham Castle, Essex in 1870. *Giannetto* (Edinburgh, 1875) appears to have been her first novel and she went on to write eight others by 1889. She also contributed to *Girls' Own Paper*.

[5]   *The Graphic*, 13 March 1875, p. 251. Collins's further response in *The World* is reprinted by Jenny Bourne Taylor as an Appendix to her edition of the novel (W. Collins, *The Law and the Lady*, ed. by J. Bourne Taylor (Oxford, 1992), pp. 414-17). For ease of reading, references to this edition of the novel are supplied in addition to references from *The Graphic*.

[6]   From *The Dead Secret* (serialized in *Household Words* from 3 January to 13 June 1857) onwards, all Collins's novels were serialized before volume publication.

place within the context of its printed appearance. In the case of *The Law and the Lady* this context is firstly that of *The Graphic* as a weekly periodical and as a collected volume, and secondly that of Collins as a serial writer and career author.

The Graphic (Figure 2) was founded in 1869 as a competitor for *The Illustrated London News* which had first appeared in 1842. Its first editor and founder William Luson Thomas wrote to the artist Luke Fildes in September 1869 that it was to be 'a new weekly journal, to be a high-priced paper, the very best we can get together by the combination of the best writers, artists, engravers and printers'.[7]

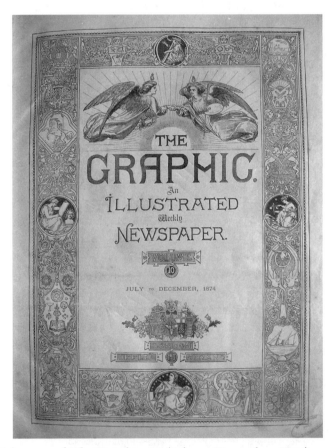

Fig. 2 Title-page of *The Graphic*, 10 (July to December 1874)

---

[7]   Cited in J. Treherz, *Hard Times: Social Realism in Victorian Art* (London, 1987), p. 53.

The Graphic and *The Illustrated London News* were weekly, middle-class, illustrated folios, described by a recent critic as 'neither review, magazine nor newspaper' but 'physical giants – [...] carefully tailored to their readers' tastes, [...] provid[ing] current events at home and abroad, high standards of illustration, and unfailing devotion to the royal family'.[8]

In the weekly *Graphic* of the 1870s there were a large number of royal references in pictures and in court news, as well as regular representations of industry, empire and the regions along with a tendency to depict dogs and other animals. The pictures were separated from the text for reasons of production and printing, and the opening section used eight groups of four hundred words to convey specific news followed by columns such as 'Topics of the Week' and 'Amusements'. The section entitled 'Our Illustrations' presented a commentary for the pictures appearing elsewhere including those within the serial which were at some remove. The layout created a need to read across the issue to link text with illustration and the eye was led from one to the other. The addition of advice on binding suggested the ephemeral and memorial functions of the sixpenny weekly as the editor defined it. The reader could subscribe for thirty shillings a year and be supplied 'across the Empire' in a vast intertext of time and space.

The 'Preface' to the initial volume of *The Graphic*, which was a collection of the first six months' issues, gave an account of the market for a collected part work and also differentiated between a book preface and a newspaper preface. The former was 'a sort of vestibule or antechamber to the literary edifice [...] intended to be read [...] before the contents of the work itself are examined'. The latter 'treats alike of the past and of the future; and while it possibly gives some indication of the entertainment to be hereafter provided, it also reminds the reader of the fare of which he has already partaken'.[9] There is the sense of an organic whole built out of reading backwards and forwards in time, in and out of everyday life. The volume edition was likened to a celebration or birthday and, juggling the two functions of periodical

---

[8]   J. R. Tye, 'The Periodicals of the 1890s', in *Victorian Periodicals: A Guide to Research*, ed. by J. D. Vann and R. T. Van Arsdel, 2 vols (New York, 1978-89), II, 13-31 (p. 19).

[9]   *The Graphic*, 4 December 1869, p. v.

and volume format, the editor claimed that the first volume was 'a Weekly Journal which shall be worthy of preservation as an artistic record of the times in which we live'.[10] Six years later this 'artistic record' would extend to Locker's printed condemnation of Collins's novel.

The volume edition was advertised as 'handsomely bound in extra cloth, and containing upwards of 500 illustrations drawn by the most eminent artists, of all the event5 [*sic*] of interest of the period'.[11] Serials within *The Graphic* were dwarfed by other material since they occupied less than three of the twenty-eight pages within an issue. The completeness of the written text was also less assured. Volume 9, for instance, contained 'the greater portion of Victor Hugo's New Romance' *Ninety Three*.[12] The whole novel could not be read, only the 'greater portion' which represented the prioritization of time-frame over serialization and perhaps some poor planning. *The Graphic* had originally resisted the inclusion of serialized fiction but began the practice in 1873 with Margaret Oliphant's *Innocent: A Tale of Modern Life* which fitted into a bound volume. Trollope's *Phineas Redux* which followed overran its planned numbers into January 1874 and Hugo's novel, not originally designed for serialization, continued until August. *The Law and the Lady* followed in late September 1874 after a six-week delay for Locker's own novella *The Village Surgeon* written in the form of a diary.[13] This meant that Collins's novel, despite being written specifically for *The Graphic*, straddled two volumes.

The advertising for Hugo suggested that a novel could be consumed through this monster of a text.[14] Reading a novel in a weighty, bound folio would not have been a comfortable experience but the *Graphic* advertisement in 1874 pointed out other advantages: 'These volumes form elegant presents, are useful works of reference, and welcome

---

[10] Ibid.

[11] *The Graphic*, 3 October 1874, p. 322.

[12] Ibid.

[13] See G. Law, *Indexes to Fiction in 'The Illustrated London News' (1842-1901) and 'The Graphic' (1869-1901)*, Victorian Fiction Research Guides, 29 (Queensland, 2001), pp. 4-8.

[14] *Cassell's Magazine* in more modestly scaled and cheaper quarto format had produced Wilkie Collins's previous novel *Poor Miss Finch* in a volume edition which reprinted and bound up the issues of the periodical itself, prioritizing novel over periodical. *Cassell's Illustrated Family Paper*, forerunner of the *Magazine*, had originally been produced as a folio (1853-57).

guests in every gentleman's family.'[15] One recent critic dubs them a 'middle class parlour mainstay' and there is a sense in which the physical bulk of *The Graphic* was enlisted as a defence against the erosion of morals in that same parlour.[16]

In its earlier issues a serial representation of the future author of *The Law and the Lady* can also be traced, suggesting some of the ways in which Collins's popularity brought the periodical and the sensation novelist into their unsatisfactory commercial arrangement. In its very first number in 1869, *The Graphic* referred to Wilkie Collins in the light of his less well-known brother, Charles who was guilty of 'Pre-Raffaellitism' [*sic*] and the 'perversion of perspective'.[17] In 1871, an illustration from a photo of Collins appeared to function as an advertisement or trailer for the novella *Miss or Mrs?*. The engraving of the author faces an illustration of a production at the Olympic Theatre of Collins's earlier hit *The Woman in White*.[18] Collins was often irked by the tag lines associated with him which suggested that he would never write anything better than *The Woman in White* published a decade before.[19] Seeing a further link, the writer of the commentary in *The Graphic* some seventeen pages before these engravings could not resist adding the reference to *Miss or Mrs?*: 'Lastly may we mention our own Christmas number [...] which by the time these lines appear will have been read by some thousands of eager purchasers.'[20]

Given that he was now a contributor, Collins was defined more positively in this 1871 piece than in 1869. This was done, however, as befitted an art-orientated newspaper, by representing him as the son of his famous father William Collins 'the well-known rustic painter' and as the nephew of Mrs Carpenter 'one of the best female portrait painters of her time'.[21] The Christmas number, containing *Miss or Mrs?*, was issued on 13 December – although dated the 25th – and was bound into the volume edition at the end. It had been advertised

[15] *The Graphic*, 3 October 1874, p. 322.

[16] N. M. Distad, 'Desiderata and Agenda for the Twenty-first Century', in Vann and Van Arsdel, *Victorian Periodicals*, II, 124-30 (p. 130).

[17] *The Graphic*, 4 December 1869, p. 2.

[18] *The Graphic*, 16 December 1871, pp. 596, 597.

[19] For example, when *The Moonstone* was serialized in *All the Year Round* in 1868, he was throughout referred to as 'the Author of "The Woman in White," &c. &c.' (*All the Year Round*, 4 January 1868, p. 73 through to 8 August 1868, p. 193) .

[20] *The Graphic*, 16 December 1871, p. 579.

[21] Ibid. Margaret Carpenter was sister to Harriet Collins, Wilkie Collins's mother.

previously in November as 'a new tale by Mr. Wilkie Collins [...] [e]qually in length a One-volume Novel, and Illustrated by Six Full-page Drawings by Messrs S.L. Fildes and H. Woods'.[22] At this point, Collins was safely categorized and accommodated within the *Graphic* mission. The illustrations and the printed word represented value for money as Christmas entertainment and Collins was even known to be a part of the original 'Christmas number' concept popularized by Dickens.[23]

At an even broader intertextual level, one particular reference in Collins's writing in the early 1870s offers an indication of the overall community of journalism in the late nineteenth century. In the same 25 November issue of *The Graphic* there was an illustration of the musical instruction of the blind in the Paris Blind School and the commentary supplied for this picture supported the Braille system.[24] During the same period in 1871-72 Collins's novel *Poor Miss Finch* was being serialized in *Cassell's Magazine*. Arthur Locker, editor of *The Graphic* and at the time more congenially disposed towards a potential author, was in correspondence with Collins about the viability of the cure for blindness which occurred in that serial during the same month as the Braille article of November 1871. In a letter to Locker, Collins blamed the 'vile periodical system of publication' for raising the hopes of the blind.[25]

When *Miss or Mrs?* appeared a few weeks later, it revisited Collins's obsession with the vagaries of marriage law which he had treated in his earlier novel *Basil* (1852) and in *Man and Wife* (1869-70). Collins wrote in apparent satisfaction to the publisher Bernard Tauchnitz that '[t]he sale in the *Graphic* newspaper was so large (I believe two hundred thousand copies) that I may have exhausted my public in England at least for 'Miss or Mrs?'.[26] Despite some earlier correspondence with Locker about the occurrence of the word 'damn' in the novella, Launce in Scene Two of *Miss or Mrs?* in the Christmas issue certainly utters the curse 'Damn him'. The phrase is even associated directly with a woman, the fifteen-year old Natalie who is pictured by Luke

---

[22] *The Graphic*, 25 November 1871, p. 519.
[23] Collins participated in the Christmas numbers of Dickens's periodicals from 1854 to 1861.
[24] *The Graphic*, 25 November 1871, pp. 513, 507.
[25] Collins, *Public Face*, ed. by Baker and others, II, 314-15.
[26] Ibid., II, 333.

Fildes on the cover with a daringly lifted skirt. She is immediately invoked within the text: 'Natalie started. A curse addressed to the back of your neck, instantly followed by a blessing in the shape of a kiss, is a little trying.'[27] At this stage in the relationship between author and editor, the scene appears to have escaped censorship whereas the attempt to kiss Valeria in the eighteenth instalment of *The Law and the Lady* three years later did not; and indeed marked the beginning of the deteriorating relationship between Collins and Locker.

As a novelist, Collins had also featured as the subject of an article in which *The Graphic* did not seem ignorant of his reputation. At a time before *The Graphic* serialized them, its Christmas number of 1869 asked 'Who writes all the bad novels?', defining 'bad' as 'morally objectionable'. Volume of output was considered an inappropriate measure – 'is Mr Trollope a demoralising novelist?' – and of Dickens the reviewer asked, '[W]as there ever a more harmless humorist and sentimentalist since novels first began?'. Margaret Oliphant, who would unwittingly collaborate in the condemnation of *The Law and the Lady*, was 'as blameless as she is touching and amusing' and Dinah Craik was 'a preacher in disguise'.[28] In the next sentence Wilkie Collins was pronounced 'a sensationalist rightly in vogue, notwithstanding his critics'. 'But,' the article continued, 'what must be the moral calibre of the girl or woman who could be damaged by puzzling out any of his terrible mysteries'.[29] It is suggested that it is the female reader who should judge the influence of a work of fiction rather than the reviewer of a sensation novel or the editor of a periodical. It is telling, however, that five years before the textual outrage against Dexter's kissing and clasping Valeria, the *Graphic* columnist regarded novels as 'the reflection of an age of intensified decencies and conventionalism', part of '[t]hat peculiar demand for propriety in print which is a striking feature of modern English life'.[30]

Concerns about 'propriety in print' may have initially deterred *The Graphic* from the serialization of novels. In 1891, the newspaper

---

27 *The Graphic*, 25 December 1871, p. 5.
28 Oliphant's *Innocent* was the first serialized novel in *The Graphic*, appearing from 4 January to 28 June 1873. Craik (as 'the author of *John Halifax Gentleman*') was the author of 'Little Mother' serialized in three parts from 5 to 19 October 1878 (see Law, *Indexes to Fiction*, pp. 59, 74).
29 *The Graphic*, 25 December 1869, p. 75.
30 Ibid.

censored Hardy's *Tess of the D'Urbervilles*, removing the illegitimate child, Sorrow, and putting the milkmaids into a wheelbarrow so that Angel Clare could transport them without making physical contact. As early as 1844 the first volume of *The Family Herald* claimed that 'A periodical for the public must be more discreet than a bound book'.[31] *The Graphic* itself remarked sternly in a review of other magazines: 'The serial stories in the *Leisure Hour*, besides being very readable, are always thoroughly wholesome, which cannot be said of all serial stories in these days.'[32] By the time of this pronouncement, it is significant that the editor Arthur Locker had already received the offending copy of the eighteenth instalment of *The Law and the Lady* which began his public confrontation with Collins.

There was thus an ongoing serial behind the appearance of *The Law and the Lady* in *The Graphic*. The newspaper's mission and the novelist's aspiration were temporarily aligned by Collins's search for new readers and Locker's quest to challenge the dominance of other periodicals such as *Cassell's Magazine* and *The Cornhill Magazine* which had already featured Collins's work.[33] Andrew Maunder concludes, however, that any study of the periodical discloses 'a world of competing, as well as complementary, discourses'. Deborah Wynne has also observed that 'new reading practices were brought about by the intertextual strategies developed by magazine editors' and it is clear that *The Graphic* was engaged in a particular form of competitive intertextuality based on its use of artworks and text.[34] Locker's intervention in March 1875 overtly supported a conventional view of womanhood and the 'propriety of print'. The intertextual arrangement of illustrations and advertisements built an alternative picture which apparently emerged without editorial sanction but at the same time

---

[31] *The Family Herald*, 1 (17 February 1844); quoted by S. Mitchell, 'The Forgotten Woman of the Period: Penny Weekly Family Magazines of the 1840s and 1850s', in *A Widening Sphere: Changing Roles of Victorian Women*, ed. by M. Vicinus (London, 1980), pp. 29-51 (p. 43).

[32] *The Graphic*, 9 January 1875, p. 42.

[33] *Poor Miss Finch* and *Man and Wife* were serialized by Cassell's in the early 1870s. The *Cornhill* had serialized *Armadale* in 1864-66.

[34] A. Maunder, '"Monitoring the Middle-Classes": Intertextuality and Ideology in Trollope's *Framley Parsonage* and *The Cornhill Magazine* 1859-60', *Victorian Periodicals Review*, 33 (1999), 44-64 (p. 45); D. Wynne, *The Sensation Novel and the Victorian Family Magazine* (Basingstoke, 2001), p. 3. Wynne discusses the illustrations for *Armadale* and an accompanying second serial, Trollope's *The Claverings* (pp. 162-65).

gave *The Graphic* an appeal to the audience of the sensation novels of its competitors. The apprehension of the alternative ideological message of text and picture by the original reader can be illustrated through a more detailed exploration of *The Law and the Lady* in its original serial appearance in *The Graphic*.

Valeria Macallan – a resourceful woman not unlike Collins's earlier heroine Marian Halcombe in *The Woman in White* – emphasizes the construction of her story with reference to documents and to the occasions for writing. She acts as a first-person intradiegetic narrator and although her commentary suggests that she is writing in instalments, she explains towards the end of her narrative: 'I write from memory, unassisted by notes or diaries.'[35] The dating of the serial and the grouped articles, commentary and advertisements within *The Graphic* also reflected the story unfolding in the lives of readers. After rewriting the discovery that she has been married under an assumed name, Valeria writes as the serial reader might be reading: 'Let me dry my eyes and shut up my paper for the day.'[36] She draws attention to an anticipated closure when she explains that her narrative act takes place '[w]riting as I do long after the events'.[37] Her task is to rewrite the text of her husband's trial at which Eustace was given the verdict 'not proven' under Scottish law. This legal middle ground has left Eustace Macallan forever under suspicion of his first wife Sarah's murder. In the novel, Eustace's diary – a serial document itself – is forcibly read out at his trial, and in reading and rewriting the court transcript, Valeria records the court reporter's opinion of the diary's 'silent evidence [...] the prisoner's daily record of domestic events, and of the thoughts and feelings which they aroused in him at the time'.[38] The periodic writing of both Valeria and Eustace lays additional emphasis on the impact of serial writing within serial reading.

Eustace's friend Miserrimus Dexter has destroyed the 'Wife's Confession' written by Sarah Macallan in the last hours of her life. Sarah is bedridden and writes of her slow poisoning from the arsenic she has bought to cure her bad complexion in an attempt to regain her hus-

---

[35] *The Graphic*, 13 March 1875, p. 250; Collins, *Law and the Lady*, p. 399.

[36] *The Graphic*, 26 September 1874, p. 302; Collins, *Law and the Lady*, p. 12.

[37] *The Graphic*, 21 November 1874, p. 495; Collins, *Law and the Lady*, p. 156.

[38] Ibid. The diary is revealed in Chapter 18 which spanned two issues of *The Graphic* (21 and 28 November 1874). For a discussion of serialization, see also C. Delafield, *Women's Diaries as Narrative in the Nineteenth-Century Novel* (Farnham, 2009), pp. 101-18.

band's affection. Her account describes those moments when he treated her with indifference although his behaviour towards her could have dissuaded her from suicide. The confessional journal letter is rediscovered and reconstructed like a novel recovered from its serialized portions but Valeria chooses that her husband should never know that he has, in effect, caused Sarah's death. Although he is exonerated from any physical involvement in it, Eustace is implicated in the death by his psychological neglect of his wife. When she shields her husband from the knowledge of his complicity, power is transferred to Valeria in a way which questions the balance of the domestic relationship. It is this representation of the dutiful wife's duplicity which is both illustrated and challenged by the presentation of *The Law and the Lady* within *The Graphic*. In *The Law and the Lady*, Valeria Macallan reads the text of her husband's trial for the murder of his first wife then seeks to prove his innocence. In that last instalment of the novel, she burns the first wife's journal letter – reconstructed from a dustheap – in an unwitting echo of the *Graphic* editor's act of destruction against the novel.

Material within the periodical operated both as a contextual reference point and in combative dialogue with the themes of the novel. After the marriage of Eustace and Valeria conducted under a false name in the first instalment (Chapters 1-3) of *The Law and the Lady*, a review of new novels by *The Graphic* included 'The Honeymoon: Remembrance of a Bridal Tour through Scotland' and *Mark Bradon's Wife* by Elizabeth J. Lysaght which is also about an identity concealed. Of *Safely Married* 'by the author of *Caste*', the reviewer concluded that Effie 'must, as a wife, have been intolerable' although the novel itself was deemed 'decidedly above the average of excellence and very well worth reading'.[39] There was also an 'EXTRA DOUBLE PAGE SUPPLEMENT' to this issue illustrating (or more properly illustrated by) a poem written by Locker himself. The poem was called 'The Foster Mother' and the picture (Figure 3) by L. Verdeyn presented a rapt and beautiful girl tending a nest of baby birds which have lost their mother. The picture was detachable from the newspaper although the full text of the poem occurred during the commentary section. That text promised a 'great bird-chorus' from a grown-up 'feathered throng' one of whom was the avian poet, previously one of the abandoned fledglings. The lines directly under the picture extracted

---

[39] *The Graphic*, 26 September 1874, p. 306.

Fig. 3 'The Foster Mother by L. Verdeyn', 'EXTRA DOUBLE PAGE SUPPLEMENT', *The Graphic*, 26 September 1874

from the poem read: 'Sadly she took us home: she fed / Us with the sweetest milk and bread, / Then kissed and put us into bed.' Locker's later objections suggest that he was not alert to the erotic undertones of this piece.

In the instalment of 3 October 1874, Chapters 4 to 6 of *The Law and the Lady* described Valeria's first apprehension about the legality of her marriage and her husband's true identity. Immediately following the episode where she meets her mother-in-law for the first time, there was a fashion column which launched into a discussion of wedding dress with the effervescent hope that 'a few hints as to the minor details of bridal attire may not be found unprofitable for those who are about to take part in wedding ceremonials!'.[40]

A week later in serial time on 10 October 1874, Chapters 7 and 8 were illustrated by the well-known artist William Small who had also illustrated Cassell's serialization of Collins's *Man and Wife*. This illustration (Figure 4) depicted the efforts of a chambermaid to transform Valeria in preparation for her first meeting with Major Fitz-

Fig. 4 Illustration for *The Law and the Lady*, in *The Graphic*, 3 October 1874, p. 349

David, a known womanizer, lover of a pretty face and keeper of Eustace's secret. Valeria wishes to influence him to reveal what he knows and the episode concludes with the arrival of the Major's

---

[40] *The Graphic*, 3 October 1874, p. 334.

mistress when '[t]he lady of the rustling dress burst into the room'.[41] Eight pages later, *The Graphic*'s advertisements for that week reinforced the chambermaid's skills. They described 'Mrs SA Allen's WORLD'S HAIR RESTORER the only preparation that will certainly revive the original and natural colour of grey or faded Hair, stop its falling off and induce a luxuriant growth'. A company in Piccadilly specializing in 'Ladies Ornamental Hair' invited 'an inspection of their Ladies Perukes or Coverings for Thin Partings, copies of Nature'. In the wake of the maid's application to Valeria of 'pearl powder', another advertisement offered a 'Clear Complexion' for all who used the 'UNITED SERVICE SOAP TABLET which also imparts a delicious fragrance'.[42] *The Graphic*'s reader was accustomed to these claims for such preparations which occurred in every issue. An earlier *Graphic* advertisement included an adaptation of Pope's 'The Rape of the Lock' with a glossary in footnotes to highlight the products used by 'Lovely Opoponax'.[43] On 6 March after the instalment describing Sarah Macallan's suicide, Hagan's Magnolia Balm made claims to be a 'toilet miracle' which could change complexions by 'infusing vitality into the skin'.[44] A long paragraph of text asserted that 'it is quite certain that a fresh and rosy complexion will attract more admiration'.[45] These separate advertisements on the back pages of *The Graphic* nonetheless interacted with *The Law and the Lady*, a novel which was itself drawing some comparisons between the two female characters in their use of such face-enhancing products. Despite the separation of the two texts and the two women, the reader would find it hard to ignore the juxtaposition between the soaps and balms and the death of Sarah Macallan. She dies as a result of arsenic poisoning from the preparation she was using to improve *her* complexion.

This competition of discourses continued for the reader in the weeks after Locker's insistence on the vulnerability of his audience on 13 March, and there were particular representations of womanhood which could be read in the light of Valeria's actions and experience. On 26 June 1875, *The Graphic* reproduced a picture (Figure 5) entitled 'To Be Left Until Called For' by A. Dixon in the exhibition of the

---

41 *The Graphic*, 10 October 1874, p. 351; Collins, *Law and the Lady*, p. 64.
42 *The Graphic*, 10 October 1874, p. 362.
43 *The Graphic*, 12 September 1874, p. 267.
44 *The Graphic*, 6 March 1875, p. 238.
45 Ibid.

Fig. 5 'To Be Left Until Called For', *The Graphic*, 26 May 1875, p. 601

Royal Academy. It was very reminiscent of John Everett Millais's paintings *My First Sermon* (1863) and *My Second Sermon* (1864). Writing in the commentary section of the newspaper, the columnist asserted that 'This picture tells its own tale plainly enough', but there were clear indications of further contradictions in the presentation of women – this time as objects of art. The girl was called 'the little woman' in the accompanying but separate text which made it appear as if she had been left there like a parcel 'until called for'.[46] She was also, however, pictured alone both as a child and as a woman, and yet she gazed confidently out at the projected purchasers of the newspaper whose numbers would increase to two hundred thousand for the Christmas issue. *The Graphic*'s 1880 Christmas supplement included Millais's 'Cherry Ripe', another depiction of a lone female child. It was claimed to have sold five hundred thousand copies.[47]

Illustrations of Valeria herself in *The Law and the Lady* tended not to allow her to face outward although this was partly because at least five artists worked on the serial. Her appearance varied until the artist was fixed as Sydney Hall in the latter third of the novel's instalments.[48] A reading of Valeria in the context of the other women pictured in *The Graphic* and in the light of Locker's concern for his audience demonstrates competitive periodical discourse at work.

On 6 March 1875 the penultimate instalment of the novel contained the 'Wife's Confession' reconstructed out of the dust heap at the Macallan family home at Gleninch. The illustration (Figure 6) by Hall depicted Valeria burning Sarah's letter with Eustace's entrance shown behind her in the mirror. On the previous page in this issue was the first in a series of illustrations called 'The Career of the White Slave' which appeared adjacent to the opening of Chapter 46 of the novel for the original reader of the serial.[49] On 20 March, a week after the novel's conclusion, the third illustration in this series was accompanied at an earlier point in the issue by an article from F. C. Lewis about 'successful women hunters' on the borders of Persia:

> We have no wish to palliate the violence and cruelty inflicted by these captures of maidens, but as the ultimate destination of the victims is not

---

[46] *The Graphic*, 26 June 1875, p. 603.

[47] See W. L. Thomas, 'The Making of The Graphic', *The Universal Review*, 2:5 (1888), 80-93 (p. 92). The 'demure little sitter' for the painting was Thomas's great niece Edie Ramage (Thomas, 'Making of The Graphic', p. 91) but critics are divided on the impact of the work between 'timeless purity' (L. Bradley, 'From Eden to Empire: John Everett Millais's *Cherry Ripe*', *Victorian Studies*, 34:2 (1991), 179-203 (p. 192) and 'pronounced paedophilic appeal' (P. Tamarkin Reis, 'Victorian Centrefold: Another Look at Millais's *Cherry Ripe*', *Victorian Studies*, 35:2 (1992), 201-5 (p. 201)).

[48] For instance, on honeymoon (*The Graphic*, 26 September 1874, p. 301) and on the beach where she confronts Eustace (*The Graphic*, 3 October 1874, p. 329). Hall was a well-known illustrator for William Thomas (Thomas, 'Making of The Graphic', p. 84).

[49] *The Graphic*, 6 March 1875, p. 219.

an unhappy one, it seems a pity that force should be necessary to complete a transaction which might be entered on voluntarily.

He defined this process as a type of 'matrimonial market' and added: 'Mothers with large families of daughters might not be sorry to see the system extended to the British Isles.'[50]

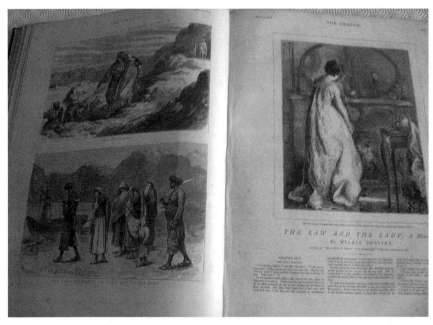

Fig. 6 'The Career of a White Slave' and 'The Last Morsel of Paper', *The Graphic*, 6 March 1875, pp. 224-25

Reading across the textual Sarah and the pictured Valeria/White Slave is a process which readers were invited to follow by the very layout of the newspaper. Other contrasting images were presented side by side such as the 'Valentine Makers' and 'Valentine Receivers' on St Valentine's Day 1875 (Figure 7) or 'Before' and 'After' pictures of children rescued from lives on the street.[51] In a letter to his solicitor William Tindall, Collins himself wrote to discuss the layout of the publicity for his novel *Man and Wife*: 'Of course the advertisement will

---

50   *The Graphic*, 20 March 1875, p. 270.
51   *The Graphic*, 13 February 1875, p. 165; 'A Girl before and after Reclamation', in 'Transformation Scenes in Real Life: Effects of the East End Juvenile Mission' (*The Graphic*, 16 January 1875, p. 64).

go "across columns" small advertisements are useless now.'[52] The reading technique of *The Graphic* also ran across columns and the binding of the journal separated commentary from illustration in a way which sought to direct the reading experience. In this way, too, Locker's positioning of his disowning paragraph built on the experience of reading in an intertextual even extradiegetic recreation of Valeria's rereading and rewriting experience within the novel.

Fig. 7 'Valentine Makers' and 'Valentine Receivers', *The Graphic*, 13 February 1875, p. 165

A more detailed example of the double standard in text and illustration can be shown in the presentation of a picture called 'The New Necklace' (Figure 8) published the week after *The Law and the Lady* concluded. This was the painting by C. Chaplin 'exhibited last year in the Gallery of French Artists', its caption suggestive of a risqué piece of continental work. The commentary three pages earlier used this picture to posit the existence of a 'chasm' between the sexes:

---

[52] Collins *Public Face*, ed. by Baker and others, II, 186.

Here is this young lady in a state of perfect rapture because of the pretty toy which she has just hung around her neck. Her fingers press it complacently, while her other hand rests on a bracelet. It cannot be vanity, for there is nobody looking at her, though her joy may arise in some measure from the anticipation of future conquests to be achieved through the aid of this magic chain of pearls; anyhow, she is completely absorbed and does not feel at all chilly about the shoulders, although she looks as if she ought to do so.[53]

Fig. 8 'The New Necklace' and 'Charles E Darwin Esq. FRS', *The Graphic*, 27 March 1875, pp. 300-1

The commentator aimed to belittle both the woman and the subject and to raise prudish concerns about bare shoulders. He tried to maintain that this was a private moment even though the painting had been publicly viewed in a gallery and now in a newspaper costing sixpence a week. The allusion to the sexes suggested that no young man could experience such delight unless he were 'an untutored savage [...] A clear proof, says some surly misogynist that women are still in the bondage of barbarism'. He could not then resist the final patroniz-

---

[53] *The Graphic*, 27 March 1875, p. 297; the illustration is on p. 300.

ing *coup de grâce*: 'Long may they continue in such barbarism, we reply, for the world will become very dull when women cease to desire to look pretty and attractive.' The whole was finally compounded by reading 'across columns' where the reader would find a portrait in the style of a masculine commemorative medallion of a resolutely male authority on barbarism in the form of Charles Darwin.

This is a complex reading. Paintings have some sanction in terms of their depiction of women as objects and it becomes clear that *The Graphic* could reproduce well-known pictures and then use print media to undermine them. The problem for Wilkie Collins appears to have arisen when he took liberties in print which the editor could not omit but which he could nonetheless undermine through the same technique 'across columns'. It was a depiction through print in adjacent columns which was used to correct the perceived impropriety which occurred in *The Law and the Lady* as a serial. Collins wrote in 1872: 'I confess (considering my recent experience of illustrations [...]) that I am always relieved to find myself working with no other interpreter than the Printer.'[54] The experience of *The Law and the Lady* in serial suggests that even print could interpret through illustration.

It has been observed that the nineteenth-century periodical created a 'textual community' with its 'deft movement among categories of address, invocation, inclusion and marginalization', and these qualities have been demonstrated in the layout and reading direction supplied by *The Graphic* newspaper in its quest for 'propriety in print'.[55] *The Graphic* also had a mission to succeed in a competitive market and to reinforce the aspirations of its readers whose appreciation of art existed within a specific and policed ideological context. Valeria Macallan was writing a serial and Wilkie Collins was writing a serial. *The Graphic* was writing within the serial life of its readers and as a mainstay of the parlour it had to reinforce that intertextual community in order to remain 'a welcome guest in every gentleman's family.'

---

[54]   Collins, *Public Face*, ed. by Baker and others, II, 347-48. It is ironic that at the time he excused *The Graphic* from this criticism – at least with reference to *Miss or Mrs?*.

[55]   L. Brake, B. Bell and D. Finkelstein, *Nineteenth-Century Media and the Construction of Identities* (Basingstoke, 2000), pp. 3, 5.

'Boz Versus Dickens': Paratext, Pseudonyms and Serialization in the Victorian Literary Marketplace[1]

ROB ALLEN

Introduction

Dickens's success as an author began with a series of sketches written from 1833-36. Published in a range of London newspapers and magazines, these sketches were praised for their humour and for capturing everyday urban life. The full title of the first volume edition – *Sketches by Boz: Illustrative of Every-Day Life and Every-Day People* – and the assertion that the sketches 'present little pictures of life and manners as they really are' both emphasised the work's claim of fidelity to contemporary experience.[2] Yet this insistence on faithful mimesis revolved around the fiction of a pseudonymous author called 'Boz'. Emerging in 1834 as a way of labelling sketches scattered across the London periodical press, Dickens's fictional pseudonym became, paradoxically, the marker for an authorial voice noted for its accurate representation of the metropolis. The use of the pseudonym allowed Dickens to maintain a respectable distance between his own name and a literary experiment he was hoping might supplement his income. Under the guise of 'Boz', Dickens could unify the sketches he was producing and build on the popular reception they received. Yet, by keeping a careful separation between pseudonym and real name, Dickens could ensure his foray into authorship would not endanger his professional career as a well-respected court reporter.[3]

Kathryn Chittick has observed that Dickens did not simply emerge as a novelist with the publication of his first serial between 1836-37.[4] His career began with sketches attributed to his pseudonym 'Boz' which, from 1834-36, functioned as a textual label specifying the name

---

[1] 'Boz versus Dickens' was the title of an unsigned article in *Parker's London Magazine*, cited in P. Collins, *Dickens: The Critical Heritage* (London, 1986), pp. 168-71 (p. 168).

[2] *Sketches by Boz* (London, 1836), title-page; reproduced in *Sketches by Boz and Other Early Papers*, ed. by M. Slater (London, 1994), p. xxxix.

[3] Kathryn Chittick, *Dickens and the 1830s* (Cambridge, 1990), p. 57.

[4] Ibid., p. ix.

of an otherwise unknown authorial figure.[5] Due to the specific conditions of their original publication, these sketches were unsupported by the kind of paratextual elements, such as illustrations, frontispieces, dedications, prefaces and portraits of the author, that would subsequently accompany the volume editions of Dickens's work. The purpose of this essay is to examine how from 1836-39 the relationship between the pseudonym, 'Boz', and the real author, Charles Dickens, was staged in the paratext to work attributed to both of them.

Gérard Genette defined 'paratext' as that which 'enables a text to become a book and to be offered as such to its readers'.[6] Characterizing the nature of this offer by metaphors of thresholds, vestibules and airlocks, Genette suggested that such transitional mechanisms provide 'a better reception for the text and a more pertinent reading of it'.[7] The assumption of this essay is that the paratextual elements of a literary work also serve to create or modify the image of the author responsible for it. As Genette's consideration of the 'pseudonym effect' suggests, such authorial representation is the province of the paratextual, a bibliographic 'apparatus' that conjures, describes and positions 'imagined author[s]' in relation to the body of work that comes to be grouped around their invented names.[8]

The Emergence of 'Boz'

Dickens's early work, from *Sketches by Boz* (1836) to *Nicholas Nickleby* (1838-39), was accompanied by the 'paratextual apparatus' substantiating the existence of 'Boz' and presenting him as what Genette calls 'an imagined author'.[9] The written correspondence between Dickens and his publishers during these years reveal an author sensitive to the implications of paratextual choices especially in regard to how they affected representations of authorship. In a letter of 1836 to his

---

[5]   A situation aptly described by Gérard Genette when he discusses one of his seven categories of pseudonymity in which 'a real author attributes a work to an imaginary author but does not produce any information about the latter except the name'. G. Genette, *Paratexts: Thresholds of Interpretation*, trans. by J. E. Lewin (Cambridge, 1997), pp. 47-8.

[6]   Ibid., p. 1.

[7]   Ibid., p. 2.

[8]   Ibid., pp. 48-9.

[9]   Ibid., p. 48.

publisher, John Macrone, Dickens tried to steer the former away from using 'bwain' in the title to the latter's first book. The author offered two other possibilities: 'Sketches by Boz and Cuts by Cruikshank' and 'Etchings by Boz and Wood Cuts by Cruikshank'.[10] Both of Dickens's proposed titles incorporated the pseudonymous author, 'Boz', and the named illustrator George Cruikshank. Proposing these titles, Dickens added: 'I think perhaps some such title would look more modest— whether modesty ought to have anything to do with such an affair, I must leave to your experience as a Publisher to decide.'[11]

Macrone finally settled on *Sketches by Boz: Illustrative of Every-Day Life and Every-Day People*, which was first published in February 1836 for a guinea. This two-volume edition was illustrated by George Cruikshank, a famous illustrator of 'London street scenes', which meant that Macrone could at once 'capitalize on Dickens's growing reputation and Cruikshank's already established one'.[12] In February 1836, after the final work on the volume's plates had been completed, the author sent the illustrator a letter which 'rejoiced' that they were so close to 'the termination of our labours in Boz's cause'.[13]

It was as 'Boz' that Dickens addressed readers in the 'Preface' to this edition, which began with a startling comparison:

> In humble imitation of a prudent course, universally adopted by aeronauts, the Author of these volumes throws them up as his pilot balloon, trusting it may catch some favourable current, and devoutly and earnestly it may *go off well* – a sentiment in which his Publisher cordially concurs.[14]

It is interesting to note how 'Boz' invokes the idea of an aerial panorama in his first paratextual description of authorship. The expensive volumes are transformed from a literary and visual product into a 'pilot balloon' sent up 'as a prudent course' to see if it 'may catch some favourable current'. Letters from Dickens to Macrone leading up to the publication of this volume reveal that Dickens was well aware of

---

[10] *The Letters of Charles Dickens*, ed. by M. House and others, 12 vols (Oxford, 1965-2002), I, 82.
[11] Ibid.
[12] Robert Patten, *Charles Dickens and his Publishers* (Oxford, 1978), p. 29.
[13] Cited in Patten, *Dickens and his Publishers*, p. 30.
[14] *Sketches by Boz*, ed. by Slater, p. xxxix, emphasis retained.

the experimental nature of the venture and the risk his publisher was taking.[15]

In the 'Preface', 'Boz' notes the cordial relationship between author and publisher before developing the metaphor of the 'pilot balloon' so that it includes a 'car' into which 'Boz' precariously places not only himself but also 'all his hopes of future fame'. Discussing the 'perilous voyage' he is taking in such 'a frail machine', 'Boz' notes the 'assistance and companionship of some well-known individual', the illustrator George Cruikshank, observing that although this 'is their first voyage in company' it may 'not be the last'. The 'Preface' ends with an acknowledgement of the experimental nature of the volume and the author's hopes 'to repeat his experiment with increased confidence, and on a more extensive scale'.[16]

This focus on the possible future efforts of 'Boz' would have been particularly relevant to Dickens at the time he wrote the 'Preface', as he had recently signed a contract with Chapman and Hall to provide letter-press, as 'Boz', for what would become *The Pickwick Papers*. Due to publish a new serial in just under two months from the date of the 'Preface', it seems that Dickens was using the publication of a volume edition of sketches by 'Boz' to prepare the public for the forthcoming serial which would be 'Edited by Boz.'

In August 1836, the second edition of the first series of *Sketches by Boz* was published with a 'Preface' ironically informing readers that they were 'guilty' if 'Boz' produced more work because they had encouraged a 'young and unknown writer, by their patronage and approval'.[17] This statement configured 'Boz' as a biographical individual ('young' and 'unknown') and as a 'writer' whose future work was dependent on the positive reaction of the reading public. The 'Preface' also suggested that 'Boz', the writer of sketches, might turn his hand to more serious work:

> If the pen that designed these little outlines, should present its labours frequently to the Public hereafter; if it should produce fresh sketches, and even connected works of fiction of a higher grade, they have only themselves to blame.[18]

[15] Patten, *Dickens and his Publishers*, p. 30.
[16] In this paragraph I draw on *Sketches by Boz*, ed. by Slater, p. xxxix.
[17] Ibid., p. xl.
[18] Ibid.

From a writer of urban sketches in London periodicals, 'Boz' was now presented as an aspiring novelist whose prospective career emerged from the public's recent reaction to his work. The promise of the original 'Preface' for writing on a 'more extensive scale' had been realized in the success of *The Pickwick Papers*. Starting as a series of episodic adventures accompanying visual caricatures, by August 1836 the serial had introduced a key plot development when Mrs. Bardell faints in Pickwick's arms thereby provoking the narrative arc of Pickwick's trial and imprisonment. The September instalment, written in August, also began to develop the relationship between Pickwick and his servant, Sam Weller, a Quixotic pairing that came to be one of the serial's chief attractions, together with the regular appearance and 'comic soliloquies' of Sam Weller from the fifth instalment in August – an instalment which had been excerpted in seven London papers in the fortnight following 10 August.[19] Thus, when composing the 'Preface' to the August 1836 edition of *Sketches by Boz*, Dickens may again have been using the paratextual platform of the volume edition to comment on the success of his current serial, a work he could justifiably consider 'of a higher grade' and more 'connected' than his previous, discrete sketches.

In early August 1836, Dickens wrote to Macrone to consult him on a prospective title for a series of sketches Dickens was planning to write for the *Carlton Chronicle*. Pre-empting any negative reaction on the part of the publisher, Dickens argued that the new sketches would convince the 'nobs' who read 'The Carlton Chronicle' to buy the forthcoming volume edition of *Sketches by Boz*.[20] Asking the publisher for his view on what would be a good title 'for our purpose', Dickens suggested: 'Leaves from an unpublished volume by 'Boz' (which will be torn out, once a fortnight).'[21] What is interesting in this proposed title is that it reverses the origin of work by 'Boz', presenting it as first produced in books and only subsequently yielding '[l]eaves [...] torn out' periodically from an 'unpublished volume'. From a pseudonym used to group together discrete sketches, 'Boz' was now being figured as an author whose work was automatically associated with the

---

[19]   Chittick, *Dickens and the 1830s*, p. 64.
[20]   *Letters*, I, 160.
[21]   Ibid.

volume editions, which, just six months earlier, had been presented as a 'pilot balloon'.

Dickens and his early publishers:
Macrone, Bentley and Chapman and Hall

By November 1836, Dickens had 'vastly overextended himself' with 'seven or eight publishing commitments' that were impossible to meet.[22] Moreover, his relationship with Macrone was becoming increasingly sour as a result of contractual disagreements. This had an impact on the publication of the second series of *Sketches,* which had been advertised as being available in two volumes from October but which was eventually released as a hurried one-volume edition in time for Christmas.[23] The main reason for the delay was Dickens's distractions with other, more lucrative, projects and the breakdown in the relationship between author and publisher.

The second series of *Sketches by Boz,* published in mid-December 1836 for fifteen shillings, was accompanied by a 'Preface' which characterized the volume in a very different style from those published with the first series.[24] Instead of asserting that the author's continued career depended on the success of the volume in question, the 'Preface' to the second series negated its own value on the grounds that 'nine hundred and ninety-nine people out of every thousand, never read a preface at all.'[25] The author nevertheless simply ventured to hope the volume might be well received and not 'considered an unwelcome, or inappropriate sequel'.[26] He then continued, as Patten notes, to make a direct allusion to the work's status as a 'Christmas Piece' before showing the dialogue that ensued when author and publisher gave 'a modest tap at the door of the public'.[27] This seemingly light-hearted scene in which, following 'the well-known precedent of the charity boys', author and publisher argued about who was to knock on the public's door in an effort to convince them to look at their Christmas Piece, allowed Dickens to dramatize a situation which he took very

---

[22] Patten, *Dickens and his Publishers,* p. 34.
[23] Ibid., p. 35.
[24] Ibid., pp. 35-6.
[25] *Sketches by Boz,* ed. by Slater, p. xl.
[26] Ibid.
[27] Patten, *Dickens and his Publishers,* pp. 35-6.

seriously: the representation of his relationship with readers.[28] Significantly, it is the publisher who is made to knock on the door of the public, begging them to take the book into their homes, and leaving as soon as they do. The author seems to care less about the success of the volume and 'lingers behind' not to promote business concerns but simply to wish 'his best friend, the Public' a merry Christmas.[29] Thus, jovial as this sketch is, there seems to be an explicit separation between the purely business interests of the publisher and the more personal relationship between the author and his public. I would like to suggest that this was part of an authorial strategy designed to mitigate any damage that might be done to the image of 'Boz' by his publisher or by the hastily and negligently compiled second series.[30] 'Boz' not only sought to disentangle himself from the publisher (note their very different activities at the door of the public) but also from this edition of the work itself. It is surely significant that, as Patten points out, Macrone and Dickens were at the time not on speaking terms and that the edition was rushed out with enough speed for Dickens's subtle distinction between author and publisher to make it past Macrone and into print.[31] Equally important was 'Boz's' current success with two other publishers: Chapman and Hall, who were publishing *The Pickwick Papers*; and George Bentley, who had recently contracted Dickens to provide him with more work attributed to 'Boz' while performing the editorial role for *Bentley's Miscellany*, which would begin publication in the following month.

'Boz': From Editor to Author

If this representation of 'Boz' depicts him as an author more focused on his relationship with his readers than with his publisher, an address in *The Pickwick Papers* in the same month represents 'Boz' as an author who prefers to keep faith with his readers rather than follow the 'sad temptations' of the market.[32] In a December 1836 announcement acknowledging that *The Pickwick Papers* had reached the halfway mark of its serial run, 'Boz' stepped out explicitly as its author (rather than

---

[28] *Sketches by Boz*, ed. by Slater, p. xli.
[29] Ibid.
[30] Ibid., pp. 35-6.
[31] Patten, *Dickens and his Publishers*, pp. 36-7.
[32] Charles Dickens, *The Pickwick Papers*, ed. by J. Kinsley (Oxford, 1986), p. 758.

the editor he was presented as on the serial's monthly cover). The address marked an important moment allowing the author to thank his readers, to make explicit his motives on their behalf and to reassure them that the second half of the work would be issued as originally promised. 'Boz' confided that the enormous success of his endeavours, increasing sales and 'the most extensive popularity' could easily lead him to 'exceed the limits he first assigned himself'.[33] However, he declared that he was determined to resist the temptation to write beyond the 'original pledge' of confining his work to twenty instalments. He gave two reasons for this: that he wanted to ensure that when published as a complete volume, the book would not have 'the heavy disadvantage of being prolonged beyond the original plan' and that he wished to 'keep the strictest faith with his readers'.[34]

At the same time as making these pledges, the image of 'Boz' was transformed from his original function as the editor of *The Pickwick Papers* to its author. Until this point, 'Boz' had been characterized merely as an editor of existing documents rather than an author of fictional characters and events. In changing his role into one revolving around authorship, 'Boz' also suggested just how this authorship should be understood. The initial advertisement for the serial described how the 'whole of the Pickwick Papers' had been 'carefully preserved' by a secretary, purchased at 'immense expense' and put into the hands of the editor, 'Boz', who was 'highly qualified for the task of arranging these [existing] important documents, and placing them before the public in an attractive form'.[35] This located value in the ability of an editor to arrange and place the various documents in an appealing manner before the public. In an image that played on the popular Victorian trope describing serial fiction as coming 'warm from the brain' of the author, 'Boz' was transformed from a purely administrative, editorial function into one characterized by the a sense of the imaginative labour necessary to continue the second half of the serial:

---

[33]   Ibid.
[34]   Ibid.
[35]   Ibid., p. 756.

The Author merely hints that he has strong reason to believe that a great variety of other documents still lie hidden in the repository from which these were taken, and that they may one day see the light.[36]

The author has eclipsed the editor, and the archive purchased at 'immense expense' has been replaced by the idea of a 'repository' from which subsequent material could be procured. The reticent 'Boz' of the Christmas edition of *Sketches by Boz*, who stands apologetically at the door of the public, has been replaced by an author in full control of his material who can hint, through the metaphor of the repository, that there will be no lack of future content for the second half of the serial. Published in December 1836, the announcement in *The Pickwick Papers* could also function as an implicit advertisement for the first issue of *Bentley's Miscellany* which was due to be published the following month.

The continued publication of serial instalments was the focus of another address to readers, accompanying the fifteenth instalment, which excused a recent delay in publication, caused by what 'Boz' called 'a severe domestic affliction'.[37] Although he did not mention it, the reason for this delay was the death of Dickens's beloved sister-in-law, Mary Hogarth, who died in his arms at the age of just seventeen. The 'Address to the Reader' counteracted the 'various idle speculations and absurdities' that had been circulating about the author and stated that he had been doing nothing more than 'seeking in a few weeks' retirement the restoration of his spirits after 'a sad bereavement'.[38] The 'Address' excused the delay in publication and situated 'Boz' in an embodied, contemporary world where grief could bring his pen to a standstill. There followed a 'Notice to Correspondents', which begged readers to stop sending the 'immense number of [...] suggestions' for *Pickwick* as these 'hints' could not be included and the author had no time 'to peruse these anonymous letters'.[39] Highlighting the author's ability to make requests of his readers, this notice also served to characterize a readership so immersed in the story that they wished to actively participate in its development.

---

[36] J. Sutherland, *Victorian Novelists and Publishers* (Chicago, 1976), p. 21; Dickens, *Pickwick Papers*, p. 758.
[37] Dickens, *Pickwick Papers*, p. 759.
[38] Ibid.
[39] Ibid.

The Emergence of Dickens

The final, double instalment of the serial transformed its authorship from the pseudonymous caricaturist of London life, 'Boz', into the real-world author, Charles Dickens. The latter emerged to take retrospective responsibility for the enormous success that had previously been accorded to 'Boz' and began a process whereby the name Charles Dickens would come to signify a particular set of values and characteristics associated with the production of Victorian fiction.

Among the various paratextual elements of the final, double instalment, an important element in the transformation of authorship from 'Boz' to Dickens was the 'Dedication'.[40] It featured Dickens's real name and address, enabling a biographical figure to take retrospective responsibility for a text that had captured the popular imagination on a grand scale. The 'Dedication' also established a position for authors and their rightful place in society. It was written to 'Mr. Serjeant Talfourd, M.P.' and acknowledged his 'efforts' to secure better copyright terms for authors and their descendants.[41] This was not just a matter of seeking to protect commercial interests. Dickens thanked Talfourd for:

> [...] the inestimable services you are rendering to the literature of your country, and of the lasting benefits you will confer upon the authors of this and succeeding generations, by securing to them and their descendants a permanent interest in the copyright of their works.[42]

Thanking Talfourd for his 'efforts on behalf of English literature' represented more than just an expression of gratitude. From the moment the name and signature of Charles Dickens emerged in connection with a publicly-endorsed production of authorship, Dickens made explicit his personal affiliations and concerns related to copyright and the future of an English literary tradition. This 'Dedication' marks what Helen Small has described as a career-long attempt by Dickens to reorient the image of contemporary Victorian authors

---

[40] The paratextual elements such as the 'Dedication', 'Preface', and 'Table of Contents' accompanying the volume edition were also included as bibliographical extras in the final double instalment of the serial to allow those subscribers who had followed the original serialization to have their instalments bound into a complete volume.

[41] Dickens, *Pickwick Papers*, p. 5.

[42] Ibid.

away from a model based on the abasement of eighteenth-century writer-patron relationships to one based directly on appeal to a contemporary mass readership.[43] This was, in other words, a model of literary production in which the barriers to publication depended less on the whims of a capricious, wealthy individual than on the tastes of an emerging mass market. This new mode of production prompted Dickens to make repeated polemical statements about the need for revised national and international copyright laws that better represented and rewarded the contributions of authors.

If the 'Dedication' of *The Pickwick Papers* helped to define the characteristics and concerns of the figure labelled as Charles Dickens, the 'Preface' engaged with contemporary debates about how to define a periodical serial that had become a book. At the same time as referring to *Pickwick* as a 'book in monthly numbers', Dickens used the 'Preface' to explain the 'author's object in this work'.[44] Initially, this seems to have been a continuation of Dickens's earlier *Sketches* and was presented in terms of 'a constant succession of characters and incidents [...] paint[ed] in [...] vivid colours' that are 'life-like' as well as 'amusing'.[45]

However, Dickens also analysed the consequences of the 'detached and desultory form of publication' on him as an author of a book in monthly, thirty-two page portions.[46] Referring to the intermingling of the serial and episodic modes, Dickens admitted that the mode of publication (lasting 'no fewer than twenty months') necessitated both a 'chain of interest' that connected the instalments and an approach that ensured that each instalment was a complete unit. In a sentence which, I would like to suggest, summarized his approach to publishing a 'book in monthly numbers', Dickens explained how the form of publication (as instalments and then a volume) 'appeared to the author' to demand that:

> [...] every number should be, to a certain extent, complete in itself, and yet [...] the whole twenty numbers, when collected, should form one tol-

---

[43] H. Small, 'The Debt to Society: Dickens, Fielding, and the Genealogy of Independence', in *The Victorians and the Eighteenth Century: Reassessing the Tradition*, ed. by F. O'Gorman and K. Turner (Aldershot, 2004), pp. 14-40 (p. 34 and passim).

[44] Dickens, *Pickwick Papers*, p. 6.

[45] Ibid.

[46] All quotations in this paragraph and the next come from Dickens, *Pickwick Papers*, p. 6.

erably harmonious whole, each leading to the other by a gentle and not unnatural progress of adventure.

Having outlined the considerations involved in publishing such a work, the 'Preface' stated that it would be unreasonable to expect 'an artfully interwoven or ingeniously complicated plot'. Responding to objections that *The Pickwick Papers* were 'a mere series of adventures' with 'ever changing' scenes and 'characters [who] come and go like the men and women we encounter in the real world', Dickens suggested that similar objections had been made 'to the works of some of the greatest novelists in the English language'.

While acknowledging possible objections to what had been a phenomenally successful serial, Dickens was also grouping his book with the picaresque novels of authors such as Fielding and Smollett. Although he did not categorize his work as a 'novel', he implicitly compared it with that of 'some of the greatest novelists in the English language'. Unlike his illustrious predecessors, Dickens emphasized that he was very much contemporary with the early Victorian reading public and affected by their positive reaction to his work: 'The almost unexampled kindness and favour with which these papers have been received by the public will be a never-failing source of gratifying and pleasant recollection while their author lives.'[47] The use of 'author' here contradicted the earlier focus on 'editor', in the same way that the 'Preface' was signed by the biographically identifiable individual, Charles Dickens, rather than the pseudonymous 'Boz'.

A similar transformation, from the editor of a serial, 'Boz', to the author of a completed work, is evident in Dickens's second serial, *Oliver Twist*, which was published from 1837-39 and overlapped first with *The Pickwick Papers* and later with *Nicholas Nickleby*. It is important to note that *Oliver Twist* was initially presented in *Bentley's Miscellany* as a continuation of 'the mudfog papers' with little indication in its early instalments that it was intended to be a novel or that it would last long enough to become one. Yet, as a result of a contractual argument the publisher of *Oliver Twist*, George Bentley, agreed that the serial could serve a double purpose simultaneously fulfilling Dickens's obligations for providing monthly text to *Bentley's Miscellany* and their agreement for a three-volume novel. Without this

---

[47]　Ibid., p. 7.

agreement, it is possible *Oliver Twist* would have been discontinued before it could become the three-volume edition published by Bentley.

This edition was published on 9 November 1838. However, as a result of comments from Dickens and Forster, it was re-issued a few days later with a new title-page replacing 'Boz' with 'Charles Dickens, author of "The Pickwick Papers"'.[48] Advertisements were also altered to match this change in attribution. In less then a week, Dickens had ensured that this volume edition (and the accompanying advertisements) would be promoted as the work of Charles Dickens instead of 'Boz'.[49] With the copyrights for the novel remaining with Bentley, a second edition (dated 1839) was published in December 1838. Bentley advertised this in *The Athenaeum* as a second edition of *Oliver Twist* by 'Charles Dickens, Esq.', a sign that he had taken on board Dickens's complaints against naming 'Boz' on the title-page.[50] The second edition was reissued both in October 1839 with an expanded reference to Dickens which included mention of *Nicholas Nickleby*, and again in March 1840 with the title-page reverting to 'Boz' a month prior to the much-anticipated publication, by Chapman and Hall, of Dickens's *Master Humphrey's Clock*, 'Edited by Boz'.[51]

By December 1839, Dickens complained to his lawyers that Bentley's indiscriminate use of his name and writing was damaging his reputation. Bentley had been busy promoting the forthcoming publication of *Barnaby Rudge*, although Dickens had not agreed to provide this novel and had only finished two chapters.[52] At the same time, Bentley had advertised Ainsworth's *Jack Sheppard* as a novel 'uniform in size and price with "Oliver Twist"'.[53] This comparison, to a popular work that had provoked critical reaction for its glamorization of 'Newgate' crime, damaged Dickens's serial.[54] Indeed, it was just this kind of negative association that Dickens attempted to dispel in the 'Preface' to the third edition of the novel published by Chapman and Hall in 1841. It is worth noting that Dickens was only able to write

---

[48] Charles Dickens, *Oliver Twist*, ed. by K. Tillotson (Oxford, 1966), p. xxiv.
[49] Ibid.
[50] *Athenaeum*, 22 December 1838, p. 917.
[51] Dickens, *Oliver Twist*, p. xxvii.
[52] Ibid.
[53] Ibid.
[54] Ibid., p. 399.

this preface as a result of Chapman and Hall buying the copyright to the novel from the original publisher.

As first his pseudonym and subsequently his biographical name developed increasing significance, Dickens was careful to guard, wherever possible, the use of these names to prevent their market value being damaged by careless publishers or bad publicity. In a letter of April 1837, Dickens asked J. P. Hartley to omit mention of 'Boz' in relation to a play the author felt anxious to avoid being linked with.[55] In June 1837, Dickens was faced with a more serious concern when Macrone decided to capitalize on his ownership of the copyright of Dickens's work and started to re-issue *Sketches by Boz* in the same green-wrapper, monthly format in which *The Pickwick Papers* was then being serialized. Dickens, as he wrote in a letter to Forster, was only too aware that his 'name being before the town' in three publications (*The Pickwick Papers, Oliver Twist* and *Sketches by Boz*) at the same time 'must prove seriously prejudicial to my reputation'.[56] As a result of Dickens's insistence, Chapman and Hall intervened purchasing the copyright from Macrone and reissuing the sketches in monthly instalments accompanied by distinctive pink wrappers with a new cover by George Cruikshank.[57]

'Boz Versus Dickens'

The earliest mention of Dickens's name in any of his serials or volumes occurred on the first page of the advertiser accompanying the eleventh instalment of *The Pickwick Papers* in February 1837 as part of an advertisement by the publisher Macrone for *Sketches by Boz*.[58] One month later, a poem in the third issue of *Bentley's Miscellany* played with the relationship between Dickens and his pseudonym:

> Who the *dickens* "Boz" could be
> Puzzled many a learned elf;
> Till time unveil'd the mystery

---

[55] *Letters*, I, 246.
[56] Cited in Patten, *Dickens and his Publishers*, p. 39.
[57] Ibid., pp. 41-2.
[58] J. Eckel, *The First Editions of the Writings of Charles Dickens: Their Points and Values* (New York, 1972), p. 33.

And *Boz* appear'd as DICKENS' self![59]

This poem was located directly underneath an article called 'The Pantomime of Life' attributed to 'Boz', which itself came beneath a headline that read 'Stray chapters by Boz'.[60] This page of the miscellany, as Michael Slater helpfully reminds us, was published because Dickens had underwritten his contribution for *Oliver Twist* and needed to fill up the sixteen pages of text stipulated in his contract with Bentley.[61] It seems fitting, in this respect, that the poem was titled 'IMPROMPTU'. Suggesting the combination of improvisation and performance that figuratively and literally produced this very page of *Bentley's Miscellany*; the title is also sufficiently theatrical to encompass the shifting authorial identity humorously depicted in the poem.

Along with this poetic meditation on authorial identity, the figure of 'Boz' was prominently displayed in a tipped in leaflet accompanying the March 1837 issue of *Bentley's Miscellany*. Entitled 'The Extraordinary Gazette', this presented a short 'speech by his mightiness', 'Boz', underneath a woodcut presenting 'Boz' exercising his editorial duties and leading a giant porter who supports the weight of *Bentley's Miscellany*. Copies of the latest issue of the magazine fly off in all directions to the delight of the eager readers crowding on all sides. Far from an anonymous, textual function, 'Boz' is depicted here as an embodied figure in the world of Victorian periodical publishing who bore a striking resemblance to the twenty-five year old Charles Dickens.

The January 1838 edition of *Bentley's Miscellany* began with a proleptic, full-plate steel engraving of Oliver being shot before proceeding to the ending to Book One of *Oliver Twist*.[62] It also included a poem entitled 'A Poetic Epistle to "Boz"'.[63] Noting how the 'potent mirth-compeller', 'Boz', had won the public's hearts 'in monthly parts', the poet implicitly declared that the work 'Boz' was producing for *Bentley's Miscellany*, such as *Oliver Twist*, was superior to his recently completed monthly serial, *The Pickwick Papers*. The rather strained verse contained a quatrain which played with the relationship

---

[59] Verse by C. J. Davids, first published in *Bentley's Miscellany*, March 1837, p. 297 and cited in *Letters*, I, 264, n. 1.
[60] *Bentley's Miscellany*, March 1837, p. 291.
[61] *Sketches by Boz*, ed. by Slater, p. 500.
[62] *Bentley's Miscellany*, January 1838, pp. 1-16.
[63] Ibid., p. 71.

between 'Boz' and Dickens, allowing the latter to emerge in a visually descriptive fashion from the pseudonym addressed in the title:

> Write on, young sage! still o'er the page pour forth the flood of fancy;
> Wax still more droll, wave o'er the soul, Wit's wand of necromancy.
> Behold! e'en now around your brow th'immortal laurel thickens;
> Yea, SWIFT or STERNE might gladly learn a thing or two from
>   DICKENS.[64]

Following an end rhyme ('flood of fancy'/'necromancy') that suggests an occult relationship between the imaginative process and the use of wit, the poem concludes with an end rhyme which reveals Dickens, conjuring the man from a metonymic representation of literary fame accruing around the figure of the pseudonym ('around your brow th'immortal laurel thickens'). The final end rhyme completes the transformation from the 'Boz' of the poem's title to the Dickens of its conclusion.

While Dickens is traditionally showered with praise as the 'genius' of *Pickwick,* the idea for the monthly serial publishing format, followed by volume reissue, had been his publishers'. For all that Dickens sought to suggest about authorship in the 'Preface' or 'Dedication' to *The Pickwick Papers,* the existence of such paratextual elements depended upon the specific form that the serial's publishers had envisaged and enabled. Dickens's later prefaces to *Sketches by Boz* (1839 and 1850), and his important 'Author's Introduction' to the 1841 edition of *Oliver Twist,* were only possible because of Chapman and Hall's willingness to purchase the copyright to these works from Dickens's previous publishers (Macrone and Bentley respectively). Thus, as we trace the transformation from 'Boz' to Dickens in the paratext to his early work, we should also acknowledge the assistance and capital investment provided by Chapman and Hall.

In what we might term a private paratextual performance, Dickens provided a signed copy of a bound first edition of *The Pickwick Papers* to Edward Chapman in November 1839, when he had finished *Nicholas Nickleby.* The copy included a humorous scene from *Oliver Twist* in which the eponymous hero naïvely hits on the truth that it would probably be 'a much better thing to be a bookseller' than a

---

[64] Ibid.

'book-writer'.[65] Declaring Chapman and Hall, the publishers of *The Pickwick Papers* and *Nicholas Nickleby,* to be 'the best of booksellers past, present, or to come', Dickens signed the 'Dedication' with his own name, while 'Boz' acted as the 'witness' at the bottom left-hand corner of the page.[66]

Such a display of cordiality between author and publisher in November 1839 contrasted with Dickens's recent dealings with Macrone and Bentley and may well have been, in part, a result of two important factors: the continued success Dickens and his current publishers were enjoying with their pioneering style of monthly serial fiction; and Chapman and Hall's involvement in the famous portrait of Dickens that accompanied the final number of *Nicholas Nickleby* in October 1839 before it was issued one month later in a volume edition. This frontispiece engraving, which had been promoted in the serial's 'Advertiser' for several months, presented a startling, signed portrait of Dickens. It marked an important stage in the process of separating the characteristics associated with Charles Dickens from those associated with 'Boz'. The iconographic associations of the portrait added Dickens to the pantheon of respected English writers, making use of the established tradition that portrayed 'poetic genius with the light of inspiration striking the eyes'.[67] It was, as Gerard Curtis has noted, a fine-art portrait indicating quite explicitly the *gravitas* of the subject's authorial presence, and implicitly asserting the move from the caricaturist, 'Boz', to the writer of serious literature, Charles Dickens.[68] As Curtis has noted, the 'appeal to the real', which was central in Victorian advertisements for literature and the fine arts, was used in this frontispiece portrait to market the real man, Dickens, instead of the pseudonymous caricature, 'Boz'.[69] Dickens also added his signature, giving a final seal of authenticity to both the product presented to the public and the originating, authorial presence behind it. Curtis points out that 'the signature and the portrait were coming to be a trademark feature for certain products

---

[65] Cited in Patten, *Dickens and his Publishers*, p. 88.

[66] Ibid.

[67] Gerard Curtis, 'Dickens in the Visual Market', in *Literature in the Marketplace: Nineteenth-Century British Publishing and Reading Practices*, ed. by John O. Jordan and Robert L. Patten (Cambridge, 1995), pp. 213–49 (p. 238).

[68] Gerard Curtis, *Visual Words: Art and the Material Book in Victorian England* (Aldershot, 2003), p. 131.

[69] Curtis, *Visual Words*, p. 130.

in the period, acting as stamps or seals in order to protect against fraudulent imitators'.[70]

Chapman and Hall commissioned Daniel Maclise to paint the *Nickleby* portrait of Dickens at a crucial time in their relationship with the author. *Nicholas Nickleby* had outstripped the success of *The Pickwick Papers* making 'Boz' their prize asset. Yet in the summer of 1839, with the serial's conclusion looming, they still had to establish an agreement with Dickens for subsequent work. Moreover, at this point in his career, Dickens had worked with three publishers in as many years.[71] He had broken irreparably with both Macrone and Bentley over disagreements that focused on a three-volume novel he had promised but not produced because of the incessant demand for his serial fiction. Commissioning this portrait and using it as an engraved frontispiece to *Nicholas Nicekleby* both staged the emergence of Charles Dickens before a reading public who were more familiar with the pseudonym, 'Boz', and was part of Chapman and Hall's strategy to deal with an author who seemed only too happy to switch publishers and who still had not written the great, three-volume novel that the visual language of Maclise's portrait suggested he was fully capable of producing. In other words, the portrait functioned as a marketing strategy aimed not only at the public but also at Dickens himself.

Once the portrait had been finished, some time in June 1839, Dickens demonstrated an eagerness to prolong his relationship with his publishers. In a letter to Forster dated 14 July 1839, he told his confidante that he was 'well disposed towards' Chapman and Hall and that if they were willing to make him a 'handsome' offer they might find him 'tractable'.[72] As Patten points out, the offer Dickens had in mind involved a percentage share in the profits for his current work, which would ensure his publishers access to future work.[73] The latter was outlined in a proposal for what would become *Master Humphrey's Clock*, a miscellany which Chapman and Hall advertised in the August

---

[70] Curtis, 'Dickens in the Visual Market', in *Literature in the Marketplace*, ed. by Jordan and Patten, p. 241.
[71] Macrone had published *Sketches by Boz* (1836); Chapman and Hall had published *The Pickwick Papers* (1836-37); and Bentley had published *Oliver Twist* (1837-39).
[72] *Letters*, I, 562.
[73] Patten, *Dickens and his Publishers*, p. 99.

1839 instalment of *Nicholas Nickleby* as a 'New Work on an entirely new plan' from 'Boz' arranged with 'Mr. Charles Dickens'.[74]

An awareness of the different associations that developed alongside these names is evident in a *Parker's London Magazine* article published in 1845 in which the reviewer pointed out his preference for the work of 'Boz' over what the reviewer judged as the inferior work associated with Charles Dickens since 1839.[75] The article suggested that Dickens was inauthentic, a fraud, while 'Boz', the pseudonym, was the true original genius: 'The style of Dickens—that which distinguishes him from 'BOZ'—is laboured and artificial, as unlike the easy natural style of the latter as a statue is unlike a living, moving man.'[76] This unusual inversion, in which the pseudonym is given primacy over the bio-graphical figure of the author, means that the *'style'* of the former is judged as more 'original' than the latter.[77] The reviewer noted how Dickens borrowed from his 'predecessor's sketches' and described this act of borrowing as 'plagiarism'.[78] According to this logic, the charac-ters found in the 'works' of Dickens are usually just 'a meagre outline' compared to the pictures drawn by 'Boz', the 'originals' upon which the plagiarised characters of Dickens were based.[79]

In a similar way, William Thackeray, using his own pseudonym, 'Titmarsh', when discussing Daniel Maclise's 1839 portrait of Dickens, noted how the artist 'must have understood the inward 'Boz' as well as the outward before he made this admiral representation of him'.[80] Thackeray was so amazed by the 'likeness' of the portrait that he compared it to a 'looking-glass' in which viewers could see 'the real identical man Dickens'. [81] Thackeray commented that the 'past and the future' were 'written in every countenance'.[82] This led to a reading of

---

[74] *Letters*, I, 562.
[75] Collins, *Critical Heritage*, pp. 168-71.
[76] Ibid., p. 170.
[77] Ibid., emphasis retained.
[78] Ibid.
[79] Ibid.
[80] *Fraser's Review*, July 1840, p. 113. Thackeray waited more than ten years before emerging from behind his pseudonymous mask of 'Michael Angelo Titmarsh' in his dedication to Charles Lever in the *Irish Sketch Book* first published by Chapman and Hall in 1843. Cited in Henry Sayre Van Duzer, *A Thackeray Library* (New York, 1971), p. 120.
[81] Ibid.
[82] Ibid.

Dickens's face, a focus on the man which, paradoxically, inspired a panegyric on the pseudonym:

> Long mayest thou, O Boz! reign over thy common kingdom; long may we pay tribute, whether of threepence weekly or of a shilling monthly, it matters not. Mighty prince! at thy imperial feet, Titmarsh, humblest of thy servants, offers his vows of loyalty and his humble tribute of praise.[83]

Thus, by 1839 the pseudonymous figure of 'Boz' had acquired a set of values and significations that did not simply disappear when the biographical author became, first identified and, subsequently, celebrated. A close reading of the ways in which the different associations of 'Boz' and Dickens were deployed by the author and his publishers demonstrates what Genette provocatively calls the '*pseudonym-effect*'.[84]

Despite the open secret, by March 1837, that Dickens was responsible for the work of 'Boz', the covers to Dickens's part-issue fiction (*The Pickwick Papers, Nicholas Nickleby, Martin Chuzzlewit*) as well as his magazine serials (*Oliver Twist, The Old Curiosity Shop* and *Barnaby Rudge*) continued to present serialized instalments as 'Edited by Boz' until 1844.[85] Thenceforward, references to 'Boz' diminished in Dickens's correspondence and in the paratext to his work (with the notable exception of the title to the *Sketches by Boz*). By 1847, in the 'Preface' to the cheap edition of *The Pickwick Papers*, Dickens reduced the pseudonym to a mere child's nickname: '[It] was the nickname of a pet child, a younger brother, whom I had dubbed Moses, in honour of the Vicar of Wakefield; which being facetiously pronounced through the nose, became Boses, and being shortened, became "Boz".'[86] Thus, originating in a reference to an eighteenth-century novel, and characterized in terms of a child's facetious mispronunciation, Dickens repositioned 'Boz' as 'a very familiar household word to me, long before I was an author'.[87]

From *The Pickwick Papers* until *Edwin Drood*, Dickens's original part-issue monthly serials were issued between distinctive green covers. These were an eye-catching feature on book-stalls and possessed such commercial value that Chapman and Hall scrambled to acquire the copyrights to *Sketches by Boz* before Macrone published them in the

---

83   Ibid.
84   Genette, *Paratexts*, p. 48, emphasis retained.
85   Eckel, *First Editions*, pp. 17-74.
86   Dickens, *Pickwick Papers*, p. 761.
87   Ibid.

same form.[88] It is clear that Dickens and his publishers were well aware of the market value of the green covers, which had an iconic significance lost in subsequent editions, and were looking to deploy this to their advantage.[89] A review of February 1839 presented Dickens's latest success with *Nicholas Nickleby* in visual terms conjuring an image of a street-scene where every 'passenger' had his copy of the monthly Dickens:

> As we were passing along the Strand on the last day of the month, the two sides of the street looked almost verdant with the numerous green covers of this popular book, which were waving to and fro in the hands of the passengers along that busy thoroughfare. "This", thought we, "is fame!"[90]

This account represents *Nicholas Nickleby* as so successful that, on the first day of a new instalment, a crowd of readers can be seen 'waving' their copies 'to and fro' in a dance of green covers that makes the Strand 'almost verdant'.

Dickens himself played with the pun inherent in the trope of 'green leaves' in the 'Preface' to *David Copperfield* where he turned the regular production of his recently completed serial novel into something more akin to a wonder of nature:

> I cannot close this Volume more agreeably to myself, than with a hopeful glance towards the time when I shall again put forth my two green leaves once a month, and with a faithful remembrance of the genial sun and showers that have fallen on these leaves of David Copperfield, and made me happy.[91]

The covers of Dickens's monthly part-issue instalments, the characteristic 'green leaves', have become the centre of a conceit which transforms a twenty-month serial into a seasonal boon producing, in

---

[88]   Curtis, 'Dickens in the Visual Market', in *Literature in the Marketplace*, ed. by Jordan and Patten, p. 220.

[89]   Dickens's rival in monthly part-issue fiction, William Thackeray, published his serials between distinctive yellow wrappers. Monthly part-issue fiction was only routinely successful for Dickens and Thackeray. Most of the serial novels issued by other authors during Dickens's career came out in weekly or monthly magazines.

[90]   *United Services Gazette* no. 317, 9 February 1839; cited in Chittick, *Dickens and the 1830s*, p. 132.

[91]   Charles Dickens, *David Copperfield*, ed. by J. Tambling (London, 2004), p. 11.

'remembrance of the genial sun and showers', a new set of leaves 'once a month'.

This metaphor, of one serial leading organically to the next, functions in a more poetic way than those used to characterize Boz's authorship in the February and August 1836 editions of *Sketches by Boz*. The difference pinpoints an essential distinction between the pseudonym and the biographical figure. In the earlier work, the metaphor was based directly on the literary marketplace. Success in the periodical press led to success in volumes, which induced more serialized work and so on. The new work, produced as a result of current success, promised connected works of fiction of 'a higher grade'.[92] In *David Copperfield* there is the same emphasis that the success of the current serial will lead to future work. However, the metaphor by which this is expressed is as far away from the commodity culture of the marketplace as could be. Instead, Dickens evokes the characteristic material quality of his serial fiction, its green wrappers, transforming this into a conceit that recasts his books as a benevolent act of natural creation. This play on the materiality of the book is a reminder that in order to understand fully the 'paratextual apparatus' involved with the construction of authorship, our analysis must combine a focus on language with attention to the material level of texts. Cloth, paper, binding, frontispieces, title-pages, illustrations and portraits play an important role in creating the images of authors.[93] In the case of Dickens, the 'physical artefact' of his serial instalments, the thirty-two pages of text, two full-plate engravings, stitched in 'Advertiser' and green covers, had a profound effect on the way his work as an author was represented, received and understood.[94]

Conclusion

As a way of publishing new writing that was subsequently re-issued across a range of formats, serialized fiction opened up paratextual spaces where new models of authorship could be represented, explored and revised. These spaces, inscribed at the material level of the book, enable us to reconstruct the development of new models of authorship

---

[92] *Sketches by Boz*, ed. by Slater, p. xl.
[93] T. Mulcaire, 'Publishing Intimacy in *Leaves of Grass*,' *English Literary History*, 60 (1993), 471-501 (p. 490).
[94] Ibid.

over the course of Victorian literary careers. The transition from 'Boz'
to Charles Dickens demonstrates how paratextual elements could
effect such a transformation as part of the staging of a literary career in
progress. As Dickens's career developed through publication in
different formats and in successive editions, he became increasingly
adroit at using paratextual spaces himself and in dealing with the
impact his publishers had in this regard. His use of the pseudonym,
'Boz', in his early work, and his repeated move between 'Boz' and
'Dickens', provides an interesting case study with which to consider
Genette's theory of pseudonyms as well as his overall approach to
paratextuality.

   With the frequent issue of weekly and monthly instalments,
together with subsequent volume editions made up from remaining
instalments, Victorian serial fiction was predicated on an industrial
mode of production that opened up certain paratextual '*site*[s]' at the
same time as it presented a new form of fiction to readers.[95] That
Dickens could emerge from behind the mask of 'Boz' in the 'Preface'
and 'Dedication' to *The Pickwick Papers* was dependent on Chapman
and Hall's scheme to republish the part-issues as a complete volume.
This was only possible due to a combination of cheap paper and recent
improvements in binding. Thus, if we wish to trace how authors'
names are deployed in discursive 'modes of circulation, valorisation,
attribution, and appropriation' necessary for the construction of
bodies of work, literary genres and national literatures, we must
acknowledge these names are presented to readers through paratextual
elements, the materiality of which are an essential precondition for the
reception and interpretation of texts and authors.[96] Printed texts have a
material form, and this always involves some type of paratextual
apparatus. There is, in other words, no way to ever have a 'transparent' encounter with texts.[97]

   With this material focus, it becomes clear that there are a range of
paratextual elements, such as the wrappers, frontispieces, vignette title-
pages, illustrations, portraits of authors and advertisements that need
to be considered in a wider sense than the '[t]raditional textual criti-

---

[95]   Cited by Richard Macksey in Genette, *Paratexts*, p. xvii, emphasis retained.
[96]   M. Foucault, 'What is an Author?' in *Authorship: From Plato to the Postmodern*, ed.
by S. Burke (Edinburgh, 2003), pp. 233-46 (pp. 244, 234-5).
[97]   Mulcaire, 'Publishing Intimacy in *Leaves of Grass*,' p. 493.

cism' Genette applies in *Paratexts*.[98] If we consider, as Genette pointed out, that features such as titles and dedications were once part of 'the text itself' before becoming paratextual elements, it becomes clear that any theory of paratextuality needs to account for this inherent generic instability.[99] Genette himself suggests a way to do this in an introduction to a special issue of *Poétique* devoted to paratext. First acknowledging the fluid nature of the text/paratext binary, and then focusing on the shifting 'threshold' between 'interior' and 'exterior', Genette comes to define the ideal point of paratextual interest:

> [...] paratext is neither on the interior nor on the exterior: it is both; it is on the threshold; and it is on this very site that we must study it, because essentially, perhaps, *its being depends upon its site*.[100]

Where Genette calls for a study that focuses on the very liminality of the paratextual 'threshold', I would like to suggest that, together with paratextual features like illustrations and serial, cliff-hanger endings, pseudonyms require an approach to paratext which focuses on the materiality of texts. Genette admits that he cannot include illustration or serialization in his survey in *Paratexts*, but these are precisely the 'liminal', paratextual examples he appears to suggest in his introduction to *Poétique*: the 'threshold' elements, like a pseudonym, which are neither 'interior' nor 'exterior' but on the 'contours' of texts.[101] Victorian serial fiction was rich in what we might call 'threshold' experiences: the implacable temporal border between the current instalment and the next; the boundaries between text and illustration, as well as between serial and advertisement; and the transformation of a serial into a volume. This focus on the 'threshold' is related to a central question that emerged from serialization as a mode of production: when did serials become novels and what kind of novels did they become?

As the generic category of the novel changed, so their paratexts provided a way of representing a new kind of fiction and the authors

---

[98]   J. McGann, *The Textual Condition* (New Jersey, 1991), p. 57.

[99]   E. Berlatsky, 'Lost in the Gutter: Within and Between Frames in Narrative and Narrative Theory', *Narrative*, 17:2 (2009), 162-87 (p. 170).

[100]   Cited by Richard Macksey in Genette, *Paratexts*, p. xvii, emphasis retained.

[101]   Genette, *Paratexts*, pp. 405-6. Foucault notes how 'the name of the author remains at the contours of texts' in 'What is an Author?', in *Authorship: From Plato to the Postmodern*, ed. by Burke, p. 235.

responsible for it. If earlier nineteenth-century writers, such as Jane Austen and Walter Scott, had employed anonymity as a device to protect their biographical identity (complicated in the case of Scott by his identity becoming something of an open secret), by the 1830s the production of serial fiction encouraged a representation of pseudony-mous authorship that, in the case of 'Boz', was manifested in prefaces, pictures and reader addresses and which survived the revelation of the real author. The persistent use of his pseudonym showed that Dickens, his publishers and reviewers found it useful to be able to discuss his work with reference to the different genres, nuances and expectations evoked by the pseudonym and the real man. From 1846, with the serialization of *Dombey and Son,* Dickens used his own name on the serial and volume covers of his work. The name was also the one he used as the 'Conductor' of his weekly journals and on the advertise-ments for the famous reading tours he undertook. 'Boz' slipped away, having performed a function that had, by the late 1840s, become incorporated into the figure of Charles Dickens.

In an obituary published a week after Dickens's death, the *Illus-trated London News* noted how readers depended on 'the man Charles Dickens for a continued supply of the entertainment which he alone could furnish'.[102] The emphasis on 'supply' is a testament to the symbolic, cultural and commercial capital represented by the man. This was encapsulated in the title and presentation of the *Charles Dickens Edition* (1867 onwards) which featured Dickens's facsimile signature stamped in gold to show the author's 'present watchfulness over his own edition'.[103] The signature, which Forster noted had become familiar to everyone, came to stand for the fame of the man behind the work. The market value of authorial anonymity, a com-mon practice for novel writers of the early nineteenth century, had been eclipsed by the power of biographical presence. Thus, Dickens's journey from obscurity to pseudonymity and, finally, celebrated onymity, provides a snapshot of the way that serial fiction changed the Victorian literary marketplace. It was a change inscribed at the mate-rial level of instalments and volumes and is a reminder that the repre-

---

[102] Collins, *Critical Heritage,* p. 516.
[103] Taken from an 1867 prospectus in the *Athenaeum* for the Charles Dickens Edition, cited in Patten, *Dickens and his Publishers,* p. 311.

sentation of authorship in serial fiction was dependent not only on text but also on paratexts and the materiality of textual production.

The Operation of Literary Institutions in the Construction of National Literary Aesthetics in Fadia Faqir's My Name is Salma (2007)

RACHEL BOWER

> 'It is not only the symbolic constructs in texts, but also of texts –
> the lives of books – that inform national literary mythologies.'[1]

Andrew van der Vlies incisively captures the importance of looking beyond the disembodied text in examining the construction of national literary aesthetics. This chapter examines how the book trade and literary institutions operate in constructing postcolonial national literary aesthetics, with a particular focus on Arab anglophone fiction. I ask how material interests shape the form and content of anglophone 'international literature' and look at how such literature is marketed in different national contexts. What is the relationship between national mythologies and the formation of 'transnational' aesthetics? How far does the twenty-first century book trade operate against cross-cultural authorial intentions? How do commercial demands and literary marketing impact upon the formation of narrative, and how are authorial and publishing decisions shaped by particular political and historical agendas?

I approach these questions through a consideration of Fadia Faqir's *My Name is Salma*, published in sixteen countries and translated into thirteen languages.[2] Faqir was born in Jordan, and has lived in Britain for twenty-five years. She writes mainly in English, but all of her novels have been published internationally. She has also edited and translated many works, particularly in her role as senior editor for the Arab Women Writers series. *My Name is Salma* narrates the experiences of a young Bedouin girl who is forced by her family to leave her home in the Levant after she becomes pregnant outside marriage. Salma's first person narrator describes her temporary refuge in prison,

---

[1]   Andrew van der Vlies, 'Introduction: The Institutions of South African Literature', *English Studies in Africa*, 47 (2004), 1–17 (p. 2).
[2]   Fadia Faqir, *My Name is Salma* (London, 2007). Further references to this edition are given after quotations in the text.

and a convent in Lebanon, before she arrives in Exeter to begin a new life, removed from the immediate threat of violence.

The novel was published by the Doubleday imprint of Transworld Publishers in the UK in 2007. Doubleday publishes bestselling fiction by authors including Monica Ali, Ian McEwan and Alexander McCall Smith, and also by 'brand-name' authors such as John Grisham and Dan Brown.[3] Doubleday clearly markets itself as 'more' than a book publisher, and utilises popular contemporary marketing methods such as social networking sites to publicise its material, describing itself as, 'book publisher, content provider, entertainment property, gate-keeper, star maker, hit factory, meme machine, icon' on the website Twitter.[4] Technological changes have enormous implications for literary institutions in the twenty-first century, and Doubleday here markets printed materials through digital means. Many small traders now operate 'virtually,' selling through international retailers such as Amazon, rather than through local independent shops. In light of the increased access to printed materials through internet sales, the growth of large, conglomerate publishing corporations such as Transworld, and the rise of online English, one might expect a parallel increase in the commissioning, production and marketing of 'transnational' narratives across national borders.[5] Indeed, the name 'Transworld' captures this aspiration. Faqir hopes to produce transnational writing and she recently described her work as cross-cultural and unclassifiable: 'I cross borders, languages, cultures and literary traditions in a blink. I belong to a rootless multi-cultural community.'[6] There is an obvious

---

[3]   The term 'brand-name author' is borrowed from John B. Thompson's illuminating study of the twenty-first century trade publishing industry: *Merchants of Culture* (Cambridge, 2010), vii.

[4]   < http://twitter.com/doubledaypub > [accessed 21 June 2011]. The rapid develop-ment of electronic literature and digital narratives is a related area, but quite distinct from the digital marketing of printed materials. See the following for some of the central debates relating to digital narratives and hypertexts: N. Katherine Hayles, *Electronic Literature: New Horizons for the Literary* (Notre Dame, Ind., 2008) and *Writing Machines* (Cambridge, Mass., 2002), and George Landow, *Hypertext 3.0* (Baltimore, Md., 2006).

[5]   Thompson's *Merchants of Culture* provides a useful commentary on some of the major changes in trade publishing over the last century, including the recent growth of book sales through retail chains in the US and UK, and the increase in transnational publishing corporations since the 1960s.

[6]   Fadia Faqir, 'Interview with Rachel Bower', *Journal of Postcolonial Writing*, 14 April 2011.

tension here between the romantic ideal of seamlessly representing a plurality of cultures and Faqir's simultaneous desire to act as a representative for Arab women's writing and experience elsewhere in her work. Nevertheless, exploring the differences and commonalities between cultures clearly motivates much of Faqir's writing.

In contrast, I suggest that literary institutions operate against such a cross-cultural intention, which does not straightforwardly produce 'international' literature but paradoxically reinforces reified cultural stereotypes that are situated within national borders. Literary marketing frequently offers a package of stock cultural 'otherness,' solidifying the boundaries that such writing initially set out to challenge. The world market here colludes with pseudo cross-culturalism, whilst utilising and reinforcing populist and nationalist sentiments in order to maximise profit. Translated books continue to be marketed in the language of national settings, and the continued growth of book sales through supermarkets and high-street chains in the UK and US demands nationally-focused marketing. Although the market for e-books is growing, the trend is currently to imitate the printed material as closely as possible. Even when imprints like Doubleday digitally present themselves as 'star makers' rather than book-sellers, online sales of e-books and printed material still rely on facsimiles of book covers, and frequently these are the only visible aspect of the book available. Cover images therefore remain the primary point of contact with a book. The cover of *My Name is Salma* varies considerably between national contexts. Although the novel is predominantly set in England, and straddles three countries, most published editions emphasise the 'otherness' of the narrative. The UK edition features a retreating barefooted and veiled young girl stepping hastily across a detailed mosaic background, above a title printed in mock-Arabic calligraphy. Other European publishers also opt for images of veils and mosaics, whilst in the Indonesian context a European image is chosen. This will become clearer as I examine the publication of the novel in more detail.[7]

The varied marketing of the novel shows how the physical book can be manipulated so that only those transnational aspects that collude with

---

[7] Facsimiles of many of the covers discussed in this chapter are available on Faqir's website. These include the UK, US, French, Indonesian and Spanish editions. < http://www.fadiafaqir.com/Books.html > [accessed 21 June 2011].

constructed national mythologies are mobilised. Sally Howell and Andrew Shryock shrewdly make a similar point in relation to the rapid change in attitudes towards Arab Americans and Islam in Detroit immediately after the attacks on the World Trade Center:

> In the post-9/11 era, transnational ties that connect the US to Arab and Muslim countries will be acceptable only insofar as they strengthen sites of belonging and social reproduction that are located in America (in the form of "ethnic communities").[8]

Similarly, the marketing of Faqir's novel in different linguistic settings constructs boundaries between imagined monolithic cultures, rather than reflecting the reality of the constant dialogue within and between cultures that is reflected by Faqir's narrative.

Faqir's novel is marketed very differently to other 'multicultural' hits such as Monica Ali's *Brick Lane* (2003) also published by Doubleday, and Zadie Smith's *White Teeth* (2000), despite examining similar issues surrounding immigration and racism. Even a cursory glance at the marketing of twenty-first century anglophone Arab literature reveals that images of veils, deserts and forlorn individual females predominate, in contrast to these colourful 'celebrations' of multicultural Britain.[9] These images suggest exotic tales of the oppressed Muslim woman, despite the divergent nature of their narratives. For instance, all of Leila Aboulela's novels are marketed with images of veiled individual women or palm trees and markets, including the 2001 edition of her novel *The Translator* which is primarily set in Aberdeen.[10] This is also largely the case with the work of other contemporary Arab anglophone writers including Ahdaf Soueif, Diana Abu-Jaber, and Rabih Alameddine. There is also a plethora of commercial novels that promise the 'true' story behind Islamic or Arab culture, and although many are not autobiographical, they strongly suggest that they contain authentic accounts of individual suffering, and salacious tales of torture and triumph over oppression.[11] This prolifera-

---

[8]   Sally Howell and Andrew Shryock, 'Cracking Down on Diaspora: Arab Detroit and America's "War on Terror"', *Anthropological Quarterly*, 76 (2003), 443–62 (p. 459).

[9]   This also contrasts with the marketing of much South Asian literature, particularly anglophone Indian fiction, where the magical and mystical are often emphasised.

[10]   Leila Aboulela, *The Translator* (Oxford, 2001).

[11]   Such books (all featuring images of veiled women) include: Qanta Ahmed, *In the Land of Invisible Women*, (Naperville, 2008); Rania Al-Baz, *Disfigured*, trans. by

tion of 'victim' memoirs, either written in English or selected for translation into English, constitutes a sub-genre, which explicitly requires the reader to feel 'sorry' for the oppressed other woman.[12] Lila Abu-Lughod sharply critiques the sense of superiority implicit in this sentiment, arguing that, 'projects of saving other women depend on and reinforce a sense of superiority by Westerners.' Abu-Lughod rightly suggests that this obsession with saving other women tends to 'plaster neat cultural icons like the Muslim woman over messy historical and political dynamics.'[13] This desire for consumable cultural symbols is clear in the publication of *My Name is Salma* in its various national contexts.

In the US the novel was published with the title, *The Cry of the Dove* (New York, 2007); a title that Faqir says she initially resisted.[14] When I pursued the title change with Faqir in a recent interview she fervently told me,

> I had two options: either reject the titles or break my contract with the American publisher. I grudgingly agreed because I wanted to be on Grove's list, a respectable publisher. The decision complicated my life and website. I will never agree to something like this again.[15]

Catherine Spencer (Oxford, 2007); Nujood Ali, *I am Nujood, Age 10 and Divorced* (New York, 2010); Sofia Hayat, *Dishonoured* (London, 2009); Rana Husseini, *Murder in the Name of Honour* (Oxford, 2007); Yasmina Khadra, *Swallows of Kabul*, trans. by John Cullen (London, 2004); Hannah Shah, *The Imam's Daughter* (London, 2009); Siba Shakib, *Samira and Samir* (London, 2004). Many of these are published by Transworld. Several of the books in this 'genre' are published under single name authors, reinforcing the focus on authenticity, including: Latifa, *My Forbidden Face*, trans. by Lisa Appignanesi (London, 2002); Leila, *Married by Force*, trans. by Sue Rose (London, 2006); and Souad, *Burned Alive* trans. by Judith S. Armbruster (London, 2004).

[12] There are, of course, exceptions to this trend, and a handful of independent publishers, including Banipal, translate a range of contemporary literature from all over the Arab world. Nevertheless, the complexity and diversity of modern Arabic literature is completely neglected in the small number of texts translated into English.

[13] Lila Abu-Lughod, 'Do Muslim Women Really Need Saving?', *American Anthropologist*, 104 (2002), 783–90 (pp. 788, 783).

[14] Faqir initially mentioned her unease with the US title in a seminar held in the Faculty of Asian and Middle Eastern Studies, University of Cambridge, 18 February 2009.

[15] Fadia Faqir, 'Interview with Rachel Bower', *Journal of Postcolonial Writing* (forthcoming).

The power of large publishers in the process of 'developing' the final novel as a product is clearly seen here. As John B. Thompson lucidly illustrates, literary agents and publishers actively create the books we receive, and are certainly not passive transmitters between authors and retailers. In terms of the 'book supply chain' the author actually plays a very minor role before their work is 'acquired,' 'developed' and promoted by publishers.[16] Narratives become 'content,' and aesthetic questions are sidelined in negotiations about 'bundles of rights,' as agents and publishers function as gatekeepers of ideas. Publishers often commission writers to carry out pre-conceived projects, or seek particular pieces of writing. The market-driven objective of selling books sidelines creativity, and intellectual independence, and the publisher's title, cover image and blurb in the US are incongruous with Faqir's narrative. The serene blue cover of the US edition features a small, lone figure veiled in black against the elaborate mosaic of a towering blue mosque. The arched, black interior of the mosque mirrors the woman's veiled shape and suggests an immense religion that oppresses the individual, echoed by the blurb, which reads, 'an evocative portrait of forbidden love and violated honor in a culture whose reverberations are felt profoundly in our world today'.

There is little resemblance between the overall effect of this dust-jacket and the sense of narrative place in the novel, which includes Salma's childhood Bedouin village and her later experiences in Exeter. The word 'dove' evokes the woman behind the tale of 'forbidden love' and suggests a cry from a peaceful, innocent creature. In contrast, the narrative focuses on the protagonist's experience of immigration, rather than providing an account of a woman suffering under Islam, or meditating upon theological questions. The rare moments in which the word 'dove' is used in Salma's narrative relate to moments of deep physiological and psychological illness, and emotional fragmentation. The word first appears half-way through the novel, in a flashback to Salma's arrival in the UK:

> Weakened by the nausea and vomiting I saw tiny spots of lights swimming around when I suddenly got out of the ex-army bed [...] I rummaged in Parvin's rucksack looking for her plastic bag full of cassettes. I picked one that had 'When Doves Cry' written on it in purple ink (p. 191).

---

16   Thompson, *Merchants of Culture*, pp. 14-22.

Parvin, who eventually befriends Salma in the hostel when she first arrives in Exeter, walks in to find Salma unsteadily dancing to the replaying song, in an episode which evokes the difficulties that Salma experiences as a result of her displacement, imprisonment and immigration. Salma stops singing and sits next to Parvin: '"I tired. I ill. I look for flowers in bloom." She held both of my hands and said, "If only you weren't losing so much weight." "Conditional sentence. I see. Express wish," I said like a schoolteacher', (pp. 191-2). Salma's fragmented English and self-conscious focus on the form of the words whilst remaining detached from their content reflects the disjointedness of her illness and the difficulties of adjusting to her new alien environment; all of which are absent from the marketing of the novel. The word 'dove' is also mentioned later in a violently fragmented flashback. This time the traumatic shards of Salma's experiences bubble to the surface as she sits on an aeroplane and feels as if she is 'drowning'. Her isolation, drinking and prison force-feeding rear themselves whilst her narrative drifts into a disjointed stream of consciousness:

> A long well, cold water, seeds popping open, a body breaking free, yielding [...] throwing up in the bin, Rock The Casbah, 'too much past', doves crying, sniffing falafel, *'Min il-bab lil shibak'*, right behind you, get married to Sadiq, eating dry bread, Noura's blood and snot running down her chin (pp. 257-8).

This traumatic jumble of English and Arabic is in tension with the US smooth cultural focus and reminds us of Lughod's critique of plastering cultural symbols over complex political situations.

In fact, Faqir suggests that the re-titling of the novel is connected to a reluctance to include an Arab name in the political climate of the US following 9/11;[17] a proposition that makes some sense in light of the media hysteria about Barack Obama having a 'Muslim' middle-name in the US elections of 2008. Arabic and Arab identity have become increasingly politicized in the European and American media, and the obsessive focus on Islam in the press was powerfully criticised by Edward Said in 1996, for its 'highly exaggerated stereotyping and belligerent hostility' and the 'strange revival of canonical, though previously discredited, Orientalist ideas about Muslim, generally non-

---

[17]   Fadia Faqir, 'Seminar,' Faculty of Asian and Middle Eastern Studies, University of Cambridge, 18 February 2009.

white, people'.[18] Such populist stereotyping has increased in recent years and the book industry has taken advantage of this. It is also possible that the US title change reflects the publisher's desire to relocate the focus from Arab to American culture by using the title of the top-selling hit 'When Doves Cry' by American musician Prince, which is presumably the song Salma listened to in the hostel. This makes the title more familiar to an American audience without losing the exotic allure of the cover.

The extent of the differences between the covers of the novel is surprising. The Spanish cover features a naked arm pressed against a window, through which the desert is visible; whilst one of the two Italian editions features an illustration of a girl looking blankly and darkly at a dove.[19] The Romanian edition of the novel continues the earlier focus on veils, featuring a bold, close-up portrait of a young woman in a black niqab veil, which frames her heavily made-up eyes as she looks wistfully skyward.[20] Such images appear to offer a tantalizing insight into the woman 'behind' the veil, rather than acknowledging the fact that the novel creates a literary account of Britain where ketchup, dustbin-lid pizza and Diet Coke are juxtaposed with the 'sizzling sound of frying, the ladle fishing out, falafel being crushed in warm pitta bread and the pungent smell of chickpeas, parsley and coriander' (p. 215, pp. 30-1). Difficult questions about the jolts and realities of immigration are elided in favour of an easy focus on difference. Faqir states that she has no control over the various cover images, and presumably she sold the rights to these in the negotiations between her agent and publisher.[21] Unlike the cover images, Salma's narrative highlights the echoes and similarities between cultures. The novel opens with a juxtaposition of 'the dewy greenness of the hills' of the English countryside and the 'deserted hills' of Hima in Salma's

---

[18] Edward Said, *Covering Islam* (London, 1997), p. xi.

[19] *Mi Nombre es Salma* (Madrid, 2008); and *Un tè alla salvia per Salma*, trans by V. Bastia (Milan, 2007). The Italian title becomes 'a sage tea for Salma.' Other editions include the French, *Mon nom est Salma*, trans. by Michelle Herpe-Voslinsky (Paris, 2007); the Arabic, *Isme Salma*, trans. by Ismail Abed (Beirut, 2009), and the Danish, *Lengslen Efter Layla* where 'Salma' becomes 'Jennifer', trans. by Ole Eistrup (Måløv, 2009). The novel has also been published in Canada, Bulgaria, Czech Republic, Bosnia and Herzegovina, India and Brazil, and a German translation has been agreed.

[20] *Ma numesc Salma*, trans. by Ilinca-Smarandita Schiopu (Bucharest, 2008).

[21] Fadia Faqir, 'Seminar,' Faculty of Asian and Middle Eastern Studies, University of Cambridge, 18 February 2009.

'distant past' (p. 7). This is one of many occasions in which parallels are drawn between the places brought together by Salma's narrative.

The predominance of veils is striking in light of the content of the novel. For the majority of the narrative Salma lives in blue jeans and a t-shirt, or later in the shorter skirts and tight clothes she wears when she sits in bars alone. In relation to the Levant, Salma describes the childhood days 'when I used to chase the hens around in wide pantaloons and loose flowery dresses in the bright colours of my village' (p. 8): a palette of colours that sits uncomfortably with the black hues of Romania's Salma. In Salma's later return to the Levant she is conscious of her 'dyed short hair, straw hat, sunglasses and short sleeves' (p. 275), and although she does arrive in Britain wearing a *white* headscarf (p. 114), she soon removes this, hoping that this will make it easier to get a job: '"We have to look for jobs," said Parvin, "but first I must ask you about this scarf you keep wearing [...] It will be much harder to get a job while you insist on wearing it"' (p. 108). This passage examines the pressures upon immigrants to assimilate and it is removed from the oriental allures of the Romanian cover. There is not a single mention of Salma covering her face in the novel. The nearest the narrative gets to supporting the Romanian image is perhaps Salma's fleeting mention of her 'mother's black shawl,' or her early description: 'My black Bedouin madraqa, embroidered with threads so colourful they would make your eyes water, was tucked away, like my past, in the suitcase on top of the wardrobe' (p. 13). Not only is the madraqa tangential to the narrative, being a once-mentioned part of Salma's 'past,' but the vivid colours of this traditional Jordanian item of clothing again contrast sharply with the Romanian image.

Why is Salma's narrative represented by a woman wearing a piece of clothing that is culturally incongruous with descriptions of her character in the novel? Implicit within this marketing decision is a refusal to engage seriously with the specificity of different cultures, conflating all 'other' cultures into the same. By implication, such an exotic image is used as an attraction which will sell books to the specific national market. Here, the reception of the text is anticipated and manipulated by the book trade, creating a complex set of expectations which coincide with social preconceptions and populist media coverage, shaping hermeneutic possibilities prior to the reading. In turn, such sales generate an increased appetite for these reified tales of suffering, and fuel the commissioning of further work that offers this consumable formula. This leads to a censoring effect as writers increasingly produce narratives they can sell, or alter their texts in light of editorial feedback, as we shall see in Faqir's experience.

The contrast between the Romanian and French editions is particularly striking. The minimalist white French cover juxtaposes the image of a Union Jack mug of milky tea with a picture of a crescent-adorned, delicate glass of sage tea. Initially, this appears to move towards the juxtaposition of cultures that I suggest the narrative explores. It is worth remembering, however, that in marketing the novel as a celebration of the joys of multiculturalism through tea, the French edition continues to side-step difficult issues of racism and immigration. This is particularly pertinent in light of the widespread rioting against racism in France, unrest about poor housing and services in immigrant communities, and the controversy over the 2004 French secularism laws which ban the wearing of conspicuous religious symbols in public.[22] Although there is a sizable market in France for Arab and Islamic victim memoirs (many of those appearing recently in English were originally written in French), perhaps the focus here reflects a willingness to publish a celebratory account of *British* multiculturalism, whilst francophone literature about immigration remains heavily focused on difference.

Such a surface acceptance of multiculturalism through cultural symbols offers a flavour of the 'other' for consumption to a national market without demanding critical reflection. As Charles Taylor suggests, such understandings of multiculturalism can paradoxically be 'homogenizing' as they 'cram the others into our categories' where 'real judgements of worth suppose a fused horizon of standards'.[23] The French marketing romanticises a cultural difference that the narrative actually satirizes. Salma gives a *mug* of sage tea to a man called Jim with whom she has a one-night stand. Even here, neat cultural symbols are refused. Jim comments, 'It has a wild strange aroma' (p. 70), enjoying Salma's exoticism before leaving and ignoring her the next time he encounters her in the street.

---

[22] These laws do not explicitly mention Islam but are frequently referred to in the press as the 'French headscarf ban'. See the French National Assembly for more details about the laws: 'LOI n° 2004-228 du 15 mars 2004', <http://www.assemblee-nationale.fr/12/dossiers/laicite.asp> [accessed 21 June 2011].

[23] *Multiculturalism* (Princeton, 1994), pp.71, 70.

Yet, presumably 'otherness' sells. Significantly, the cover with the most striking use of the Islamic veil is published in Romania where Orthodox Christianity is the dominant religion and only a tiny minority have Islamic heritage.[24] By contrast, the lack of Islamic symbolism on the French cover is published in a country where the Muslim population is the largest in Western Europe, at an estimated 8-10% of the population.[25] These figures tentatively suggest a trend in which publishers select cover images to market that which is 'other' to major cultures within that society. This is particularly interesting in relation to the Indonesian edition, published in a country where Islam is the state religion and the majority of people are Muslim.[26] In sharp contrast with the Romanian edition, the Indonesian cover features a reclining sensual light-skinned model in a crimson dress. This image uses light skin to sell the novel and neglects the anxieties that Salma feels about her skin colour, and the related societal pressures.[27] Parvin instructs

> 'Lighten up! Groom yourself! Sell yourself! [...] You are now in a capitalist society that is not your own.' She was right. Most hair colour was designed for blondes, and a dark woman like me, who had gone prematurely grey, found it hard to match the original colour of her hair (p. 46).

The narrative critiques racial constructions of beauty. In the mirror Salma sees 'a face dripping like honey wax, a face no longer young. My hair was dark, my hands were dark and I was capable of committing dark deeds' (p. 46). Salma's subjective interiorising of her own 'dark-

---

[24]   Less than 0.9% of people in Romania are Muslim. *CIA World Factbook*, < https://www.cia.gov/library/publications/the-world-factbook/geos/ro.html > [accessed 21 June 2011].

[25]   The French Government does not keep statistics on religious adherence but various sources, including the *CIA World Factbook* estimate that the number of Muslims is approximately 5-6 million. In comparison, the UK's Muslim population is approximately 2.8% (UK Census 2001, Office for National Statistics). < http://www.state.gov/g/drl/rls/irf/2005/51552.htm > [accessed 21 June 2011].

[26]   According to the United Nations, Indonesia has 'the largest Muslim population in the world.' The *CIA World Factbook* estimates Indonesia's Muslim population to be 86.1%. < https://www.cia.gov/library/publications/the-world-factbook/geos/id.html > [accessed 21 June 2011].

[27]   There are many products for sale in Indonesia which claim to 'lighten' skin. Globally, the digital lightening of skin of celebrities and models in fashion magazines is also widespread.

ness' in the pressures of the 'light' context surrounding her, is neglected by the Indonesian cover.

The potential for subversion within translation of literature from
one language to another in colonial settings has been much discussed.[28]
Within the Indonesian colonial context, Doris Jedamski suggests that
there has been a scholarly neglect of the 'counter canonical discourse'
generated by 'indigenous translations' of Western novels such as
Robinson Crusoe.[29] The subject of translation and the book trade
demands further investigation, but in the postcolonial context it is also
important to acknowledge the way in which book-trade processes
complicate any analysis of abstracted 'discourse'. The 'indigenous' is
not hermetically sealed from transnational market forces, and in the
postcolonial book trade we must also ask how translated literary
works circulate as commodities. The Indonesian translation of *My
Name is Salma* cannot be situated as a clear point of postcolonial, or
indeed feminist, resistance to the forces of global capitalism, by virtue
of the fact it is translated, without considering the hermeneutics of the
life of the book in which it is bound. Undeniably, the book has
undergone a transformation in its movement from Europe to Indonesia, but one might argue that the Indonesian marketing presents a
European female stereotype in a similarly fetishistic way, in a parallel
desire to sell commodified 'otherness'. This constitutes not only a
problematic marketing of cultural difference, but also a profitable
circulation of books through the stereotyped images of women.

Why *does* a single novel have so many different covers? It would be
wrong to suggest that cover images should somehow transparently
represent narrative content, and an infinite number of images, symbols
or moments could be chosen to represent the text of a novel. However, these editions do not select different objects to represent the text.
Rather, all of the editions, excepting the French cover, attempt to
represent the same thing: namely, the female Muslim Arab body. The
point therefore, is not to demand a uniformity of marketing in which
covers should become more 'accurate,' but to question why, in the
insistence on representing *My Name is Salma* through the body of

---

[28]   Useful studies include Román Álvarez and M. Carmen-África Vidal, *Translation,
Power, Subversion* (Clevedon, 1996) and *Postcolonial Translation: Theory and Practice*,
ed. by Susan Bassnett and Harish Trivedi (London, 1999).
[29]   Doris Jedamski, 'Popular Literature and Postcolonial Subjectivities', in *Clearing a
Space*, ed. by Keith Foulchar and Tony Day, (Leiden, 2002), pp. 19–48 (p. 45).

Salma herself, all of the covers vary so vastly in the representation of this body. We must ask ourselves, what is at stake in the representation of a Bedouin, Muslim woman who spends most of her life in England? The fact that the French publisher chooses not to represent this body is perhaps as telling as the publishers that choose sexualised or religious symbols to represent narrative content.

This raises questions about how far Faqir's narrative is complicit in the production of fantasies of Arab women as helpless victims. Perhaps literary institutions exaggerate a tendency inherent within her writing, rather than inventing stereotypes. The plot of *My Name is Salma* is driven by an initial threat of an honour killing, a subject which frequently holds an exotic place in the 'western' imagination. Although Faqir states that she started the Arab Women Writers series to counter westerners' stereotypes of Arab women's lives, the mistreatment of Arab women is also a prominent feature of much of her fiction.[30] In response to such criticism, Faqir has suggested that the 'honour killing' was primarily a literary plot-device and a feasible way of completely displacing a character:

> I wanted an excuse for an Arab woman to arrive totally unprepared in Britain. Escaping an honour killing was only a justification. It is the second part of the book, dealing with her immigrant experience, which is important.[31]

Even though the honour killing is not the main focus of the narrative, perhaps it is naïve of Faqir to utilise this controversial subject as a literary trope without anticipating criticism, or expecting literary institutions to focus exclusively on this aspect or use it as a sales 'hook.' Although the novel was not widely reviewed by the British press, most reviews, including a sensational one in *The Telegraph*, focused squarely on Salma's 'passionate affair' and 'death sentence'.[32] This approach offers a deep insight into the expectations surrounding those authors who are positioned as 'different'. Assessing Faqir's narrative in relation to her cultural heritage confuses her sharp critique of a specific domestic situation in which a woman is subjugated, with the facile condemnation of an entire culture, and situates Faqir's work

---

[30] Fadia Faqir, 'Interview with Rachel Bower,' *Journal of Postcolonial Writing*, 14 April 2011.
[31] Fadia Faqir, 'Interview with Sally Bland,' *Jordan Times*, 16 October 2007.
[32] Sophie Ratcliffe, 'A Fading Map of Africa,' *The Telegraph*, 24 May 2007.

as representative of all Arab writing. Such a burden of representation is frequently projected onto postcolonial authors who are perceived as representing their entire cultures, in the same way that racism makes individuals responsible for 'their' race, as Frantz Fanon so powerfully articulated: 'it is not I who make a meaning for myself, but it is the meaning that was already there.'[33] Faqir's narrative complicates the blanket use of culture, particularly in its sustained critique of Salma's repugnant boss who condemns 'them Arabs' before expressing his surprise when she responds: '"I don't know any Arabs here," I said and sat down. "That's strange. Why not?"' (p. 152).

Faqir's negotiations with her UK and US publishers about the inclusion of the word 'novel' on the cover, relates directly to this burden of representation.[34] Faqir suggests that, in her experience, publishers often demand a particular type of literary aesthetic from Arab writers; which translates into a demand for 'autobiographical' and 'realist' texts that portray women as victims, and can be marketed in the vein of Nawal El Saadawi's *Woman at Point Zero*, recently re-published with a cover similar to the victim memoirs above, and with an almost identical cover to the Romanian edition of *My Name is Salma*.[35]

The word 'novel' was eventually included in small letters under the title in the US edition, and embedded within the cover type of the blurb of the UK edition. The title does not reflect a confessional narrative, but indicates Salma's defiant declaration of her name and repeated refusal of the names 'Sally' and 'Sal' in the UK: '"Name? Sally Asher." "No. Salma Ibrahim El-Musa"' (p. 161). Close attention to the text shows how the 'Salma' of the title is not a thinly veiled reference to the author's own authentic experience, but a refusal to assimilate. However, the institution of literary reviews often extends the demand for authenticity from authors like Faqir, assessing their work by how accurately it is deemed to tell the 'true' story, or 'speak for' a cultural

---

[33] Frantz Fanon, *Black Skin, White Masks*, trans. by Charles Lam Markmann (London, 2008), p. 102. Also see Etienne Balibar's account of the development of a 'neo-racism' where 'culture' begins to substitute 'race'. Etienne Balibar, 'Is There a "Neo-Racism?"', in *Race, Nation, Class: Ambiguous Identities*, ed. by Etienne Balibar and Emmanuel Wallerstein, trans. by Chris Turner (London, 1991), pp. 17–28.

[34] Fadia Faqir, 'Seminar,' Faculty of Asian and Middle Eastern Studies, University of Cambridge, 18 February 2009.

[35] Nawal El Saadawi, *Woman at Point Zero*, trans. by Sherif Hetata (London, 1983).

collectivity, rather than by aesthetic merit. This was particularly the case with Ali's high-profile *Brick Lane* which was heavily censured for 'misrepresenting' the Bangladeshi community in Tower Hamlets.[36]

Understanding *My Name is Salma* as a *literary* text as Derek Attridge so often urges us to do, shifts the focus from whether Faqir accurately represents Arab culture, towards an examination of the honour-killing as a 'literary device' within the context of the entire novel.[37] Salma is not a passive victim, and emerges as a complex character as the narrative progresses. Although many of the characters remain one-dimensional, Layla Al Maleh rightly argues that the novel 'manages to avoid the stock sensationalism' that often accompanies the 'now exhausted stereotypical story of honour crime' because it broadens the protagonist's experience to 'encompass the harsher realities of immigration and the arduous quest for a foothold on foreign soil'.[38] Challenging the primacy of expectations that Arab women's writing will be transparent and authentic widens the scope for examining the historical and political aspects of such texts.

However, whilst urging more serious consideration of the discrepancies between the narrative and the hermeneutics of marketing, we must also be suspicious of the narrative itself. Publishing and marketing constraints by literary institutions cannot be separated from theoretical considerations of the actual language we receive. Faqir has described how the original manuscript of *My Name is Salma*, which had two endings, was rejected by the publisher, because it was considered 'too experimental' and 'not realist enough' for Arab literature.[39] Although Faqir's ending remains ambiguous and impossible, we should be aware that this is not the ending that she insists originally belonged to the novel. This renders an abstracted consideration of the narrative ludicrous without an accompanying consideration of the impact of the commissioning and editing processes.

---

[36]   For example, see Sukhdev Sandhu, 'Come hungry, leave edgy,' *London Review of Books*, 9 October 2003.

[37]   In particular, see Attridge's oft-cited *The Singularity of Literature* (London, 2004).

[38]   Layla Al Maleh, 'Anglophone Arab Literature: An Overview', in *Arab Voices in Diaspora: Critical Perspectives on Anglophone Arab Literature*, ed. by Layla Al Maleh (Amsterdam, 2009), pp. 1–65 (p. 15).

[39]   Fadia Faqir, 'Seminar,' Faculty of Asian and Middle Eastern Studies, University of Cambridge, 18 February 2009.

The financial imperative is clear: like other authors, Faqir needs to sell her books. The importance of archival work on authors' drafts and manuscripts prior to publication remains valuable here and reveals much about the impact of publishers. The interpretation of received texts, and analysis of the intricate web of institutional processes in which they are embedded, complement and enhance textual analysis. However, we must also be aware of the impossibility of extracting a 'pure' text prior to the interventions of the book trade as these increasingly permeate the writing process. The operation of literary institutions affects the narratives, language and aesthetics we receive, as well as the way in which we receive them. The consideration of a single novel reveals how the processes of commissioning, editing and marketing are crucial factors in exploring hermeneutic questions about a text. Narrative content and material appearance are inextricably linked in our interpretations of postcolonial aesthetics, and the marketing of books is influenced by national and international commercial and political agendas. In particular, the marketing of novels often presents seemingly transnational narratives that actually reinforce popular national stereotypes or ideas about particular cultural groups, masking complex political and historical questions beneath stock cultural symbolism. Ultimately, understanding the impact of literary institutions is essential in moving towards a fuller appreciation of postcolonial literary aesthetics.

PART 2
To Collectors

'La conquest du sang real': Edward, Second Viscount Conway's Quest for Books

Daniel Starza Smith

As Sears Jayne and Francis R. Johnson have observed, 'A large and careful English library catalogue is [...] the shortest and most accurate route to a knowledge of what was known in Renaissance England about any subject.'[1] A private library catalogue indicates the books that were available to an autodidact, and suggests which were considered valuable purchases worthy of storage and maintenance. Furthermore, a 'careful' library catalogue can provide crucial evidence about the manner in which early modern collectors arranged their libraries, both physically and mentally. A catalogue embodies an ordering system, and reveals the book-owner's conceptual methodology. The collection catalogued must also be 'large' in order to present a useful sample of the material in circulation. However, this conclusion immediately invites an important question: what, in fact, constituted a large library in the early modern period?

In their examination of private libraries owned by the gentry and nobility between 1560 and c. 1640, Pamela and David Selwyn ask precisely this question. They argue that an impressive pre-1600 collection contained around 400-600 books, specifying the libraries of Sir Thomas Smith (1566), Francis Russell, second Earl of Bedford (1584), Richard Stonley (1597) and William Gent (1600). Just two English noblemen before the seventeenth century, Henry Fitzalan, twelfth Earl of Arundel (d. 1580), and William Cecil, first Baron Burghley (d. 1598), are known to have owned over 1000 books. Between 1600 and 1640, predictably, libraries increased in size:

My work on the libraries of Edward, second Viscount Conway, has been assisted by grants from the Bibliographical Society, the Malone Society and the Central Research Fund of the University of London, to whom I wish to express my gratitude. Thanks are also due to Carol Conlin and the Governors and Guardians of the Armagh Public Library, who have generously helped facilitate my research, and to Henry Woudhuysen for comments on earlier drafts of this chapter.

[1] *The Lumley Library: The Catalogue of 1609*, ed. by Sears Jayne and Francis R. Johnson (London, 1956), pp. 28-9.

The largest for which evidence exists is that of the [14th] earl of Arundel, Thomas Howard (1646), at some 4,500 books, and that of the Sidney family at Penshurst may have been of a similar size. Earlier, [John, first Baron] Lumley's library at Nonsuch had consisted of about 3,000 items in 1609 (excluding earlier donations and disposals), and Sir Thomas Tresham's (*c.* 1605), [...] has been estimated by Sears Jayne as about 2,600.[2]

As Jayne and Johnson predict, the library catalogues of these collections offer a wealth of information both about individual habits of acquisition and systematization, and about the contemporary availability of 'knowledge'. Germaine Warkentin, for example, has written persuasively about the interplay between 'the world and the book' at the Penshurst library of Robert Sidney, second Earl of Leicester.[3] The other outstanding collection mentioned by Selwyn and Selwyn is that of Arundel, a library that in both size and content reflected the Earl's pioneering and hugely successful acquisition of art.

However, two names are notable by their absence: Henry Percy, ninth Earl of Northumberland, and Edward, second Viscount Conway.[4] No contemporary catalogue of Northumberland's library survives before the 1690s, but G. R. Batho estimates that it comprised between 1500 and 2000 volumes.[5] Given the lack of definitive evidence about Northumberland's stock, his omission is perhaps understandable. In contrast, the libraries of Edward Conway represent some of the best-documented bibliographical collections of the age, and together they number almost three times Arundel's 1646 collection. Conway's 1636 and 1641 library catalogues together record around 13,000 volumes, with upwards of 8000 books held at his estate in Lisnagarvey (now Lisburn, co. Antrim, Northern Ireland), and a further 4700 items in London. Numerous letters survive in which Conway ordered or mentioned specific volumes, identifying the agents and booksellers he bought from, and commenting on the conditions in which his acquisitions were made.

---

[2]   Pamela Selwyn and David Selwyn, '"The Profession of a Gentleman": Books for the Gentry and the Nobility (*c.* 1560 to 1640)', in *The Cambridge History of Libraries in Britain and Ireland*, ed. by Peter Hoare, 3 vols (Cambridge, 2006), I, 489-519 (p. 502).
[3]   Germaine Warkentin, 'The World and the Book at Penshurst: The Second Earl of Leicester (1595-1677) and his Library', *The Library*, 6th ser., 20 (1998), 325-46.
[4]   After 1609, Lumley's books were incorporated into the existing collection of Henry, Prince of Wales, establishing him as an important collector, too.
[5]   G. R. Batho, 'The Library of the "Wizard" Earl: Henry Percy Ninth Earl of Northumberland (1564-1632)', *The Library*, 5th ser., 15 (1960), 246-61 (p. 251).

H. R. Plomer published some of these documents in 1904, and Conway's collections have since been examined by Ian Roy, T. A. Birrell, Arthur Freeman and Paul Grinke, and Barra Boydell and Máire Egan-Buffet.[6] This paper re-evaluates Conway's collecting methodology; it also presents new information about his relations with the book trade, and the place of book buying within the wider pattern of his purchases.

'Well versed in all parts of learning': the second Viscount Conway

Edward Conway was born in 1594 in Arrow, Warwickshire, and educated at The Queen's College, Oxford, matriculating in May 1611. He served as General of the Horse in Scotland in the 1640s, and published a short report on the rebellions in Ireland in 1642. Knighted at Whitehall in 1618, he was raised to the peerage after his father's death in 1631.[7] Clarendon accurately summarized contemporary opinion of the second Viscount:

> there was no action of the English either at sea or land in which he had not a considerable command; and always preserved a more than ordinary reputation, in spite of some great infirmities [...] for he was a voluptuous man in eating and drinking, and of great license in all other excesses, and yet was very acceptable to the strictest and the gravest men of all conditions. And, which was stranger than all this, he had always from his pleasure, to which his nature excessively inclined him, and from his profession, in which he was diligent enough, reserved so much time for his books and study that he was well versed in all parts of learning, at least appeared like such a one in all occasions and in the best companies.[8]

---

[6]   H. R. Plomer, 'A Cavalier's Library', *The Library*, new ser., 5 (1904), 158-72; Ian Roy, 'The Libraries of Edward, 2nd Viscount Conway, and Others: An Inventory and Valuation of 1643', *Bulletin of the Institute of Historical Research*, 41 (1968), 35-46; T. A. Birrell, 'Reading as Pastime: The Place of Light Literature in Some Gentlemen's Libraries of the Seventeenth Century', in *Property of a Gentleman*, ed. by Robin Myers and Michael Harris (Winchester, 1991), pp. 113-31; Arthur Freeman and Paul Grinke, 'Four New Shakespeare Quartos?', *TLS*, 5 April 2002, p. 17; Barra Boydell and Máire Egan-Buffet, 'An Early Seventeenth-Century Library from Ulster: Books on Music in the Collection of Lord Edward Conway (1602-1655)', in *Music, Ireland and the Seventeenth Century*, ed. by Barra Boydell and Kerry Houston (Dublin, 2009), pp. 95-108.

[7]   James Knowles, 'Edward Conway, 2nd Viscount Conway', *ODNB*, < http://www.oxforddnb.com > [accessed 21 June 2011].

[8]   Edward Hyde, *The History of the Rebellion and Civil Wars in England Begun in the Year 1641*, ed. by W. Dunn Macray, 6 vols (Oxford, 1888), II, 82.

Conway stayed loyal to the monarchy during the Civil War and in 1643 was implicated in the Waller Plot to restore it. He died in France in 1655 after spending several years in retirement at Petworth, the seat of his closest friend Algernon Percy, tenth Earl of Northumberland, the brother-in-law and sometime book-buying agent of the second Earl of Leicester.[9]

Conway's father, Edward, first Viscount Conway, was an important soldier and statesman, a secretary of state to both James I and Charles I. The elder Edward Conway owned a significant library at his Low Countries military garrison at the Brill, some or all of which was sent back to the family's Warwickshire seat, Ragley Hall, and catalogued in 1610 as part of a wider inventory of his property.[10] He owned books in four languages other than English, had extensive connections with the Low Countries, and translated Spanish poetry into English. Secretary Conway was for a time in charge of licensing English books and owned a significant collection of literary manuscripts, including poetry by Donne and Jonson. The younger Edward Conway was thus born into an atmosphere particularly congenial to literature, to a family conversant with a variety of European languages and which owned a considerable number of books. He inherited his father's collection of literary and non-literary manuscripts, adding to it many verse libels, political squibs and ballads; over the years, the two men's documents have become mixed together, and have suffered significant physical deterioration.[11] Similarly, books owned by both men can be identified, but are now widely dispersed.[12] The evidence suggests, however, that in his own time

---

[9]   On this latter point, see Warkentin, 'World and the Book', p. 325.

[10] London, National Archives, SP 14/57/114B, 'A cathalogue of such bookes / as were brought from Briell / And left at Raggely the / [   ] of [   ] 1610'; the square parentheses indicate blanks in the MS. There are 213 entries in the inventory, neither grouped by subject matter or language, nor arranged alphabetically. Cf. James Knowles, 'Jonson's Entertainment at Britain's Burse', in *Re-Presenting Ben Jonson*, ed. by Martin Butler (Basingstoke, 1999), pp. 114-51 (p. 124).

[11] For accounts of the Conway Papers and their inherent technical difficulties, see Peter Beal, *Index of English Literary Manuscripts*, 4 vols (London, 1980), I:I 247-48; Daniel Starza Smith, 'How Do You Know if John Donne has Been in Your Archive?', *Lives and Letters*, 3 (2011), < http://journal.xmera.org/volume-3-no-1-spring-2011 > [accessed 21 June 2011]; Daniel Starza Smith, '"...another part rotten, another gnawed by rats...": Tidying up the Conway Papers', *Moveable Type*, 5 (2009), < http://www.ucl.ac.uk/english/graduate > [accessed 21 June 2011].

[12] The second Viscount bequeathed some of his books to George Rawdon (see below), whence they derived to the estate of the Marquis of Hastings at Donington

Edward, second Viscount Conway, took great care over the purchase, storage and classification of his extensive library collections.

'How hard a task you lay vpon mee': The Lisnagarvey Catalogue, 1636-40

The Conway family's Irish estate had been established in the province of Ulster by Sir Fulke Conway. He died in 1624 and the property passed to his brother Edward, later the first Viscount. The second Viscount inherited the estate in Lisnagarvey in 1631 along with its manager, George Rawdon (later created baronet in 1665), who married Conway's eldest daughter in 1654. Conway and Rawdon's colonial ambitions in Ireland were challenged after a decade of their steward-ship. On 23 October 1641, Sir Phelemy O'Neil, Sir Connor Maginnis and Major-General Plunkett led a force of almost 9000 men in rebel-lion, targeting Conway's estate *en route* to Carrickfergus. Conway repulsed the attack, virtually annihilating the enemy forces but, as W. P. Carmody notes, the retreating rebels 'fired Brookhill house, and the Lord Conway's library in it, and other goods, to the value of five or six thousand pounds, their fear and haste not at all allowing them to carry any thing away'.[13] Conway and most of his men survived, but the library, kept at Rawdon's Brookhill House, was severely damaged. Fortunately, Conway had arranged for his collection to be catalogued five years earlier, and the large manuscript inventory, a folio volume, has survived in perfect condition at Armagh Public Library.[14]

In the early spring of 1636, Conway engaged two local men in a large-scale, four-year cataloguing project. Philip Tandy was a schoolmaster in the village; his co-worker was William Chambers, Conway's chaplain, also vicar of Magherall in 1635 and curate of Lisnagarvey church between

---

Park, and were sold at auction in Nottingham in 1868. However, the second Viscount probably left the majority of his collection to his son, Edward, later first Earl of Conway, as part repayment for debts. I have not yet traced this collection. Several of Conway's books can be traced to other collections: one (now St. John's College, Oxford, shelfmark P. scam.2.B7) was owned by Philip Ayres (1638-1712), another (St. John's College, shelfmark K.4.2), by Nathaniel Crynes (1685/6-1745), and a third (Worcester College, Oxford, shelfmark HH.7.18), by George Clarke (1661-1736).

[13] W. P. Carmody, *Lisburn Cathedral & its Past Rectors* (Belfast, 1926), p. 109.

[14] Armagh, Armagh Public Library, MS KH II 39: *Tituli catalogi sequentis in theologia; Library Catalogue of Edward, 2nd Viscount Conway*. Several of Conway's books, bearing his stamp of a Moor's head in profile, also survive at the library.

1633 and 1636. It was a daunting undertaking, as Chambers revealed on 14 March 1636:

> How hard a task you lay vpon mee my Lord indeed you doe not knowe. I wil heartily & in y^e feare of God set my self to doe my duty in it. seeing if you wil have it \so/ And fro*m* y^e promise wch you are pleasd to make mee of remembring mee if a better occasion offer it self [...][15]

While the concept of professional librarianship was not yet fully formed in the early seventeenth century, a job like this required education and a degree of sophistication. Gilbert Spencer, who catalogued Leicester's Penshurst library (*c.* 1653-55), was a gentleman and the family's secretary, while Alethia Talbot, Arundel's wife, commissioned no less a scholar than William Dugdale to 'sett her librarie in some order, and to make a catalogue of all the books that were in it'.[16] Tandy may initially have been unequal to the task: Chambers revealed that Conway's 'chiding of him hath wrought much wth him hee seems to mee to bee more careful of yor bookes then before'.[17] Nevertheless, by December at the latest work was underway, and a letter from Tandy to Rawdon on 26 December indicates the methodology employed:

> His Lord*shi*ps bookes are better now then when hee left them. I am set-tinge them as speedily as that little time I have fro*m* my schoole will give mee leave in an Alphabeticall ordere distinguished notwithstandinge both by volumes and sciences.[18]

Tandy's claim that he was 'setting' the books, and the exhortation for him to be more delicate with them, imply that the volumes were physically put 'in a place allotted or adapted to receive [them]'.[19] The natural assumption is that they were shelved but, then as now, shelves were just one storage option among many; Thomas Tresham is known to have specified books 'For my closett drawer' in 1582, noting others

---

[15]   London, National Archives, SP 16/316/37.

[16]   Linda Levy Peck, 'Uncovering the Arundel library at the Royal Society: Changing Meanings of Science and the Fate of the Norfolk Donation', *Notes and Records of the Royal Society of London*, 52 (1998), 3-24 (p. 7).

[17]   London, National Archives, SP 16/316/37.

[18]   London, National Archives, SP 63/255/79.

[19]   'Set', v., 15. a. *OED Online* available at < http://www.dictionary.oed.com > [accessed 21 June 2011].

as 'left on the shelfe' or on the 'table in yo[r] closett'.[20]

Although little evidence survives about the physical appearance of Conway's library, a few inferences can be made. As Elisabeth Leedham-Green and David McKitterick note,

> For much of the seventeenth century it was still quite usual, even in great houses, for books as items of relative rarity to be kept in closets and indeed in chests, and some of the earliest seventeenth-century bookcases are in the form of shelved cupboards.[21]

We do not know whether Chambers and Tandy worked directly from a shelving system, but Tandy's letter does reveal that some of Conway's books were kept out of view: 'the chested bookes I have in this Christmas vacation unchested againe, and put into the dininge roome, where they are as oft as they need aired by good fires/'.[22] The term 'chested' may imply that the books were usually kept in closed trunks and occasionally brought out for airing, or that they had been transported to Ireland in trunks or boxes and were only just being unpacked. In March 1636, Conway's sister Brilliana, Lady Harley, wrote to ask:

> have I mistoake in rwiteing [*sic*] or you in readeing for I sent a Box of Pyes and not Papers, but I thinke if I Could a found out a Box of Boockes that has not yet bine seene my Lord would have bine as well pleased with them as with any other Present.[23]

Most likely, Tandy's specification of 'the chested books' defines them as a separate group from those kept on shelves *and* in cupboards: given the size of his collection, Conway probably used all available storage space at Brookhill.[24]

However, we can surmise that the books were physically arranged by subject matter. In March 1636, Chambers explained that Tandy

---

[20]   Nicholas Barker and David Quentin, *The Library of Thomas Tresham & Thomas Brudenell* (London, 2006), p. 66.

[21]   Elisabeth Leedham-Green and David McKitterick, 'Ownership: Private and Public Libraries', in *The Cambridge History of the Book in Britain*, ed. by John Barnard, D. F. McKenzie, with the assistance of Maureen Bell, 6 vols (Cambridge, 2002), IV, 323-38 (p. 325).

[22]   London, National Archives, SP 63/255/79.

[23]   London, National Archives, SP 16/316/87.

[24]   An inventory of Henry VIII's books records 'I[te]m. undre the table cvij bookes'; this suggests books were often kept wherever they would fit. Sears Jayne, *Library Catalogues of the English Renaissance* (Goldaming, 1983), p. 6.

placed the books 'in their several faculties alphabetically because yor Lord^p. was bringing yor catalogues to y^t method when I came from England'.[25] The Lisnagarvey catalogue is not ordered alphabetically (unlike Leicester's 1646 catalogue), so Chambers and Tandy must have been referring to the placement of books within Brookhill House: they were actually re-ordering the library as well as creating the catalogue. Furthermore, it would appear that Conway had been compiling his own catalogues before employing Chambers, indicating Conway's personal familiarity with library or bookshop catalogues. Chambers referred to a two-tier organizational principle: first 'faculties' ('volumes' and 'sciences') and then alphabetical order within each faculty. Unlike Leicester's Penshurst catalogue, which mingles quartos and folios, and is not ordered by subject class, Conway's Lisnagarvey catalogue was not simply a list of his property – it was a finding aid and an attempt at classification. The catalogue itself, which records no books published after 1640, notes various bibliographical identifiers: title, date, size and place of printing. It begins with a contents list written in Latin, noting sixty class subdivisions. Each of these is further ordered by size of volume, which confirms Sears Jayne's claim that 'books were shelved in the most attractive and economical way possible, that is, by size'.[26] Volumes recorded at the end of each subject section tend to be dated 1639 or 1640, suggesting that the catalogue was mostly complete by 1638, and had new acquisitions added subsequently at the end of the document.[27]

The sixty subdivisions are ordered thematically. The first eleven sections deal with religion and are followed by books on magic and demonology (12) and philosophy (13). The catalogue progresses to include science (subdivisions 14-20), including natural history (14), medicine and horse medicine (17, 15), and mathematics (19, 20). It continues from science to music (21), architecture (22) and military and naval arts (23 and 24). There follows a loosely connected group, 'Libri critici' (25), hieroglyphics and mythology (26) and 'De re memnario ponderibus, mensuris, de re vestiavia, etc' (27). A group of early modern social sciences, 'Ethici, Economici, Politici, de nobilitate,

---

[25]   London, National Archives, SP 16/316/37.

[26]   Jayne, *Library Catalogues*, p. 35.

[27]   Leicester's answer to the problem of additions had been to leave blank pages opposite each complete catalogue page (Warkentin, 'World and the Book', p. 330).

Legato' (28) forms the bridge to a group of rhetoric and language books (29-33). A long run of literature sub-divisions (34-43) begins with satirical writings (34), then continues quite deliberately as follows:

35	Poetae Graeci et Latini
36	Poetae Anglici
37	Poetae Gallici
38	Poetae Italici
39	Poetae Hispanici
40	English Plaies
41	Commedie Italiane
42	Comedios Espagnolas
43	Commedies Françoises[28]

It is interesting to note the difference between the poetry, all entered in Latin, and the drama, where the language of composition is used for the catalogue entry. Both poetry and plays were divided by language; within each language they were grouped by size – quartos and octavos each given separate headings, and duodecimos and sextodecimos listed together. The remaining section headings (44-60), with two exceptions,[29] treat history, mostly divided by geographical area. In fact, the catalogue contained a further twenty-one sections not listed in the contents, another thirteen history subdivisions, two on biography, a section each on 'Libri Viatory' and 'Libri Genealogici', one on 'Raræ et incertæ materiæ scriptores', a section on romances, another on famous libels – and one on 'Bibliotecæ', suggestive evidence about Conway's interest in other libraries.

Conway's library was informed by and reflected contemporary theories of knowledge, which underpinned the structure of other major libraries, as Leedham-Green and McKitterick note:

> The organization of the Bodleian was simple: theology, jurisprudence, medicine and arts, the books in each to be shelved according to size and then in alphabetical order of author.[30]

Similar systems of classification had been around for many years, even in private collections. Matthew Parker's gift of books to Corpus

---

[28] Armagh, Armagh Public Library, MS KH II 39, fol. 2^v.
[29] Item 44 lists legal books, item 47 geography books.
[30] Leedham-Green and McKitterick, 'Ownership', p. 334.

Christi College, Cambridge, in 1574 was divided as follows: 'Theologica, Historica, Iuridica, Medica, Philosophica, Ethica, Physica, Metaphysica, Mathematica, Poetica'.[31] The fact that a whole section of the Armagh catalogue was given over to other catalogues suggests that Conway refined his methodology by reading about other libraries. George Lord Digby, showing familiarity with his friend's ordering system, sent Conway 'a Catalogue of such Spanish bookes as are thought the best [...] many of them I thinke for my part to be Pamphletts but you may bee pleasd to range them amonge y^r volumes of Balletts' (i.e. ballads).[32] John Lanyon, in March 1639, instructed his patron that there would be a delay in the arrival of printed catalogues from Frankfurt, and Fulke Reed sent a similar, but more detailed, explanation about the delay of another catalogue in August 1637.[33] Conway's agent Miles Woodshaw noted on 5 September 1650 that Conway had asked John Donne junior for a green bird and a 'catalogue of his bookes', presumably an inventory of his library.[34] It seems likely that Conway enjoyed reading about books, and thinking about how to arrange or classify them, as much as he enjoyed owning them.

The Lisnagarvey manuscript has been very carefully prepared, and there are barely any mistakes. Numerous means have been employed to facilitate its readability, such as page numbers, an index, and running titles across the tops of pages, e.g. 'Poetae Anglici, 8°'. The neat, elegantly structured and easily readable Irish catalogue contrasts strikingly with the other principal document listing Conway's books, created against his will in 1643.

'All the Papists and delinquents Bookes seized': the sequestered books of 1643-45

Conway's second major repository was a London-based collection impounded by the Parliamentary Committee for Sequestration.

---

[31] Jayne, *Library Catalogues*, p. 34.

[32] London, National Archives, SP 16/409/55.

[33] London, National Archives, SP 16/415/2; Fulke Reed wrote to Conway, 'I haue spoken wth M<^{r}> Bellers for the catalogue of bookes he promist to send yor. Lo^p., ... but there is none drawne as yett, for that Mr Burges (who oweth them) is litle time where is [*sic*] bookes are; and that M^r. Roberts ... one whose asistance & iudgm^t. in the drawing of a catalogue M^r. Burges doth much relie, is now residing nere Birmingeham' (London, National Archives, SP 16/365/39).

[34] London, National Archives, SP 18/11/8.

Official confiscation occurred twice in 1643, first on 27 March against individuals at war with Parliament or actively contributing to the King's cause, then again on 18 August.[35] Conway had been imprisoned until July 1643 on suspicion of plotting with the poet Edmund Waller, then rode to Oxford to join the King. It was at this point that his goods were taken. The Committee for Sequestration created a list of books confiscated, with contemporary estimates of their worth, a folio manuscript book which survives in its original binding, with 230 pages of writing.[36] It lists approximately 7360 titles across twenty-six sequestered libraries. Conway's accounted for about 65% of these: of more than 4700 volumes, 3010 of his books were specifically named in the inventory.

It is not clear whether these books represent the totality of Conway's London collection, as we might assume he carried some of his imperilled volumes away from the capital. The later date also provokes speculation that there had been cross-pollination in the intervening years since Lisnagarvey had been catalogued; we know, for example, that Conway sent across almost 500 'double and imperfect' books in November 1637.[37] However, numerous eye-catching volumes in this latter list (e.g. *Othello*, *Ignatius his Conclave*) are not found in SP 20/7, and Boydell and Egan-Buffet agree that 'Conway's Ulster (Lisnagarvey) and London libraries appear to have been substantially independent collections'.[38]

The London inventory is written in two or three hands over eighty-nine folios. The writers arranged books broadly according to size; they gave titles and language of composition in the shortest possible form, did not order alphabetically, and only occasionally mentioned dates of publication. The committee's valuer, Robert Bostock, was a London bookseller already overwhelmed by impounded books.[39] Twenty or thirty volumes were frequently lumped together for a couple of shillings and several times vague groupings – '18. bookes scarce worth

[35]   Roy, 'Libraries', p. 36.
[36]   London, National Archives, SP 20/7.
[37]   London, National Archives, SP 18/372/111. For discussion of the elimination of duplicates during the merger of Lumley's collection into Prince Henry's, and thence with the Old Royal collection, see Jayne and Johnson, *Lumley Library*, pp. 17, 19.
[38]   Boydell and Buffet, 'An Early Seventeenth-Century Library', p. 37.
[39]   Roy conjectured that Bostock was the compiler; in fact, Bostock's signature appears on fol. 229[v].

walluing' – are used.[40] As a result, Conway's London library was artificially priced at £200.[41] As an indicator of value, therefore, the document is misleading – or, rather, its evidence is very time- and situation-specific. Conway does not seem to have kept accounts of the prices of his books, as other collectors, like Humphrey Dyson, sometimes did in their catalogues.[42] However, a number of booksellers' accounts survive among the Conway Papers.

'Any bookes yr lo: would have, he will fitt you': Conway and the booksellers

Conway's search for printed matter took him to Westminster, St. Paul's, Temple, Fleet Street, Bedlam, Little Britain and Duck Lane. It also extended well beyond London, to Birmingham, Penshurst and Lyndhurst; Paris, Lyon and Douai; Antwerp, Dublin, Frankfurt and Florence; and even to a ship anchored off the Plymouth coast. T. A. Birrell notes a variety of English booksellers whom Conway patronized:

> Philemon Stephens for religious books; Humphrey Moseley for English literature, especially plays; Robert Martin presumably for foreign books; and James Allestree [...] for foreign as well as English books. When in London, Conway went in person to the Latin warehouse and bought quantities of imported books direct[.][43]

To these we can add 'Mr. Cave' (perhaps John Cave) at the 'Sign of the Mermaid' in the Strand, active in 1642, and the unidentified Parisian 'Cottard'. Sir Kenelm Digby, Conway's friend and sometime agent in Europe, used Cottard's brother to deliver letters to the Viscount in 1637, claiming that the Cottard brother who remained in France was

---

[40]   London, National Archives, SP 20/7/79[v].
[41]   Conway's brother-in-law, Sir Robert Harley, as Master of the Mint safeguarded Conway's library, which Conway repurchased in 1645 for a fine of £20 (Roy, 'Libraries', p. 44). The manuscript's binding features Conway's gilded stamp and Conway possibly acquired the inventory when he recovered his books.
[42]   Oxford, All Souls College, MS. 117. See Francis R. Johnson, 'Notes on English Retail Book-Prices, 1550-1640', *The Library*, 5th ser., 5 (1950), 83-112 (p. 86).
[43]   Birrell, 'Reading as Pastime', p. 124. The 'Latin trade' was the trade in all Continental books, although the *OED* does not record this meaning of 'Latin'. Julian Roberts, 'The Latin Trade', in *Cambridge History of the Book in Britain*, ed. by John Barnard, D. F. McKenzie, with the assistance of Maureen Bell, IV, 141-73.

the chiefe booke seller in Paris for curious bookes; and hath correspondence in Italy, Germany, Spaine, and everywhere; so that any bookes yr lo: would have, he will fitt you withall better then any man I know if you please to employ him.[44]

Another Paris-based seller in 1636 was John Trundle, perhaps the same dealer in 'ballads, news-books, plays and ephemeral literature' who had a shop at the 'Sign of Nobody' in the Barbican in 1613.[45]

One of Conway's regular booksellers is less of a mysterious figure – James Allestree.[46] In July 1653 Allestree forwarded 'Altorfij Harmonia' (12s.), 'Grotius de Imperio' (3s.) and news gazettes from France, at 1s. each.[47] He also let Conway in on a bookseller's secret. His much-valued customer had spent hours copying out a wish-list of books from a catalogue sent to him by Allestree.[48] However, Allestree explained, 'it is a very vsuall thing for the Bookesellers in Germany to send the Titles of Bookes to be put into the Catalogue before they are printed so that they are not there to be had'.[49] Allestree had been able to acquire some of the items, including Johan Jonston's *Historiæ naturalis de insectis et serpentibus* (Frankfurt, 1653). Conway had also requested Zwelfer's *Animadversiones* (Gouda, [1653?]), and Wilhelm Langius's *De annis Christi* (Leiden, 1649), but Allestree realized the former was the same edition the Viscount already owned, and that he had already seen the other.[50] This suggests not only that Conway collected multiple editions of books, but that booksellers remembered his previous purchases. Instead,

---

[44] London, National Archives, SP 16/343/28.

[45] *A Dictionary of Printers and Booksellers in England, Scotland and Ireland, and of Foreign Printers of English Books 1557-1640*, ed. by R. B. McKerrow (London, 1968), p. 269.

[46] H. R. Plomer, *A Dictionary of the Booksellers and Printers Who Were at Work in England, Scotland and Ireland from 1641 to 1667* (London, 1907), pp. 2-3.

[47] The books were Christoph Althofer, *Harmonia Evangelistarum emedullata* (Jenae, 1653) and Hugo Grotius, *De imperio summarum potestatum circa sacra* (Hague, [1652?]).

[48] English translations of the Frankfurt Book Fair catalogues had become available since John Bill's editions, 1617 to 1628. See John L. Flood, '"Omnium totius orbis emporiorum compendium": The Frankfurt Fair in the Early Modern Period', in *Fairs, Markets and the Itinerant Book Trade* ed. by Robin Myers, Michael Harris and Giles Mandelbrote (New Castle, Del., 2007) pp. 1-42 (p. 21).

[49] London, National Archives, SP 18/38/76.

[50] The books were Johan Jonston, *Historiæ naturalis de insectis* (Frankfurt, 1653), probably *Pharmacopœia Augustana reformata, et eius mantissa. Cum animadversionibus Johannes Zwelferi [...] annexa eiusdem autoris Pharmacopœia regia* (Gouda, 1653), and Wilhelm Langius's *De annis Christi* (Leipzig, [1651?]).

Allestree added, 'We haue a Booke intitled Bibliotheca Portabilis, siue totius Theologiæ Nucleus et Systema Integrum qo. 1653 3ᵛᵒˡ. which sells excellently well, & is much esteemed of.'[51] The amount of bibliographical information listed by Allestree is noteworthy, as it indicates that he thought Conway was not only interested in a book's subject matter, but also its size ('qo.', '3 vols'), novelty (a 1653 book would be brand new) and how well it was judged by contemporaries. In other words, Conway was thinking like a bookseller.

There is further fascinating evidence to support this claim. A letter from Allestree in October 1652 strongly suggests that Conway was selling books as well as buying them. Referring to a copy of Bartholomaeus Platina's *Delle vite de' Pontefici*, Allestree advised his customer,

> your Lᵒᵖ knowes very well the old edition can neuer honestly be sold since there are so many additions to this new one, neither is there any thing in it that should prouoke gentlemen to buy it, but the liues of these late Popes, which being not in yours, it will be altogether unfitt for my sale.

Conway's copy was evidently one of those that pre-dated the 1612 edition, which added the lives of Leo XI and Paul V, and was itself made obsolete by the 1622 edition, with a life of Gregory XV. Allestree continued:

> Your Lubini Antiquarius is imperfect, as yoʳ. Loᵖ knowes, and if I knew of whom it was bought I would endeauour to get them make it perfect, or change it for some other Booke but I haue taken notice what leaues it wants, & shall in my next letters to Lyons desire my Corrispondents there to send them amongst the Bookes they are to send to me[.][52]

Not only could a book be resold or given as part exchange, it could also be reconstructed to order, with the insertion of gatherings or specific leaves to make it complete. It is unclear whether Conway's *Antiquarius* was destined for sale, but the fact that someone of his resources would consider having it restored so painstakingly is remarkable.

Conway's book-purchasing habits should not be considered too distinctly from his wider programme of acquisitions. A detailed

[51] Allestree was alluding to Jacobus Rauppius, *Bibliotheca portabilis* (Erfurt, 1653).
[52] London, National Archives, SP 18/25/21. The book referred to was Eilhard Lubin, *Antiquarius sive prinscorum* (Amsterdam, 1594 or Cologne, 1609).

account of household payments between 7 July 1634 and 19 March 1635 is highly revealing.[53] It includes details of one trip from Lisnagarvey to London taken by the Viscount with twelve servants, costing £690 19s. 10d. Examples of expenditure include hats, garters, gloves; perfume, a pistol and sword blades; and tips to coachmen, porters and musicians. Most revealing for a bibliographical study, though, are the following items:

> For gilt paper, 6d.
> For books, 14s. 6d.
> For books in Westminster Hall, 1s. 6d.
> For three books in Paul's Churchyard, 1s. 8d.
> For three books at the Temple, 1s. 3d.
> For books in Fleet Street, 2s.
> Paid to Mr. Bee for a great book, £1 5s.
> More to Mr. Huggens for his books, 5s.
> To a porter that brought books from 'Beadlum', 1s.
> Given to my Lord Goring's footman that brought books, 5s.
> To a porter that brought books from Duck Lane, 6d.
> Paid to the French bookbinder, 10s.
> Paid to the book-binder with withered hand, £2 11s.
> For the writing of a book, 10s.
> For the copying out of verses, 4s.
> For writing out of a masque, 1s. 6d.
> For ballads and a play book, 3s. 6d.
> For five play books, 4s.

These accounts show that Conway's haunts included the bookshops around Westminster, St. Paul's, Temple, Fleet Street, Bedlam and Duck Lane, but that he did not necessarily visit the shops himself. Vendors included Mr. Bee and Mr. Huggens/Huggins; the latter is not mentioned in Plomer's *Dictionary* or the *British Book Trade Index* (might the correct spelling have been Huygens?), but the former was probably Cornelius Bee (1636-71/2), of Little Britain.[54] Conway had unbound volumes taken to several bookbinders, including a Frenchman and another with a 'withered hand'.

---

[53]   London, National Archives, SP 16/285/19. Cf. London, National Archives, SP 16/346/105, bill of Edward Burgh, Conway's servant, 11 February 1637.
[54]   Plomer, *Dictionary* (1968), pp. 19, 251-52, 255.

David Pearson has shown the relative lack of contemporary scholarly interest in bindings from 1550 to 1650, but it seems that Conway was interested in the physical attractiveness of his books, whether or not he always bought the finest option available to him.[55] Sir Kenelm Digby wrote to him in 1637 from Paris:

> I am promised La conquest du sang real for you, and the Legend of S^r. Tristran, and can procure you an entire collection of all the bookes knowne here of that kind, and in particular a curious Amadis in 12 volumes; but least j should buy what you haue already, j beseech y^r. Lo: lett me know what you want and what is y^r. store; (for these are of the deerest bookes here) be pleased also to lett me know if you would haue such of them as are extraordinarily bound for curiosity and cost, or whither the vulgar meanest binding will serue y^r. turne.[56]

Perhaps most interesting, however, is the evidence that Conway had works copied out by hand: a masque, verses and a book, the latter presumably a long work, as it cost him 10s., significantly more than the 4s. and 1s. 6d. he paid for the other items. A notable collector of manuscript separates, Conway was commissioning manuscript copies of works, both professionally, as above, and within his own household. 'Let Tandy write out Sr Iosias Bodleys iourney,' he instructed Rawdon, 'and bring it with you'.[57]

Conway's tastes in literature were not just the sedentary pleasures of book collecting: his theatre-related expenditure shows an avid attendance at performances when he was in London. While there is practically no drama in the London catalogue, Conway's Irish library is particularly impressive for its theatrical content. Conway owned 350 English plays published between 1560 and 1640 – more than half the 600 printed by

[55]   David Pearson, 'Scholars and Bibliophiles: Book Collectors in Oxford 1550-1650', in *Antiquaries, Book Collectors and the Circles of Learning*, ed. by Robin Myers and Michael Harris (Winchester, 1996), pp. 1-26.

[56]   London, National Archives, SP 16/344/58. *Tristran* may be Jean-Pierre Camus, *A Discours Hapned. Betwene an Hermite Called Nicephorus & a Yong Louer Called Tristan* (Paris, 1630), and the 'Sang Real' perhaps an edition of the *Morte D'Arthur*. London, National Archives, SP 16/372 lists a 14-book *Amadis*.

[57]   London, National Archives, SP 16/271/79. Josias Bodley was brother to the more famous Thomas, founder of the Bodleian Library. This was probably a manuscript text. One example of a printed book Conway had copied out for him survives at London, National Archives, SP 16/415/31.

1640 – and, in total, 619 plays in four languages.[58] Conway's collections appear to have included three Shakespeare quartos unrecorded elsewhere, including a first edition 1597 *Love's Labour's Lost*, a combined 'Henry 4 the first and second parte' from 1619 (probably a pirated version), and 'The Taminge of the Shrew by W: Sh:' (1621), though the latter may be the known 1631 edition, mis-written. Using a list of plays supplied by Moseley to 'an unknown customer', Birrell has shown that Conway was in fact buying books on standing order, using Moseley as a centralized retail bookseller.[59]

'The joy of my life': books as an organizing principle

As I have shown, Conway thought about his book collections very deliberately, researching the availability of particular books, establishing a network of informed purchasers and arranging his libraries to suit his reading habits. He clearly had a deep emotional attachment to his collections. Complaining of deafness in 1652, he explained, 'I haue not delighted in any thing so mutch as reading and discoursing if I loose my hearing I loose the one halfe of the ioy of my life'.[60] Books defined Conway, and on a straightforward anthropological level his collections embodied his character: Conway was omnivorous by nature, a man as much humoured by rude jokes and scandalous gossip as he was well-read in theological debates and military theory. Nevertheless, his catalogues clearly represent serious repositories of information about the seventeenth century. Writing about the Lumley catalogue, Jayne and Johnson note

> there is only one type of literature which is not present [...] the type read by the uneducated man: the street ballad, the play, the broadside news-sheet, the literature of low-life which did not get into any large library, private or institutional.[61]

In addition to being stores of serious history and jurisprudence texts, the Conway libraries abounded in plays, romances and jest-books, and

---

[58]   Freeman and Grinke, 'Four New Shakespeare Quartos?'.
[59]   W. W. Greg, *Bibliography of English Printed Drama*, 4 vols (London, 1957), III, 1317-18. Cf. Freeman and Grinke, 'Four New Shakespeare Quartos'; but also note the retraction of one of their claims in 'Shakespeare Quartos', *TLS*, 14 June 2002, p. 17.
[60]   London, National Archives, SP 18/25/15.
[61]   Jayne and Johnson, *Lumley Library*, pp. 31-2.

these were not discriminated against when it came to making a catalogue. Taken in conjunction with the ballads and ditties in the Conway Papers, Conway's libraries offer a more democratic representation of the knowledge available in seventeenth century Europe than almost every other private repository. They constitute 'the shortest and most accurate route' to knowledge of what was known in Renaissance England – and Ireland – about virtually *every* subject.

Who was Dr James Fraser of Chelsea?

Iain Beavan

James Fraser was born into a clerical family in September 1645. His father was the minister of the Parish of Petty in north-east Inverness-shire, and his mother was the daughter of one of the ministers of Inverness itself. According to Ker and Henderson, (*pace* Moffat) the couple had five sons and three daughters and James was the third of the five boys. After some time at Inverness Grammar School, he entered King's College Aberdeen in 1660, aged fifteen, and graduated four years later. Then, from graduation in 1664 there is a gap of some eleven, clearly formative, years as Fraser drops out of sight.[1]

The 1732 eulogy, published a year after his death (he died aged 85), said that after graduation Fraser struck out for England.[2] From 1675 to 1678/9, Fraser, then in his early thirties, was tutor and companion to Charles Berkeley, eldest son of the soldier and ambassador, John, Lord Berkeley of Stratton, and he almost certainly also acted in some form of secretarial capacity to his Lordship himself. During these three years, father, son, and Fraser, travelled to Continental Europe, and can be placed in Amsterdam in 1676.[3] The association probably explains the presence, amongst Fraser's papers in Aberdeen University, of transcripts of mediators' proceedings leading to the Treaty of Nijmegen, which John Berkeley attended in a governmental capacity.[4]

The scholar and diarist John Evelyn noted that it was he who recommended Fraser to the Berkeley family.[5] Fraser had, then, succeeded in becoming recognised by, and accepted within, the learned

---

[1]   Fraser has been eulogised in J. Ker, *Frasereïdes; sive funebris oratio & elegia* (Aberdoniae, 1732), and his life summarised in J. M. Henderson, 'James Fraser, 1645-1731', *Aberdeen University Review*, 25 (1937-38), 138-46, and B. Moffat, 'Fraser, James (1645-1731)', in *ODNB* <http://www.oxforddnb.com> [accessed 21 June 2011]. J. R. Pickard, *A History of King's College Library*, 3 vols (Aberdeen, 1987), II, 44-155 is an indispensable resource.

[2]   Ker, *Frasereïdes*, p. 7; F. Douglas, *A General Description of the East Coast of Scotland* (Aberdeen, 1782; repr. 1826), commented that Fraser 'went into England to push his fortune' (p. 168).

[3]   London, British Library, MS Egerton 3682, fol. 15.

[4]   Aberdeen, Aberdeen University, MS K257/44/6.

[5]   *The Diary of John Evelyn*, ed. by A. Dobson, 3 vols (London, 1906), III, 105.

and distinguished circles in London, and had also been sufficiently regarded to be entrusted with the tutelage of children of the aristocracy. Fraser's employment subsequently took him towards the very centre of the court, and he recorded that he was honoured to have been appointed governor for three years (to 1682) to Charles Beauclerk illegitimate son of Charles II and Nell Gwyn.[6]

After his years with Beauclerk, Fraser was appointed, in 1682, companion to the influential Paston family. Robert Paston, a politician, became the first Earl of Yarmouth, and his eldest son, William, married one of the king's illegitimate daughters. One of Paston's sons, possibly William, met Prince William (of Orange) and Mary in The Hague in March 1683, accompanied by James Fraser (who wrote to Lady Yarmouth about it) and who smoothed the entry to the Dutch court through his 'old friend and acquaintance' Thomas Chudleigh, British envoy there.[7]

Parallel with his various duties as governor and companion, James Fraser was using his contacts and travels abroad to nurture another source of income. Edmund Bohun described Fraser's other chosen activity: he was buying and selling books, sometimes speculatively, sometimes on commission. Fraser had seemingly started out as a 'poor broker of books' – possibly to supplement his income as tutor – and carried them round, as Bohun described,

> in a satchel to the chambers of the nobility, and there sold them, and paid the money for them to the stationers, and lived by the profit. The book-sellers also trusted him with 2 or 300£ to buy books for them in Paris.[8]

Evidently, Fraser had found a small niche in part of the commercial world of the seventeenth-century European book trade.[9] It is therefore

---

[6]   Charles Beauclerk, 1670-1726, Earl of Burford, Duke of St Albans. The King's College copy of A. Menjot, *Febrium malignarum historia et curatio* (Paris, 1662) is inscribed on the title-page, 'Liber Collegij Regii Aberdonensis, ex dono Mri Jacobi Fraserij Tutoris Comitis de Burford in Anglia'.

[7]   London, British Library, MS Additional 36988, fol. 227.

[8]   E. Bohun, *The Diary and Autobiography* (Beccles, 1853), p. 115.

[9]   T. A. Birrell intriguingly notes Fraser as acting for a Continental buyer in at least one auction in 'Books and Buyers in Seventeenth-Century English Auction Sales', in *Under the Hammer: Book Auctions since the Seventeenth Century*, ed. by R. Myers, M. Harris and G. Mandelbrote (New Castle, Del., 2001), p. 52, citing *l'Histoire des bibliothèques françaises*: T.2: *Les bibliothèques sous l'Ancien Régime*, sous la direction de C. Jolly (Paris, 1988), p. 178, n.98.

no surprise to find that when in the Netherlands, Fraser mixed his duties to the English gentry and Dutch royalty with book buying: three days after a meeting with Prince William, he attended the auction of the library of the eminent Dutch polymath and diplomat Nicolaas Heinsius in Leiden. Fraser's own copy of the sale catalogue (of over 12,500 lots) is still present in Aberdeen, and John Evelyn tells us that Fraser bought some 'Herbals in miniature' and some texts on Verona.[10] It is probably no coincidence that, within Fraser's copy of the auction catalogue, at least eight botany books are not just priced, but further annotated, as are the entry for the 1622 *Musaeum Calceolarianum Veronese* and a 1540 history of Verona.[11] This voyage to the Netherlands was also referred to by Samuel Pepys when he recorded that,

> Mr Frazier being just from the auction of books in Holland, says that there is a great collection in a private hand there of maps of all sorts through all the World [...] and particularly of the King of Spain's dominions abroad. For this is demanded as much as comes to £2,000.[12]

It is unlikely that Pepys, who had previously been a senior official at the Navy Board and Admiralty, regarded the maps and plans as objects of curiosity, but more likely that he saw their potential benefit as instruments of military or economic advantage.

Fraser was a regular dinner guest in educated circles, and took commissions to procure desired items.[13] A friend and regular visitor to the second Earl of Clarendon (Henry Hyde), they often took supper together, and Fraser kept his lordship abreast of recent and forthcoming publications, sometimes, when necessary, by letter. During 1692, Fraser told Hyde of the 'the historicall dictionary that is now a printing [that] is the substance of the last Edition of the grand Dictionnaire historique', of the continuation of John Rushworth's *Historical Collections*, and in a letter of 12 May, of the 'new Relation of Siam in 2 vol. 8° with variety of cutts come over, writt by Mr. Loubere

[10]   *Diary of John Evelyn*, III, 105.
[11]   Fraser's annotated copy of the catalogue is now in Aberdeen University as Nicolaas Heinsius, *Bibliotheca Heinisiana* (Leiden, 1682), shelfmark, Historic Collections, π 0182 Hei.
[12]   *The Tangier Papers of Samuel Pepys*, ed. by Edwin Chappell, The Navy Records Society, 73 (London, 1935), p. 309.
[13]   *Elias Ashmole (1617-1692): His Autobiographical and Historical Notes*, ed. by C. H. Josten, 5 vols (Oxford, 1966), IV, 1800.

[...] and it is done with the greatest exactness & judgement that I have observed in any author of that kind'. Fraser's commendation worked, as five days later, he noted, 'The new Relation of Siam [...] shall be sent your Lordship by the first.'[14]

Fraser indeed quietly traded in books and manuscripts well into the 1720s. In 1726 he told the Scottish church minister and historian Robert Wodrow, with whom he had a considerable correspondence, that he had purchased a manuscript of Buchanan's 'History of Scotland' from the Duke of Lauderdale's Library when it went up for sale, and sold it on to the Earl of Cholmondly, and a manuscript copy of the Acts of the General Assembly of the Church of Scotland, which he could have sold to the Earl of Oxford (Robert Harley) for forty guineas, but chose not to, instead presenting it to the 'Theological Library at Edinburgh, for the publick use of the nation'.[15] At least one Edinburgh bookseller, David Randie, made his way down to London, with 'severall scarce and curiose books' and was more than prepared to meet with Fraser. This was in 1728, and Fraser in his eighties.[16]

The scientists Robert Hooke, Robert Boyle and Fraser (amongst others) frequented the various London coffee-houses where book auctions were held. Hooke recorded his crossing paths with Fraser at one of Hussy's auctions in 1689, and of subsequently borrowing topographical books from him.[17] They had in fact already met, as the scientist had been allowed by Fraser to examine 'the Impressions of several of the King of *France*'s Medals, in a thin transparent Substance, much like *Muscovy* Glass'.[18] Fraser presumably had access to collections not immediately available to Hooke. Fraser's letters of 1695 to Hans Sloane, also, show him borrowing botany and travel books, including an edition of Verbiest's *Voyage de l'empereur de la Chine dans la Tartarie*, and an unidentified 'Journal of the Caravan from Musco to China'.[19]

---

[14] Glasgow, Glasgow University Library, MS Hunter 73, items 87-90. The book was Simon de la Loubère, *Du royaume de Siam* (Amsterdam, 1691).

[15] *Analecta Scotica*, ed. by J. Maidment, 2 ser. (Edinburgh, 1837), ser. 1, pp. 313, 317-18, 323.

[16] *Analecta*, ser. 1, p. 321.

[17] *The Diary of Robert Hooke* [...] *1672-80*, ed. by H. W. Robinson and W. Adams (London, 1935), pp. 142, 147, 170, 174, 175.

[18] R. Hooke, *Philosophical Experiments* (London, 1726), p. 111.

[19] London, British Library, Sloane MS 4036, fol. 224, fol. 250.

Fraser's career (and political affiliations) developed during the four years covering Charles II's death in February 1685, the withdrawal of James VII & II to France in late 1688, and the coronation of William and Mary in the spring of 1689. Here three major matters emerge. Did he become the Royal Librarian? How did he become settled in Chelsea? And, finally, how thankless a task was it to be a licenser of the press?

Fraser was nearly forty when Charles II died. With the accession of James VII & II, he sought the post of Royal Librarian, or at least tried to gain privileged entry to the royal collections. There is evidence that he succeeded, though it falls short of being conclusive. Prof. John Ker's eulogy explicitly states that James put Fraser in charge of the Royal Library, though the author throughout was at pains to demonstrate the connections Fraser had with the crown, and the respect in which he was held.[20] Previous scholars have drawn attention to Fraser's letter of October 1685 to Sir Robert Southwell in which he commented that,

> The King has been graciously pleased to renew to me the assurances of being shortly in possession of the Library at St James's & he told me that last week he overcome the difficulties that Mr Thynne had formed ag[ains]t it.[21]

The great majority of the Royal Library had certainly been housed in St James's Palace for some considerable time previously, and the letter implies that Henry Thynne, Royal Librarian since 1675, was about to vacate his post. Yet, on a dispassionate reading, the king's reported assurance is scarcely a solemn guarantee, and is not further developed in a letter which ranges over a number of broadly political topics. Further evidence in support of Fraser can be adduced in the form of his 'Catalogue of all the Mapps, Plans of Towns, Harbours, Itineraries and other unprinted MSS in his Majesty's Closet at Whitehall', dated 27 April 1685.[22] The title is misleading, as it lists nearly 100 manuscript maps, over 500 printed texts, and over 40 other literary or historical works. These maps and printed books may have been removed from the Royal Library and transferred to Whitehall – either by Charles or James – and they certainly speak to Fraser's privileged access to the

---

[20] Ker, *Frasereïdes*, p. 8.

[21] London, British Library, MS Additional 28569, fol. 56ᵛ.

[22] Aberdeen, Aberdeen University, MS K257/44/4. MS K257/44/9/2 is a single letter of 1686 addressed to, 'Monsieur fresur Bibliothecaire de sa M[ajes]te Britannique a Londres'.

royal apartments, but overall this again falls short of conclusive proof of his being Royal Librarian. On the other hand, Fraser was working for the king, members of the court and government officers as a book agent throughout this period. In January 1687, the Customs Commissioners were petitioned by Fraser to:

> Deliver, Customs free, such of the following books as are for private use and not for sale [...] five bales and one box of old books [...] lately come from France, some for the King, some for the Lord President, the Earl[s] of Arran [...] of Middleton [...] of Melfort, and some for the petitioner: all of which have been visited by the Archbishop of Canterbury's officer deputed thereto.[23]

The balance of evidence suggests that Fraser shared the duties of Royal Librarian jointly with Henry Thynne who remained in post during James's short reign. First appointed by Charles II, Thynne was still called 'Keeper of the Library at St James's' in letters issued in July and August 1687, when he was instructed to allow the king's chaplains, the Benedictine monks at St James's, the use of such books out of the library as they desired, and was directed to deliver the required texts.[24]

As king, James was prepared partially to honour some of his deceased brother's debts. In September 1688 James Fraser was given the post of Secretary and Register for the Royal Hospital at Chelsea, a situation he held for thirty years. It was a complete sinecure, as the Pay Office in a round of attempted government savings in 1712 and 1713 recognised, when it tried unsuccessfully to have the post permanently removed from the establishment when Fraser was finally to vacate it.[25] At the time, Fraser was drawing £80 per annum as part of the establishment's salary costs, and the little work involved, was done by others.[26] Fraser, however, proffered his resignation in 1718, as he

---

[23] *Calendar of Treasury Books Preserved in the Public Record* Office, ed. by William A. Shaw, 32 vols (London, 1904-57), 8:3 (1923): *1685-89*, p. 1169.

[24] *Calendar of State Papers Domestic James II*, ed. by E. K. Timings, 3 vols (London, 1960-72), 3 (1972): *1687-89*, entries 115 and 279. See *The Lumley Library: The Catalogue of 1609*, ed. by S. Jayne and F. R. Johnson (London, 1956), Appendix B for notes on the sequence of royal librarians. Henri Justel (see *ODNB*) was appointed Royal Librarian by William and Mary, and took up post in July 1689.

[25] London, British Library MS Additional 5940 letters therein, J. Howe, Pay Office, 13 August 1712 and 4 June 1713 to Robert Harley, Earl of Oxford.

[26] D. Ascoli, *A Village in Chelsea: An Informal Account of the Royal Hospital* (London, 1974), pp. 94-95, 129, 136.

needed to travel to Scotland on business,[27] and, in his submission acidly explained that he had accepted the position,

> At the Rate of £750: which was a Dept [*recte* Debt] owing him from King Charles the Second, in consideration of his Services for Three Years [...] of being Governour to the presant [sic] Duke of St Albans, with the promise of £250 Sallery per annum as Standing and Board wages and never to this day was payd any part of it.[28]

As part of his resignation letter Fraser also successfully proposed that the post be offered to his son-in-law, Elijah Impey of Hammersmith.[29] Summarily, though, there can be little doubt that for three decades the post had given Fraser a secure base from which to continue trading in books, and to busy himself as a government official.

It says much about the strength and steadfastness of Fraser's allegiance, and of his trustworthiness, that he was to assist the government at a pivotal and extremely fraught political and constitutional moment. Fraser, clearly convinced that he must withdraw whatever support he had previously had for James VII & II, accepted a commission to become a licenser of the press even before the coronation of William and Mary, and began work in March 1689. His particular role, renewed annually by a Secretary of State, needed considerable sensitivity and discretion.[30] He was required to pass judgement on works of 'profane history'; in effect, recent and current affairs other than those strictly theological, though there was a considerable variety in what he actually licensed.[31] The months of March to December 1689 were by far the busiest for him as he licensed at least eighty items, from broad-

---

[27] R. B. Litchfield, 'Dr James Fraser, of Aberdeen and Chelsea and Sir E. Impey', *Notes and Queries*, 9th ser., 3 (1899), 301-02, confirms that Fraser vacated the post in May 1718.

[28] London, British Library, MS Additional 61632. Submission undated, but 1717 or 1718.

[29] *Weekly Packet*, 17 May 1718, p. 2, col. 2.

[30] D. F. McKenzie and Maureen Bell, *Chronology and Calendar of Documents Relating to the London Book Trade, 1641-1700*, 3 vols (Oxford, 2005), III, 55. The necessary authority was issued by the Earl of Shrewsbury, 19 March 1689; by the Earl of Nottingham, 12 June 1690. Bohun (*Diary and Autobiography*, p. 115) states that Fraser was offered the licenser's post because of his preparedness to go to King James's wife with the news that his majesty had retreated to France.

[31] A. Wood, *Life and Times of Anthony Wood* [...] *1632-1695*, 5 vols (Oxford, 1891-1900), IV, 17.

sheets to major publications, from Edmund Bohun's 176-page *The History of the Desertion*, to the broadside *A New Song Lately Come from Ireland*, and from Gilbert Burnet's sermon, delivered as Bishop of Salisbury, at the coronation of William and Mary, to *An Examination of the Scruples of Those who Refuse to Take the Oath of Allegiance*, and *A Brief Vindication of the Parliamentary Proceedings against James II*.[32] One important feature relating to the book trade that emerges from this, is that many printers, though unconcerned to register their copies at Stationers' Hall, nevertheless felt it imperative to get the protection of a license before they offered their material for sale. An interesting case in point is *A True Account of the Behaviour of the Nine Criminals that were Executed at Tyburn*. The author was Samuel Smith, who, as chaplain of Newgate Prison, benefited from the customary right to compile and profit from such execution sheets.[33] Nevertheless, either Smith or the printer made sure that the work was licensed (by Fraser) before it reached the streets. Overall, Fraser licensed at least 170 items, including periodicals and newspapers.[34] John Dunton, the bookseller, thought very highly of him, and commented that Fraser was, 'our Chief Licenser for several years, and it was pity that he had not continued longer in the same post, for his treatment was kind and impartial'. Dunton found himself paying Fraser £30 a year for getting his books, serials and weekly *Athenian Mercury* licensed, though he did not resent it, 'I suppose', he wrote, 'other booksellers were as forward as myself to have recourse to him, which made his salary very considerable; and he deserved every penny of it.'[35] However, Edmund Bohun, staunch royalist, and a subsequent licenser of the press, was hostile towards Fraser, and regretted that, 'In the beginning of this

---

[32] Edmund Bohun, *The History of the Desertion; or, An Account of all the Publick Affairs in England from the Beginning of September 1688 to the Twelfth of February Following* (London, 1689); Anonymous, *A New Song Lately Come from Ireland* (London, 1689), Gilbert Burnet, *A Sermon Preached at the Coronation of William III and Mary II* (London, 1689); Pierre Allix, *An Examination of the Scruples of Those who Refuse to Take the Oath of Allegiance*, (London, 1689); Anonymous, *[A Brief] Vindication of the Parliamentary Proceedings against the Late King James II* (London, 1689).

[33] Samuel Smith, *A True Account of the Behaviour of the Nine Criminals that were Executed at Tyburn* (London, 1689), available at <http://www.oldbaileyonline.org> [accessed 21 June 2011].

[34] *A Transcript of the Registers of the Worshipful Company of Stationers from 1640-1708*, ed. by G. E. B Eyre, 3 vols (London, 1913-14), III, passim.

[35] J. Dunton, *The Life and Errors of John Dunton*, 2 vols (London, 1818), I, 266-67.

revolution, one Frasier, a Scot, was made licenser. Under him the Whigg party had golden days. They printed what they pleased, and he licensed whatever they could write.'[36] In Bohun's opinion, he

> licensed all that came to hand [...] except the Jacobite; so that we had swarmes of the worst books written in the rebellion of 1640, reprinted with authority; the monarch run down and vilified; all government made to be the gift of the people and subject to them; the divine right of government was ridiculed and bantered every day.

High Tory that he was, he concluded by accusing Fraser of blatant partiality and inconsistency, 'At first he licensed books on both sides, but, being once settled, he rejected the loyal papers and would suffer little to pass on that side, except the party were too big to be contested'. Other booksellers and printers, claimed Bohun, had to go behind Fraser's back to another licenser to get permission for their work to be published.[37]

In April 1692, Fraser made an uncharacteristic error of political judgement, and gave his detractors exactly the excuse they sought. It is *prima facie* odd that he got involved in the controversy surrounding the authorship of the *Eikon Basilike* at all – not because the text had no political reverberations (as patently it did) – but because other texts integral to the debate had been licensed by churchmen. However, it may also be that the text in question was referred to him precisely because of its potential for political upset. The influential views of Dr Richard Hollingworth – that Charles I was the sole author of the *Eikon Basilike* – appeared in early 1692, in his *Defence of King Charles I*, an edition of which carries the imprimatur of the senior cleric, Dr Zacheus Isham.[38] There is no doubt that Fraser licensed the subsequent book on the controversy, Anthony Walker's *A True Account of the Author of a Book Entituled Εικων Βασιλικη*, which stood as the first major, compelling and persuasive defence of the controversial view that the *Eikon Basilike* had not been entirely the work of Charles.[39]

---

[36] Bohun, *Diary and Autobiography*, p. 110.

[37] Ibid., p. 115.

[38] Richard Hollingworth, *A Defence of King Charles I* (London, 1692), ESTC R223243 has the imprimatur.

[39] *Transcript*, ed. by G. E. B. Eyre, entry under 19 April 1692, confirming Fraser's license. Anthony Walker, *A True Account of the Author of a Book Entituled Εικων Βασιλικη*, (London, 1692).

Not that Fraser's name appeared within the book, which exists in three issues,[40] only one of which records the author's name, and notes, 'Licensed, and Entred [sic] according to Order'.[41] The riposte to Walker was quick, in the form of *Dr. Hollingworth's Defence of K. Charles the First's Holy and Divine Book* licensed on 2 May 1692 by Charles Alston, chaplain to the Bishop of London.[42] Fraser's license was seen to have allowed the publication of a text that caused needless offence, and as a result, he, apparently along with other licensers (who had also been too relaxed with their powers), was summoned to the Chief Justice (Sir John Holt).[43] As Anthony Wood, the antiquarian tartly (but characteristically) noted, 'James Frazer, a Presbyterian Scot [...] was bound over to appear at the sessions in the Old Baylee, for licensing this pestilent pamphlet & afterwards [was] deprived of his place.'[44] Though Fraser was removed from his post, he licensed, over his three years' tenure, some texts of lasting consequence, including the 1690 English translation of Buchanan's *History of Scotland* (so he should have; he is said to have translated it), John Locke's *Letters on Toleration,* (licensed 1689, 1690, and 1692), his *Two Treatises on Government,* 1690 (licensed the previous August, as recorded on leaf A1ᵛ (p.[2])) and his *Some Considerations of the Consequences of the Lowering of Interest,* 1692. Moreover, Fraser saw no reason to inhibit the publication of Tonson's 1691 edition of Rochester's *Poems.*[45]

Fraser, according to his will, had been minded 'to give something back to 'mankind in general and [... his] own country in particular'.[46] One opportunity had already arrived with the initiative to establish presbytery- and parish-based libraries in the Highlands of Scotland. So,

---

[40]   ESTC numbers R186154; R221937; R24591.

[41]   Walker, *True Account,* ESTC R221937. See also *The Term Catalogues, 1668-1709,* ed. by E. Arber, 3 vols (London, 1903-06), III, 404, where the author's name was given.

[42]   F. Madan, *A New Bibliography of the Eikon Basilike of King Charles the First* (London, 1950), Appendix 1 and entries 165-68.

[43]   R. Astbury, 'The Renewal of the Licensing Act in 1693 and its Lapse in 1695', *The Library,* 5th ser., 33 (1978), 296-322 (p. 298); R. B. Walker, 'The Newspaper Press in the Reign of William III', *Historical Journal,* 17 (1974), 691-709 (p. 696).

[44]   As recorded in Wood's own copy. See N. K. Kiessling, *The Library of Anthony Wood* (Oxford, 2002), entry 6389.

[45]   For Buchanan see *Transcript,* ed. by G. E. B. Eyre, August 1689; For Locke *Two Treatises* see *Transcript,* ed. by G. E. B. Eyre; Locke, *Letters,* licensed April 1695; Locke, *Some Considerations,* recorded April 1695; Rochester, *Poems,* November 1690.

[46]   Litchfield, 'James Fraser', pp. 301-02.

between 1708 and 1713, he made a series of six donations (comprising some 320 books) to the incipient library in Inverness, sending them up by sea to Robert Baillie, minister there.[47] He also made two financial donations, 1000 merks in 1712, and six years later, a further 900 merks, the interest on which was to go towards a librarian's salary and the purchase of yet more books. The second of these financial gifts (1718) was made from his deceased brother's financial estate over which he had control.[48] His younger brother, William, who died unmarried, and who appears to have been a dislikeable and divisive character, had held senior office in the East India Company, and had been Acting Governor of Fort St George (now part of Chennai) – undoubtedly a lucrative post. He returned to England, having managed to cause considerable friction, in 1713.[49] The books sent north by James Fraser were largely theological, but he made sure that other disciplines and debates were not ignored. The 1708 and 1709 donations to Inverness included 'Lock de Intellectu humano. opt. ed. 1701' – Locke throughout seems to have been a favoured author of Fraser – an edition of Milton's *Eikonoklastes* (an interesting selection given Fraser's fate over the publication of Anthony Walker), Dioscorides, 1549, Avicenna, 1569, and the folio edition, 1587, of Holinshed's *Chronicles*.[50] There were also some grammars, geographical and topographical texts. Subsequent donations included a finely bound and coloured *English Atlas* published by Moses Pitt, which alone cost Fraser £20 sterling, Blaeu's map of Scotland and Ireland, 'finely illuminated bound in fine velome gilt on the leaves, back and filleted', and descriptions of Jamaica and Canada, and, so that they were conversant with events, 'a large bundle of Gazzets containing above 2000 of the best papers'.[51] In 1719, the Kirk Session, wishing to recognise his benefactions, ordered a portrait of Fraser, and had it hung in the Church Hall.

---

[47] *Inverness Kirk-Session Records, 1661-1800*, ed. by A. Mitchell (Inverness, 1902), pp. 193-97; *Catalogue of the Inverness Session Library*, 1897 (Inverness, 1897), passim.

[48] Douglas, *General Description*, p. 169.

[49] H. D. Love, *Vestiges of Old Madras*, 4 vols (London, 1913), I, 554, 589; II, 103.

[50] Presumably the 4th edition of the *Essay on Human Understanding*, in Latin, issued by Awnsham and John Churchill, London, 1701.

[51] 'Library Catalogues and Lists of Books', Aberdeen, Aberdeen University, MS K272/3, details the shipments of books to Inverness by Fraser; also listed in the separate, and more extensive, 'Catalogue and Borrowers' Register, Inverness Presbytery Library, 1706-30', AU MS 1066.

However, the Inverness Kirk Session was not the only institution to appreciate Fraser's beneficence. Between 1712 and 1715, he made three donations, totalling some 250 books, to the new Theological Library, formed in 1700 (financially helped by the Aberdeen Synod) to benefit divinity students at both King's and Marischal Colleges.[52] Anglican and Episcopal thought was well represented with editions of works by Thomas Barlow, White Kennett, Hugh Latimer, John Patrick, Richard Stillingfleet, Jeremy Taylor, John Tillotson, and James Ussher. Yet in some contrast, *Sions Plea against the Prelacie* (1628), by the religious controversialist and anti-episcopalian, Alexander Leighton, the writings of the Presbyterian, Richard Baxter, and George Gillespie's *Assertion of the Government of the Church of Scotland* (1641) were also included. Fraser also packed up 'several controversial pieces about the Trinity', and included a number of books commenting on the Society of Jesus, with the donation list annotated by the compiler, 'The Jesuits Catechisme [,] a rare book', and 'Watson the priest's quodlibets agt the Jesuits. A choice piece'.[53] As a reminder of the effects of moral and institutional repression, a copy of the 1601 edition of *Index librorum expurgatorum* also arrived in Inverness. However, exactly how the Aberdeen divinity students were to benefit from the serial publication, *Le Mercure françois*, 1621-29, is unclear.

James Fraser came back to Scotland twice before his death: first, in 1718, then again in 1723 when he bought the estate of Wester Moy (to the west of Inverness) to provide an income for his grandson, William, who unfortunately died within a year of the purchase.[54] During his passage north in 1723 he paid a visit to his old college, King's, in Aberdeen, and was struck by the dilapidated state of the 200-year-old library (it was leaky and damp) built along the south side of Chapel, and also by the poor quality of its stock. At the time, the estimate for repairs, renovation and expansion was said to have been about £3000

---

[52] MS K272/3, 'Library Catalogues and Lists of Books' itself contains a separate listing, 'A Catalogue of Books [...] Sent to the Theological Library Lately Erected at Aberdeen for the Use of Students in Divinity and Others of North Britain, and Delivered to Mr Blackwel Professour of Divinity in the University of Aberdeen'.

[53] Etienne Pasquier, *The Jesuites Catechisme*, trans. by William Watson (London, 1602); William Watson, *A Decacordon of Ten Quodlibeticall Questions Concerning Religion and State* (London, 1602).

[54] Aberdeen, Aberdeen University, MS K257/25/2, entitled 'Copy, Dr James Fraser his Will and Testament'.

sterling.[55] So, to help, over a period of seven years, 1723-30, Fraser gave over £1250 sterling, and signed over the rents during his lifetime of the lands of Wester Moy. Additionally, he gave money for the purchase of scientific instruments, and established a number of student bursaries.[56] The library was indeed rebuilt, and Fraser's money allowed for a wider buildings programme, but unfortunately the new library itself did not out-last the century. It was pulled down in 1772, because of 'innumerable defects' but Fraser's other major benefactions to King's College still exist.[57] Over that same seven-year period, Fraser donated nearly 1000 books to King's College Library (all copies dutifully annotated) and raised the stock to an estimated 3900 titles.[58] Few of the donated books that were published in Britain, were issued after 1710, and this is undoubtedly because Fraser knew very well that King's College had recently gained the right of legal deposit.[59] King's College was not prosperous, and was necessarily more preoccupied at the time with maintaining the fabric of its buildings, its levels of income, and its ability to pay bursaries and salaries, than it ever was with building up the strengths of its library. Moreover, the book trade in Aberdeen itself was extremely small, and (until 1710) the College had no regular correspondents or agents to call upon to inform it of, or supply it with, new publications. Without Fraser's regard for his old college, and his intimate knowledge of, and expertise within the British and Continental book trades, the library's stock simply could not have been raised by over thirty percent, as happened as a result of this series of donations.

There are two notable features to the books that Fraser sent to enhance and enlarge the library. (A catalogue of King's College Library

---

[55] W. Orem, *A Description of the Chanonry, Cathedral, and King's College of Old Aberdeen in the Years 1724 and 1725* (Aberdeen, 1791), pp. 181, 187.

[56] Douglas, (*General Description*, pp. 168-69) also confirms that Fraser's donations to the Society in Scotland for Propagating Christian Knowledge came to 600 guineas.

[57] C. A. McLaren, *Rare and Fair: A Visitor's History of Aberdeen University Library* (Aberdeen, 1995), p. 13.

[58] Fraser's donations are listed in King's College Library, List of Accessions, 1710-50, Aberdeen, Aberdeen University, MS K112; neatly transcribed, with other donations, in AU MS K115. Statistics based on P. J. Anderson's analysis of the 1717 King's College catalogue, which listed some 2857 books, 'Aberdeen University Library Manuscript Catalogues', *Aberdeen University Library Bulletin*, 4 (1918-22), 242.

[59] Strictly speaking this right was granted to the University of Aberdeen (which at the time did not exist as a legal entity) but in practice, the books went to King's College.

had been especially prepared for Fraser, presumably so that he could identify gaps and avoid duplication).[60] First, the majority came from the Continent and the single largest subject was, unsurprisingly, theology, but both Catholic and Reformed traditions were present, often enough, with a controversial twist.[61] Fraser was not afraid to have acquired and sent on to King's College works touching on Catholicism, Episcopalianism and Nonconformism, and included the Presbyterian Richard Baxter's *A Treatise of Episcopacy*, 1681; the 1660 reprinting of Gillespie's *Dispute Against the English-Popish Ceremonies* (a reaction to Charles II's moves towards the restoration of episcopacy); *A Short Account of the Complaints and Cruel Persecutions of the Protestants in [...] France*, 1707; *Pietas Romana et Parisiensis; or, A faithful Relation of the [...] Charitable and Pious Works [...] in Rome and Paris*, 1687; *The Bishop of London, his Legacy. Or Certain Motives of D. King [...] for his Change of Religion and Dying in the Catholike and Roman Church*, 1623, issued from the recusant English College Press at St Omer; and Andrew Marvell's *An Account of the Growth of Popery and Arbitrary Government in England*, 1677.[62]

However, some of the more textually significant titles were not theological, but came from other disciplines. It was through Fraser that King's College acquired early issues of *Le journal des sçavans*, seventeenth-century editions of Spinoza, John Locke's *Two Treatises of Government*, 1694, one of his *Letters on Toleration*, 1690, and Naudé's *Considerations politiques sur les coups d'estat*, 1667, which may well have made challenging reading at the time. Architectural design was also represented, with Vitruvius, *De architectura*, 1522 and Alberti, *I dieci*

---

[60] The King's College Library catalogue is probably London, British Library, MS Sloane 3298.

[61] Fraser's donations to King's, by publication origin: Continental European: 62%; London and other British: 38%. The largest two Continental publication areas were Paris and other French: 27%; Amsterdam and Low Countries: 20%.

[62] Richard Baxter, *A Treatise of Episcopacy* (London, 1681); George Gillespie, *A Dispute Against the English-Popish Ceremonies Obtruded on the Church of Scotland* (Edinburgh, 1660); Jean Claude, *A Short Account of the Complaints and Cruel Persecutions of the Protestants in [...] France*, trans. by Hilary Reneu (London, 1707); Theodor van Meyden, *Pietas Romana et Parisiensis; or, A faithful Relation of the [...] Charitable and Pious Works [...] in Rome and Paris* (Oxford, 1687); *The Bishop of London, his Legacy. Or Certain Motives of D. King [...] for his Change of Religion and Dying in the Catholike and Roman Church*, (Saint Omer, 1623); Andrew Marvell, *An Account of the Growth of Popery and Arbitrary Government in England* (Amsterdam, 1677).

libri de L'archittetura, 1546; as was garden and landscape design with the attractive – and rare – *Brabantia illustrata*, reissued in London about 1705 by David Mortier. The major early detailed and illustrated description of North America, *Admiranda narratio de commodis et incolarum ritibus Virginiae*, by de Bry and Harriot, had been published for over 100 years before King's College acquired a copy through Fraser's donation. Natural science also was not neglected, with the 1603 printing of Aldrovandi's *Ornithologiae* [...] *tomus tertius* and Edward Tyson's *Orang-outang; sive, Homo sylvestris*, 1699. The King's College professoriate was understandably effusive in its appreciation, and, in 1725, gave Fraser an honorary doctorate on the strength of his benefactions already made and in the hope (which was fulfilled) of further donations. The following year, 1726, the Senatus (rather like the Inverness ministers previously) arranged with him to get his portrait painted, and indeed, he paid for it himself.[63]

The second issue concerns the books themselves which were in the most part published some thirty-fifty years previously, and this provokes two major questions: when and where did Fraser obtain them?[64] We cannot yet specifically say. We know of some of his travels abroad – he was probably in France in 1695, as 'The Lord Steward proposed that leave be given to Mr Frazer to go to [...] an auction of Thuanus's library' – and again in 1698, but there is clearly more to be elucidated.[65] The precise nature of his diplomatic mission to Paris in 1698, is not clear, but Fraser was able to write to 'Mr Ellis at the honourable Mr Secretary [James] Vernon's Office at Whitehall', that there were many things to report, as 'being 2 days at Fontainbleau where King James, his queen & most of his St Germain's Court were, I had the opportunity of [...] observing severall things not unworthy of

---

[63] J. Ker, *Donaides; sive, musarum Aberdonenium, de eximia Jacobi Fraserii J.U.D. in Academiam Regiam Aberdonensem munificentai, carmen eucharisticum* (Edinburgh, 1725) includes details of Fraser's degree, and expresses the hope of a memorial to Fraser. Fraser's portrait, and its cultural surroundings are fully discussed in M. R. Pryor, 'Painting the Profile: Imagery and Identity in the Collections of King's and Marischal Colleges, 1495-1860', 2 vols (unpublished Ph.D. thesis, University of Aberdeen, 2002), I, 224-37; II, fig. 51.

[64] Median dates of publication of books donated to King's College: Paris 1685; other French 1664; Amsterdam 1675; other Low Countries 1661; Geneva 1592; other European 1618; Germany 1663; London 1683; other British 1674.

[65] McKenzie and Bell, *Chronology and Calendar*, III, p. 199 (*sub* 18 July 1695). The De Thou sale is unidentified.

your knowing'. Fraser, tantalisingly, gave no more information. The letter however, involves comments on the French book trade.[66] After asking what Vernon would have Fraser 'get of books or Prints before I leave this place', he continued,

> You can hardly imagine how very scarce they are at Paris the good ones; but as for devotionary and church books they are the only ware their shops are stuffed with, & dear too. But as for good classick, Greek or latin [...] no such is to be met with here; there being a sort of Inquisition in books & learning, as well as in Religion prevailing every where.

Moreover, Fraser's books to King's College are very clean. There are few annotations, and only infrequently can a binding assist with previous ownership, so in that respect, the royal binding of Henry Frederick, Prince of Wales (d. 1612) on Dubravius, *Historia Bohemica*, 1602 is exceptional.[67]

The sale of most of Fraser's personal library seemingly began on 11 February 1732, organized by the bookseller and auctioneer Olive Payne at his shop in the Strand. The sale itself had been advertised for some days previously, and, in order to maximise interest, the bookseller rearranged and changed the order of the list of important titles within the sale advertisements themselves.[68] The printed catalogue to accompany the sale listed nearly 2000 lots, mostly single items.

This was not the collection of an antiquarian, but the library of a person with wide interests beyond the expected theological and political interface, and included philosophy (Locke, Descartes and Bacon were all present); geography, topography and travel (Stow's *Survey of London*, Sanson's *Atlas maritime*, *Description des Indes et de Malabar*); architecture (editions of Palladio, Vitruvius and Wotton); science and mathematics (Newton, Hauksbee, and Kepler); some medicine, histories and constitutional histories of Britain and Europe; a run of the *Tatler*; and works by Swift and Defoe. Fraser did, however, occasionally succumb to an outstanding provenance. His copy of a Tremellius and Junius Bible of 1603, was noted by the bookseller, as 'King William's book' and Tasso's tragedy, *Torrismondo* was described

---

[66]   London, British Library, MS Additional 28902, fol. 114.

[67]   J. Dubravius, *Historia Bohemica* (Hanover, 1602), Aberdeen University, shelfmark π f9(4371) Dub.

[68]   *Daily Journal*, 21, 26 January; then 1, 2, and 11 February, 1732. All advertisements printed on p. [2], col. 3 of relevant issue.

as with manuscript notes, and was listed as 'the famous Milton's book'.[69]

Some writers and diarists were antipathetic towards Fraser. Bohun obviously had a dislike for him, driven by sharply divergent political views. Anthony Wood called him 'a clamorous, covetous fellow, a great roundhead, never contented', but this trenchant view may again have been driven by differing opinions on matters of state and church.[70] Most found him sociable, gossipy on occasion, though he was occasionally disapproving, immensely knowledgeable of the British and Continental book trades, and helpful to authors. Michael Geddes, chancellor of Salisbury diocese, described him as one who 'knows books the best of any man that I am acquainted with'.[71] The final word rests with Sir John Percival, referring to a meeting with Fraser in April 1730:

> Old Catalogus Frazer called on me. He is eighty-four years old, and has his health and memory, sight, and parts as brisk as when young. There scarce has been published a book he has not read, or does not know, for which reason the world have fixed on him the name Catalogus. He is a great searcher into anecdotes, and a relator of not a few. He is a Presbyterian, but not rigid.[72]

---

[69] Olive Payne, *Viri praeclarissimi* [...] *Jacobi Fraser* [...] *nuper defuncti, librorum catalogus* (London, 1732). The sale continued with Payne, *A Catalogue of Part of the Library of the Lord Londonderry* [...] *to which are Added* [...] *Scarce Old Pamphlets Being the Remains of the Library of* [...] *James Fraser* (London, [1732(?)]).

[70] Wood, *Life and Times*, III, 398.

[71] M. Geddes, *Miscellaneous Tracts*, 2nd edn, 3 vols (London, 1714), I, 225.

[72] Historical Manuscripts Commission. *Manuscripts of the Earl of Egmont: Diary of Viscount Percival, afterwards First Earl of Egmont*, 3 vols (London, 1920-23), I, 95.

Titus Wheatcroft: An Eighteenth-Century Reader and his Manuscripts

MAUREEN BELL

On 16 February 1723 Titus Wheatcroft, a forty-two year old parish clerk and master of an elementary school in Ashover, Derbyshire, began to compile a catalogue of his books.[1] For the next twenty years or more he added to his catalogue, which eventually amounted to nearly four hundred entries. About half the books listed by Titus were religious or devotional and about a fifth were schoolbooks and educational texts, in keeping with Titus's interests as parish clerk and schoolmaster. A significant proportion, about a third, were of other kinds, including poetry, music, romance, morality, emblems, heraldry, history, politics, law, popular medicine, geography and travel. The catalogue thus provides valuable evidence of what printed books were accessible to a literate but relatively humble rural reader in the first half of the eighteenth century.[2]

At the Newcastle conference in 2000 I presented a paper on the question of access to books in Derbyshire in the late seventeenth century, referring to the catalogue but concentrating on Titus's father, Leonard Wheatcroft (1627-1706), well-known locally as a poet and 'character'.[3] My purpose then was to investigate the seventeenth-century books described in the catalogue (at least some of which can reasonably be assumed to have belonged originally to Leonard before passing to Titus on Leonard's death in 1706/7), in order to consider the question of rural access to books in the provinces in the late seventeenth century. More recently I have been concerned with understanding the catalogue

---

[1] I am very grateful to Margaret O'Sullivan, Archivist, and her staff at the Derbyshire Record Office, Matlock for access to the manuscript material discussed in this paper and for permission to reproduce images from the Wheatcroft manuscripts. I owe thanks to many former colleagues in the Department of English at the University of Birmingham, and especially Marilyn Washbrook for helping with research materials, and to George Parfitt for his unflagging enthusiasm.
[2] Titus was born in 1679 and died in 1762.
[3] 'Reading in Seventeenth-Century Derbyshire: The Wheatcrofts and their Books', in *The Moving Market: Continuity and Change in the Book Trade*, ed. by P. Isaac and B. McKay (Oak Knoll, 2001), pp.161-68.

in its entirety and in its eighteenth-century context, focussing on Titus Wheatcroft as its maker; and with exploring the catalogue as evidence of Titus's own life-long engagement with books. An annotated edition of the catalogue as a whole, identifying the printed books and analyzing them by subject, language, age, format and price, has now been published.[4]

While most of the items Titus recorded in his catalogue were printed books, twenty-five of them are described as 'written', including manuscripts both by his father Leonard and by Titus himself.[5] This paper is concerned with the surviving Wheatcroft manuscripts and the ways in which they can both supplement the information gleaned from his catalogue and contextualize our understanding of his everyday uses of printed material. The manuscripts offer us a glimpse not only of Titus's books and reading, but also of a world of cheap and popular print, through his activities as a *writer*. 'Writing', as will be seen below, is to be broadly understood, encompassing penmanship, copying, imitation and adaptation as well as composition.

The manuscripts

First, it is necessary to give a brief description of the surviving manuscripts. Titus's book list, entitled 'A Catalogue or Roll. Of the names of All the Books that I Titus Wheatcroft have Feb. 16. 1722. With the Number and price of them, which are as followeth [...]', appears in his manuscript entitled 'Church and School or The Young Clarks Instructor'.[6] The volume is mainly concerned with describing the parish of Ashover and the parish clerk's duties but also contains a number of other more personal memoranda, including the catalogue of books and two inventories (of Titus's household goods and 'shop' goods) also taken in 1722/3.[7] In addition to this 'Church and School' volume, there are three more surviving manuscripts written by Titus, making a total of four:

---

[4]   *A Catalogue of the Library of Titus Wheatcroft of Ashover*, ed. by Maureen Bell, Derbyshire Record Society, XXXV (Chesterfield, 2008).

[5]   It is possible that one or two other manuscripts are included but not described as such.

[6]   Matlock, Derbyshire Record Office (hereafter DRO), D5433/2, pp. 55-69, 90-93 and 107-110.

[7]   Titus's 'shop' seems to have been a carpenter's workshop. The inventories appear on DRO, D5433/2, pp. 94-105.

1. 'Church and School or The Young Clarks Instructor';[8]
2. 'Wheatcroft's Divine and Profitable Meditations';[9]
3. an untitled commonplace book of more than 300 pages, catalogued by the Derbyshire Record Office as 'Wheatcroft's collections';[10]
4. a large compilation volume (pulling together more than forty gatherings apparently written over a long period, amounting to more than 700 pages in total and indexed by Titus) deposited in the Record Office in September 2006.[11]

Although the cover of this last and largest manuscript has the inscription 'begun june. 6. 1744', it seems likely that the date refers to the point at which Titus gathered and indexed the volume, rather than the actual date of writing of much of the contents. It is obvious from his catalogue that Titus wrote other manuscripts, now lost, but these four surviving volumes represent a sizeable body of material through which Titus's literacy and bookish interests can be explored.

In addition to his own manuscripts, Titus's hand also appears in two surviving books written by his father. In Leonard's volume of poetry, 'The Art of Poetry, or Come ye gallants', Titus occasionally filled up a page left partly empty by his father.[12] He used a blank part of a page, for example, to inscribe his poem on Leonard's death, 'A Single Epitaph on my Honoured father'; and further on in the volume has written out 'The Motto's of the 4 Bells in Ashover Church'.[13] The other surviving work by Leonard, an autobiography, was continued, though rather more tersely, by Titus after Leonard's death in 1706/7, the last entry being for 1751.[14] Beyond these domestic and family manuscripts, Titus's hand also, of course, appears – this time in his official capacity as parish clerk – in the Ashover parish registers for many years from 1708 onwards.[15]

---

[8] DRO, D5433/2.

[9] DRO, D5775/1.

[10] DRO, D5775/2. Though there is no such title on the manuscript itself, the Record Office's title 'Wheatcroft's collections' is used here for ease of identification.

[11] DRO, D5775/3.

[12] This is the title of Leonard's volume as given by Titus in his catalogue. The volume (DRO, D5433/1) now has no title-page, but many openings have a variation of the running head first found on pp. 33-4, 'Cum you galants looke and by [*verso*] hear is myrth and melody [*recto*]'.

[13] DRO, D5433/1, pp. [133], 137.

[14] DRO, D2079/1.

[15] DRO, M77/1.

Penmanship

That the act of writing was itself a skill much prized and much practised by the Wheatcrofts is abundantly clear from Titus's catalogue of books, which lists a number of seventeenth-century works on penmanship, each valued by him at 2s. 6d.: Edward Cocker's *Multum in parvo. Or, The Pen's Gallantrie* (item 19) and two unidentified 'Cocker's Copy-Books' (21); Jeremiah Rich's *The Penns Dexterity* (31); Cocker's *Penna volans: Or, The Young Man's Accomplishment* (73); and James Seamer's *A Compendium of All the Usuall Hands Written in England* (74).[16] An interest in shorthand is also evident from the entry '4 books of Short-writing' (87), which include William Hopkins's *The Flying Pen-man* and Samuel Botley's *Maximum in minimo*.[17] The appearance of all these seventeenth-century books in the early part of the catalogue suggests that they were perhaps the books from which Titus (born in 1679) learnt his penmanship as a boy, and were possibly originally his father's.

Concern for the materials of writing is shown in Titus's occasional annotation of his catalogue to show how much paper he had used in producing a manuscript. His 'The Clerk & his Companions, or a book of my own Composing', which no longer survives, for example, is annotated with 'Contains 5½ Quire of paper'.[18] His large compilation volume contains two recipes (differing only very slightly) for the making of ink:

> How to make a Quart of good Ink.
>
> | | |
> |---|---|
> | Take, One quart of clear Rain-water | d |
> | One Ounce of the Best fine blue indigo | 1½ |
> | Four Ounces of Green Galls | 4 |
> | Two Ounces of Copperas | --- |
> | 2 Ounces of clear Gum | 2 |
>
> Pound them very small, and mix and stir them all together, for the space of a Month, then put it into an Earthen pot, or Glass Bottles to keep, and

---

[16] Dates of first editions are as follows: Edward Cocker, *Multum in parvo. Or, The Pen's Gallantrie* (London, 1660); Jeremiah Rich, *The Penns Dexterity* (London, [1659(?)]); Cocker's *Penna volans: Or, The Young Man's Accomplishment* (London, 1661); James Seamer, *A Compendium of All the Usuall Hands Written in England* (London, 1683).

[17] William Hopkins, *The Flying Pen-man* (London, 1674); Samuel Botley, *Maximum in minimo* (London, 1674).

[18] Item 235 in the catalogue.

I shall have excellent Ink, when strain'd through a flannel, or strainer. Probatum est. &c.[19]

This recipe, which appears on p. 593 of the manuscript, has also been copied out almost exactly (but without the prices) onto a separate slip of paper, which is pasted into the inside of the front cover and carefully cross-referenced 'see. p. 593'. A surviving fragment of a poem in his other commonplace book, 'Wheatcroft's collections', suggests that – either as a schoolboy, or later in life as a schoolmaster; or, most probably, in both capacities – the acquisition of good habits of writing and of study were important to him:

[When?] you write cleare some fine Gum sandrack dust
Upon your paper rubb, or pounce you must

Xact Observers of those Rules shall find
Their hands improve, to writing well inclin'd

Your hand your head, and all your study bend
To make the Action of your penn transcend

Zealously mind what doth you most concerne
Th'Examples imitate, The precepts Learne[20]

The end of this rhyming alphabet poem is followed by a line of fine capitals (A-N only), Titus's signature, and the motto 'Scribere Iussit Amor' (from Ovid, *Heroides XX*, 'love had commanded me to write').

That Titus practised often with the pen is amply demonstrated by his manuscripts, and the books by both Leonard and Titus reveal their shared interest in the production of well-written texts. Leonard's volume of poems and Titus's 'Wheatcroft's Divine and Profitable Meditations' are both carefully presented texts, and Leonard's is particularly elaborate in its layout with rules, rubrication, running heads and keen attention to presentation throughout. That Titus – probably in his youth – practised his penmanship assiduously is obvious both from the commonplace book known as 'Wheatcroft's collections' and from the more recently discovered larger manuscript, both of which seem to have been assembled from a miscellany of gatherings of paper written over a long period.

---

[19] DRO, D5775/3, p. 593.
[20] DRO, D5775/2, verso of unpaginated leaf apparently inserted at beginning of volume. The beginning of the poem is missing, as is the beginning of the first line given here (corner torn off).

Some of this material looks like school exercises in penmanship, with many alphabets written in different scripts and many pages of sayings, poems and proverbs set out very carefully as if to offer a sampler of writing hands. Whether these were youthful exercises by Titus or teaching materials he used as a schoolmaster it is impossible to tell. Perhaps they were both. A good example is a page from 'Wheatcroft's collections' (Figure 1) which sets out seven sayings in different scripts, punctuated by repetitions of Titus's signature.[21]

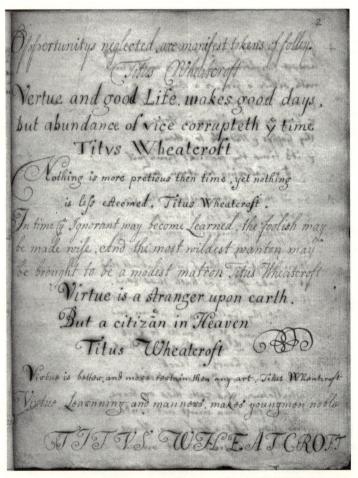

Fig. 1 Titus Wheatcroft, 'Wheatcroft's Collections', page of aphorisms, DRO, D5775/2, fol. 1ʳ. Reproduced with the permission of Derbyshire Record Office

---

21   DRO D5775/2, [fol. 2ʳ].

Six of the seven aphorisms on the page are traceable to one printed book which is listed as item twenty-two in Titus's catalogue: *Politeuphuia. Wits Common-wealth*, a compilation of proverbs, similes and moral sayings arranged by topic and much used as a schoolbook.[22] The fact that the aphorisms he has copied out appear only in the 1598 edition of *Politeuphuia* suggests that this must be the edition he owned and catalogued. That the final aphorism on the page, 'Virtue, Learnning [*sic*], and manners, makes youngmen noble', is his own composition is perhaps signalled by the extra-large, bold, flourished capitals of his name beneath it. It is also possible, however, that this too derives from the same printed text, perhaps being adapted from *Politeuphuia*'s 'True nobility consisteth [...] in wisdom, knowledge, & vertue, which in man is very nobility [...]'.[23] More likely than claiming authorship, however, the emphatic repetition of Titus's name beside or beneath each saying perhaps suggests nothing more than his approval – his moral ownership – of the sentiments he has selected to place so prominently on the page. Other material in the same volume – apparently copy-book practice, exercises in arithmetic and short rhymes – suggests that in constructing it Titus was gathering together material stretching back to his youth. Such rhymes as

> Titus Wheatcroft is my name
> Great Britain is my Station
> Ashover is my dwelling place
> And Christ is my Salvation[24]

and the many signatures and flourishes suggest a youthful delight in penmanship.

Copying and adaptation

The hundreds of pages of surviving manuscript offer, sadly, no direct comment on Titus's books or reading habits. He recorded no helpful

---

[22] Nicholas Ling, *Politeuphuia: Wit's Common-wealth* (London, 1598). Ian Michael, *The Teaching of English* (Cambridge, 1987), p. 140, describes *Politeuphuia: Wit's Common-wealth* and Francis Meres's *Palladis Tamia: Wit's Treasury* (London, 1598) as English versions of the kind of collection previously used as sources of themes for Latin. Adam Fox, *Oral and Literate Culture* (Oxford, 2000), pp. 119 and 124, notes that '*Politeuphuia* was, in effect, a printed commonplace book for schoolboys containing aphoristic sentences and observations listed under different heads'.

[23] Ling, *Politeuphuia*, 1598, p. 73v.

[24] DRO, D5775/2, p. 10.

remarks on books he liked or disliked, on his acquisition of books, or about his borrowing and lending. *Indirectly*, however, the manuscripts do offer some insight into how some of the books he listed in his catalogue were used. For, as with the examples from *Politeuphuia* above, in his manuscripts we find Titus copying, imitating and reworking texts which – from the catalogue evidence – we know he owned in printed form. *How* he used his printed books is thus at least, in part, recoverable from his own writing.

Perhaps the most striking example of Titus's use of print is the manuscript volume entitled 'Wheatcroft's Divine and Profitable Meditations' which has an elaborate title-page as seen in Figure 2:

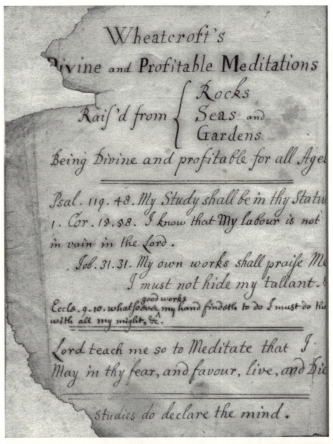

Fig. 2 Titus Wheatcroft, 'Wheatcroft's Divine and Profitable Meditations', DRO, D5775/1, title-page. Reproduced with the permission of Derbyshire Record Office

Despite its title emphatically claiming it as 'Wheatcroft's Divine and Profitable Meditations', the manuscript is in fact a partial copy of a work by William Prynne, written during Prynne's imprisonment at Mount Orgueil Castle on Jersey and published after his release in 1641 (Figure 3).

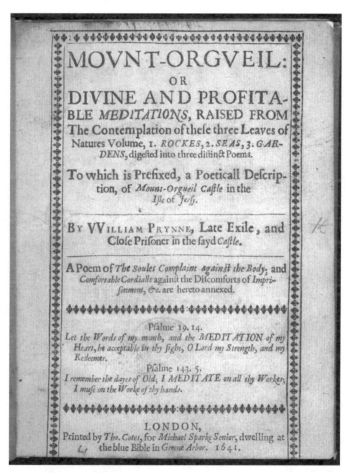

Fig. 3 William Prynne, *Movnt-Orgveil: Or Divine and Profitable Meditations* (1641), title-page. Reproduced with the permission of the British Library

Prynne's title is: *Movnt-Orgveil: Or Divine and Profitable Meditations, Raised from the Contemplation of These Three Leaves of Natures Volume,*

*1. ROCKES, 2. SEAS, 3. GARDENS, Digested into Three Distinct Poems
[...].*[25]

Prynne's *Movnt-Orgveil* appears as number 175 in Titus's catalogue of his books, where it is listed *not* as *Movnt-Orgveil: Or Divine and Profitable Meditations* but as 'Rocks improved, composing certain poetical meditations' and priced at 2s. 6d. Prynne's *Movnt-Orgveil*, although continuously paginated, has three main parts ('Rockes'; 'Seas'; 'Gardens'), each with its own title-page, the first of which is *Rockes Improved, Comprising Certaine Poeticall Meditations* (Figure 4).

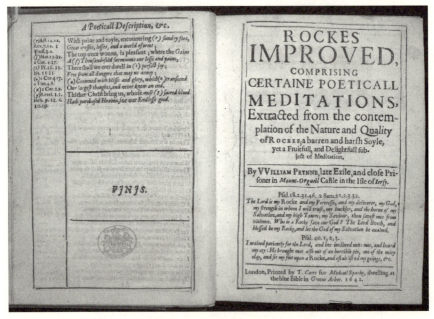

Fig. 4 William Prynne, *Movnt-Orgveil: Or Divine and Profitable Meditations* (1641), title-page of section 'Rockes Improved'. Reproduced with the permission of the British Library

Titus's entry of the 'Rocks Improved' title in his catalogue suggests that he had only a partial copy of the printed text, missing (at least) the title-page and preliminary pages (a dedicatory letter and a poem). At some stage prior to its entry in the catalogue, though, the text must have had its title-page, since Titus's manuscript follows part of

[25] Donald R. Wing, *Short-Title Catalogue of Books Printed in England* [...] *1641-1700*, 2nd edn, 3 vols (New York, 1972-88) entry P4013ff.

Prynne's title-page closely – apart, of course, from its substitution of Wheatcroft's name as author for Prynne's and the addition of its 'Being Divine and profitable for all Ages'.

This should not be dismissed as a simple case of literary theft. Titus presents the text as his own because, in a sense, it is: his appropriation of Prynne's book involves work of his own (not least, of course, in the labour of penmanship). Prynne's printed volume presents a sequence of poems with copious marginal Biblical references, linked to the poems typographically by a system of lower-case letters in parentheses (see Figure 5).

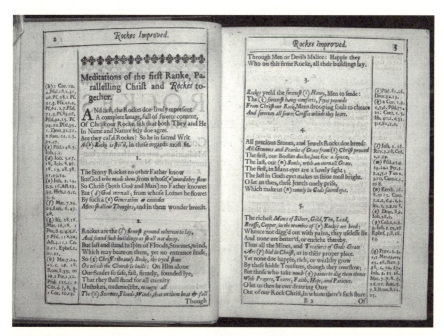

Fig. 5 William Prynne, *Movnt-Orgveil: Or Divine and Profitable Meditations* (1641), first opening of 'Rockes Improved' section. Reproduced with the permission of the British Library

Wheatcroft's version does more. Titus has indeed copied part of Prynne's text (the whole of the first, 'Rockes Improved' section; and part of the second section, 'A Christian Sea-Card'); but he has *expanded* Prynne's marginal Biblical references so as to ·give the complete quotations from the Bible alongside the poems (see Figure 6).

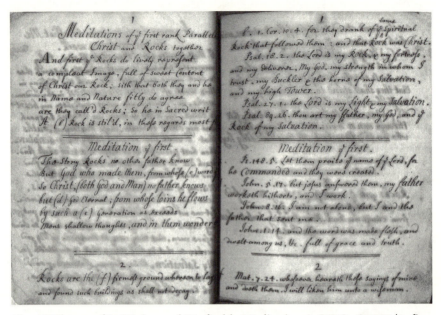

Fig. 6 'Wheatcroft's Divine and Profitable Meditations', DRO, D5775/1, first opening of 'Rockes Improved' section. Reproduced with the permission of Derbyshire Record Office

The manuscript entitled '*Wheatcroft's* Divine and Profitable Meditations' is indeed Titus's own in that he has enhanced Prynne's printed version by his own endeavours: he has copied each poem, has looked up the Biblical references signalled by Prynne, and transcribed them into his own text. Wheatcroft's manuscript is thus a product of his own meditative practice, in which his reading of both Prynne's poems and the Biblical citations produces an expanded version of a text which, as far as Titus is concerned, becomes the product of his own manual, intellectual and spiritual effort.

That Titus is alert to the differences between copying and composition is clear from his descriptions of the manuscripts listed in the catalogue. Some works in manuscript are simply described as 'written': 'Quarles Poims written' (236); 'Francis Quarles Emblems written' (244); 'The English Traveller written' (320); and 'Senecas Moral written' (355). The identity of the scribe in such cases is unclear, though the description of 'Francis Quarles Emblems' as being 'written, in the poor-mans penny well-bestow'd', a volume which is entered separately as item 233 in the catalogue and is described as 'of my writing', suggests that in this case at least Titus was the copyist. The phrases 'written by me' and 'of my writing' seem more ambiguous, however, possibly containing the claim to authorship made more explicit by a phrase such as 'a book of my own Composing'.[26]

So far this discussion of Titus's use of printed books has shown him copying and adapting texts he owned in printed form, and many more examples of this kind could be offered. That Quarles was a favourite author, for example, is obvious from the catalogue, which lists two 'written' copies of Quarles's poems as well as a printed edition added, and presumably acquired, later in life. Copies of Quarles's poems also appear in the manuscript 'Wheatcroft's collections' on pp. 122-23 and in a sequence later in the volume (pp. 214-28) with an intermittent running head 'Quarles Emblems'.[27] Fables from Aesop such as 'a story of the Fir-tree', 'A Miller and a Rat' and 'Love and Death' have also been copied into the same volume, and a later owner has obligingly pencilled in references to identify them as being taken from L'Estrange's translation.[28] The catalogue shows that in fact Titus owned multiple editions of Aesop. Several unidentifiable editions in both Latin and English occur near the beginning of his catalogue (items 11-14) and later acquisitions include more Aesops in English and in Latin, including a new translation published in 1705 (228, 300) and an Aesop 'with the Reflections' (380). No doubt with further research many more of the masses of proverbs, stories and aphorisms accumulated in the commonplace books could be traced to specific printed texts listed by Titus in his catalogue.

---

[26] As, for example, 'the Praise of Wisdom . . . written by me' (no. 201); 'A Description of the Church and School of Ashover, written by me' (202) and 'the Art of Poetry, or Come ye gallants Look and buy, here is mirth & Melody, written by Leo W.' (205). The latter two volumes both survive and contain some material copied out or imitated, but consist largely of authorial compositions. Compare 'The Clerk & his Companions, or a book of my own Composing in question & answer [. . .]' (235), which does not survive.

[27] This sequence possibly represents all or part of one of the 'written' copies of Quarles which Titus catalogued separately, presumably before this volume was assembled.

[28] DRO D5775/2, p. [343], identified in pencil by a later hand as L'Estrange's Aesop IV. 237; p. [346] identified as Aesop no. 500; p. [347] identified as L'Estrange's 'second pt no. 130'.

Popular print

That Titus had an interest in historical and political events is clear from the books he collected in his maturity: works on military heroes like the Duke of Marlborough (items 154, 251) and his ally Prince Eugene (249, 347, 348) occur particularly in the later parts of the catalogue. It is not surprising, therefore, to find snippets of historical information – presumably copied from printed sources – in his commonplace books. The larger commonplace volume contains, for example, a description of the damage occasioned by the Great Fire of 1666, headed 'Upon the dreadful fire of London/burned by the Papists sep. 2. 1666', apparently extracted from a printed account.[29] Given his devotion to books it is interesting that Titus notes the losses in the fire 'espetially of Books, (of which alone were Lost the value of near 150000ˡⁱ[)]'. As well as the extracts from Quarles and Aesop already mentioned, the manuscript known as 'Wheatcroft's collections' assembles a wealth of information including mnemonic poems, anecdotes, aphorisms, precepts and lists (of, for example, the seven wonders of the Peak, and dates of local fairs).[30] Many items were no doubt copied from printed sources, though these are rarely attributed. One attribution occurs on pp. 202-12, where 'a Twelvemonth's observations for every Month in the year' are given 'as they are noated by Poor Robin', presumably a reference to 'Poor Robins Almanac', which appears as the penultimate entry in the catalogue.[31] In another case Titus's attribution tells us something of his reading beyond the books listed in the catalogue: one of his questions and answers ('Q. Whence comes the proverb, As drunk as David's Sow?') he accurately notes as being taken from *The British Apollo*, p. 572, which is also the source of others of his questions and answers.[32]

---

[29]   DRO, D5775/3, p. 26. Titus's account follows almost exactly that given by Benjamin Harris in *The Protestant Tutor*, which appeared in many editions 1679-[1720?].

[30]   DRO, D5775/2.

[31]   The position of 'Poor Robins almanac' at the end of the catalogue suggests that the almanac was acquired in the late 1740s or early 1750s. No copy of the almanac with the verses noted by Titus has, however, been found.

[32]   *The British Apollo: Containing about Two Thousand Answers to Curious Questions in Most Arts and Sciences, Serious, Comical, and Humorous, Approved of by Many of the Most Learned and Ingenious of Both Universities, and of the Royal Society*, 3rd edn (London, 1718). (Three-volume editions appeared in 1726 and 1740).

Other passages, unattributed by Titus but identified using Early English Books Online, indicate that Titus was drawing much of his material from a range of popular printed texts which, judging by his catalogue, he seems not to have owned. These include printed repositories of sentences and moral sayings such as Curray's *Sententiae selectae*, 1732; the compendium *The British Apollo* mentioned above; and Nathaniel Crouch's *The Vanity of the Life of Man* from which he copied two lengthy poems.[33] Notable is his frequent use of older texts, such as *Recreation for Ingenious Head-peeces*, 1654, one of the *Wits Recreations* series of collections of epigrams, epitaphs and fancies; *Westminster-drollery*, 1671; and Owen Felltham's *Resolves*, first published in 1623[?], from which Titus copied Felltham's poem on dreams.[34] It is, however, amongst the items more difficult to identify that Titus's manuscripts are perhaps most valuable: as evidence of lost editions of known printed texts, and of printed texts (particularly cheap broadsides and chapbooks) now apparently completely lost. One example of this is a gathering in 'Wheatcroft's collections' which appears after p. 318. The whole gathering has had its top right-hand corners removed, presumably to excise pre-existing page numbers, but has not been re-paginated after being added to the volume. The gathering is incomplete, and begins part-way through a poem:

> Then starts up the Priest demure
> who of mens Souls takes Care & Cure
> and packs them all to heaven besure
> therefore of Right challenges he
>   to have the Superiority.

This is from a satirical poem printed as a quarter sheet and listed in the Dicey catalogue of 1754 as 'The Tripple Plea: Or, The Lawyer, Physician, and Divine, striving for Superiority, worthy utmost Observation'.[35] The only printed copy so far found in the UK appears

---

[33] Edward Curray's *Sententiae selectae* (London, 1732); *British Apollo*; Nathaniel Crouch, *The Vanity of the Life of Man* (London, 1698). 5th edn.

[34] Anonymous, *Recreation for Ingenious Head-peeces* (London, 1654); Anonymous, *Westminster-drollery* (London, 1671); Owen Felltham, *Resolves* (London, 1647), p. 165.

[35] William and Cluer Dicey, *A Catalogue of Maps, Prints, Copy-books, Drawing-books, &c. Histories,* [...] *Printed and Sold by William and Cluer Dicey, at their Warehouse* (London, 1754) where it is listed as no. 127 in 'Copper Royals' (p. 19) and no. 132 in 'Wood Royals', p. 32.

at the end of *The History of a Good Bramin*, published by the radical publisher Daniel Isaac Eaton in 1795. ESTC, however, lists the same item, now in the Huntington Library, California, as printed by Samuel Keimer in Philadelphia with the suggested date '[1723?]'. In this and several other cases Titus's manuscripts offer new evidence for apparently fugitive and ephemeral items, pre-dating surviving printed copies and pointing to the earlier circulation in England of popular texts now known only in survivals from the later eighteenth century.

The most striking and tantalizing example of material of this kind is a page headed 'These 12 Good Rules were found in the Studdy of King Charles ye first of Blessed Memory' (Figure 7).[36] Not surprisingly, no such title is listed in Titus's catalogue of books; and, in any case, had he owned any broadsides he would no doubt have displayed them as wall decorations, constantly present to the eye, rather than needing to record them in his memorandum book. The rules as listed by Titus are as follows:

Prophene	. . . . .	No Divine Ordinance.
Touch	. . . . .	No State-matters.
Ourge	. . . . .	No Healths.
Pick	. . . . .	No Quarrels.
Maintain	. . . . .	No Opinions.
Incourage	. . . . .	No Vice.
Repeat	. . . . .	No Grievances.
Reveal	. . . . .	No Secrets.
Make	. . . . .	No Comparisons.
Keep	. . . . .	No bad-company.
Make	. . . . .	No long-meals.
Lay	. . . . .	No wagers

These Rules observ'd, thou wilt obtaine
thy Peace and everlasting gaine.

Adam Fox notes that 'the ubiquity of King Charles's Twelve Good Rules was [...] indicative of the popularity of sententious advice on the printed sheet'.[37] That 'King Charles's rules' were popularly associated with humble homes, cottages and inns and were recognisable by all levels of society in the eighteenth century is suggested by the many

---

[36] DRO, D5775/2, p. 175. The attribution to Charles I is discussed below.
[37] Fox, *Oral and Literate Culture*, p. 149.

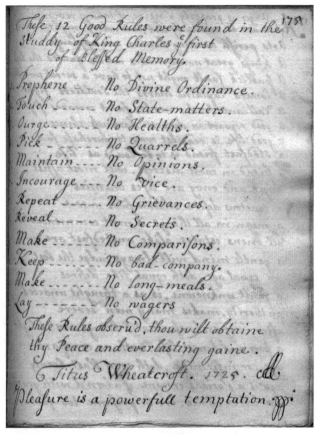

Fig.7 Titus Wheatcroft, untitled commonplace book known as 'Wheatcroft's Collections', DRO, D5775/2, p. 175. Reproduced with the permission of Derbyshire Record Office

casual references made to them by writers such as George Crabbe and Oliver Goldsmith.[38] Thomas Bewick, describing in his *Memoir* the variety of woodcuts he had known as a boy, says: 'A constant one in every house, was "King Charles' Twelve Good Rules".'[39]

---

[38] George Crabbe, *The Parish Register*, Part 1 (1807); Oliver Goldsmith, *The Deserted Village*, l. 232 (1770) and see also his 'Description of an Author's Bedchamber', l. 12 (1760).

[39] Thomas Bewick, *A Memoir of Thomas Bewick, Written by Himself* (Newcastle, 1862), p. 246.

It is ironic, if unsurprising, that only three printed copies of a text apparently so widely distributed have so far been found, of which only one is in a public collection. One of these three copies was Bewick's own. The sale catalogue of Bewick's effects in Newcastle lists as item 341 'Twelve Good Rules, found in the Study of King Charles the First of Blessed Memory. A rare and interesting Broadside. Surmounted by a large and curious woodcut of the King's Execution', which was stamped with Bewick's mark.[40] Morris Martin reports that it was sold to a Mr Price for £2 1s. 0d. and, having turned up in 1987 in an antique shop in Cambridge, is now in private hands.[41] A second surviving copy was reported in the 1950s as hanging in the Equerries' Entrance to Windsor Castle and its survival there, varnished and framed, was confirmed in 1987.[42] There, the rules are listed in exactly the same order as that in which Titus lists them, and the title is arranged around an inset dropped-in woodcut of Charles's execution. The third known copy is in the British Library, in the collection of Miss Sarah Sophia Banks.[43] By a curious coincidence Miss Banks (1744-1818), collector of broadsides and other antiquarian printed items, was the sister of the naturalist Sir Joseph Banks and great-granddaughter of William Hodgkinson of Overton in the parish of Ashover, Derbyshire.[44] This is the William Hodgkinson who, in 1703/4, built the Ashover school to which Titus was appointed master at its opening and which is in part the subject of his 'Church and School' manuscript.[45] Titus must have had many dealings with William Hodgkinson over the business of the school, and wrote an epitaph on Hodgkinson's death in 1731

---

[40] Morris Martin, 'The Case of the Missing Woodcuts', *Print Quarterly*, 4 (1987), 342-61.

[41] Martin, 'The Case of the Missing Woodcuts', fig. 229.

[42] Its presence was first reported in 1952 in Ray Nash, 'An American Colonial Calligraphic Sheet of King Charles's Twelve Good Rules at Dartmouth College Library', *The Library*, 5th ser., 7 (1952), 111-16 (pp. 114-15). Martin, 'The Case of the Missing Woodcuts', p. 357, reproduces the Windsor Castle copy (as fig. 239), examined in 1987, arguing that it predates the Banks copy described below.

[43] Item 12 in British Library shelfmark LR 301.h.10; illustrated in Martin, 'The Case of the Missing Woodcuts', p. 351. The order of the 'rules' is the same as in the Windsor copy and the inset of the execution scene is also present, but Martin judges this to be an earlier copy than that at Windsor. 'No. 88' is printed in the top right corner.

[44] John Gascoigne, 'Sarah Sophia Banks', in *ODNB* < http://www.oxforddnb.com > [accessed 21 June 2011]

[45] Philip Riden, 'William Hodgkinson', *ODNB* < http://www.oxforddnb.com > [accessed 21 June 2011]

included in his 'Church and School' volume.[46] The Overton estate was bequeathed to William Banks, the father of Joseph and Sarah Sophia. In 1741, while Titus was still schoolmaster, the family moved from Overton to Revesby in Lincolnshire, and Overton was eventually inherited by Sir Joseph, with whom his sister Sarah lived for much of her adult life. To suggest that the copy of the 'rules' now in the British Library and collected by Miss Banks originated in Ashover is no more than speculation. Nonetheless, its survival in her collection is a tantalizing hint of a possible source at Overton for the rules Titus carefully copied out.

Not surprisingly, given their wide circulation, the 'rules' are to be found in the catalogues of the Diceys, the most prolific producers of cheap print in the eighteenth century. The 1764 Dicey and Marshall catalogue lists, as number fifty-one among the 'Copper Royals', a sheet entitled 'King *Charles's* Rules'.[47] Martin notes that it also appears as number eighty-eight in the Dicey catalogue of 1754, as the second of a set of ten royals all concerned with Charles I.[48] The extensive nature of the Diceys' export trade to America probably accounts for the appearance of the 'rules' across the Atlantic. A calligraphic copy made in 1759 by Richard Rogers, first schoolmaster of Oxford, Massachusetts, and headed 'Twelve good Rules found in

---

[46]   DRO, D5433/2, p. 40, epitaph for William Hodgkinson of Overton, buried on 9 December 1731.

[47]   Cluer Dicey and Richard Marshall, *A Catalogue of Maps, Prints, Copy-books, Drawing-books, Histories, Old Ballads, Patters, Collections &c Printed and Sold by Cluer Dicey and William Marshall* (London, 1764). The catalogue, with a substantial introduction, has been made available by Richard Simmons at:
http://www.diceyandmarshall.bham.ac.uk/index.htm. The Copper Royals are described as mostly 'excellently well Engraved, And Printed on good Paper, Each beautifully Ornamented and Embellished, according to the Subject'. The wholesale price was two shillings per quire 'plain' and four shillings per quire 'coloured'. See, 'Copper Royals' and 'Wholesale Prices' at < http://www.diceyandmarshall.bham.ac.uk > [accessed 21 June 2011].

[48]   Simmons notes that the status of the 1754 catalogue is unclear: 'internal evidence suggests that it was in fact issued in about 1760, more than three years after the death of William Dicey and seven years after William and Cluer Dicey had entered into a partnership with Richard Marshall'. ('The Diceys: Cheap Print in the Era of the Eighteenth-century Consumer Revolution', available at < http://www.diceyandmarshall.bham.ac.uk > [accessed 21 June 2011]). Martin assumes that a set of ten 'prints of the reign of Charles I' advertised by John Bowles in 1728 was probably the same as those sold by the Diceys, but offers no evidence of their individual titles.

the Study of King Charles the First of Blessed Memory' survives in Dartmouth College Library. There are only very slight differences between this and the version copied by Titus, and the border at the foot of the sheet has a variation of the couplet found on printed copies: 'These Rules Observed may obtain / Thy Everlasting Peace and gain'.[49] In this calligraphic copy, however, the inset woodcut of the execution scene found in the printed copies is replaced by a crude drawing of Charles I at prayer, reminiscent of the *Eikon Basilike* engraving by William Marshall.

The similarity of these eighteenth-century 'King Charles's rules' to a much earlier single printed sheet entitled *Table-obseruations*, c. 1615, (Figure 8) surviving in a unique copy in the library of the Society of Antiquaries, was noted as early as 1863.[50] Some of its precepts are also found in Burton's *Anatomy of Melancholy*, 1621: 'Be not opinative [*sic*], maintaine no factions. Lay no wagers, make no comparisons. Find no faults [...].'[51] Attempts in 1863 and, more recently, by Morris Martin in 1987 to attribute the *Table-obseruations* to another royal author, James I, are surely wishful thinking, there being no foundation for the attribution except for the (assumed) Jacobean date of *Table-obseruations*, the identification of one of the three variant rules, 'Take no Tobacco', with James's tendency to offer moral instruction and his known anti-tobacco stance, and the existence of a copy in Windsor Castle.[52] It is much more likely that a set of moral precepts already familiar in print in the early seventeenth century was at some point dusted off by an enterprising printer and repackaged as belonging to Charles I for commercial reasons.

The date at which this attribution to Charles I was made, however, is intriguing: it seems to have nothing to do either with an effusion of

---

[49]   Nash, 'An American Colonial Calligraphic Sheet', Plate II. Titus's concluding couplet is: 'These Rules observ'd, thou wilt obtaine / thy Peace and everlasting gaine', exactly the same version as found in the Banks and Windsor copies.

[50]   STC 23634.7. See *Notes and Queries*, 3rd ser., 3:63 (1863), 215; Nash, 'American Colonial Calligraphic Sheet', p. 113; Martin, 'The Case of the Missing Woodcuts', p. 354; and see Tessa Watt, *Cheap Print and Popular Piety, 1550-1640* (Cambridge, 1991), p. 234. The image in *Fig. 8* is produced by ProQuest as part of Early English Books Online. Inquiries may be made to: ProQuest, 789 E. Eisenhower Parkway, Box 1346 Ann Arbor, MI 48106-1346 USA.

[51]   Robert Burton, *The Anatomy of Melancholy* (London, 1621), sig. 2D7^v.

[52]   Martin makes no reference to the suggestion of attribution to James I in *Notes and Queries*, 3rd ser., 3:63 (1863), 215, but elaborates the same arguments.

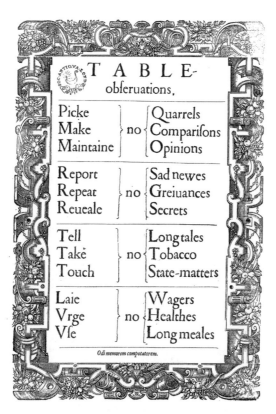

Fig. 8 *Table-obseruations*, c. 1615, Lemon Collection, Society of Antiquaries. Image published with permission of the Society and of ProQuest. Further reproduction is prohibited without permission

sympathy immediately following the execution in 1649, which made *Eikon Basilike* a best-seller, or with a revival of enthusiasm for the Stuarts expressed at the Restoration. In fact, *no seventeenth-century copy* of the text presented in the eighteenth century as 'King Charles's rules', or even an allusion to it, has been found. The earliest mention of 'King Charles's rules' is an advertisement in the *Daily Courant* of 23 July 1703, where they are offered for sale as

> Pious instructions, which were found hanging up in a black Ebony Frame, written in Gold, in King Charles the First's Closet soon after his death 1648 [*sic*], neatly printed upon a Broad-side with his Majesty's pic-

ture, to be put into Frames. Sold by George Sawbridge in Little Britain price 6d.[53]

Titus's copy, dated by him as being made in 1725, is the earliest known and is perhaps therefore a copy of Sawbridge's broadside. Certainly, Titus provides us with much earlier evidence of the popularity of the 'rules' than was previously known, all references to which (the Dicey catalogues and the allusions in memoirs and poems, discussed above, and the pictorial evidence described below) date from 1754 or after.[54] If the timing of their attribution to King Charles is uncertain, however, the persistence of the 'rules' beyond their eighteenth-century heyday is clear. In nineteenth-century America, as late as 1869, Harriet Beecher Stowe's novel *Oldtown Folks* has a scene in which the rules, framed and hung on a wall beneath a copy of a Van Dyck portrait of Charles I, are read aloud and memorized by a boy whose attention to these 'good rules for a man to form his life by' is heartily commended.[55]

Pictorial evidence from the eighteenth and early nineteenth centuries shows the rules *in situ* as wall hangings. They are depicted in an engraving entitled *Saint Monday*, which forms the frontispiece to *Low life or One Half of the World Knows Not How the Other Half Live* (c. 1742) and illustrates the interior of an inn; and in Rowlandson's print *Easter Tuesday or the Parish Meeting Dinner*, showing the interior of a workhouse.[56] A modern calligraphic copy of the 'rules' hangs today in All Saints church in Cotgrave, Nottinghamshire. The original set of rules, hanging beneath the ringing chamber, was destroyed in a catastrophic fire in 1996, which ruined much of the church. As part of the restoration project a replacement copy, painted on wood, was made. The relationship between this modern copy and Cotgrave's original version is unclear. The Cotgrave 'rules' have the usual twelve rules as found in the printed texts (though in a different order) but add

---

[53] I am grateful to Mark Knights for this reference, which he found in C. H. L. George, 'Topical Portrait Print Advertising in London Newspapers and the Term Catalogues 1660-1714', (unpublished Ph.D. thesis, University of Durham, 2005), p. 163.

[54] This omits Martin's suggestion that the 'rules' were included in the set of ten prints of Charles I's reign advertised by Bowles in 1728; but even were the identification in the Bowles catalogue secure, Titus's copy made in 1725 would remain the earliest evidence yet found for their circulation beyond London.

[55] Harriet Beecher Stowe, *Oldtown Folks* (Boston, 1869), ch. 25.

[56] Both illustrations are given in Martin, 'The Case of the Missing Woodcuts', figs 232 and 234.

a thirteenth ('Do nothing in anger'). This addition suggests that the usual 'Twelve good rules' heading was missing from the copy lost in the fire. Moreover, their identification as 'King Charles's Rules' is attributed to the Society of King Charles the Martyr, which again suggests that the usual heading was absent from the original Cotgrave hanging.[57] The modern replacement copy is headed 'for bellringers', but whether this was present in the original text or was added in the modern replacement to reflect the original association and position of the rules at Cotgrave is unclear.[58] Their presence in a church – and in connection with bell-ringing – suggests, of course, another possible source for Titus's copy. Perhaps All Saints in Ashover, like All Saints in Cotgrave, displayed such a set of rules for the edification of its bell-ringers. Certainly the behaviour of ringers was a concern of both Titus and his father. Titus's interest in bell-ringing is evident from his 'Church and School' manuscript, and Leonard includes a set of rhyming rules (with details of fines for breaking them) as well as oaths for ringers in his book of poetry.[59]

Original composition

Titus's use of printed texts becomes more difficult to demonstrate once we move from copying and adaptation to Titus's own original compositions; but here, too, the influence of printed models is at least a possibility. Cedric Brown's work on the poetry of Leonard Wheatcroft shows that as a poet Leonard moved from copying and imitation towards composition, and in some of Titus's own work the influence of printed models seems likely.[60] The use of running heads in manuscripts produced by both Leonard and Titus and the deployment of

---

[57] *All Saints Cotgrave: A Guide* (2005), p. 19. Crediting the Society with the identification of the rules as King Charles's suggests that the original was either the printed broadside with its title missing, or a calligraphic copy. The Cotgrave rules are listed on the Society of King Charles the Martyr website, available at < http://www.skcm.org/SCharles/Statements/statements.html > [accessed 21 June 2011].
[58] For a photograph of the modern hanging see *All Saints Cotgrave: A Guide* (2005), p. 19.
[59] DRO, D5433/1, last bifolium [unnumbered] contains: 'These orders I made when I was Clerke in 1683'; 'The. 12. Artickells for all Ringers to be sworne unto'; and 'The Ringers oath and covenant' [dated 1680].
[60] Cedric C. Brown, 'The Black Poet of Ashover, Leonard Wheatcroft', *English Manuscript Studies, 1100-1700*, 11 (2002), 181-202.

subtitles and generic titles indicate their awareness of printed form and genre and a desire to emulate the books and authors they read. Titles such as Leonard's 'the Art of Poetry, or Come ye gallants Look and buy, here is mirth & Melody', or Titus's 'the Poor-mans Peney well bestow'd, or a pound's-worth of witt for a penney' and 'The Clerk & his Companions, or a book of my own Composing in question & answer, it is titled Good-Company' suggest the Wheatcrofts' emulation of commercial book titles in framing their own manuscripts.[61]

Such is the intermingling of copying, adaptation and composition in Titus's manuscript volumes that differentiating them is problematic and, arguably, hopelessly anachronistic in assuming a neat separation between the media of print and manuscript. It is the case, for example, that much of what Titus wrote in his 'Church and School' volume seems to be of his own composition and is a mixture of recording, describing and systematizing local information (some of it gleaned orally, from stories told him by his father) so as to produce what is, overall, a new and original work. In particular, his description of the school at Ashover built by the Hodgkinsons is his own composition, a proud record of his place of work for more than half a century. However, the volume contains much copying out of information, too: a midwife's certificate, oaths to be taken by church officers, the coronation oath, a 'terrier' of glebe lands owned by the church, visitation presentments and many other memoranda which no doubt had written or printed antecedents, some of them perhaps in parish records long since lost or destroyed. Anecdotes and information supplied orally, often by his father, are also included, and in his lists of epitaphs and the mottoes of church bells he was recording for posterity 'written' information from other sources altogether: the words inscribed on the very fabric of the church and its churchyard.

Conclusion: the Wheatcroft manuscripts as evidence

In order fully to understand Titus's practices as an owner of books and as a reader we have to take account not only of his catalogue but also of his reading as represented by the sometimes fragmentary evidence of his memorandum books. The manuscripts are powerful evidence of

---

[61] See DRO, D5433/2, item 205 (surviving as DRO 5433/1); items 233 and 241 (possibly duplicate entries); and item 235.

the Wheatcrofts as readers and also as *writers* in every sense: practising their penmanship, copying and adapting material from printed sources, and composing their own work in verse and prose. Moreover, in these manuscript volumes we have tantalizing evidence of a world of print, much of which – because of its ephemeral nature – has been lost; and it is in this area of popular cheap print that Titus Wheatcroft's manuscripts have a particular value in relation to the study of printed texts.

Several longer texts copied by Titus and so far unidentified are possibly survivals of texts otherwise completely lost, such as a 'Dance of Death' and the set of poems, mentioned above, on the twelve months which he attributes to 'Poor Robin'. His verse history 'of Joseph and his Brethren', in twelve sections, looks very like a chapbook text but is unlike any so far found. In other cases, such as 'King Charles's rules', Titus's manuscript copies indicate the existence of earlier, lost editions. Another such example is the poem 'The masters advice to his scholars', which appears in the 1789 edition of Dilworth's *A New Guide to the English Tongue*, but not in earlier surviving editions, indicating that the copy listed in Titus's book catalogue was perhaps from an edition which does not survive. The extended discussion of the example of 'King Charles's rules' suggests something of the complex interactions between popular print and manuscript writing in which Titus participated. It is necessarily inconclusive in terms of his sources: Titus could have been copying from a set of the 'rules' he had bought or borrowed, or a set that he had seen on display in a variety of possible places, such as a local inn, a church, a schoolroom or indeed a house such as Overton Hall. Whatever his source, Titus's copy made in 1725 predates the evidence for their widespread popularity by a quarter of a century.

Titus's manuscripts also give us at least a partial glimpse of the uses to which he put some of the printed books he recorded in his catalogue. That list of titles comes more vividly to life in the context of his own writing, and seeing the catalogue in its manuscript context confirms that reading and writing were central preoccupations in Titus's working life as Ashover's schoolmaster, in his local status as parish clerk, and in his intellectual and devotional life. This extract from his 'A Prayer for a Youth at School', summing up his heartfelt love of books and learning, provides a fitting conclusion:

Keep me from abusing my pen, and defiling my hand, in writing useless and hurtful stuff which will Corrupt my fancy, and spoil my relish of better things [...]

Communicate to me that true knowledge & Grace which shall raise me above a fondness for fine Clothes, or any childish vanities; and make me thankfull that I have Books.[62]

---

[62] DRO, D5775/3, p. 261.

Singing by the Book: Eighteenth-Century Scottish Songbooks, Freemasonry, and Burns

STEPHEN W. BROWN

The Rise of the Scots Song Immediately After the 1707 Union

A song that appears in a number of eighteenth-century collections begins with the following declaration:

> This world is a stage, where all men engage,
> And each acts his part in the throng;
> There is naught but confusion, mere folly, delusion,
> And the rest of it all is a song.

In the course of its ten verses, parsons, statesmen, doctors, soldiers, ship-masters, drovers, prudes, and coquettes give over long-winded piety, beguiling promises, quackery, preferment, grog, cheating, pride, and vanity to come together in a final, democratic chorus of grotesques:

> Let's each fill our glasses taste life as it passes,
> And each of us sing a good song.[1]

While the notion that singing contributes fundamentally to the making of community was certainly not a discovery of the Enlightenment, the eighteenth century did see popular music become a curiously powerful vehicle for the expression, even fomenting, of social change, most notably in Methodist hymn-singing and the marching songs of emergent radical-ism.[2] In eighteenth-century Scotland, popular song was the site for two conflicting linguistic embodiments of nationhood: the English of Britain and the Scots of Scotland. On the eve of the Union of 1707, James Watson issued the first volume of his *Choice Collection of Comic and Serious Scots Poems* (three parts, 1706, 1709, 1711; 2nd edition of Part One, 1713), inspired, no doubt, by the London success of Thomas D'Urfey's

---

[1] 'A Collection of Scots and English Songs', *The Free-Masons Pocket Companion* (Glasgow: Printed by Joseph Galbraith, 1765), pp. 210-11.
[2] See William Donaldson, *The Scottish Jacobite Song: Political Myth and National Identity* (Aberdeen, 1988), pp. 1-4, 72-125; W. Hamish Fraser, *Scottish Popular Politics: From Radical-ism to Labour* (Edinburgh, 2000), pp. 1-25; Bob Harris, 'Print and Politics', in *Scotland in the Age of the French Revolution*, ed. by Bob Harris (Edinburgh, 2005), pp. 164-95.

serial publication, *Wit and Mirth: Or Pills to Purge Melancholy* (six volumes, 1698-1720), which his 'Preface' surely denotes in deriding 'the
frequency of Publishing Collections of Miscellaneous Poems in our
Neighbouring Kingdoms'.[3] Although Watson's anthology is something of
a mishmash of Scottish and English poems mingled with a few Latin
selections, he asks his reader to 'give some Charitable Grains of Allowance' on account of the work 'being the first of its Nature which has been
publish'd in our Native Scots Dialect'.[4] The nationalist inclination here is
strong. Watson had been jailed for printing anti-English pamphlets in
1700 and his Jacobite motivation in publishing the *Choice Collection* is
indisputable.[5] He, in fact, initiated the century-long identity politics that
roots Scottish native pride in vernacular song and poetry (even if most
urban Scots required detailed glossaries to negotiate their way through the
printed vernacular).[6] Watson's sources are unclear and he only vaguely
refers to his dependence upon 'Generous Helps [...] from the Repositories
of some Curious and Ingenious Gentlemen' and 'Poems as had been
formerly Printed most Uncorrectly, in all respects, but are now copied
from the most Correct Manuscripts'.[7] The intention of making his *Choice
Collection* accessible to the common reader was no doubt the reason

---

[3]   'The Publisher to the Reader', in *A Choice Collection of Comic and Serious Scots Poems*
(Edinburgh, 1706), p. iii. In view of Watson's political position and his dislike for the
coming Union, his decision to publish these Scots poems when he did in 1706 can hardly
be considered mere coincidence. The subsequent volumes that appeared after the 1707
Union with their increasing inclusion of dialect pieces would only have reasserted the
Choice Collection's reputation as an act of resistance.

[4]   'The Publisher to the Reader', in *Choice Collection*, p. iii.

[5]   Watson's crime was printing the pamphlet *Scotland's Grievance Respecting Darien*.
Along with his prison sentence and fine, Watson was banned 'from entering within ten
miles of Edinburgh during the particular session of Parliament' in 1700-01, although he
appears to have continued printing during this period (Alastair Mann, *The Scottish Book
Trade 1500-1720: Print Commerce and Print Control in Early Modern Scotland* (East Linton,
2000), p. 185). Watson had also been summoned and sentenced for 'pseudo-Jacobite
printings' in 1690-91, see Mann, *Scottish Book Trade*, p. 184. James Hogg drew on
Watson's Jacobite reputation when alluding to the printer in *The Private Memoirs and
Confessions of a Justified Sinner* (Oxford, 1981), pp. 220-21.

[6]   The convention of glossing Scots poetry in print increased incrementally throughout
the century after Watson's publication, a phenomenon evident in both antiquarian
collections such as David Dalrymple's *A Specimen of a Book Intituled, Ane Compendious
Booke, of Godly and Spiritual Sangs* (Edinburgh, 1765) and such popular ones as William
Darling's *The Gold-Finch: A Collection of the Most Celebrated Songs, Scots and English*
(Edinburgh, 1777).

[7]   'The Publisher to the Reader', in *Choice Collection*, p. iv,

Watson sold it at a shilling per part or at 2s. 6d., for all three parts in calf-skin bindings. That price was certainly within the reach of tradesmen. Three aspects of Watson's strategy would become crucial to all subsequent editions of popular poetry and songs in Scotland: sources (were the texts traditional, contemporary or faux-traditional?); language (was Scots granted a privileged status and was the Scots authentic or put on?); and market (was the text designed for a wide or a restricted readership?). One might add 'affordability' to the list since it was rare for Scottish song collections – William Thomson's London-published *Orpheus Caledonius* (1725) is one of the exceptions – not to strive for a democratic chorus through inexpensive pricing. The vogue for Scots verse initiated by Watson, whether as poems or songs – and the distinction is not always clear – would ebb and flow throughout the eighteenth century until it achieved canonical status with the collections prepared by Burns, Hogg, and Scott, among others.

Watson was followed in Edinburgh by two major anthologies in the 1720s, each of which claims to be addressing the profound inadequacies of their common predecessor, the *Choice Collection*. One is well-known: Allan Ramsay's ubiquitous *Tea-table Miscellany* (1723); the other is the now quite rare and seldom discussed, despite its extraordinary merits, *Edinburgh Miscellany* (1720).[8] Both works targeted a female market, with the *Edinburgh Miscellany* actually promoting itself as having been published at the behest of 'a Society of Edinburgh Ladies'.[9] This group was, in fact, the Fair Intellectual Club, a secret women-only reading circle distinguished for being probably Edinburgh's first gathering of bluestockings. Curiously, however, while Ramsay's work emphasizes its Scots content, the *Miscellany* was proud to be devoid of the Doric. It was none the less assertively Scottish, insisting that it contained less 'refuse' than readers had come to anticipate 'in many English Collections of Poetry'.[10] The *Edinburgh Miscellany*'s 'Preface' also took aim at Watson. Where he had warned the reader that his collection's Scots verses might 'come not up to such a Point of Exactness as may please an over nice Palate', the editors of the *Miscellany* took up Watson's metaphor to insist that 'tho' some of the[ir] Dishes (as a certain Author writes) be not served in the

---

[8]   Allan Ramsay, *The Tea-Table Miscellany* (Edinburgh, 1723); Anonymous, *The Edinburgh Miscellany; Consisting of Original Poems, Translations, etc. by Various Hands* (Edinburgh, 1720). No volumes were issued beyond this first one.

[9]   Anonymous, *Edinburgh Miscellany*, p. iii.

[10]   Ibid.

exactest Order and politeness, but hash'd up in haste, there are a great many accommodated to every particular Palate'.[11] Elsewhere, the 'Preface' punned upon the phrase 'Scot-free (to use our own Idiom)', further distancing itself from the native coarseness of Watson's anthology.[12] Yet, despite this disdain for dialect, the *Miscellany* still declared, 'we are conscious of the Integrity and Generosity of our Endeavours for the Honour of *our Country* and the Improvement of the Youth' [emphasis mine].[13] The *Miscellany* thus appears to have considered both its attention to women readers and its suppression of the native tongue crucial to its national (and clearly Unionist) project; it seems to have been determined to present a native alternative to the overt Jacobitism of the *Choice Collection* by promoting a vehemently Scottish identity, but doing so within a self-consciously British context, and without the brogue. Certainly, as we shall see, many popular songbooks in eighteenth-century Scotland both targeted female readers and considered themselves nationalist publications. Although Watson and the Society of Edinburgh Ladies may have disagreed about the literary value of vernacular Scots, they were allied in making the forceful denigration of English miscellanies (and thus the implicit promotion of Scottish ones) a crucial part of their marketing strategies. The *Edinburgh Miscellany* is noteworthy for printing some early work by both John Home and James Thomson, as well as David Malloch, who would be engaged by Allan Ramsay to assist him with his own later and far more successful compilations, before going on to a career as a playwright in London where he anglicized his name to 'Mallet'. The nationalistic nature of the *Miscellany* is perhaps most evident in its two subtly Jacobite poems, 'Str....'s Farewell to the Hermitage' and 'The Holy Ode', which were both suppressed in the anthology's second printing, thus possibly underscoring the anonymous editor's support, however reluctant, for the recent Union; after all, more than a decade had passed since that historic change, and Edinburgh (if not the rest of Scotland) was beginning to reap its economic and cultural benefits. The *Edinburgh Miscellany* is an interesting early instance of establishing an aggressively Scottish cultural identity while encouraging the use of English in place of Scots as the preferred medium of literary communication in a united Britain. The eminent success of Malloch and especially

---

[11] Anonymous, 'Preface', in *Edinburgh Miscellany*, pp. iii-iv.
[12] Anonymous, 'Preface', in *Edinburgh Miscellany*, p. iii.
[13] Ibid.

Thomson as British, rather than Scottish, authors in London would demonstrate the wisdom of that strategy. It was left to Allan Ramsay, however, to find a way of being more culturally accommodating while still making the use of Scots, an acceptable novelty act under the marquee of Britishness.

This awkwardness about the literary place of Scots in an English literary world may be explained in part as an Edinburgh reaction to the London taste at the time for 'Scotch songs', or what David Johnson has described as 'somewhat debased popular songs of allegedly Scottish origin, some with fake tunes, all with fake words'.[14] Johnson's succinct description of the opportunism of Ramsay's reshaping of Scotland's musical tradition into something palatably nationalistic bears repeating here:

> A national song is usually made by taking a folk-song and rewriting first the words and then the tune, bringing them into line with the latest fashion, until nothing is left of the original but the use to which it is put, like the spade with the new blade and the new handle.[15]

Scots as a tongue was thought by the English to be archaic, quaintly historical, with something of the past echoing through its coarse musicality. Allan Ramsay – who had tested the post-Watson market with a small volume entitled *Scots Songs* in 1718 – followed the modestly successful *Edinburgh Miscellany* with his own hugely successful collection, the *Tea-table Miscellany*, in 1723. While Ramsay did not eschew Scots in the manner of his immediate predecessor, the Fair Intellectual Club, his inclusion of works in the native tongue was far from the raw authenticity of Watson and as such not wholly straightforward. He reworked many of D'Urfey's fashionably faux-Scots lyrics into something that would pass in his local Edinburgh market, used English texts abundantly, and proved surprisingly selective in the genuine Scots songs that he did include in his first issue of the *Tea-table*. Their numbers increased with subsequent editions, but in his use of Scots Ramsay was always genteel and sensitively aware of his urban readership – not unlike his renowned Shepherd – leaving the bulk of that sort of thing to his later two-volume *Ever Green*, with its antiquarian justification.[16] In making 'Doric' the fashionable term

---

[14]   David Johnson, *Music and Society in Lowland Scotland in the Eighteenth Century*, 2nd edn (Edinburgh, 2003), p. 130.

[15]   Ibid.

[16]   Allan Ramsay, *The Ever Green, Being a Collection of Scots Poems*, 2 vols (Edinburgh, 1724).

for the native Scots dialect, he deliberately linked its use in poetry with the pastoral echoes (and correctness) of classical Greek verse.[17] Many of Ramsay's earliest and most inauthentic native offerings, like 'The Yellow-haired Laddie', would reappear in almost every eighteenth-century collection of Scots songs – no matter how provincially obscure the imprint – until James Johnson's and George Thomson's collaborations with Burns.[18] Consequently, the study of the publication of Scots songs in the eighteenth century must carefully separate out such ersatz lyrics from genuine examples, which is where Burns's own reliable research proves so useful to the modern scholar. Ramsay was not unaware of the distinction himself. A 1724 proposal receipt for his *Ever Green* pocket volumes emphasizes the historical pedigree that the Ballantyne manuscripts provided for this new compilation, which he sold for six times the cost of Watson's *Choice Collection*. He cited Watson disdainfully in observing the need to recover some of the *Ever Green*'s texts 'from their Sufferings, by careless Publishers, ugly Types, and gray Paper'.[19] Ironically, although Watson is credited with vastly improving Scots printing through his own example and his publication of the *Art of Printing* (Edinburgh, 1713), his anthology in three parts is rather more reminiscent of past worst than future best practices in the trade.

---

[17] Johnson, *Music and Society*, p. 133; see Ramsay's 'Preface' to the 1728 two-volume collection of his own poetry where he argues for the placement of Scots 'Doric' alongside Hebrew, Greek and Latin as an 'heroick' tongue. Allan Ramsay, *Poems by Allan Ramsay* 2 vols (Edinburgh, 1728), I, pp. iii-v. Ruddiman was an antiquarian scholar and publisher, whose family firm would be responsible for much of the authentic Scots published before Burns.

[18] David Johnson's analysis (*Music and Society*, pp. 133-45) remains the best discussion of Ramsay's creation of the 'canon' of quasi-Scots poems that included 'The Yellow-haired Laddie'. On that canon's late dimensions see Donald Low, 'Introduction', *The Scots Musical Museum, 1787-1803, James Johnson and Robert Burns* (Aldershot, 1991), pp. 1-28. Burns made significant contributions to both James Johnson, *The Scots Musical Museum* (Edinburgh, 1787-1803) and George Thomson, *A Select Collection of Original Scottish Airs* (London, 1793-99).

[19] Ramsay's 'Proposal' for the *Ever Green* volumes also claimed that one of his primary sources ('a very curious old Book, quite out of Print') was a very rare copy, the rest 'having been gather'd up and burnt by the *Roman Catholicks*, in the Reign of Queen Mary'. A surviving Proposal Receipt, signed by Ramsay, is held in the National Library of Scotland (RB.s.1240). The 'Preface' to the *Edinburgh Miscellany* had already complained of the 'Patience [required] to peruse [Watson's *Choice Collection*] with all the Disadvantages that [its] bad Paper and Types afforded' (p. ii).

The publication of the *Ever Green* volumes would only have confirmed one of the primary attractions of Scots songs in print, and thus furthered the reputation of the *Tea-table*, by illustrating – as the latter's 'Preface' asserts – that 'their antiquity' is 'what further adds to our esteem for them'.[20] Ramsay, possibly following the example of the *Edinburgh Miscellany*, recognized the appeal of such collections to women. His 'Preface' ends by urging his songs to 'steal your selves into ladies bosoms', while the dedicatory poem with which he introduced the *Tea-table Miscellany*, explicitly pursued 'ilka lovely British lass' and enjoined that 'E'en while the tea's fill'd reaking round [...] Treat a' the circling lugs wi' sound, / Syne safely sip when ye have sung'.[21] One wonders if Ramsay actually imagined the members of the Fair Intellectual Club themselves 'sipping tea' in an Edinburgh drawing room and singing rounds from his collection. Here, we perhaps see a first instance of the resetting of folk culture to suit refined taste, something very much at the heart of George Thomson's agenda in producing the song collection for which he enlisted Burns's assistance, although this practice was vigorously resisted in another distinctive area of Scots song anthologies: masonic songbooks. Ramsay went on in his 'Preface' to identify himself as a compiler and editor who had 'kept out all the smut and ribaldry' that made earlier collections (particularly Watson's and D'Urfey's) unsuitable for women readers, so 'that the modest voice and ear of the fair singer might meet with no affront [...] the chief bent of all my studies being to gain their good graces'.[22] In closing his 'Preface', Ramsay predicted 'a thousand editions' for the *Tea-table Miscellany* which would, he hoped, 'be assured of favourable reception wherever the sun shines on the free-born chearful [sic] Briton'.[23] If those 'thousands' were a little wishful, Ramsay's *Miscellany* did see scores of editions, both legitimate and pirated, and his polite Scots became the measure by which native song would be judged for much of the eighteenth century, at least in Edinburgh. Indeed, he secured a place for Doric lyricism as a quaint aspect of the emerging democratic, optimistic vernacular of the true Briton, which survived the occasional incursions of the real thing by the likes of Robert Fergusson, until Burns

---

[20] Ramsay, *Tea-table Miscellany*, p. v.
[21] Ibid., p. viii; Ibid., 'Dedication', no page number.
[22] Ibid., p. vii.
[23] Ibid., p. viii.

set about collecting genuine examples of Scots songs from appropriate, and often oral, sources.[24]

Scottish Freemason Song Collections and the Vernacular 'Canon' Before Burns

One likely source for Burns's song collecting has been oddly neglected by scholars, despite – or perhaps because of – its origins in one of his own favourite social haunts, masonic lodges, where both oral and written transmission of authentic Scots had been unbroken from the late-seventeenth through the whole of the eighteenth century. The song anthologies most readily to hand in Scotland after 1750 were often those attached to masonic pocket histories. Taken as a group, they are perhaps the most representative expression of this eighteenth-century Scottish genre, with some twenty different editions bearing the imprints of more than a dozen publishers in ten different locations from Aberdeen to Falkirk.[25] The songbooks are also distinctively Scottish, differing from their English counterparts in ways that reflect the three criteria that were identified in the earlier discussion of Watson's *Choice Collection*: they draw on traditional sources alongside what they take from Ramsay's *Tea-*

---

[24] Fergusson's success did much to promote the printing of Scots songs and poems by returning a substantial profit to his publishers. The inclusion of a Fergusson poem or song (however spurious) guaranteed a volume's sales; Burns's name would do the same a generation later. Thus, in 1777, William Darling advertised his miscellany of Scots poems and songs as: '*The Gold-Finch* [...] to which is added, The Edinburgh Buck: An Epilogue, Written by *Mr. R. Fergusson*' [emphasis Darling's]. The advertisement is bound in with the copy in the National Library of Scotland. While Walter Ruddiman Jr was taking financial advantage of Fergusson's popularity to increase the circulation of his family's newspaper and magazine (*The Caledonian Mercury* and the *Weekly Magazine, or Edinburgh Amusement*), Fergusson may have attempted to print some of his poetry as chapbooks on James Tytler's home-made press. A drinking companion of Fergusson and fellow ne'er-do-well, Tytler published other Fergusson work and an obituary for his friend in the Edinburgh periodical the *Gentleman and Lady's Weekly Magazine* (Edinburgh, 1774-75), which he edited for John Mennons. See Rhona Brown and Gerard Carruthers, 'Robert Fergusson and *The Gentleman and Lady's Weekly Magazine*', *Eighteenth-Century Scotland*, 21 (2007), 10-13; also Stephen Brown, 'James Tytler's Misadventures in the Late Eighteenth-Century Edinburgh Book Trade, *Printing Places: Locations of Book Production and Distribution Since 1500*, ed. by John Hinks and Catherine Armstrong (New Castle, Del., 2005), pp. 47-63.

[25] For a bibliography of these song collections see Stephen W. Brown, 'Scottish Freemasonry and Learned Printing in the Later Eighteenth Century', *Worlds of Print: Diversity in the Book Trade*, ed. by John Hinks and Catherine Armstrong (New Castle, Del., 2006), pp. 71-89 (pp. 88-9).

table Miscellany; for the most part, they include respectable and occasionally significant amounts of authentic Scots, with the exceptional cases explicable through the peculiarities of their sites of publication; and they are inclusive, always priced to be affordable to a socially representative readership, while assuming – as the printer himself often tells us in notes to the reader – that women will make up a considerable portion of their market. In fact, these song collections were commonly published separately from the masonic histories that they appear designed to complement and, even when sold together, usually had their own title-page, imprint, and individual pricing, because most booksellers felt that non-masons, and women in particular, would be more interested in the songs than the history of the Lodge. The prefatory remarks of one compiler speak for his colleagues in declaring his decision 'to subjoin a few of the most Celebrated Scotch and English Songs for [the] amusement' of readers 'not initiated into the Mysteries of Free-Masonry'.[26] Such would include women, whose names are sometimes inscribed on the title-pages of surviving copies of these anthologies. Masonic song collections were also ultimately closer to Watson's than Ramsay's, and thus anticipated Burns's in emphatically distinguishing themselves from the parallel English tradition. They established a Scottish character for masonic songbooks that reflected authentic regional identities and espoused an historic respect for what separated Scottish masonry from its belated English and continental cousins.[27]

The first masonic songbook to appear in Scotland was probably *A Pocket Companion for Free-Masons*, issued at Glasgow in 1748, which was nothing more than a piracy of the song selection printed with Smith's English handbook at London in 1735.[28] It is only with William Cheyne's edition of 1752, and the lapse of the copyright on the fourteen original masonic songs printed with James Anderson's *Constitutions*, that the true line of Scottish masonic song collections commenced, although Cheyne, who along with the Donaldsons, was among the period's chief Scottish literary pirates, still poached most of his volume's content.[29] There were

---

[26] Anonymous, *The Young Free-Mason's Assistant, Being a Choice Collection of Mason Songs* [...] *to which are Added Celebrated Songs, Scotch and English* (Dumfries, 1784), p. 5.
[27] On the distinguishing characteristics of Scottish freemasonry see David Stevenson, *The Origins of Freemasonry: Scotland's Century, 1590-1710* (Cambridge, 1988).
[28] William Smith, *A Pocket Companion for Free-Masons* (London, 1735).
[29] James Callendar, *The Free-Mason's Pocket Companion* (Edinburgh, 1752); James Anderson, *The Book of Constitutions* (London, 1723).

no fewer than five collections and reprints in Leith, Edinburgh, and Glasgow through 1760, including one brought out that year by Robert Bremner who published the first handbook of music theory in Scotland in 1755.[30] None of these, however, compiled anything but ceremonial or self-referential masonic songs, and no examples in Scots were anthologized to this point. The 1750s also saw a dramatic resurgence in the printing of musical scores in Scotland, principally through the arrival in Edinburgh of Robert Bremner; Scottish masonic songbooks, however, never included musical notation, unlike other increasingly sophisticated Scottish song collections of which James Johnson's *Scots Musical Museum* (1787-1803) and its immediate imitator, *The Edinburgh Musical Miscellany* (1792), are prime examples.[31] Starting in 1761, William Auld printed in Edinburgh three consecutive editions of what would be, for over forty years, the Grand Lodge of Scotland's 'official' handbook, expanding with each printing his selection of masonic songs.[32] Although the total reached fifty-five items with the 1772 third edition, Auld never anthologized Scots lyrics and stayed strictly with masonic pieces; he did, however, print many more songs than one would find at the time in any equivalent English masonic handbook. In 1766, the year after his second edition of masonic songs, Auld, again in partnership with William Smellie, printed *The Chearful Companion*, for William Gibb in Edinburgh, a collection of over one hundred popular songs that included several Scots examples and had little in common with its English namesakes.[33] Thus, Auld was not averse to Scots songs, however deliberate he may have been in excluding them from his masonic publications. The absence of vernacular songs from the Edinburgh masonic collections of the 1750s, 1760s, and 1770s may have to do with the insistence on English as the town's literary language during the period and the association of Scots with Jacobitism

---

[30] *A Collection of the Songs of Masons* (Edinburgh, 1752); *A Collection of the Songs of Masons* (Leith, 1754); *A Choice Collection of Songs to be Sung by Masons, Some of which were Never before Published* (Glasgow, 1755); *A Collection of Free Masons Songs* (Edinburgh, 1758); and *A Collection of Free Masons Songs* (Edinburgh, 1760).

[31] James Johnson. *Scots Musical Museum*, 6 vols (Edinburgh, 1787-1803); Anonymous, *The Edinburgh Musical Miscellany*, 2 vols (Edinburgh, 1792).

[32] The editions were William Auld, *The Free-Masons Pocket Companion* (Edinburgh: Ruddiman, Auld and Company, 1761); *The Free-Masons Pocket Companion* (Edinburgh: Auld and Smellie, 1765 and *The History of Masonry; Or, The Free-Masons Pocket Companion*, 3rd edn (Edinburgh: William Auld, 1772). William Smellie, like Auld, was a prominent Edinburgh masonic publisher.

[33] Anonymous, *The Chearful Companion* (Edinburgh, 1766).

and the disruption of 1745. The 1770s saw a scholarly and popular reclamation of the vernacular through Walter Ruddiman Jr's publication of Robert Fergusson's poetry in his *Weekly Magazine* with its circulation of over 3000 copies per issue and David Dalrymple's two anthologies of classical Scots poetry, among other works.[34] However, the notion that Scots was not the language of the literati persisted in Edinburgh, passing from Adam Smith and David Hume to Henry Mackenzie and Dugald Stewart.[35] Whatever the reason, and it may simply have been an adherence to convention in Edinburgh as the home of Scotland's Grand Lodge, no masonic songbook printed in Edinburgh in the eighteenth century included any Scots items, with the sole exception of the eccentric compilation put together by, and printed for, Gavin Wilson in 1788. Among eighteen songs of his own composition and some forty from other sources, he had a single Scots item: 'Pate Herron was a gauger trim / And Glasgow town ne'er kent his match'.[36] The reference here to Glasgow is a pleasing coincidence since the practice of including popular and authentic Scots lyrics in masonic songbooks originated there in 1765 with the printer Joseph Galbraith.

---

[34] The Ruddimans were notoriously Jacobite and their family newspaper, the *Caledonian Mercury*, had openly supported the Pretender, Charles Stuart, in 1745 (W. J. Couper, *The Edinburgh Periodical Press*, 2 vols (Stirling, 1908), II, 45-9). For a discussion of the *Weekly Magazine*'s circulation, see Stephen W. Brown, 'Wrapping the News: *The Historical Register* and the Use of Blue Paper Cover Wrappers on Eighteenth-Century Scottish Magazines', *Journal of the Edinburgh Bibliographical Society*, 1 (2006), 61-5. Works supporting the use of the vernacular were *Ancient Scottish Poems*, ed. by David Dalrymple (Edinburgh, 1770) and *Specimen of a Book* (Edinburgh, 1765). Another influential antiquarian collection of the 1770s was David Herd, *Ancient and Modern Scottish Songs, Heroic Ballads*, 2 vols (Edinburgh, 1769-76). William Tytler's 'Dissertation on the Scottish Musick', first published in Hugo Arnot, *History of Edinburgh* (Edinburgh, 1779) was much reprinted, often as an introduction to song collections.

[35] These attacks on and prescriptions against Scotticisms proliferated in the late eighteenth century and contrast with the vernacular song revival. James Beattie's *Scoticisms, Arranged in Alphabetical Order: Designed to Correct Improprieties of Speech and Writing* (Edinburgh, 1787) is best known. Its first edition in Edinburgh ironically coincided with the first Edinburgh edition of Robert Burns, *Poems, Chiefly in the Scottish Dialect*, (Edinburgh, 1787). See, also, Marina Dossena, *Scotticisms in Grammar and Vocabulary* (Edinburgh, 2005).

[36] Gavin Wilson, *A Collection of Masonic Songs, and Entertaining Anecdotes* (Edinburgh, 1788), pp. 67-8. The appearance of his work in 1788 was no doubt facilitated by the vogue for 'natural' poetry written by working men, established the year before in Edinburgh by Burns.

Galbraith issued his *Free Masons Pocket Companion* in Glasgow that year which incorporated much of what Auld had published in his Edinburgh text earlier in 1765, including his collection of masonic songs. However, Galbraith added as an appendix with its own pagination, a new compilation of popular songs in Scots and English that had nothing to do with masonry, although they were no doubt commonly sung in lodges. He provided this section with its own title to distinguish it from the masonic text and songs that preceded it: 'A Collection of Scots and English Songs', prioritising in that title the Scots over the English.[37] Galbraith's songs were reprinted in 1771, once again in Glasgow, by Peter and John Tait and their partner James Brown, and their edition was Auld's sole competition in Scotland's lucrative masonic pocket-book market for well over a decade, until 1784, when *The Young Free-Mason's Assistant,* appeared in Dumfries, printed by Robert McLachlan.[38] This publication was followed by four further masonic song collections, all offering Scots vernacular lyrics, and printed in 1788, 1791, 1792, and 1798, at Edinburgh, Aberdeen, Ayr, and Glasgow, respectively.[39] It is probably no coincidence that all of these texts appeared on the heels of the 1787 Edinburgh edition of Burns's *Poems, Chiefly in the Scottish Dialect.*[40]

The explicitly masonic songs in each of these anthologies vary somewhat, although only the Tait/Brown edition of 1771 actually mixed in a few drinking songs with no references whatsoever to masonry, notably 'The Bottle Preferr'd, or Proud Woman I Scorn You'.[41] Thus, songs actually about masonry are never ribald themselves and their allusions to

---

[37] *Free Masons Pocket Companion* (Glasgow, 1765), pp. 202-38.

[38] Anonymous, *Young Free-Mason's Assistant.* McLachlan acknowledged Galbraith's example by placing 'Scotch' ahead of 'English' songs, but not all the subsequent masonic collections did so.

[39] Gavin Wilson, *A Collection of Masonic Songs and Anecdotes for the Use of All the Lodges* (Edinburgh, 1788); Anonymous, *The Entertaining Songster; Consisting of a Selection of the Best Masonic Songs Now in Use Among the Very Worthy Brethren of Free Masons, to which is Added a Very Considerable Collection of the Best Miscellaneous Songs, Serious and Comic, among which are All Those New and Much-Admired Songs of the Celebrated Dibdin, Edwin, and Others; with Many Admired Comic and Other Songs, that Never Appeared in any Other Collection. Together with a Very Great Variety of the Most Approved Masonic and Miscellaneous Toasts and Sentiments* (Aberdeen: Andrew Shirrefs, 1791); Anonymous, *The Free Mason's Pocket Companion* (Ayr: John and Peter Wilson, 1792). Anonymous, *The Free-Mason's Pocket Companion* (Glasgow: William Bell for Richard Scott, 1798).

[40] Robert Burns, *Poems, Chiefly in the Scottish Dialect* (Edinburgh, 1787).

[41] This song is one of the early print examples of the many progenitors of Burns's 'Big-Bellied Bottle'. *A Collection of Scots and English Songs* (Glasgow, 1771), p. 188.

drink are always restrained, in keeping with the tone of the English examples of the period and especially the official directives given by William Preston. He was a London-based Scot who had apprenticed as a printer in Edinburgh before settling in England and writing his *Illustrations of Masonry* which, in its many editions, encouraged moral correctness in all masonic entertainments.[42] Scottish masonic texts apparently respected that practice in so far as they relegated their ribald and vernacular songs to appendices and supplements once Galbraith initiated the practice of including these kinds of popular lyrics with masonic ones. Across the border, however, official English collections of masonic songs never anthologized any questionable or popular materials; thus the choice by Scottish masonic printers to do so was unique, and perhaps nationallistically motivated. Galbraith's 'Collection of Scots and English Songs' fills thirty-eight pages and includes thirty-nine songs of which twelve are in authentic Scots and twenty have content that ranges from mildly sexual to openly ribald. I have seen one surviving copy annotated in a contemporary hand describing the text of these songs as 'Very incorrect' and offering emendations that make the scandalous sections even more explicit.[43] While the Tait/Brown collection, as already noted, made some alterations to Galbraith's masonic songs, it reprinted the Scots and English popular ones exactly, including their apparently 'Very incorrect' passages. Of the thirty-eight songs, only a dozen appeared in any of Allan Ramsay's anthologies, and the rest have no readily identifiable source. It is likely that all were songs regularly sung in Glasgow lodges and collected there by the anonymous editor. Likewise, those songs also found in Ramsay's anthology are more probably derived from their performance in lodges and elsewhere than copied from his collections, although Peter Tait had reprinted the Edinburgh edition of Ramsay's *Poems* in 1770, the year before his masonic edition which he sold from his Glasgow shop near the Head of the Saltmarket.[44]

---

[42] William Preston, *Illustrations of Masonry* (London, 1772). See my discussion of William Preston's conservative attitude towards masonic song collections in, 'Scottish Freemasonry and Learned Printing', p. 80.

[43] The observation, 'Very incorrect', is written in a contemporary hand beneath the title, 'A Collection of Scots and English Songs', in, *Free Masons Pocket Companion* (Glasgow: John Galbraith, 1765), p. 202. Subsequent annotations in this copy suggest that the printed text was taken from an oral source; the errors noted in the marginalia are certainly not typographical. The volume is in a private collection.

[44] Allan Ramsay, *Poems by Allan Ramsay* (Glasgow, 1770).

The Tait/Brown pocket companion of 1771 probably found its way to Edinburgh where its competitive presence would have encouraged a turf-conscious Auld to reprint his own 1761 companion for a third time in 1772;[45] but it may just have served as the standard text for the Glasgow lodges in the way that the 'Auld' did for those in Edinburgh. Whatever the case, the Tait/Brown songbook with its savoury Scots appendix of popular songs suggests that Glasgow's masons (and its citizens) may have been readier to accept their coarser vernacular song tradition than were their Edinburgh counterparts. Certainly, by the 1770s Glasgow had significantly surpassed Edinburgh as a production centre for cheap literature, while the capital seemed uncomfortable with the whole business of printing the 'voice of the people'.[46] This should not be surprising when we recall that both Fergusson and Burns were outsiders who brought their Scots revival to Edinburgh from provincial towns, rather than discovering it there. However, all Scottish collections, regardless of their site of publication, agree on one point: no ceremonial or identifiably masonic songs, however comic, are ever recorded in Scots. Masons in Scotland clearly accepted the convention of using English to distinguish serious literature and must have placed masonic lyrics in that category; at the same time, all but one of the masonic songbooks printed outside Edinburgh after 1765 appended a miscellany of popular songs of which as much as thirty percent of the content in some instances, was in Scots. Even if Edinburgh's masons decried dialect in the printed songs they sang during their ceremonies, we know from Boswell's accounts that Scots lyrics were preferred when the rituals of the lodge had passed. With considerable glee Boswell records having sung 'my non-sensical Scotch song "Twa Wheels"' upon one such occasion.[47] One other point is absolutely essential to note: neither the Galbraith nor Tait/Brown editions indicated on their title-pages that their volumes included additional popular songs in Scots and English. These simply appeared at the end of the masonic materials, with only a modest running headnote to introduce them. This would seem to add some circumstantial weight to

---

[45] *History of Masonry*, 3rd edn (Edinburgh, 1772).

[46] John Scally points out that Glasgow produced nearly five times as many chapbooks as did Edinburgh in the second half of the eighteenth century. See his 'Cheap Print on Scottish Streets', in *The Edinburgh History of the Book in Scotland: Enlightenment and Expansion, 1707-1800*, ed. by Stephen W. Brown and Warren McDougall, (Edinburgh, 2011).

[47] James Boswell, *Boswell's Edinburgh Journals*, ed. by Hugh M. Milne (Edinburgh, 2001), p. 190.

the argument that including such material with the masonic text was, at the very least, unconventional. While the songs no doubt substantially helped sales and widened the appeal of the collection beyond the immediate masonic readership, announcing the inclusion of the songs on the title-page was something both printers chose not to do.

Three substantial masonic song anthologies (mentioned briefly above) appeared at Dumfries in 1784, Aberdeen in 1791, and Ayr in 1792, printed respectively by Robert McLachlan, Andrew Shirrefs, and John and Peter Wilson.[48] The first barely acknowledges Scots lyrics, but the other two were repositories for vernacular songs and would have been available to Burns while he was collecting materials for Johnson and Thomson in the 1780s and 1790s. McLachlan's *Young Free-mason's Assistant*, avoided anything racy or drunken, getting no more rowdy than some calls to 'bumper filling', and preferring the late Augustan artificiality of 'aethereal tours' and 'roseated bowers' to encounters coming through the rye.[49] The majority of its ninety-eight songs are conventionally masonic, but mixed in for the benefit of non-masons are a number of popular pieces, including two in Scots, 'Come gie's a sang' and 'Deil tak the wars', the former often associated with Robert Fergusson and both subsequently printed in Shirrefs' 1791 collection.[50] In fact, Shirrefs's Aberdeen volume *The Entertaining Songster* has the largest selection of Scots songs to appear in any masonic publication during the eighteenth century.[51] Among its twenty-five masonic and eighty-four miscellaneous lyrics, this anthology contained twenty-eight songs in Scots of which only four originated with Ramsay while one was from Burns ('Green grow the rashes'). The printer clearly conceived the anthology in two parts, carefully separating his masonic items from the miscellaneous ones and providing each with separate title-pages, their own pagination, and individual indices. Both sections bound together sold very cheaply at nine pence, stitched, but could easily have been sold separately at an even

---

[48] Anonymous, *Young Free-Mason's Assistant* (Dumfries, 1784); Anonymous, *The Entertaining Songster* (Aberdeen, 1791); Anonymous, *Free Mason's Pocket Companion* (Ayr, 1792). Anonymous, *The Free-Masons Pocket Companion* (Glasgow, 1798)

[49] Anonymous, *Young Free-Mason's Assistant*, pp. 110, 37.

[50] Ibid., pp. 126, 142.

[51] Andrew Shirrefs also vigorously promoted Scots verse in his short-lived but innovative *Caledonian Magazine or Aberdeen Repository* (1788-90). In 1790 he brought out his own collection with the, by-then widely recognized, title, *Poems, Chiefly in the Scottish Dialect*. My thanks go to Dr Iain Beavan for sharing with me his thoughts on Shirrefs's contributions to the vernacular revival in the Northeast of Scotland.

lower price. The paper quality is the poorest of any masonic publication that I have ever examined and the inking is bad. This was definitely a song collection for the masses and, for that very reason, an important one. It demonstrates that the masonic brand must have helped to promote the sales of even low-end printing. It also reaffirms the extent to which masonic publications outside Edinburgh were far more at ease with the inclusion of vernacular material than those printed in the capital. Shirrefs's miscellany was obviously intended for a local readership but it is none the less tempting to speculate about its having come to Burns's attention. Regardless, it is indisputably an emphatic instance of the regional popularity of Scots songs in print in the late eighteenth century. It is also interesting to note that masonic song collections – Shirrefs's is no exception – never included glossaries of Scottish words, perhaps because their regional readership was assumed to be familiar with the dialect.

The Wilson edition published at Ayr in 1792 meets much higher standards as a printed book, and unlike the Dumfries and Aberdeen anthologies, was intended for a wide distribution across central and southern Scotland, listing on its imprint, the booksellers 'J. & J. Fairbairn, Edinburgh; W[illiam] Anderson, Sterling; J. Duncan & Son; J. & M. Robertson; J. & W. Shaw, and A[ndrew] Macaulay', all of Glasgow, as joint partners in the publication.[52] The volume was also the first *Free Mason's Pocket Companion* published in Scotland since the third edition of William Auld's renowned *History of Masonry* in 1772. This new Wilson edition appears to have used the 1765 Auld version as its copy text and is satisfied with the forty-three masonic songs that originally appeared there. Its masonic history thus continued to derive from John Entick's London version of 1754 and bears his identifying motto.[53] The Wilsons save their innovations for the final section of their book where they append 'A Collection of the Most Approved English, Scotch, and Irish Songs', as described on the title-page, and thus make their volume the first official masonic companion to proclaim its breach of decorum so openly, as well as being the first one printed for an Edinburgh firm to include songs in Scots. It is important to note, however, that although sold in Edinburgh

---

[52]   Anonymous, *Free Mason's Pocket Companion* (Ayr, 1792), title-page.
[53]   Smith's motto, reprinted on the title-page of all the masonic texts that accepted his order of content, was: *Deus Nobis Sol & Scrutum*. See, Brown, 'Scottish Freemasonry and Learned Printing', pp. 86-7.

the work was not printed there, thus keeping up the practice of Edinburgh printers avoiding Scots songs in masonic collections. Galbraith, the Taits, and Brown, as we have seen, had diverted attention from their inclusion of popular lyrics in their volumes by neglecting to mention them on their title-pages. The Wilsons compiled one hundred miscellaneous songs, all indexed separately from the forty-three masonic ones. Of that one hundred, thirteen are in authentic vernacular with a further two derived from Ramsay in his faux-Scots. Among the former are two variants on sources for classic Burns songs: 'And gin ye meet a bonnie lassie' and 'I'll lay thee o'er the lea rig'.[54] Among the English songs is another variant source, 'One kind kiss before we part',[55] which is closer to Burns's 'Ae fond kiss' than the Dodsley poem usually cited by scholars as Burns's chief source.[56] The Wilsons also selected several politically controversial songs for their volume, including one on unfair taxation and an anti-war satire on the reality of military heroism, dangerous steps for printers to take in the early 1790s.[57] If nothing else, the politically radical aspects of the Wilsons' anthology provide a context for reasserting forcefully Burns's own undeniable radicalism, and the volume's Ayr imprint only underscores the argument set out here for bringing masonic collections into any discussion of the song-writing culture that surrounded and influenced Burns in his work for Johnson and Thomson.

Conclusion

Most of the Scottish masonic song anthologies examined in this essay are exceptionally rare because, unlike the compilations made by Ramsay and Burns, they were produced exclusively for mass consumption and not to be bound and placed on library shelves. Only Auld's 1772 collection turns up fairly often, occasionally finely bound, because it was the one edition likely to be owned by one of Scotland's Grand Masters or be part of a laird's library because of its quasi-official status. It is the very ephemerality of the other editions that testifies to their importance as social

---

[54] Anonymous, *Free Mason's Pocket Companion* (Ayr, 1792), pp. 230, 247.

[55] Ibid., p. 254.

[56] James Kinsley first argued for Dodsley's 'The Parting Kiss' as Burns's source in the commentary for his *Poems and Songs of Robert Burns*, 3 vols (Oxford, 1968), III, 1379.

[57] Anonymous, *Free Mason's Pocket Companion*, (Ayr, 1792), p. 259 ('Hard, hard are the times') and p. 267 ('What a charming thing's a battle'). The collection also included the popular Cape Breton song, 'In the garb of old Gaul', p. 247.

documents. No doubt owned representatively across the classes because of the emphatically democratic nature of Scottish masonry, and used by both mason and non-mason (including women) because they provided cheap access to the most popular songs of the day, these books were also regionally printed and thus probably reflect local tastes in music quite accurately. Some of the copies often also contain manuscript versions of songs not recorded elsewhere.[58] Few of these songbooks have survived paradoxically because they were so popular in their own day and often so cheaply produced that they were handled until they disintegrated. As a group, these Scottish masonic songbooks from Galbraith of Glasgow to the Wilsons of Ayr provide book-trade scholars with a rare and authentic glimpse into popular culture as well as offering possible alternative sources to those normally cited by historians narrating the genealogy of Scots songs.[59] Masonic songbooks assumed that the secular chorus that came together to 'sing a good song' from their pages would include folk of all sorts.[60] Where Watson or the *Edinburgh Miscellany* or Ramsay strategically undertook to shape Scottish culture with their collections, the printers of the masonic songbooks were simply responding to what that culture actually was, and theirs may be the best record available to us of the musical ethos that sustained Burns and which he tried to reflect as an anthologist of popular songs.

---

[58] See the National Library of Scotland's copy of Anonymous, *The Chearful Companion* (Edinburgh: Auld and Smellie for William Gibb, 1766), shelfmark Mus.E.s.61. Bound in with the text are seventy pages of manuscript transcriptions of eighteenth-century Scots and English songs in the hands of the volume's two successive owners.

[59] Claire Nelson's otherwise fascinating study is typical in this regard ('Tea-table Miscellanies: The Development of Scotland's Song Culture, 1720-1800', *Early Music*, 28 (2000), 596-620). Ironically, the most important scholarly studies of eighteenth-century masonic songbooks downplay the contributions of Scottish anthologists and ignore the role of the vernacular completely. See H. Poole, 'Masonic Songs and Verse of the Eighteenth Century', *Ars Quatuor Coronatorum*, 40 (1938), 7-29; and A. Sharp, 'Masonic Songs and Songbooks of the Late Eighteenth Century', *Ars Quatuor Coronatorum*, 65 (1953), 84-95.

[60] Anonymous, *Free-Masons Pocket Companion* (Glasgow, 1765), p. 211.

The Sale of James West's Library in 1773

WILLIAM NOBLETT

In an age of great collectors, one of the more significant was James West. Today he is relatively unknown but he was, in his own time, distinguished in a number of fields. He was born in 1703, called to the Bar in 1728 and admitted at Lincoln's Inn ten years later. He was the MP for St Albans from 1741 until 1768, and under the patronage of the Duke of Newcastle, he held various important offices during that period. In 1743 he was appointed Secretary to the Chancellor of the Exchequer (an office he held until 1752) and from 1746-56 and 1757-62, he was Joint Secretary to the Treasury. He was elected to both the Royal Society and the Society of Antiquaries in November 1726, and served as the President of the former from 1768 until his death in 1772. In 1738 he had married Sarah Steavens, the daughter of a very wealthy timber merchant, and it is said that this marriage brought him £100,000 on top of his own inheritance of £1000 a year. Added to his generous Treasury stipend, and later pension, this enabled him to indulge fully his collecting instincts.[1]

He is chiefly remembered for this and in particular as the owner of an exceptionally fine library which graced the shelves of his town house in Covent Garden and his country villa at Alscot, Warwickshire. His collections were justly famous and, when it became rumoured that after his death they were not to be sold, his fellow connoisseurs became concerned that they would not have the chance of enriching their own collections. James Granger was one. In a letter to Richard Bull, 18 July 1772, he reported that a 'good authority' had told him 'that Mr West had an estate of £12000 a year' and Horace Walpole suggested to William Cole that everyone thought West was 'so rich

---

[1] For biographical details of West, see W. P. Courtney, rev. by Patrick Woodland, 'James West' in *ODNB* <http://www.oxforddnb.com> [accessed 26 June 2011]. See also Sir Lewis Namier and John Brooke, *The House of Commons, 1754-1790*, 3 vols (London, 1964), III, 624-26; Mark Girouard, 'Alscot Park, Warwickshire', 3 parts, *Country Life*, May 15, 22 and 29, 1958, pp. 1064-67, 1124-1127, 1184-1186 and John Nichols, *Literary Anecdotes of the Eighteenth Century*, 6 vols (London, 1812), VI, 344-45. For West's library see R. Charles Lucas, 'Book-Collecting in the Eighteenth Century: The Library of James West', *The Library*, 5th ser., 3 (1948), 265-78.

that nothing will be sold'.[2] Walpole however was to be proved wrong. 'I understand', wrote Bull to Granger, October 1772, 'that Mr West has by no means died in affluence [...] for it seems his Pictures and Books are to be sold by Auction next April.'[3]

Bull was almost right. In fact, all of West's collections, not just his pictures and books were sold over forty-five days, 19 January to 24 April 1773. The auction of the library had originally been scheduled to run from Wednesday 3 February to Friday 2 April. However, Messrs Langfords, the auctioneers, decided to postpone the sale, according to the newspapers, 'in order that a more correct and descriptive catalogue of the said library may be formed' and commissioned Samuel Paterson to compile it.[4] The choice of Paterson was not surprising. He had been involved in the London book trade for twenty-five years and although he achieved little as a bookseller, he was successful as an auctioneer and was well known for the quality of his catalogues. John Nichols claimed that 'few men of this country had so much bibliographical knowledge', that 'his talent at cataloguizing was unrivalled' and some of his better-known catalogues were 'justly regarded as models'.[5] Dibdin was also a great admirer and characterised him as the 'renowned Champion of Catalogue makers'.[6]

The new catalogue was certainly an improvement. On both his title-page and in his 'Preface', Paterson highlighted three subjects within the collection that he believed to be particularly rich and important. The title-page pointed out that the library comprehended 'a choice collection of books [...] especially such as relate to the History and antiquities of Great Britain and Ireland, The early navigators, discoverers and improvers and Ancient English literature'.[7] It included a great number of books 'elucidated by Manuscript Notes and Original Letters' and 'embellished with scarce portraits and devices, rarely to be found'. Here also were to be found the works of 'Caxton [...] Wynkin de Worde, Pynson [...] and

---

[2]   Quoted in Lucy Peltz, 'Engraved Portrait Heads and the Rise of Extra Illustration: The Eton Correspondence of the Revd. James Granger and Richard Bull, 1769-1774', *Walpole Society*, 66 (2004), 1-161 (p. 98); *The Yale Edition of Horace Walpole's Correspondence*, ed. by W. S. Lewis, 48 vols (New Haven, 1937-83), I, 265.

[3]   Peltz, 'Engraved Portrait Heads', p. 100.

[4]   *Gazetteer and New Daily Advertiser*, 15 January 1773, p. 5.

[5]   Nichols, *Literary Anecdotes*, III, 735.

[6]   T. F. Dibdin, *Bibliomania*, 2 vols (London, 1842), II, 396.

[7]   *Bibliotheca Westiana; A Catalogue of the Curious and Truly Valuable Library of the Late James West, Esq.* (London, 1773).

the rest of the old English typographers'. In his 'Preface', Paterson expanded these observations and stated that many of the annotated works contained the notes 'of some our most respectable antiquaries' and mentioned, among others, Dugdale, Hearne, Stukeley and West himself. He concluded by observing that collectors of portraits ('Heads') would also not be disappointed.[8]

The bulk of the books on the early 'Navigators, discoverers and improvers', 171 titles, were sold over three days, the quartos on day fourteen, the octavos day fifteen and the folios on day seventeen. The small number of 'improvers' were mixed in amongst other works on philosophy, mathematics, husbandry and natural history. All the major explorers were represented and travels in most parts of the world covered. Pride of place in this section of the catalogue, however, must go to lot 3186, a beautiful atlas published in twelve folio volumes in Amsterdam in 1663 which sold for eighteen guineas. Yet in many respects the most unusual item here was a vellum copy of Breyden-bach's journal of his trip to Jerusalem, published in Mainz in 1486, and described by Paterson, quoting West's own words as a 'most rare book of Travels of the Religious in the Holy Land [...] contains the oldest views engraved that I have seen' – it sold for a mere fifteen guineas.[9]

The sale of Paterson's featured category of English literature – not necessarily confined to the 'Ancient' genre – was spread over five days and saw the disposal of 336 lots. Included was 'a fine copy in moroc' of the St Albans Schoolmaster Printer's '*Bokys of haukyng and huntyng*' published in 1486, but the real highlight here was without doubt three of Chaucer's works printed by Caxton.[10] A further seven editions of Chaucer were sold on the same day as these three Caxtons and in-cluded one edited by John Urry and published by Bernard Lintot in 1721 and five printed by Pynson between 1493 and 1526. To some extent, however, the most interesting was lot 2275, Thomas Godfray's 1532 edition which contained 'dyurs workes which were neuer in print before' and had tipped in 'two MS letters from Mr Rudd to Mr Ames, Oxon 1746; containing Accounts of some early Editions of Chaucer

[8]   Ibid., pp. iii-iv.
[9]   Ibid., p. 167. The atlas was *Le grand atlas ou Cosmographie Blaviane*, 12 vols (Amsterdam, 1663). The Breydenbach is now in the British Library. See *Treasures of the British Library*, compiled by Nicholas Barker and the Curatorial Staff, new edn (London, 2005), p. 59.
[10]   *Bibliotheca Westiana*, p. 130.

[and] an antient Portrait of Chaucer, upon vellum, illuminated by Tho. Occleve his Contemp'.[11]

Several other items within this class also contained additional manuscript material while others had interesting provenances. West's copy of Shakespeare's first folio (a 1664 re-issue of the third impression) contained '*MS notes on* the Tempest, *corrections and explanations of the Tragedy of* Hamlet [and] *some Account of the* Life *and Writings of* Shakespeare *MS*'.[12] The copy of 'Puttenham's Arte of English Poesie *ded to* Lord Burghley *by the Printer* Rich. Field 1589' contained a manuscript '*Catalogue of* Puttenham's *Books by* Ben Jonson'.[13] Lot 1047 'Hall (Bp) *Virgidemiarum*, 6 Books, *impr. by* Harison, 1599-1602, *rare Edit.*' had once belonged to Alexander Pope who had given it to West, '*telling him that he esteemed them the best Poetry and the truest Satire in the English Language*'.[14]

Other items did not necessarily need to rely on manuscript additions or an unusual provenance to make them interesting. A sixteen-volume compilation of William Prynne's pamphlets – '*Prynne's Tracts*, 16 vol., 104 *Pieces*' – was described thus: 'There are besides three Catalogues of his printed publications; the first in 1643, containing 31 – the second in 1653, comprising 68 – the third setting forth in alphabetical order 173 Books'. A unique collection, it was sold to an unknown buyer for seven guineas.[15] Notwithstanding an extremely concise description for lot 2112 – '*A curious collection of Old Ballads, in number above* 1200, b.l. *with humerous Frontispieces,* 3 vols' – it must have led to some very competitive bidding for it was sold for £20.[16] Likewise Francis Peck's *Desiderata curiosa*, '2 vol, large paper, 1732-1735' – admittedly with Paterson's added note, 'very scarce' – fetched a good price, in this case, eight guineas.[17]

[11]   Ibid.; The work was *The Workes of Geffray Chaucer Newly Printed, with Dyuers Workes which Were Neuer in Print Before*, ed. by William Thynne (London, 1532).

[12]   *Bibliotheca Westiana*, p. 141. It was lot 2488.

[13]   Ibid., p. 109. The work was George Puttenham, *The Arte of English Poesie* (London, 1589).

[14]   Ibid.,, p. 59. Probably, Joseph Hall, *Virgidemiarum Six Bookes. First Three Bookes, of Toothlesse Satyrs* (London, 1602). Despite the title, Harrison only printed the first three books and these may have been bound with a copy of Joseph Hall, *Virgidemiarum. The Three Last Bookes, Of Byting Satyres.Corrected with Some Additions* (London, 1599).

[15]   *Bibliotheca Westiana*, p. 111, lot 1839.

[16]   Ibid., p. 124.

[17]   Ibid., p. 140, lot 2477, Francis Peck, *Desiderata curiosa*, 2 vols (London, 1732-35).

The sale of the books described by Paterson as the 'History and Antiquities of Great Britain and Ireland' was spread over four days and, with the English topography sold on day twenty-three, brought the whole sale to its profitable close.[18] This group was the largest single category within the library, and if you add Paterson's class of 'Government, Parliament and parliamentary debates' – which could justifiably be called 'modern history' – this category becomes even bigger and numbers some 1121 lots. Included here were many volumes of real quality and distinction, and many annotated copies.

Day twenty, for example, saw the sale of an excellent collection of thirty-six octavo titles edited by Thomas Hearne.[19] Within these thirty-six titles were two editions of Leland's nine volumes of *Itinerary*, a three volume set of Camden's 'Annales Elizabethac' and the most expensive item here, *The History and Antiquities of Glastonbury*, which sold for £4 5s. 0d.[20] On the following day nine editions of Stow's 'Summarye of the Chronicles of Englande', published between 1565 and 1604, were sold.[21] On the penultimate day a large collection of eighty-seven lots relating to the history of London came under the hammer while the final day saw a selection of titles dealing with Scotland and another collection of Irish material.

In many respects, the most interesting titles in this 'History' section were the many annotated copies. Paterson had been quite right to draw attention to them and mentioned annotations by, among others, Le Neve, Stukeley and Dugdale. West had been present at the sale of Le Neve's library in 1731 and had there purchased a number of items. The most valuable, which sold for £1 7s. 0d., was 'Anstis's Register of the Order of the Garter, *cuts*, 2 vol in 1, *with original Papers, Petitions &c by* Mr Anstis, Garter, *and MS Notes by* P. Le Neve, Esq. Norroy – 1724'.[22]

---

[18] Ibid., p. 239.

[19] West and Hearne had befriended each other while West was an undergraduate at Oxford.

[20] *Bibliotheca Westiana*, pp. 182-183. The editions of these works owned by West, were John Leland, *Itinerary*, 9 vols (Oxford, 1710-12); William Camden, *Annales rerum Anglicarum, et Hibernicarum, regnante Elizabetha, ad annum M.D. LXXXIX*, 3 vols (Oxford, 1717); and Charles Eyston, *The History and Antiquities of Glastonbury* (Oxford, 1722).

[21] *Bibliotheca Westiana*, p. 193, lots 3770-78. The first edition was John Stow, *A Summarie* [sic] *of Englyshe Chronicles* (London, [1565]).

[22] Ibid., p. 185. *The Register of the Most Noble Order of the Garter, Usually Called the Black Book*, ed. by John Anstis, 2 vols (London, 1724).

Stukeley's '*Medallic History of Carausius*, 2 vol. *interleaved*, 1757' was described as 'The Author's copy, *with MS Notes in his own hand-writing, and several original Letters and Papers*' and knocked down for £3, while an impressive thirteen guineas was raised by Dugdale's annotated copy of his own 'Baronage of England, 2 vol. l.p. in moroc. 1675'.[23]

Bishop White Kennet was another strongly featured antiquarian. In the 'Preface' to the catalogue Paterson had highlighted the presence of works from the Bishop's own library, writing with his usual hyperbole, that his 'intense application and unwearied Diligence [...] so apparent throughout this collection, furnish Matter even to astonishment', and claimed that these annotations 'were alone sufficient to establish the Reputation [...] of that illustrious Prelate, without any other Monuments of his Greatness'.[24] It certainly was an impressive and large collection. All told, forty-nine lots had formerly belonged to the Bishop. Not surprisingly, it was Kennett's annotated copies that aroused the most interest. Some were Kennett's own works. Lot 453 comprised two copies of his *Case of Impropriations*, one being described as 'with large MS additions by the Author', the other as 'interleaved with great additions by the Author', and they were sold together for nine shillings.[25] From time to time Kennett's additions were joined by other hands. John Le Neve's publication of *Some Short Memorials Concerning the Life of that Reverend Divine Doctor Richard Field* was sold, along with 'Walton's Life of Hooker' as Lot 675, with 'large MS Additions and Alterations by the Editor [i.e. Le Neve] and Bp Kennett' for four shillings.[26] At other times, some lots were sold with accompanying manuscripts, usually in the form of letters. Lot 3949, 'Bp Tanner's *Notitia Monastica*, 1744' also contained '*two original letters of the Author to* Bp Kennett, 1720-1723'.[27] This sold for £4 10s. 0d.

[23] Ibid., pp. 200, 185. William Stukeley, *The Medallic History of Marcus Aurelius Valerius Carausius, Emperor in Brittain*, 2 vols (London, 1757-59); William Dugdale, *The Baronage of England*, 2 vols (London, 1675-76).
[24] *Bibliotheca Westiana*, p. iii.
[25] Ibid., p. 31. The books were copies of White Kennett, *The Case of Impropriations* (London, 1704).
[26] Ibid., p. 42. The books were Nathaniel Field, *Some Short Memorials Concerning the Life of that Reverend Divine Doctor Richard Field*, ed. by J. Le Neve (London, 1716-17); Izaak Walton, *The Life of Mr. Rich[ard] Hooker* (London, 1665).
[27] Ibid., p. 201. This was Thomas Tanner, *Notitia Monastica* (London, 1744).

Manuscript additions such as these were not the only way in which some of the works in West's library had been altered. In his 'Preface' Paterson had noted that 'the lovers of engraved English portraits [...] may here look to find a considerable number of singular and scarce heads, and will not be disappointed in their search'.[28] The majority of the prints in West's possession had been sold earlier at a separate sale and those on offer here were the extra-illustrated books from West's library. The eighteenth century craze for extra-illustration is well documented.[29] James Granger's *A Biographical History of England* had provided a suitable medium in which to indulge in this pastime for it had been specifically designed to be disbound in order to provide for the insertion of extra 'heads', hence the phrase 'Grangerisation'.[30] Granger's work had been partially based on West's collection – widely 'considered a benchmark among the first generation of portrait head collectors' – and in gratitude Granger had presented West with a copy.[31] West had, in fact, two copies of the work, the second of which (lot 3841) had '5 original Papers relative to the work' tipped in and it sold to a cash buyer for £1 16s. 0d.[32]

Neither of these copies of Granger's work was 'grangerised' but other items had been. Day twenty-two (Thursday 22 April) was the climax of the whole sale and the 226 lots on offer made £323 18s. 6d. – by far the biggest single day's receipts. Extra-illustrated volumes contributed to this amount. 'Ludlow's Memoirs, 3 vols 1722' which was said to be embellished with extra portraits 'of all the chief characters of that Time [...] in number 122' sold for £5, while a 1627 edition of Speed's 'Hist of Great Britaine', 'further embellished [...with] in all sixty-two prints' sold for £6 10s. 0d.[33] However, the real star of this day, indeed of the whole sale in terms of amount raised, was lot 4136, an edition of 'Rapin's Hist and Tindal's continuation' which was described thus: 'This matchless set of Books, besides the usual Cuts, is

---

28 Ibid., p. iv.
29 See, for example, Robert R. Wark, 'The Gentle Pastime of Extra-Illustrating Books', *Huntington Library Quarterly*, 56:2 (1993), 151-65 and Peltz, 'Engraved Portrait Heads', passim.
30 James Granger, *A Biographical History of England* (London, 1769).
31 Peltz, 'Engraved Portrait Heads', p. 90.
32 *Bibliotheca Westiana*, p. 196.
33 Ibid., pp. 206, 211. The books were Edmund Ludlow, *Memoirs of Edmund Ludlow Esq*, 3 vols, 2nd edn (London, 1720-22); John Speed, *The History of Great Britaine*, 2nd edn (London, 1627).

embellished with several hundred Portraits, Plans, Maps, Views, Public Buildings, Medals &c *many of which are exceedingly scarce.*'[34] It sold for fifty-two guineas.

These extra-illustrated works, along with the Caxtons and the other early printed items, the annotated and association copies, oozed quality. There is no doubt that the collection was both rich and diverse. Equally diverse, and many very rich, were the customers who crowded into West's house in Covent Garden where Langford had decided to conduct the auction. Who were these people, what were they purchasing and what did they have to pay? There is one group of these customers who cannot be named, let alone identified. Those whose purchases are merely recorded in the marked-up sale catalogues as 'Money' or 'Cash' and they, not surprisingly, were buying at the lower end of the market.[35] The purchasers who can be identified on the other hand were a mixture of members of the book trade and private collectors.[36]

John Thane of Gerrard Street was one member of the trade. Although he was best known as a print-seller and publisher he also dealt in second-hand books, and here he purchased 168 lots for £69 5s. 6d.[37] He also had an extensive trade in engraved portraits and consequently purchased a number of books that contained these 'Heads', including lot 4011, '*England's Worthies*, under whom all the Civil and Bloody Warres since 1642 to 1647 are related, *with their portraits*' which cost him £1 13s. 0d.[38] He likewise had a reputation as an expert on coins. He was therefore, and not surprisingly, particularly active when West's books on 'ancient inscriptions, gems, coins and medals,

---

[34] Ibid., p. 212. The edition of Tindal and Rapin which had been extended was ESTC T140785. *The History of England, by Mr. Rapin de Thoyras: Continued from the Revolution to the Accession of King George II by N. Tindal*, 4 vols (London, 1744-47).

[35] Known customers, whether members of the book trade or collectors would have had accounts with the auctioneers. Unknown customers, or those not deemed creditworthy, would not have had this facility. The highest price paid by a cash customer was £11. Only thirty-nine lots in the whole sale sold for more than ten pounds.

[36] Unless otherwise stated, details of the booksellers are taken from the *ODNB*, Ian Maxted, *The London Book Trades, 1775-1800* (Folkestone, 1977) and H. R. Plomer and others, *A Dictionary of the Printers and Booksellers [...] 1726 to 1775* (London, 1910; repr. 1968).

[37] For Thane see also Peltz, 'Engraved Portrait Heads', p. 78.

[38] *Bibliotheca Westiana*, p. 205. This was John Vicars, *England's Worthies* (London, 1647).

weights and measures &c' appeared.[39] He bought twenty-seven of the 167 lots for £4 14s. 6d., his most expensive single purchase here being Francois Le Blanc's *Traite historique des monnoyes de France* which set him back £1 2s. 0d.[40] All of these acquisitions later found their way into *Thane's Second Catalogue for 1773* [...] *out of the Cabinets of the Late Mr West and Others.*[41]

Like Thane, Peter Molini of Covent Garden was something of a general dealer trading in other goods as well as modern and second-hand books. For example, he represented William Hunter at various continental coin auctions during 1764, but in 1765 he had issued a small catalogue of the books he had recently imported. At West's sale he was successful in purchasing just two lots. On day twenty-one he purchased for eighteen shillings a fine, 1729 edition, printed by William Bowyer, of Matthew Parker's *De antiquitate Britannicæ ecclesiæ et privilegiis ecclesiæ Cantuariensis.*[42] Sixteen days earlier he had bought lot 722, which contained two separate titles. It was enhanced with the following: 'the last of these pieces [Giordano Bruno's *Spaccio de la Bestia Triofante* [...] 1584] may be justly reckoned among the scarcest books extant – This identical copy was sold at the sale of the library of Ch. Bernard, Esq; An 1711 for £28.'[43] Molini paid just £9 15s. 0d.[44]

Barnes Tovey, bookseller at the Dove, Bell Yard was, unlike Molini, something of a specialist. At first in partnership with John

---

[39] Ibid., p. 151.

[40] Ibid., p. 154. The book was Francois Le Blanc, *Traité historique des monnoyes de France* (Amsterdam, 1692).

[41] John Thane, *Thane's Second Catalogue for 1773* [...] *out of the Cabinets of the Late Mr West and Others* (London, 1773).

[42] *Bibliotheca Westiana*, p. 201. The work was Matthew Parker, *Matthæi Parker Cantuariensis Archiepiscopi de antiquitate Britannicae ecclesiae et privilegiis ecclesiae Cantuariensis* (London, 1729).

[43] *Bibliotheca Westiana*, p. 64.

[44] The sale of this book at Dr Charles Barnard's auction aroused controversy (marked up copy of the catalogue in the British Library, shelfmark 126.a.8). *The Spectator* for 27 May 1711, recorded 'nothing has more surprised the Learned in *England*, than the price which a small Book, Entitled *Spaccio della Bestia trionfante*, bore in a late auction', and concluded that 'there must be something in it very formidable' (*The Spectator*, ed. by D. F. Bond, 5 vols (Oxford, 1965), III, 459-60). Thomas Hearne hinted why it was controversial: 'Aug. 7 [1711] (Tue.) Memorandum [...] bought by on[e] Mr Clavell of the Middle-Temple, a great Crony (unless I am misinform'd) of Toland, Stevens, Tyndale & other Atheistical & ill men' (*Remarks and Collections of Thomas Hearne*, 10 vols, ed. by C. E. Doble (Oxford, 1889), III, 201-02, 209).

Worrall, and later trading on his own, he concentrated on publishing and selling legal books and monographs. In 1768 he and Worrall had produced the definitive catalogue of 'all the common and statute law books of this realm', the *Bibliotheca legum*.[45] Given this, it is not surprising that Tovey did not appear at West's sale until the law books were sold. Here he purchased twenty-one lots for £5 2s. 6d., his most expensive, at two guineas, being a collection described thus: 'Bills, Cases, Private Acts, &c. 24 vol. *including many scarce Tracts*, and a large bundle of ditto *from* 1710 to 1760, but *chiefly between* 1710 and 1720'.[46]

Another member of the trade, Benjamin White, of Horace's Head, Fleet Street, also had the reputation of a specialist, in his case natural history.[47] Somewhat surprisingly, at this auction he was not particularly pursuing this line and only five of the sixty-six lots he bought can be categorised as natural history. Of them, the most expensive items, at £2 and £1 11s. 6d. respectively, were a seven volume edition of Linnaeus's *Amoenitates academicae* and John Morton's *Natural History of Northamptonshire*.[48] The rest of White's purchases included many editions of the classics (including a twenty volume set of Cicero's works, which cost £2 14s. 0d.), three copies of Vertue's *Medals, Coins, Great-Seals Impressions from the Elaborate Work of Thomas Simon* and his most expensive purchase, at sixteen guineas, 'State trials, 8 vol, 1730-36, *with a MS Catalogue of Trials omitted in this collection digested chronologically* from Edw II to Geo I *inclus*'.[49]

---

[45]   Worrall had first published this bibliography in 1732. The 1768 edition was the first in which Tovey was involved. *Bibliotheca legume; or, a Compleat List of All the Common and Statute Law Books of this Realm* [...] *A new edition* (London, [1768]).

[46]   *Bibliotheca Westiana*, p. 180, lot 3540. Tovey, it appears, was purchasing bargains. For example, five of his purchased lots (seven titles in total) cost him £1 11s. 0d. In his *Bibliotheca legum*, published just five years before this sale, these seven titles were valued at £2 19s. 6d., making Tovey's purchase a potential mark down of 65%.

[47]   For White, see also William Noblett, 'Benjamin White – A Biographical Sketch', *Newsletter, Friends of the Wakes Museum*, 18, (May 2000), pp. 7-11.

[48]   Carl Linnaeus, *Amoenitates academicae*, 7 vols (Leiden, 1749-69); John Morton, *The Natural History of Northamptonshire* (London, 1712).

[49]   Cicero, *M. Tullius Ciceronis opera*, 20 vols (Glasgow, 1748-49); George Vertue, *Medals, Coins, Great-Seals, Impressions from the Elaborate Works of Thomas Simon* (London, 1753); possibly, *A Complete Collection of State Trials*, 2nd edn, 8 vols (London, 1730-35). Since the library contained ten copies of Vertue's work which had been 'engraved at the instance of Mr West' he may have had a financial stake in the

These four members of the trade – Thane, Molini, Tovey and White – were the mere tip of the iceberg. The dealers who attended the sale reads like a *Who's Who*, of the London book trade.[50] Yet one figure stood out – George Nicol. By the time of West's sale, Nicol was well established and he took a very prominent part in the auction, buying 320 lots for a massive £437 19s. 0d. Well over half of this total - £227 19s. 0d. – was spent on behalf of King George III, purchasing ten choice items, six of which had been printed by Caxton. These included Caxton's edition (1476-77) of Chaucer's *Canterbury Tales* which was described as the 'only perfect copy known in England' and cost £47 15s. 6d.[51] At a mere thirty-one guineas was the same printer's *The Recuyell of the Historyes of Troyes* and at a few shillings less, for £32 0s. 6d., *Game and Playe of the Chess*.[52]

The six Caxtons Nicol acquired for George III cost £153 6s. 0d. and their acquisition was not without controversy. 'Mr George Nicol', Dibdin later wrote in *Bibliomania*,

> told me with his usual pleasantry and point, that he got abused in the public papers by Almon and others, for his having purchased nearly the whole of the Caxtonian volumes in this collection for His Majesty's library. It was said abroad that a 'Scotchman had lavished away the King's money in buying old black-letter books'. A pretty specimen of *lavishing* away royal money, truly!

---

publication. It was dedicated to him and published at his suggestion and with his encouragement. Some of the plates depicted coins in West's collection.

[50] I have identified the following other members of the book trade who were active at the sale: Baker, Conant, Davis, Donaldson, Elmsley, Fox, Hayes, King, Lane, Manson, Murray, Payne, Robson, Snelling, Vandenburgh and Wingrave.

[51] *Bibliotheca Westiana*, p. 130, Geoffrey Chaucer, [*The Canterbury Tales*], ed. by W. Caxton, ([London, 1476-77]). West purchased this Chaucer at Baker & Leigh's auction, on 3 May 1771 for £15. It is a perfect copy and now in the British Library. Having bought this copy, West then sold his existing copy privately to John Ratcliffe. At Ratcliffe's sale in 1776, Walter Shropshire (print-seller and publisher of New Bond Street) paid £6 for it on behalf of the Marquess of Rockingham. It is now in the Wormsley Library. See *The Wormsley Library; A Personal Selection by Sir Paul Getty* (London, 1999), item 16, pp. 44-47.

[52] *Bibliotheca Westiana*, pp. 131, 209. Raoul le Fèvre, *Here Begynneth the Volume Intituled and Named the Recuyell of the Historyes of Troye*, trans. by W. Caxton (London, 1474); Jean de Vignay and Jean Ferron, [*Game and Play of Chess*], trans. by W. Caxton (Bruges, 1474).

However, Dibdin was quick to defend Nicol and the King and concluded

> in his directions to Mr Nicol [the King] forbade any competition with those purchasers who wanted books of science and belles-lettres for their own professional or literary pursuits: thus using, I ween, the powers of his purse in a manner at once merciful and wise.[53]

This may well have been the case. Nicol certainly did not purchase 'the whole of the Caxtonian volumes' of which there were thirty-one.[54] The King was the definite purchaser of only six and Nicol himself bought a further three which might have been destined for the Royal Library although there is nothing to indicate this. Even so, this was not even a majority of the 'Caxtonian volumes' let alone all of them.

Indeed, there was one other collector, John Ratcliffe, who purchased more Caxtons than Nicol/George III. Ratcliffe was a prosperous chandler from south London whose fascination with early printing, it is believed, had been stimulated by admiring the scraps of old books he acquired as waste paper. Ratcliffe's own collection was almost as rich as West's in Caxtons and other incunabula and he added significantly at this sale.[55] He purchased for £112 10s. 6d., 119 lots which included sixteen incunabula, ten printed by Caxton and six by Wynkyn de Worde. The ten Caxtons cost £61 10s. 6d. and the six de Wordes £3 4s. 6d. The most expensive of the Caxtons at £13 was *Thystorye and Lyf of the Noble and Crysten Prynce, Charles the Grete*, the cheapest, the letter of Alain Charetier which cost a mere £3.[56] By contrast, the de Wordes fetched modest prices; Ratcliffe's most expensive costing just 16s. 6d.[57]

---

[53]   Dibdin, *Bibliomania*, II, 382.

[54]   Strictly speaking, there were thirty-two Caxtons in the sale, but one – a 1481 printing of the *Myrrour of the World* - was so imperfect that Paterson did not credit it with the status of a separate lot. It was sold, for £2 13s. 0d. as part of a 'volume of miscellaneous tracts' (*Bibliotheca Westiana*, p. 22, lot 336).

[55]   Ratcliffe's own library was sold by James Christie 27 March to 6 April 1776. The Catalogue comprised 1675 lots which sold for £1070 7s. 6d. It contained over fifty Caxtons which attracted Ralph Willett who purchased the three most expensive.

[56]   Anonymous, *Thystorye and Lyf of the Noble and Crysten Prynce, Charles the Grete*, trans. by W. Caxton (London, 1485); Alain Charetier, *Here Foloweth the Copye of a Lettre whyche Maistre Alayn Charetier Wrote to Hys Brother*, trans. by W. Caxton (London, 1483).

[57]   This was lot 1531, '*The Meditacyons of Saynt Bernarde*, b.l. *emprynted at* Westminster *by* Wynkyn *the* Worde 1496'. *Bibliotheca Westiana*, p. 96. Lot 1532, on the other

Another particularly active collector was the pioneering bibliographical scholar, William Herbert.[58] His purchases – 304 lots –
dwarfed Ratcliffe's in number but were much less expensive and cost
just £93 1s. 6d. Herbert was working on an 'augmentation' of Joseph
Ames' *Typographical Antiquities* and some of his purchases reflect this
interest in early printing.[59] He bought an intriguingly described lot of
'Sundry fragments of old Black-Letter Books', and paid two guineas for
the equally intriguing 'Portraits and Devices of old English Printers
[and] A collection of antient English Paper Marks'.[60] Nor was Herbert
averse to buying less serious material and his acquisitions included a
treatise on gout (lot 2208), an edition of Beaumont and Fletcher's plays
(lot 2110) and a slim volume on the 'Witch of Walkerne' (lot 2197).[61]
He was also interested in works annotated by Bishop Kennett which
were held in considerable number, and he purchased six lots for £1 1s.
6d.

Another large purchaser, the noted antiquary Richard Gough, was
also seeking annotated works. He paid out £104 19s. 6d. for 143 lots.
One particularly attractive purchase was lot 3946 - 'Dugdale & Dodsworth *Monastica Anglicanum*, 3 tom, *fig.* Lond. 1655-61-73' - which
came with '*some* MS *Papers, Prints &c* relative to the work', and cost
thirteen guineas.[62] Gough was also very interested in Kennett's
annotations and purchased sixteen lots that had been annotated by the
Bishop. Lot 4219 was Kennett's own copy of his *Parochial Antiquities*
that not only contained his corrections and additions, but also '*several
original letters* by Bp Fell, Sir Will Glynne, Bp Kennett (*then Vicar of*

---

hand, comprised six de Wordes (of which three were incunabula) which cost all
together just £1 15s. 0d.

[58] For Herbert, see Robin Myers, 'William Herbert: His Library and His Friends', in
Property of a Gentleman, ed. by Robin Myers and Michael Harris (Winchester, 1991),
pp. 133-58.

[59] The resulting work was Joseph Ames, *Typographical Antiquities* [...] *Considerably
Augmented* [...] *by William Herbert*, 3 vols (London, 1785-90).

[60] *Bibliotheca Westiana*, pp. 103 and 116, lots 1672 and 2208.

[61] Ibid., pp. 127, 124 and 127.

[62] Ibid., p. 201, William Dugdale and Roger Dodsworth, *Monasticon Anglicanum*, 3
vols (London, 1655-73), now Bodleian Library, shelfmark Gough Eccl. top. 90-92.
Most of Gough's library and papers are in the Bodleian Library. For Gough, see
Rosemary Sweet, *Antiquaries: The Discovery of the Past in Eighteenth-Century Britain*
(London, 2004), passim.

Ambrosden) &c *and other MS Papers'*.[63] The most expensive of Kennett's annotated copies, however, was not sold to Gough. Lot 4438 was a copy of 'Gunton's Hist of the Church of Peterborough', which had been interleaved and contained '*MS Notes and additions* by Bp Kennett, *far exceeding in quantity the printed work'*.[64] The Dean of Peterborough, Charles Tarrant, made a special journey to London in order to buy this, and only bought this one item, finally acquiring it for twenty guineas, one of the most expensive items in the whole sale.[65]

Another customer at the sale who was particularly focused, but not quite so single minded, was Ralph Willett.[66] Willett was the owner of a truly splendid library, kept at his country house at Merly in Dorset, and a very rich man, and his purchases hinted at this. Although they were modest in number – a mere eighteen titles – they were of high quality and cost £34 9s. 0d. - nearly three pounds a lot. They included five incunabula (two Caxtons and one each from the presses of de Worde, Pynson and de Machlinia) the most expensive being Caxton's *Polycronycon,* which notwithstanding that it was imperfect, cost Willett fifteen and a half guineas.[67]

Two other customers at the sale, Keyser Mole and Peter Romilly, like Willett, purchased a small number of lots, but unlike Willett, did not spend a great deal. Romilly, a watchmaker of Frith Street in Soho bought ten lots for £3 9s. 6d. His most expensive item – a four volume edition of Bishop Sherlock's *Sermons* – cost 16s. 6d., while his interest in gardening was revealed by the purchase of Young's *Farmers Guide* and the same author's four-volume *Six Months Tour Thro' the North of England*, 1770.[68] Mole was a prosperous milliner and hat-maker from

---

[63]   *Bibliotheca Westiana*, p. 217, White Kennett, *Parochial Antiquities Attempted in the History of Ambrosden, Burcester, and Other Adjacent Parts* (Oxford, 1695), now Bodleian Library, shelfmark Gough Eccl. top 67b.

[64]   *Bibliotheca Westiana*, p. 229. This was Simon Gunton, *The History of the Church of Peterburgh* (London, 1686) and is now in Cambridge University Library, shelfmark Peterborough Cathedral Library MS.24.

[65]   Seven items in the sale made higher prices than this work.

[66]   For Willett, see Alan G. Thomas, 'Portrait of a Bibliophile. X. Ralph Willett of Merly, 1719-1795', *Book Collector*, 12 (1963), 439-48.

[67]   *Bibliotheca Westiana*, p. 209, Ranulf Higden, [*T*]*henne Followyng This for Breton Booke of Prolicronycon* (Westminster, 1482).

[68]   It is hard to identify the four volumes of Sherlock's sermons. No collection was published in four volumes so this may have been a composite collection. The other works were Arthur Young, *The Farmer's Guide in Hiring and Stocking Farms*, 2 vols (London, 1770); Arthur Young, *A Six Months Tour Through the North of England*, 4 vols

North London who collected medals and coins as well as books. He spent a little more than Romilly, £12 6s. 6d., on seventeen lots of at least sixty books. A parcel of twenty-one miscellaneous items cost a mere 1s. 6d., while two copies of '*The Prymer of Salysbury*' (one imperfect) cost £1 17s 0d.[69] His most expensive purchase, however, was lot 4118, which comprised two Wynkyn de Worde printings from 1515 (the 'St Alban's Chronicle' and the description of 'Bretane' respectively) and cost £5 10s. 0d.[70]

Another modest purchaser, albeit a focused one, was 'Capt Phipps'. Constantine John Phipps (later Lord Mulgrave), was a Naval officer, a Lord of the Admiralty, 1772-1782, whose 'library of nautical books was famous and considered to be the best in England'.[71] At this sale he bought eight lots for £6 9s. 6d. A small treatise on the 'Ferroe' islands cost a mere 1s. 6d., while his most expensive was lot 2077, costing £4 11s. 0d.[72] This comprised seven sixteenth-century titles relating to navigation, mapping and compasses, and the intriguingly entitled 'Safegarde of Saylers, or great Rutters'.[73]

As focused as Phipps, were Sir William Musgrave and Richard Bull, but in their cases, their eyes were firmly fixed on those lots that

---

(London, 1770). Romilly's own collection of prints, drawings and book of prints was auctioned by Hassil Hutchins in February/March 1785. For Romilly, see Patrick Medd, *Romilly: A Life of Sir Samuel Romilly, Lawyer and Reformer* (London, 1968), pp. 20-22.

[69] *Bibliotheca Westiana*, p. 49. Lot 829, the imperfect copy, cost 17s. The copy bought at the auction was later mentioned in Richard Gough's *British Topography. Or, an Historical Account of What Has Been Done for Illustrating the Topographical Antiquities of Great Britain and Ireland*, 2 vols (London, 1780), II, 360 where it is identified as *Here After Foloweth the Prymer in Englysshe, and in Latin Sette Out Alonge: After the Use of Sarum* (Rouen, 1556). Perhaps Gough and Mole spoke about this book at the auction?

[70] *Bibliotheca Westiana*, p. 211. The works were *Here Endeth This Presente Cronycle of Englonde with the Fruyte of Tymes, Compyled* [...] *by One Somtyme Scole Mayster of Saynt Albons* (Westminster, 1515); and probably a version of *The Descrypcyon of Englonde Here Foloweth a Lytell Treatyse the whiche Treateth of the Descrypcyon of this Londe whiche of Olde Tyme was Named Albyon and After Brytayne and Now is Called Englonde* (Westminster, 1498).

[71] Ann Savours, '"A Very Interesting Point in Geography": The 1773 Phipps Expedition towards the North Pole', *Arctic*, 37:4 (1984), 402-28 (p. 407).

[72] *Bibliotheca Westiana*, p. 164. The 'Description of the Islands and inhabitants of Ferroe' was part of lot 3095.

[73] Ibid., p. 122, Cornelis Antoniszoon, *The Safegarde of Saylers: or, Great Rutter*, trans. by Robert Norman (London, 1590).

contained 'Heads'.[74] Both men were among the leading 'Head hunters' at this time. Musgrave, a successful civil servant in H. M. Customs and a long term and dedicated Trustee of the British Museum, spent £9 4s. 0d. on eleven lots (twenty-five titles), all of which contained portraits. The majority of these were ordinary rather than famous or distinguished individuals – 'Armelle Nicolas a poor ignorant country maid of France' for example – but from time to time the engravers were among the better known members of that trade.[75] Lot 1124 contained the following: 'Mossom's *Plant of Paradise*, the Funeral of John Goodhand Holt, only Child of Tho. Holt of Grislehurst in Lancash. Esq., *with his portrait* by Loggan'.[76] One work contained a number of portraits: lot 1509, *Certamen seraphicum provinciæ Angliæ*, was described as '*with the Portraits of the English Recollects*, Bullaker, Heath, Bell, Woodcock, Colman'.[77]

Richard Bull was as dedicated as Musgrave in his pursuit of portraiture.[78] Bull's appetite for engraved portraits, it was claimed by Horace Walpole, was one of the chief reasons why their price was so high.[79] At this sale, however, his purchases were modest and ran to a mere three lots costing £5 18s. 0d. Lot 699, purchased for only five shillings, contained the portraits of a 'Ja Owen of Salop', a 'Mr Tho Cawton', and 'Funeral sermons and characters by sundries', the latter no doubt containing other portraits.[80] Costing £1 17s. 0d. was *The Cosmographi-*

---

[74]   For Musgrave, see Antony Griffiths, 'Sir William Musgrave and British Biography', *British Library Journal*, 18:2 (1992), 171-89, Arline Meyer, 'Sir William Musgrave's "lists of Portraits", With an Account of Head-Hunting in the Eighteenth Century', *Walpole Society*, 54 (1998), 454-502, and C. J. Wright, 'Sir William Musgrave (1735-1800) and the British Museum Library', in *Libraries Within the Library*, ed. by Giles Mandelbrote and Barry Taylor (London, 2009), pp. 202-21.

[75]   *Bibliotheca Westiana*, p. 42.

[76]   Ibid., p. 62. Probably, Robert Mossom, *A Plant of Paradise, Being a Sermon Preached* [...] *at the Funeral of John-Goodhand Holt* (London, 1660).

[77]   *Bibliotheca Westiana*, p. 96, Angelus, a Sancto Francisco [Richard Mason], *Certamen seraphicum provinciæ Angliæ* (London, 1649).

[78]   For Bull, see Peltz, 'Engraved Portrait Heads' and Wark, 'Gentle Pastime', passim. See also R. P. Evans, 'Richard Bull and Thomas Pennant: Virtuosi in the Art of Grangerisation or Extra Illustration', *National Library of Wales Journal*, 30 (1998), 269-94.

[79]   Another person Walpole thought responsible for the high price of 'Heads' - Joseph Gulston - was also present at this sale, although his purchases were modest in number.

[80]   *Bibliotheca Westiana*, p. 43.

cal Glasse which contained a map of Norwich as well as a portrait.[81] However, it was lot 1920, a collection of title-pages put together by Ames, which really pleased Bull. It cost him £3 16s. 0d. and he was absolutely delighted with it. 'I purchased yesterday in West's sale', he wrote to Granger on 9 April, 'the collection of Title pages, got together by the late Mr Ames, to the amount of 30,000, & many more I believe, among which I hope to find many Portraits and titles of books I have been looking after.'[82]

To some extent, this last quoted letter is almost symbolic of the whole library and its sale. The mention of Ames points toward the library's very substantial strength in early printing. The letter also shows the importance of association copies to the collection, not only in relation to Ames but also other antiquaries such as Le Neve, Dugdale and, above all, Kennett. The good price paid (notwithstanding Bull's pleasure in his purchase) reflects the fine prices reached generally and Bull's delight in telling Granger of his good fortune reveals how much interest the sale had generated amongst the London connoisseurs. Indeed, in the context of the year in which it was sold, for the impressive sum of £2927 1s. 0d., the sale of West's library stands out. To be sure, there were other auctions, some of outstanding collections, but as Dibdin put it: this one comprised 'books which for rarity and value [...] have never been equalled'.[83]

---

[81]   Ibid., p. 147, lot 2644, William Cuningham, *The Cosmographical Glasse* (London, 1599). In a letter to Granger, 26 April 1773, Bull reported that this work was a 'Fine copy [...] with a curious head of the Author, Dr William Cunningham [sic] of Norwich, engraved by J.B. whom I take to be the John Bettes mentioned by Walpole', (Peltz, 'Engraved Portrait Heads', p. 121).

[82]   Peltz, 'Engraved Portrait Heads', p. 115.

[83]   Dibdin, *Bibliomania*, II, 376.

The Linen Hall Library: Provincial-Metropolitan Connections in the Late Eighteenth Century

S. C. ARNDT

During the 1790s, Belfast was a town on the move. The population was approximately 18,000 and the area was rapidly transforming from a country town to a manufacturing hub. The port was increasingly important for exporting linen to England and importing flax seed from both England and America. The town was also a centre for radicalism in Ireland: home of Samuel Neilson, and founding place of the United Irishmen. Belfast was the centre of the Presbyterian community in Ireland, a group that valued education and self-improvement. This was an urban world rich in Enlightenment tradition and full of radicals and reformers. It should come as no surprise, then, that in 1788 the citizens of Belfast formed a reading society.

Overall, we know very little about this early group though a letter written by Martha McTier, sister to Dr William Drennan, stated that the founding members were mostly craftsmen, or, as she put it, 'there was not among them one of higher rank than McCormick the gunsmith, or Osborne the baker'.[1] Dr Alexander Haliday described the Society as a product of the 'sanculottes' [sic] of Belfast, stating that 'It originated many years ago among some sensible and reading mechanics who, by paying a crown at first, and a shilling monthly, had got up a tolerable collection of good books before the society was known out of their own walls'.[2] However, this was not merely a reading society or a subscription library; its members had higher aspirations. They wished to model their society on Benjamin Franklin's Library Company of Philadelphia, founded in 1731. True to their Enlightenment spirit, they sought self-improvement and the betterment of their community.

From these humble origins the Belfast Reading Society grew into a cultural institution. Today it is known as the Linen Hall Library, an

---

[1]   *The Drennan-McTier Letters*, ed. by Jean Agnew and Maria Luddy, 3 vols (Dublin, 1998-99), I, 418-19.

[2]   Cited in John Killen, *A History of the Linen Hall Library 1788-1988* (Belfast, 1990), p. 11.

organization that is still very active in Ulster life. This society, much like Belfast itself, has had a somewhat problematic relationship with London. For its early members, London represented the political and cultural centre of the English speaking world, but as radicals and nonconformists they could not fully embrace it. In order to explore the links between this provincial society and the metropolitan centre of London, it is helpful to examine the library and its collections. The trading relationships, inherent in the library's purchases, illuminate the complex interactions between the Belfast Reading Society and London. This paper explores what items were being sought by the library members, where they were purchased, and why, in the period 1792 to 1798 when the Society underwent a phase of growth and transition that led to a great increase in acquisitions. This time-frame coincides with a very formative period in Anglo-Irish relations.

In 1792 the 'worthy plebeians' of the Belfast Reading Society, described by Martha McTier, were joined by a large influx of new members. The reason for the Society's sudden popularity is unknown, but McTier suggested that professional men wished to take advantage of the valuable collection of books that had already been assembled by the original members.[3] These new members consisted of many leading merchants and professionals including some of the town's most prominent citizens. Dr Alexander Haliday, elected as president in 1792, was typical: he was the wealthy son of a Presbyterian minister who had studied medicine at Glasgow and now supported Catholic emancipation in Ireland.[4]

These new men brought increased professionalization to the Belfast Reading Society. The meetings, originally held at the Donegall Arms, were moved to a private residence, where the minutes began to be recorded. In 1792, the Society voted to change its name to the Belfast Library and Society for Promoting Knowledge, and at the same time, articulated its objectives. As printed in their first catalogue, 'The great and first object of this society being to form a library', the Society was to undertake 'the collection of an extensive library, philosophical apparatus, and such productions of nature and art as tend to improve

---

[3]   *Drennan-McTier Letters*, ed. by Agnew and Luddy, I, 419.
[4]   Killen, *History of the Linen Hall Library*, p. 194.

the mind, and excite a spirit of general enquiry.'[5] This statement maintained the original purpose of collective self-improvement that the founders intended. However, it also expanded the horizons of the Society from one focused solely on the reading of books to one that sought knowledge through experiment, observation and participation in the international learned community. Evidence for this enlarged view of their objectives can be inferred from some of the early purchases of 1792. In March, the Society resolved to purchase the Proceedings of the Royal Society of London, the Royal Irish Academy and the Bath and Manchester Societies as far back as it could.[6] This demonstrates a desire on the part of the members to see themselves as participants in a geographically dispersed scholarly network, and to form connections to this larger community, and to the metropolitan centre. This will be discussed further as part of the collection policies of the library.

In March 1793 James Bryson and John Templeton were ordered to make a catalogue of books owned by the Society.[7] The catalogue was printed in April and distributed to members shortly afterwards along with a copy of the rules. It contained 135 titles, and a list of the books ordered but not yet received. This early catalogue is the first record of the library's collections and serves as a base line for the Society's library, since most of the titles listed would have been part of the pre-1792 collection. The 1793 catalogue allows us to tease out the types of materials that were purchased by the original Reading Society. Most titles in the collection fall into four main categories: histories, travel literature, fine arts and literature, and scientific and philosophical discourses. The catalogue also contains a number of biographies, reference works such as the *Encyclopaedia Britannica*, and a few periodicals.[8] This collection constitutes a basic canon of 'essential

---

[5] *A Catalogue of the Books Belonging to the Belfast Society for Promoting Knowledge* (Belfast, 1793), p. 1.

[6] Belfast, Linen Hall Library (LHL), MS Linen Hall Minutes 1 November 1791 to 28 October 1793, (3 March 1792).

[7] Ibid.

[8] *Catalogue*, passim. No records were kept of the newspapers subscribed to by the library members. However, by 1819 a Bradshaw's *Belfast Directory* mentions a newsroom in the White Linen Hall that stocked a wide variety of Irish, Scottish, and London newspapers. See Thomas Bradshaw, *Belfast General and Commercial Directory for 1819: Containing an Alphabetical List of the Merchants, Manufacturers, and Inhabitants in general [...] with a Directory and History of Lisburn* (Belfast, 1819), p. xxiv.

reading', including works by many of the prominent Enlightenment writers such as: Smith, Hume, Smollett, Blair, and Montesquieu. It is consistent with the practice of similar institutions in Scotland and America, where acquiring such a range of writing was one of the first actions undertaken by subscription libraries.[9]

However, it is perhaps more interesting to see what was not included in the early Belfast catalogue. There are very few items of a religious nature. The Society deliberately refrained from collecting religious works, because of the possibly controversial nature of such items. This is one area where the Belfast Society was different from many contemporary comparable libraries, and is perhaps a reflection of the increasing tension between religious factions in Ireland. Comparison with the Manchester Circulating Library exemplifies this. In its 1794 catalogue it had 138 titles under the category of divinity and sermons.[10] There were also no foreign language items in the Belfast Society's collection, though there were a few works in translation. This makes sense if one considers the original membership, which contained many individuals, such as Osborne the baker, who may not have been classically educated and therefore would not have been able to read works in Latin or French. This situation changed quickly under the new leadership.

In September 1792 the Society resolved that up to a fifth of its budget could be used to purchase foreign language or ancient works.[11] Another category of material that was missing was entertaining literature or novels. This was an issue on which the Society developed a very strong view, believing, with many others of its time, that reading novels was harmful to the mind and destructive of the aim of

---

[9]   For more information on Scottish subscription libraries and Enlightenment texts, see Mark R. M. Towsey, 'Reading the Scottish Enlightenment: Libraries, Readers and Intellectual Culture in Provincial Scotland *c.* 1750-1820', (unpublished Ph.D. thesis, University of St. Andrews, 2007), p. 94; For examples within American subscription libraries, see James Raven, *London Booksellers and American Customers: Transatlantic Literary Community and the Charleston Library Society, 1748-1811* (Columbia, South Carolina, 2002), p. 161.

[10]   The Manchester Circulating Library, *A Catalogue of the Present Collection of Books, in the Manchester Circulating Library; a Copy of the Laws; and a List of the Subscribers* (Manchester, 1794), p. 11. The figure for the titles under the category of divinity and sermons represent approximately seven percent of the overall collection.

[11]   LHL, MS Linen Hall Minutes 1 November 1791 to 28 October 1793, (7 September 1792).

improvement through reading. Editors of the *Belfast Monthly Magazine*, a periodical run by members of the Reading Society, were of the same opinion, saying that 'pleasure is rendered subsidiary to improvement'.[12] In a later edition they went even further stating that, 'for of all the creatures that ever nature gave birth to, a novel writer [...] is the most disgusting'.[13] To its own detriment, the Belfast Society for Promoting Knowledge maintained this stance on entertaining literature well into the nineteenth century.[14] These missing categories can tell almost as much about the Society's goals as the works they did choose to collect. Conveniently for our purposes, a second catalogue was published in 1795 and by that point the number of titles in the Society's library had more than doubled, from 135 to 296. This second catalogue allows us to track changes in the Society's acquisitions and to determine what types of materials the post-1792 members thought were important given the Reading Society's newly articulated objectives and better-educated membership (see Table 1).

Table 1 **Distribution of Titles by Category in the 1793 and 1795 Belfast Society Catalogues**

General Category	Percentage of Total 1793 Catalogue	Percentage of Total 1795 Catalogue
History	30	19
Scientific and Philosophical	22	24
Fine Arts and Literature	16	17
Travel Literature	14	16
Reference	10	15
Biography	5	4
Periodicals	3	3
Foreign Language	0	2

---

[12] *Belfast Monthly Magazine*, 1:1 (September, 1808), p. 3.
[13] *Belfast Monthly Magazine*, 7:2 (February, 1809), p. 141.
[14] Killen, *History of the Linen Hall Library*, pp. 5, 60.

When we look at the works present in the 1795 catalogue the general categories are nearly identical to what had gone before. Scientific and philosophical works, travel, histories, and fine arts and literature make up about seventy-five percent of the collection. The only new category of work was foreign language titles, of which there were five. However, if we look more closely at the new acquisitions there are trends that can be identified. As mentioned earlier, the Society had invested in the Proceedings of several other learned societies. In 1793 it owned the Bath Society papers on agriculture, a history of the Academie Royale at Paris, the *Transactions* of the Royal Society of London and of the Royal Irish Academy. By 1795, it had expanded on the original set of papers and added essays from a society in Edinburgh and from the Society of Physicians in London, *Transactions* from the Antiquarian Society of Scotland, the Philadelphia Philosophical Society, and the Academy of Arts. It had also added catalogues of other institutions' collections, such as the Liverpool Society Library. Taken together this is confirmation that the members wanted to feel a part of the wider learned community. Not only were these texts excellent sources for the latest academic discoveries, but they allowed provincial readers a kind of participation in the cultural life of the metropolis. Furthermore, the acquisition of these items was an act of trade where purchase of these texts also endowed their readers with cultural and political status. These were not provincial reproductions, but authentic artefacts from the centres of knowledge and power. These items also allowed the Society to keep its collections in line with what other institutions had purchased, continuing the process of creating a canon of 'essential reading'. In October 1792, John Templeton compared the literary pursuits of the Library Company of Philadelphia to that of the Belfast Society.[15] The Society members definitely had an awareness of what items other institutions owned and there is a sense that they were trying to emulate the collections of these other institutions; this may explain the presence of the Liverpool Library catalogue and the similarities between the Belfast Society's collections and those of the Philadelphia Library

---

[15] John Killen, 'The Reading Habits of a Georgian Gentleman, John Templeton, and the Book Collections of the Belfast Society for Promoting Knowledge', in *The Experience of Reading: Irish Historical Perspectives*, ed. by Bernadette Cunningham & Máire Kennedy (Dublin, 1999), pp. 99-108.

Company. The Belfast Society wanted to be seen as an equal partici-
pant with other provincial or colonial institutions, while at the same
time trying to foster a direct relationship with London.

This leads us to the question of how the Society chose which items
to purchase for its collections? Books were added in one of two ways:
first through purchase and second as donations, sometimes in lieu of
subscription fees. Books donated to the Society may account for some
of the more idiosyncratic items in the collection, such as the manuscript copy of the Gaelic Bible donated by Charles Lynd.[16] However,
most items were simply purchased. The only firm guideline offered for
the purchase of books was that they must be of an improving nature.
The Society did employ a full-time librarian, but his job was merely to
keep the books in good order and manage lending; he did not have the
power to set collection policies and purchase items. Thus, the decision
of exactly which books to purchase was very much up to individual
members. In March 1793, just a week before constructing its original
catalogue, the Society resolved to purchase a blank book where any
member, in good standing, could write the title of a book he wished
the library to purchase. These items were then approved or rejected by
a general committee and, as funds allowed, ordered.[17] Individuals who
were more aware of new titles, had a firm grasp of their own needs, or
had ties to the committee had the potential to be more influential in
acquisitions policy than their fellow members.

Because of this it is possible to see where certain individuals may
have left their personal imprint upon the library collections. One
example is John Templeton. He joined the Society in 1792 and was an
avid natural historian and practitioner of scientific experiments. He
corresponded regularly with well-known British naturalists in whose
works some of his discoveries were included. Because of his personal
connections, Templeton was unofficially placed in charge of procuring
scientific equipment and specimens for the Society. As part of its new
objectives, the Society wished to build up a collection of natural
specimens and scientific apparatus (just as Franklin's society in Philadelphia had done) to facilitate learning and discovery among its

---

[16] John Anderson, *History of the Belfast Library and the Society for Promoting
Knowledge* (Belfast, 1888), p. 22.
[17] LHL, MS Linen Hall Minutes 1 November 1791 to 28 October 1793, (2 March
1793).

members. Templeton also advised on the latest works in his field which the Society should purchase. This is another example of trade with London, because most of the items Templeton requested had to be purchased from outside of Belfast, in some cases Dublin but more often London.[18] Evidence for Templeton's success in integrating the Society into the international academic community can be found in the form of donations. Scholars and interested amateurs from around the globe sent specimens to the Belfast Society. One example is a box of fossils donated by Dr Forester of Hamburg in 1796. In return the Society sent him a sample of Wicklow gold.[19] Here we can see not only Templeton's personal imprint on the collections but also ways in which the Society, using Templeton's connections, participated in an extended scholarly network.

The Society's minutes give a strong sense of the constant struggle between participation in these networks of intellectual exchange, especially with London, and promotion of the local interests of its members. One of the ways that this struggle manifested itself was in the purchase of books. In April 1792, the Society borrowed one hundred pounds on credit for the purchase of books, particularly the *Transactions of the Royal Academy of London*. They bought some items at auctions in Dublin and soon after began to correspond with Alderman John Boydell of London, whom they made an honorary member and who served as a consultant for works on fine arts.[20] The Society clearly sought connections with London and in February 1793 it 'resolved, that Mr. Robert Jameson be appointed an Agent for the Society in London', although whether or not it intended to purchase a large number of books there can be questioned.[21] The Society had very clear standards for the books they did acquire. Books were rejected if any flaws were detected in the production and the Society had all their books bound and embossed in a particular way. The best books, it was believed, came from London: whether or not this was empirically true,

---

[18]   Examples include a hygrometer and a eudiometer. LHL, MS Linen Hall Minutes 7 November 1793 to 3 September 1812, (19 November 1795).
[19]   Anderson, *History*, p. 27.
[20]   LHL, MS Linen Hall Minutes 1 November 1791 to 28 October 1793, (18 April 1792 to 2 January 1793); for more information, see the *ODNB* entry on Alderman John Boydell.
[21]   LHL, MS Linen Hall Minutes 1 November 1791 to 28 October 1793, (20 February 1793).

it was a perceived truth and one reason why the Society might have wished to purchase books from the capital.

However, two weeks after Jameson's appointment in 1793, William Magee, the largest printer and bookseller in Belfast, was admitted to the Society. In fact, every major bookseller and printer in Belfast joined. At the next meeting the Society apparently reversed its plan to establish connections with London, and declared 'that such books as shall be ordered by the committee may be purchased in Belfast, if possible, and that such as cannot be so procured shall be ordered through the correspondence of the Belfast book sellers'.[22] So, almost from the moment of Jameson's appointment, he was destined not to be the primary source of provision for the Society's books.

According to the intermittent accounts from these years it appears that Magee was in fact the main conduit for book purchases.[23] Unfortunately, the place of publication for the Society's books cannot be easily identified. The catalogues do not include this information and due to a continuous policy of weeding the library's collections, many of these early acquisitions are no longer part of the library's holdings.[24] Therefore, we can only conjecture whether most of the items were original London editions, Dublin reprints, or even local Belfast prints. Examples of all three types of publications exist within the early collections. We must also speculate as to what percentage of items was purchased through Magee's connections. What were the benefits of purchasing items locally through Magee or one of the other Belfast booksellers? There seem to have been very few other than the promotion of local business and personal connections for the minutes are full of complaints about the slow speed of orders, the poor quality of the materials received and their cost. At one point the minutes recorded that Magee's account was to be paid, but that he should be 'shown the difference between the prices he has charged and the London prices'.[25] This suggests a possible abuse of the relationship by Magee, and also awareness, on the part of the Society, of the London book market.

---

[22] LHL, MS Linen Hall Minutes 1 November 1791 to 28 October 1793, (7 March 1793).

[23] Fragmentary 1790s accounts in binding of LHL, Linen Hall Library Accounts and Order book 1811 to 1829.

[24] Killen, *History of the Linen Hall Library*, p. 136.

[25] LHL, MS Linen Hall Minutes 7 November 1793 to 3 September 1812, (6 November 1806).

However, according to Máire Kennedy's work on book-trade networks in the south of Ireland, local printers served as one of the
primary means by which both new and second-hand books were
distributed throughout provincial Ireland.[26] This suggests that Magee,
and the other Belfast printers and booksellers, were using established
networks and business practices to fulfil the Society's orders.

If Magee was the primary conduit for book purchases during this
period, what role did Robert Jameson play as the Society's London
agent? Jameson himself is quite a mysterious figure, for, though there
are several mentions of him in the Society's minutes, all the correspondence has been lost. There is also no Robert Jameson to be found
among the guides to the London book trade. Although there was a
Robert Jameson listed in the London Directory during the dates of this
relationship, he was a merchant living on Iron-monger Lane in Cheap-
side.[27] What we know of the Society's agent fits well with this individual, though there is no way to confirm that the two Jamesons are the
same person. Robert Jameson completed purchases for the Society,
both of books and scientific equipment ordered from London dealers.
He also had periodicals delivered to his home, and sent them on to
Belfast in packets. These are things that a merchant could reasonably
accomplish, and since many members of the Society were merchants
specializing in shipping we can conjecture that they may have had a
contact with another merchant in London who would act as their
agent.

Whether they did or not, we do know that Robert Jameson, the
agent, did not seem to have any real knowledge of the print trade. In
1793 the Society sponsored a harp festival in Belfast to preserve
traditional Irish music. They hired Edward Bunting to record the
songs as they were being played. Some of the records made then were
the only known written versions, and so the Society resolved to assist
Bunting in having them printed. Though they got quotes from Irish
printers, it was determined that it would be preferable to have the

---

[26]   Máire Kennedy, 'Book Trade Networks in the South of Ireland', in *Branches of
Literature and Music: Proceedings of the Thirteenth Seminar on the History of the
Provincial Book Trade held in Bristol, 11-13 July 1995*, ed. by M. T. Richards (Bristol,
2000), pp. 25-46.
[27]   *A London Directory, or Alphabetical Arrangement; Containing the Names and
Residences of the Merchants, Manufacturers, and Principal Traders, in the Metropolis and its
Environs* (London, 1797), p. 83.

work done in London.[28] Jameson was assigned the task of supervising this process, a task which he quickly botched. Within a few months he had produced a proof copy of the music which was completely unacceptable to both Bunting and the Society, as it had not been 'executed with that elegance which the society had designed'.[29] Bunting personally travelled to London where he took over supervision of the production from Jameson, who was never again given a task of this type.

Jameson's relationship with the Society continued in one form or another until at least 1804. He received orders and made purchases under the Society's supervision, but his role was very limited. I would argue that this was a direct result of the struggle between local interests and the desire to be connected with London. If the Society had chosen a better-connected agent or one who was willing to assume a larger role in their acquisitions it would have threatened the local booksellers, who as members of the Society would not have allowed that to happen. They may have maintained Jameson as an agent because they desired a connection with London, despite, or perhaps because of, the fact that he was of very limited use to their organization.

Nearly all of the Society's business was suspended around the time of the 1798 rebellion. The radical sympathies of many of its members such as the librarian, Thomas Russell, who had been arrested for treason in 1796 while inside the library, meant that the organization had to keep a low profile or risk being destroyed by loyalist mobs.[30] As a result of the rebellion and the 1801 Act of Union, the atmosphere of the Society changed considerably. For a time, the active membership seemed to have retreated from a direct connection with the metropolis in favour of Irish goods. There is no mention of Robert Jameson in the minutes between the years 1797 and 1804. After 1800 there are several resolutions by the Society to purchase books locally in Belfast, through the Irish post-office, or in Dublin. The Society even specified that for Roscoe's *Life of Lorenzo de Medici* they 'prefer the Dublin edition if published'.[31] This subtle retreat highlights some of

---

[28] LHL, MS Linen Hall Minutes 7 November 1793 to 3 September 1812, (27 December 1793).
[29] Ibid., (4 November 1794).
[30] Killen, *History of the Linen Hall Library*, p. 213.
[31] LHL, MS Linen Hall Minutes 7 November 1793 to 3 September 1812, (20 February 1800).

the cultural and political undercurrents of the relationship with London for a liberal Irish institution. Though the Society seemed to desire the connection, it was a troubled one both for pragmatic reasons of trade and because of the political realities of eighteenth-century Ireland. London still represented the centre of this international scholarly community, but the members of the Society would have felt compelled by their own political beliefs to resist that relationship. Perhaps this is why they chose to emulate the Library Company of Philadelphia rather than a similar institution in the British Isles. In this way the Society could establish a connection with London without fully acknowledging it as the dominant influence. Further investigation must go into whether the Belfast Society and its complex relationship with London is representative of provincial institutions' interactions with the metropolis or whether this is a unique case.

The Belfast Library and Society offers a rare example for those interested in the history of print culture, since this institution has been in continuous use as a subscription library since the eighteenth century. Its collections, though not in their original state, are a constantly evolving opportunity for historians to trace changes in attitudes about reading and book consumption over a period of two hundred years. The small window of time during the 1790s examined in this paper provides insight into the establishment of these collections, the beliefs and attitudes about reading that shaped the acquisitions and the forces of trade and politics that influenced how they were assembled.

Was Sir Walter Scott a Bibliomaniac?

LINDSAY LEVY

Abbotsford library has always been considered as Scott's personal reference library. During his life time, when he was beset with financial problems and resolved to write his way out of debt rather than accept bankruptcy, his trustees exempted the contents of the library from the rest of his estate because they were considered to be the tools of his trade, and, as such, the means whereby he would eventually repay his creditors. After his death the first Abbotsford catalogue, which had been compiled by George Huntley Gordon, was edited and published by J. G. Cochrane. Cochrane annotated the entries for each relevant book with the title of the work of Scott in which it was referenced, and ever since Scott scholars have combed the shelves in search of the sources of his literary output. This is still the most frequent reason given by researchers who want to use the library. Undoubtedly Scott did use his books as a reference tool, and the library is an invaluable resource for those studying his writing, but this perspective has obscured the importance of Abbotsford library of itself as a collection, and of the light it sheds both on aspects of nineteenth-century book culture, and on Scott's perception of himself.

It has been argued that because, from the eighteenth century, library rooms were also used for entertaining, and 'a gentleman's library shelves were thus exposed to the inquisitive gaze of his guests,' the interpretation of a private library as part of the owner's biography is no longer possible.[1] By the early nineteenth century, at the time Abbotsford library was being created, a gentleman's library was not only public, but also prescribed. Books such as T. F. Dibdin's *Library Companion*, Isaac D'Israeli's *Curiosities of Literature*, and William Beloe's *Anecdotes of Literature and Scarce Books* began to make an appearance, containing bibliographies of suitable volumes for the discerning gentleman, and sometimes how much they were likely to cost. [2] Scott owned many

---

[1]   T. A. Birrell, 'Reading as Pastime', in *Property of a Gentleman: The Formation, Organisation and Dispersal of the Private Library 1620-1920*, ed. by Robin Myers and Michael Harris (Winchester, 1991) pp. 113-31 (p. 129).

[2]   T. F. Dibdin, *Library Companion, or the Young Man's Guide and the Old Man's Comfort in the Choice of a Library* (London, 1824); Isaac D'Israeli, *Curiosities of*

bibliographical books, and it is obvious from his marginal notes that he read them closely. His annotations are sometimes triumphant – as when he added to a statement in Dibdin's *English De Bure* that there are only two copies of *Britannicarum gentium historiae antiquae scriptores tres* in Britain – 'And one in my library purchased at Johnstones sale in Ireland' (Figure 1). [3]

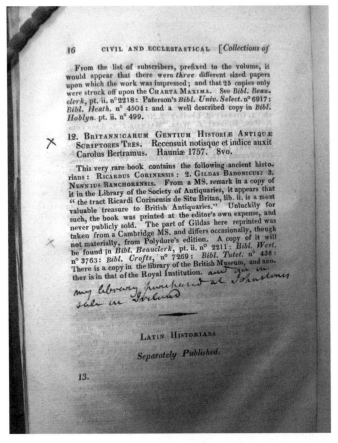

Fig. 1 Scott's annotation in his copy of Dibdin's *English De Bure*. Published by kind permission of the Faculty of Advocates and the Abbotsford Project Committee

---

Literature (London, 1791) (Scott owned the 6th edition, published in 1817); William Beloe, *Anecdotes of Literature and Scarce Books*, 4 vols (London, 1807-10).
[3]   T. F. Dibdin, *Specimen of an English De Bure* (London, 1810). Only 50 copies were printed.

At other times they were informative: 'That [copy of *Biblia sacra Latina*, published Moguntiae, 1462] in the Advocates Liby cost only £150.'[4] He was also conscious of the anomaly of keeping books in a public space where they were likely to be treated as commodities. As he commented in a letter to Anna Seward:

> But books are no longer respected for their insides, as they have been honoured with admission into the drawing-room which although a very pleasing and sensible transition from the stiffness of ancient manners when every guest was obliged to sit with hands across and listen to the prosing of such as could prose, has nevertheless contributed greatly to render books as expensive as elegant pieces of furniture.[5]

Despite these caveats I would like to follow Alberto Manguel who claims in his wonderful book *The Library at Night*, that every library is autobiographical.[6]

For, surely, Scott's library is one of the most autobiographical libraries to be found? He designed every part of the structure himself; it is his collection alone, rather than the product of subsequent generations of the same family, as many of the great Scottish libraries are, and the books in it span his entire life time, starting with those he received from his mother, aunt, and other family members, and ending with the journals and tracts that were left wrapped up at his death, waiting to be sent to the binder. In fact, the time-span of Scott's library extends just slightly beyond the grave, as the Bannatyne Club decided to continue sending their publications after his death to complete the set. For, as they stated in a letter of 26 June 1838:

> It has been a matter of great satisfaction to Lord Chief Commissioner Adam (one of the presenters of this work to the Bannatyne Club) to be able to place in the Abbotsford Library, this volume, whereby he understands that the Bannatyne Collections, will be fully completed in that Library; - so that the great and illustrious founder, alike of the Library and of the Club, will have handed down to posterity, in the seat of his creation, a work of antiquarian learning and curiosity which has been esteemed by the Club, as a most valuable addition to its eminent collection.[7]

---

4   Manuscript annotation in Beloe, *Anecdotes,* I, 31.
5   Cited in Heather Jackson, *Romantic Readers* (New Haven, 2005), p. 29 and note.
6   Albert Manguel, *The Library at Night* (New Haven, 2008), p. 194.
7   From a holograph letter bound into the Abbotsford copy of *Instrumenta publica,*

Probably the most straightforward biographical approach to Scott's book collection is through his marks of ownership. His childhood books are signed 'Walter Scott Junr.'. In 1792, when he qualified as an advocate, he began signing himself 'Walter Scott Advocate'. In later life his acquisitions are signed simply 'Walter Scott'. From around 1810 Scott's fame as a writer grew to an unprecedented level. As, ill health permitting, he continued to practise as Sheriff of Selkirk until his death, it seems reasonable to assume this change of signature indicates that, at a point yet to be discovered, he switched his self identification from advocate to that of writer.

There is also an observable progression in his use of bookplates. As a young man already obsessed with romance and chivalry, he used a bookplate made from the arms of Scott of Harden, from whom he claimed descent. It was printed on paper, cut out into a rough circle and pasted into the endpapers. In 1808 he created a portcullis crest with the motto *Clausus tutus ero* – 'I will be safe when I am enclosed' – which he intended to be applied to a few copies of every work he wrote or published.[8] These 'portcullis copies' were never produced, but at some yet to be discovered time, he added the gold-stamped device onto the spines of the books that were bound for his library.

Another possible biographical approach to Scott's library is to trace his intellectual development by examining the changing pattern of his book acquisitions and purchases, but it is difficult to formulate a coherent history of Scott's book buying as there is no accessions book at Abbotsford. Tantalisingly, Scott does appear to have kept some kind of purchasing record, as in a journal entry from 1 July 1827, he described himself as 'airing my old bibliomaniacal hobby of entering all the books recently acquired into a catalogue so as to have them shelved and marked'.[9] Perhaps this catalogue is yet to be found, but until it is we have to rely on the clues that are scattered throughout his journal and correspondence, in booksellers' records and in the library itself.

One extant record of Scott's early, eclectic book collecting is his first account with the Edinburgh bookseller Bell and Bradfute, which covers the period 1790 to 1793, when Scott was aged between nineteen

---

ed. by Thomas Thomson (Edinburgh, 1834).

[8]   *The Letters of Sir Walter Scott*, ed. by H. J. C. Grierson, 12 vols (London, 1932-37), II, 168-69.

[9]   *The Journal of Sir Walter Scott*, ed. by W. E. K. Anderson, 2nd edn (Edinburgh, 1998) p. 366.

and twenty-two. Scott was called to the Bar on 11 July 1792, and the account heading of 'Mr Walter Scott Junr' has been amended accordingly to 'Mr Walter Scott Advocate'. The account includes the binding of six volumes of sermons and Robert Lindsay of Pitscottie's *History of Scotland*, as well as the purchase of David Dalrymple's *Remarks on the History of Scotland* and Paul Henri Mallet's *Northern Antiquities*. In 1792 Scott purchased Thomas Evans's ballad collection, and the following year he bought three volumes of English songs with music, and the second Edinburgh edition of Burns.[10]

Occasionally, details of the ways in which individual volumes entered the library at Abbotsford can be determined from the books themselves because Scott has annotated them with the date, place and price of purchase, but this is rare. He sometimes noted in his journal that he had acquired certain volumes, but was often vague on how he obtained them. There is a similar problem with his letters, which can sometimes produce as many questions as answers. For example, the existence of five books at Abbotsford with the provenance of the Duke of Roxburghe is puzzling in the light of Scott's letter to T. F. Dibdin, written on 3 May 1812, in which he says:

> The Roxburghe sale sets my teeth on edge. But if I can trust mine eyes, there are now twelve masons at work on a cottage and offices at this little farm, which I purchased last year. Item, I have planted thirty acres, and am in the act of walling a garden. Item, I have a wife and four bairns crying, as our old song has it, 'porridge ever mair.' So, on the whole, my teeth must get off the edge, as those of the fox with the grapes in the fable.

But the presence of the Roxburghe books is explained by the letter he wrote to Richard Heber a mere eleven days later:

> As I conclude you will be a constant attendant on the Roxburghe sale I will make no apology for troubling you with the care of looking after a few trifling articles for me or putting the commission into such hands as you may think safe [...] I cannot resist sporting forty or by our lady fifty

---

[10] Anonymous, 'Scott's Early Book-buying', *Sir Walter Scott Quarterly*, 1 (1927), 107. Of the works cited only Robert Lindsay, *History of Scotland*, 3rd edn (Edinburgh, 1778), Thomas Evans, *Old Ballads, Historical and Narrative*, 2nd edn, 4 vols (London, 1784) and Robert Burns, *Poems, Chiefly in the Scottish Dialect* (Edinburgh, 1787) remain in the library.

pounds in St James's Square [the location of the Roxburghe sale]. I shall content myself with inclosing a list of the books I should like to have marking with a cross X concerning which I am anxious and leaving the prices entirely to you.[11]

Notwithstanding the costs of his new house, in 1812 Scott could well afford to indulge his passion for book buying, but in 1825, facing financial ruin, he noted plans for economies in his journal. 'No more building. No more purchases of land till times are quite safe. No buying of books or expensive trifles. I mean to any extent'.[12]

This ambiguity towards spending money is typical of Scott's journal and correspondence, and arouses suspicions that he was, at the very least, economical with the truth when it came to book buying. On 6 December 1827 he noted paying £1 10s. 0d. for Thomas Beard's *Theatre of God's Judgments*, (London, 1612) commenting: 'I think that Beard's Judgements is the first book which I have purchased voluntarily for nearly two years so I am cured of one folly at least.'[13] What then is to be made of his entry for the previous day, which includes the line 'To bill to Terry for books £32'? Is this perhaps involuntary book purchasing?

In the period November 1825 and April 1832, when Scott was writing his journal, and writing and publishing to discharge his debts, he punctuated his diary entries with brief accounts of debits and credits. A considerable number of these debits are to booksellers or bookbinders. Some of his comments show an ingenious approach to accounting. Beside an entry of July 1826 for a debt of £96 to Stevenson bookseller, Scott noted, 'Of this sum £70 was incurred last year so I am only accountable for £26 wilfully expended.' Beneath this particular entry he has added: 'My clumsy way of book-keeping answers very well. I find the balances come out accurate. I never bother myself with the silver.'[14]

Scott bought books from auctions and booksellers, and he also used his friends to search for him, notably Daniel Terry, the actor and theatrical impresario, who is given a grateful mention in the endpapers of several items. Terry was tasked at one time with finding the books

---

[11] *Letters*, XII, 333.
[12] *Journal*, p. 18.
[13] Ibid., p. 440.
[14] *Journal*, p. 196.

which Scott remembered from his childhood, including the rather charming book recording the journey of William Bingfield to the land of the dogbirds (Figure 2). Occasionally, it seems, Scott overrated the ability of his long-suffering friends to source the items he was seeking. Robert Jamieson, in a letter from Riga, complained to Gr′imur Thorkelin, the Icelandic scholar and antiquarian:

> In the last letter I recd from Walter Scott, he says:
> "There is a Collection of Old German Romances in Verse published by C. M. Müller in Berlin; I have the two first Numbers in 4to – Were ever more published? - I also want very much a copy of Musaeus's Popular Tales in the original German, & generally any works connected with Old Poetry or Chivalry." - I told Mr. Scott that Riga was the city upon the face of the Earth which furnished the least of any thing connected with Poetry or Chivalry; but that I wd apply to Professor Thorkelin, who was the most likely of any Gentleman I knew to advise or assist me in Procuring such thing.[15]

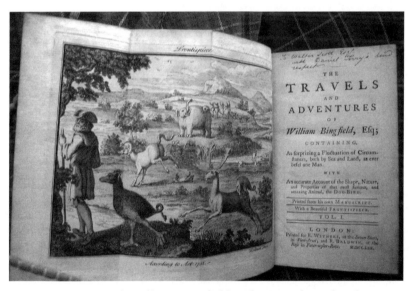

Fig. 2 Frontispiece of William Bingfield, *The Travels and Adventures of William Bingfield* (London, 1753). Published by kind permission of the Faculty of Advocates and the Abbotsford Project Committee

---

[15] Edinburgh, Edinburgh University Centre for Research Collections, MS La. III.379, fols 876-77. Thanks are due to Dr Susan Rennie McKillop who drew my attention to this letter.

Scott also acquired books from publishers on the topics he was researching, and as Peter Garside has noted in his essay *The Baron's Books*, he did not expect to have to return them. In a letter to Thomas Campbell, written in 1806 in connection with some items he required, Scott commented: 'I always experienced on such occasions that if the work is executed on my part with diligence and accuracy such books shall remain my private property.'[16] One book which certainly remained his private property was the first collection of Irish prose and poetry to be translated into English. The book, entitled *Poems: Translated from the Irish Language into the English by C. H. Wilson*, was published in Dublin in 1782 and sent to Scott by the Anglo-Irish antiquarian Joseph Cooper Walker. The pitiful letter that accompanied it was not bound into the book, but is preserved in the National Library of Scotland, and reads:

> I had begun a transcript of O' Rourke's noble feast in Irish but I think it better to send you the pamphlet in which it is printed, as it contains some Irish Tales which you or Mr. Weber might wish to see. Of this little publication I never saw but the copy which I send, & which I must beg of you to return whence a safe conveyance shall occur, but not until you have entirely done with it.[17]

It was certainly inadvisable to suggest to such an avid book-collector as Scott that he should keep any item for as long as he wished. Nineteen volumes of the collections of Massachusetts Historical Society intended for the Advocates Library sent to him with a similar message still remain at Abbotsford.

It is undoubtedly true, however, that many donors did not want their books returned for, as the Reverend William Parr Greswell wrote in a letter which accompanied the gift of his Annals of Parisian Typography, published in 1818, '... what author would not be ambitious of gaining a place for his productions on the shelves of Sir Walter Scott's library?'[18] Yet, as Scott was perfectly aware, such gifts came at a price, as they were usually accompanied by requests. It was also unfortunate for his intended economies, that until after 1840, postage

[16]   Peter Garside, 'The Baron's Books', *Romanticism*, 14:3 (2008), 245-258.
[17]   Edinburgh, National Library of Scotland, MS 881, 77: 11-17. Thanks are due to Professor Micheal McCraith who drew my attention to this letter.
[18]   Holograph letter bound into William Parr Greswell, *Annals of Parisian Typography* (London, 1818).

was paid for by the recipient rather than by the sender. In his journal for 6 January 1828 he noted:

> I am annoyed beyond measure with the idle intrusion of voluntary correspondents; each man who has a pen, ink, sheet of foolscap and an hour to spare flies a letter at me. I believe the postage costs me £100 besides innumerable franks; and all the letters regard the writer's own hopes or projects, or are filled with unasked advice or extravagant requests.[19]

None-the-less Scott bound most of the dedicatory letters into the books that they accompanied, even, in some cases, when the pages of the book were uncut. These gifted books and the letters that accompany them are another valuable biographical source, tracing as they do, the rise to fame of a man whose name would become so well known throughout the world that he would receive the first printed works from both Australia and Tasmania: Barron Field's *First Fruits of Australian Poetry* (Sydney, 1818) presented by the author, and Thomas E. Wells's *Michael Howe, the Last and Worst of the Bush Rangers of Van Dieman's Land* (Hobart, 1818) sent to him by Lachlan Macquarie.

In 1830 Scott suffered a stroke, and his publisher, Robert Cadell, in trying to find a project that would interest him without being too taxing, suggested that he compiled a *catalogue raisonnée* of his collections. Scott agreed immediately and set to work the following day, but he compiled his catalogue in the form of a novel entitled *Reliquiae Trotcosienses; or, the Gabions of the Late Jonathan Oldbuck Esq. of Monkbarns*. The stroke had left Scott with a mild aphasia and the work was muddled and difficult to read. Publication was suppressed by Cadell and J. G. Lockhart, who did not want to display what they interpreted as a diminution of the great man's intellectual powers. *Reliquiae Trotcosienses* was finally edited by Alison Lumsden and Gerard Carruthers and published in 2004. It is a complex tale narrated to us by the antiquarian Mr Jonathan Oldbuck, who states in his 'Preface' that he is borrowing from an anonymous friend, the description of a house in the South of Scotland, instead of describing his own collections. In this mischievous and convoluted way we are given Scott's personal guide to the antiquities and library of Abbotsford.

Scott's selection of the individual items amongst his books that were worthy of mention is curious, as they did not always represent the rarest

---

[19] *Journal*, p. 462.

or the most valuable items in his collection. He began his section on the contents of the library by commending his collection of historical works relating to Scotland and England as extensive and valuable. He was proud too, of his collection of Restoration drama, mentioning in particular an edition of Settle's *Emperor* [sic] *of Morocco*, the first play ever to be published with engravings, a copy of which he donated to the library of the Duke of Devonshire, commenting 'I question if there is another fair copy in the world'.[20] Special mention was given to fifteen volumes of a French work on antiquities, presented to him by George IV, and one hundred and thirty-nine volumes of a variorum edition of classical authors, the gift of Archibald Constable. Scott celebrated the collections of ballads, both Scottish and English, and those that he collected, mostly in the form of chapbooks, from John Bell of Newcastle; his collection of books on demonology and witch trials, and what he termed 'eccentric biography,' namely the lives of criminals, pirates, gypsies, and other such outsiders.[21] His section of early romances and works of chivalry he described as the 'Dalilahs' of a collector's imagination, and one of those receiving special mention was *Huon de Bordeaux,* a black-letter romance published in Paris in 1516, and one of the books purchased for him at the Roxburghe sale by Richard Heber.[22]

In conclusion, on the basis of this brief overview of the Abbotsford library and Scott as a book collector, can he be described as a bibliomaniac? A bibliomaniac can be defined as one who has an obsessive compulsive disorder involving the collecting or hoarding of books, who purchases multiple copies of the same book and edition, and accumulates books beyond possible capacity of use or enjoyment. Bibliomania as a malady was first noted by the physician John Ferriar in 1809, in a poem dedicated to Richard Heber, Scott's old friend and go-between in the Roxburghe sale, the man who famously declared that no gentleman could do without three copies of each book, one for his show copy which he would keep at his country seat, one for his own studies, and one for the service of his friends.[23] Scott owned a

---

[20] Scott almost certainly means Elkanah Settle, *The Empress of Morocco* (London, 1673); Walter Scott, *Reliquiae Trotcosienses,* ed. by Alison Lumsden and Gerard Carruthers, (Edinburgh, 2004) p. 47.

[21] *Reliquiae Trotcosienses,* pp. 52, 64.

[22] Ibid., p. 69-71.

[23] Cited in Nicholas A. Brisbanes, *A Gentle Madness: Bibliophiles, Bibliomanes, and the Eternal Passion for Books* (New York, 1999), pp. 110-11.

copy of Ferriar's poem and was familiar enough with it to inscribe in the endpapers of his own unsullied copy of Vere's *Commentaries,* (Figure 3)

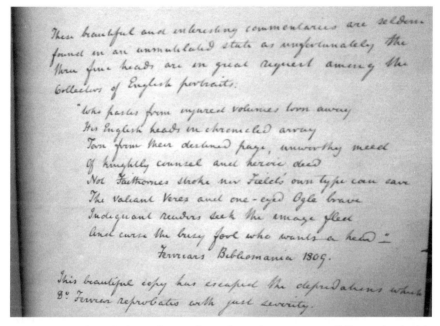

Fig. 3 Scott's inscription of a section of Ferriar's poem 'Bibliomania' in his copy of De Vere's *Commentaries.* Published by kind permission of the Faculty of Advocates and the Abbotsford Project Committee

the verse condemning the person

> Who pastes from injured volumes torn away,
> His English heads, in chronicled array.
> Torn from their destined page [...][24]

Ferriar has been largely forgotten and Thomas Frognall Dibdin is usually associated with the invention of the term 'bibliomania'. In the same year that Ferriar's poem appeared, Dibdin published his *The Bibliomania; or, Book-Madness* (Figure 4), and republished it in 1811, much enlarged; both editions are in the Abbotsford library.

---

[24] John Ferriar, *The Bibliomania, an Epistle, to Richard Heber, Esq.* (London, 1809); Francis Vere, *The Commentaries of Sr. Francis Vere* (Cambridge, 1657).

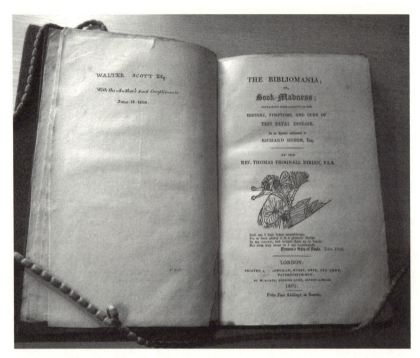

Fig. 4 Scott's copy of Thomas Dibdin's *The Bibliomania; or, Book-Madness* (London, 1809). Published by kind permission of the Faculty of Advocates and the Abbotsford Project Committee

Bibliomania became a fashionable term, as book madness swept Great Britain, much as tulip mania had in the Netherlands in the seventeenth century. It reached its apotheosis in the Roxburghe sale where Earl Spencer and the Duke of Devonshire bid against each other for a 1471 Venetian edition of Boccaccio's *Decameron*, which reached an unprecedented price of £2260. Dibdin wrote a humorous account of the sale in *The Bibliographical Decameron* (London, 1817), and later founded the Roxburghe Club, of which Scott was a member, dedicated to the republication of classic texts.

Sir Walter Scott built himself a house dominated by its library. Although he seems to have persuaded himself to the contrary, he continued to buy books even when his financial situation was so dire that he was effectively working himself to death to repay his debts. He accumulated books from authors and publishers around the world, and occasionally forgot to return those that had been lent to him. Does this make him a bibliomaniac? At least one of his contemporaries thought so, and wrote to him in a letter dated 19 February 1811: 'If you find yourself numbered amongst the most terrible and dangerous of bibliomaniacs, don't blame me – blame yourself!'[25] The writer of that letter was Thomas Frognall Dibdin.

---

[25] Edinburgh, National Library of Scotland, Edinburgh MS 3880, fols 51-2.

'Several Tons of Books':
The Creation, Travels and Rediscovery of
Thomas Cassidy's Recusant Library

JOSEPH MARSHALL

In 1992 the National Library of Scotland received on deposit a collection of some 5000 books, which had been in the library of Fort Augustus Abbey, which lies between Fort William and Inverness in Scotland. Most of these books were printed before 1700, including ten incunabula. They are mainly works of Catholic theology and controversy, and the focus of the collection is on English recusant books. Many are in contemporary bindings and have early provenances. The Cassidy Collection is virtually unknown and has been inaccessible to scholars for years. However, work is now underway on a database of the collection which will be available on the internet, and which will allow readers to consult the books. A by-product of this database has been the discovery of more information about the curious origins of the collection, in large part thanks to the obsessive inscriptions and annotations of the collector, the Reverend Thomas Francis Cassidy.[1]

Cassidy was a Franciscan friar in Dublin, who created his large collection between the 1820s and his death in 1873. As a Franciscan, who should have taken a vow of poverty and should not have owned any worldly goods, how was he able to acquire and retain such a large library? It has been suggested that in the early nineteenth century the Irish Franciscans' 'style of living became a source of scandal'.[2] If a Franciscan lifestyle could extend to the purchase of thousands of rare and finely-bound books – and presumably a building in which to keep them – then it is not surprising that there was controversy. Cassidy's career is thus of

[1] I wish to record my thanks to Fr Ignatius Fennessy OFM, whose help has been invaluable in preparing this paper. Fr Fennessy has provided considerable information as well as allowing sight of copies of letters and documents. In return, Fr Fennessey was shown an earlier draft of this paper, and is making use of some of the information about Cassidy's books in a forthcoming article of his own. Thanks are also due to Fr Francis Davidson OSB, Richard Yeo OSB, Andrew Nicoll, Noelle Dowling, Alastair Cherry.

[2] Patrick Conlan, 'Vocations to the Irish Franciscans 1800-1980', *Archivium Hibernicum*, 42 (1987), p. 30.

considerable interest, not just for librarians or book historians, but for anyone with an interest in the church in nineteenth-century Ireland.

According to Fr Ignatius Fennessy, Librarian of the Franciscan Library in Killiney, Thomas Francis Cassidy was probably from Donegal. Thomas was probably his baptismal name, Francis the name given him on profession. On 5 December 1829 he was professed, as was usual for Irish Franciscans, in St Isidore's College, Rome, and was ordained priest there on 18 December 1830.[3] It was at Rome that he seems to have started collecting books. His copy of *Regula et testamentum seraphici* [...] *Francisci* was inscribed with the year 1828.[4] It was an appropriate book to start the collection of a Franciscan.

Cassidy was subsequently appointed titular guardian to various vacant friaries in Northern Ireland; Strabane being the first, on 14 July 1834, and Carrickfergus being the last, to which he was re-appointed for the last time on 23 January 1851. He had vacated this position by the chapter meeting of 13 October 1852.[5] These sinecures gave him the right to vote in chapter meetings, but did not involve the responsibility of running an active friary. According to the official records of the church, then, he was nominally affiliated to the Franciscan order, but what did he actually do?

Some of the gaps in this picture can be filled in by the marks of ownership in the books. The vast majority of the books have his inscription, with an address and a date. Sometimes there are two or more dates, which may indicate that he added a date when he read a book as well as, or instead of, the date he acquired it. There are often other notes as well, such as the price he paid; he bought books from booksellers' catalogues, local individuals and contacts in Paris and Rome. Fr Fennessy remarks: 'For a Franciscan, the normal custom was for him to get permission to use a book given to him. It could be inscribed "Ad usum Patris / Fratris NN" [...] and be later deposited in the library of a friary where he was stationed.'[6] It is clear, however, that Cassidy thought he had personal ownership of these books.

---

[3] Killiney, Du Mhuire Fransican Library, MS Richard L. Browne notebooks 36, entry 32; Discretorium Minutes, St. Isidore's.

[4] *Regula et testamentum seraphici* [...] *Francisci* (Antwerp, 1644), shelfmark Cassidy.2156.

[5] Anselm Faulkner, *Liber Dubliniensis: Chapter Documents of the Irish Franciscans 1719-1875* (Killiney, 1978), p. 260.

[6] Letter of 18 January 2006.

Furthermore, the bookplate added to the Cassidy books by Fort Augustus Abbey, (Figure 1) gives him the initials 'R. P.' ('*Reverendus*

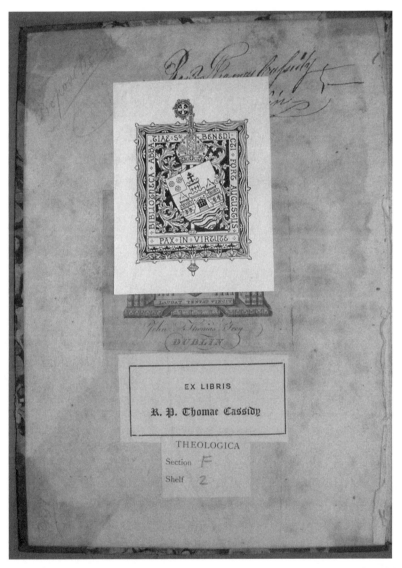

Fig. 1 Bookplates of John Thomas Troy, 1739–1823, Archbishop of Dublin, Fort Augustus Abbey Library and the Thomas Cassidy Collection (Lotharius Franciscus Philippus Marx, *Propositiones dogmatico-politico ex universa theologia* (Rome, 1787)). The Cassidy Collection under the custodianship of the English Benedictine Congregation, on deposit in the National Library of Scotland, with thanks to the Scottish Catholic Archives.

Pater') rather than 'O. F. M.' ('*Ordo Fratrum Minorum*') as might be expected of a Franciscan. Fr Fennessy notes further:

> The Provincial Reports do not say that he was ever officially secularized or given permission to leave the Franciscan Order; neither is there any sign of an official permission to live outside a friary (exclaustration). The Reports refer to him as a Franciscan living outside a friary and exercising pastoral function under a bishop; but there is no legal document confirming his legal right to do that.

It would appear that Cassidy's position was somewhat anomalous.

Most of the inscriptions include the address 'Harold's Cross', which is an old Dublin suburb. Nicholas Donnelly discusses the parish of Harold's Cross, and notes a directory entry for 1836 for 'Father Thomas Cassidy, ex-Franciscan, Chaplain to the Poor Clares in Harold's Cross'.[7] It would seem that Cassidy had taken up this position as chaplain in early 1833, partially severing his links with the Franciscans. The first inscription to mention Harold's Cross appears to be that in Cassidy's copy of William Robertson's *An Attempt to Explain the Words*, which is dated March 1833, and which, uniquely, also specifies St Clare's Convent.[8] Since most of the books are inscribed with later dates it would seem that this career move marked the real start of Cassidy's collecting career. Perhaps the duties of convent chaplain were not particularly onerous, and allowed him time to indulge in more literary pursuits such as building a library. In 1837 Cassidy appears as a subscriber to Samuel Lewis, *Topographical Dictionary of Ireland*, as 'Cassidy, Rev. Thomas, Harolds-cross, near Dublin'. He subscribed to an ordinary rather than a large-paper copy.[9]

The nuns had come to Harold's Cross in 1804, to start a girls' orphanage, and were supported by rich and powerful benefactors.[10] In 1837, there were seventeen professed nuns in the convent and ninety

---

[7]   N. Donnelly, *A Short History of Some Dublin Parishes. Part 6, Parish of St Nicholas Without, Francis Street. Section Three*, Carraig Chapbooks, 15 (Blackrock, [1979?]), pp. 88, 90.

[8]   William Robertson, *An Attempt to Explain the Words* (London, 1766), shelfmark Cassidy.1355.

[9]   Samuel Lewis, *Topographical Dictionary of Ireland*, 2 vols (London, 1837) I, xvi, available online at < http://www.booksulster.com/library/topog/subsc.php > [accessed 12 January 2010].

[10]   Patrick Conlan, *Franciscan Ireland* ([Dublin], 1988), p. 93.

children in the orphanage, and this private orphanage seems to have flourished.[11] However, records in the Dublin Diocesan Archives indicate that Cassidy's career in this apparently congenial setting was not smooth. On 28 March 1840, Fr Murphy wrote from Harold's Cross to Archdeacon John Hamilton asking for help:

> In consequence of the unfortunate action brought against the Revd Mr Cassidy, and his inability to meet the demand, a few friends have come forward and set a subscription on foot to liquidate in some degree the heavy expense incurred; Could I have your influence and that of the Revd. Gentlemen of the House, as also in a pecuniary way it would serve him and oblige Revd. Fr.[12]

By 1840, according to the inscriptions, Cassidy's book buying was in full swing, so if this is the same Cassidy, perhaps his bibliophilia had led him into what sounds like serious legal and financial trouble.

Cassidy apparently stayed on as chaplain, but not without controversy.[13] On 11 December 1846 we find Sr M. Murray writing from the orphanage to Archbishop Daniel Murray explaining her reason for writing was

> Revd. Mr Cassidy's Quarter will terminate the 21st of this month, hoping that if possibly convenient, some ultimate change may be made by that time. But we must earnestly entreat for many very serious causes, [...] that in the interim 'till something is conclusively arranged, the Orphans may not be desired to go to confession to Mr Cassidy. I made this observation in Low Week when Doctor Mayler called here, he appeared anxious they should do so, but soon as we mentioned that the case had been laid before your Grace, he immediately acquiesced. We shall anxiously await your decision on the matter.[14]

---

[11] Joe Curtis, *Harold's Cross*, 3rd edn (Dublin, 2004), p. 33; Lewis, *Topographical Dictionary*, II, 2.

[12] Drumcondra, Archbishop's House, MS Dublin Diocesan Archives (hereafter DDA), File 36/3: Papers of Archdeacon John Hamilton, 1840, No. 49; see Mary Purcell, 'Dublin Diocesan Archives: Hamilton Papers (7)', *Archivium Hibernicum*, 50 (1996), p. 64.

[13] He was still chaplain in 1846, according to the Arch-Diocese of Dublin, Roman Catholic Directory for Dublin, 1846 'State of Religion', available at <http://www. from-ireland.net/diocs/1846/dubreleducation1846.htm> [accessed 12 January 2010].

[14] Drumcondra, Archbishop's House, MS DDA File 32/2: Murray 1846. No. 113; see Mary Purcell, 'Dublin Diocesan Archives: Murray Papers (4)', *Archivium Hibernicum*,

This raises more questions: what exactly were his terms of employment at the convent, and why was his position apparently being terminated at the end of the 'Quarter'? What was the 'case' laid before the Archbishop? That the nuns did not wish the orphans to make their confessions to Cassidy suggests he had an unfavourable character. Nevertheless, he seems to have remained in Harold's Cross, judging by the inscriptions although, the 'Index of Clergy' in the Dublin Diocesan Archives, indicates that he ceased to be chaplain at some point in 1847. He does not appear in the 'Index' again until 1867.

In the summer of 1847, perhaps with his services no longer required at the convent, Cassidy seems to have travelled to Rome, inscribing books with that city as the address in August and September 1847. The inscription on Romano, *De Sacro Sigillo* dated 28 August 1847, specifically mentions the College of St Isidore.[15] Cassidy was back in Harold's Cross by 7 January 1848 – perhaps a wise decision, in view of the revolutionary turmoil that was about to engulf Rome and much of Continental Europe. One has the impression that Cassidy had some kind of private income that enabled him to travel and collect books without having to rely totally on his clerical employment.

There are several different addresses which appear over the years after 1847, without any particular consistency. It looks as though Cassidy continued to reside at Harold's Cross – we know from one inscription that he was living at no. 84.[16] However, he also inscribes books naming the Adam and Eve Franciscan monastery church on Merchant's Quay in Dublin, particularly from 1848 to 1850. In early 1848 he stood in for the Franciscan Minister Provincial when he was ill.[17] Other addresses appear in his hand during the same period, such as 21 Black Hall Street, Dublin where he may have kept his library. A copy of *A Life of the Lady Warner* is inscribed twice: Adam and Eve, 1849, and 21 Black Hall Street, 21 September 1849.[18] Was he living at Harold's Cross, working at Adam and Eve, and storing books at no. 21 Black Hall Street? A further address which appears in the books dated

---

39 (1984), p. 79.

[15]   Romano, *De Sacro Sigillo* (Milan, 1611), shelfmark Cassidy.1191.

[16]   The inscription is in Paul Jasz-Berenyi, *A New Torch to the Latin Tongue* (London, 1670), shelfmark Cassidy.1605.

[17]   Killiney, Du Mhuire Franciscan Library, MS J1, n. 93.

[18]   Edward Scarisbrike, *A Life of the Lady Warner* (London, 1692), shelfmark Cassidy. 973.

1851 onwards is 21 Arran-quay. This may be the place of purchase rather than Cassidy's place of residence. Shaw's 1850 Directory suggests that Arran-quay was a step down in the world from Black Hall Street (drapers and merchants rather than barristers and solicitors). Within living memory, there were bookstalls on the Dublin quays, so the inscriptions may refer to the site of a stall rather than to a building.

By 1 May 1860, Cassidy seems to have moved to 1 Fortview Avenue, Clontarf (near Dublin). The 1862 report of the state of the Irish province records that he was living outside a friary, but engaged in pastoral ministry, and with his bishop's permission to hear confessions and celebrate Mass.[19] Fr Kenner's report, on his general visitation of the Irish friars in 1864, noted that Cassidy was 'a difficult man to live with'.[20] Perhaps because of his difficult character, the Franciscans seem to have avoided challenging his anomalous lifestyle. Living outside a friary, collecting books on a vast scale, travelling across Europe – Cassidy nonetheless kept returning to his connections with the order. A number of books purchased at Clontarf are inscribed with his name and 'O. S. F.', indicating that he saw himself as a Franciscan at this period. Between 1867 and 1869 he was a chaplain at 'Jervis Street', according to the Dublin 'Index of Clergy'; this probably refers to the hospital run by the Sisters of Mercy there.[21] In 1870 he seems to have moved to Blackrock, another village near Dublin, where he was chaplain to the Carmelite Convent until his death on 30 September 1873.[22] The last date inscribed on a book is 1872.[23]

Cassidy's difficulties with his religious order are implicit in his only surviving will of 19 September 1852. A most curious document, it may have been made in the heat of the moment following a dispute between Cassidy and his order which was subsequently smoothed over. He was particularly concerned about his books:

> I Thomas Cassidy bequeath all my books to the Most Rev Paul Cullen, Roman Catholic Archbishop, for the intended Irish Roman Catholic

---

[19] Personal correspondence from Fr Fennessy.

[20] Personal correspondence from Fr Fennessy.

[21] Available at < http://www.chaptersofdublin.com/books/OldDub/chapter5.htm > [accessed 3 July 2010].

[22] MS Richard L. Browne notebooks 36, entry 32.

[23] The inscription is in a copy of Christian Kruik van Adrichem, *Vita Jesu Christi* (Antwerp, 1578), shelfmark Cassidy.138.

University or some similar Roman Catholic public Institution. From this bequest I emphatically exclude the Franciscan Order and all other religious Orders save and except the Orders of Jesus, and Saint Vincent de Paul [...]. These books constitute my whole property, having no money whatever. I hereby solemnly declare that I have got a release from the Franciscan Order in May last.[24]

Cassidy's intention was, it seems, to transfer the books to Paul Cullen (1803-1878), Archbishop of Dublin, so that they could become part of the library of the new Catholic University which John Henry Newman and others were trying to establish. There seems to be no evidence that Cullen or the Archdiocese ever came into possession of the books. Well before Cassidy's death in 1873, it had become clear that the original vision of the Catholic University would not be realized. The university had failed to obtain a charter and Newman had left as rector.[25] There would have been little point giving the books to a semi-functioning university in 1873 (and in any case, it might have been reluctant to acquire such a large collection of controversial English works). Indeed, by 1882, the 17,000 volumes in the Catholic University's library were in storage.[26] It seems highly likely that in view of these circumstances Cassidy made a subsequent will or codicil which does not survive. The best guess is that it was probably destroyed in the fire in the Irish Public Record Office in 1922. In any case, the collection did indeed pass to a 'Roman Catholic public Institution' – but it was to Fort Augustus Abbey in Scotland, rather than an Irish university.

There is a gap in the records between Cassidy's death in 1873 and the books' arrival at Fort Augustus in Scotland in 1885. On 24 August 1885, Prior Jerome Vaughan of Fort Augustus wrote to Judge John O'Hagan:

When the late Lord O'Hagan did me the honour of paying me a visit at Fort Augustus last summer he told me of a certain interesting library

[24]   Edinburgh, Scottish Catholic Archives, (SCA) FA 59/29.1.
[25]   Colin Barr, *Paul Cullen, John Henry Newman, and the Catholic University of Ireland, 1845-1865* (Notre Dame, Ind., 2003), p. 2; see also *Struggle with Fortune: A Miscellany for the Centenary of the Catholic University of Ireland, 1854-1954*, ed. by Michael Tierney (Dublin, [1954]).
[26]   Norma R. Jessop and Christine J. Nudds, *Guide to Collections in Dublin Libraries: Printed Books to 1850 and Special Collections* (Dublin, 1982), pp. 30-31.

which had been left to him & to others of his family in succession, but which had for years been stored up in boxes in a certain warehouse in Dublin, & consequently was doing no service to anyone but the warehouseman. His Lordship expressed to me a desire of his on three different occasions that this library should be brought out into light & made use of in the service of religion, & wished that it should be at all events during the rest of his lifetime located at S. Benedict's Abbey. His Lordship's sad illness & death a few months later prevented his wish being realised, & I understand that Mrs Judge O'Hagan has succeeded to the library according to the will of the original owner, & that she also would be glad to see it turned to the care of religion & thinks it could be better cared for in our Abbey than in the Dublin warehouse. If Mrs O'Hagan would kindly assert that we have the loan of this interesting & valuable library, I can assure her that we should keep it as a sacred trust & would be willing to undertake the cost of transit of the boxes from Dublin to Fort Augustus. I need hardly point out that to have the use of such a library would be a great boon to our Abbey for which we should be extremely grateful & certainly the books would be kept in better preservation on the shelves of our library than confined in boxes in a warehouse. Hoping that my proposal may meet with a favourable reply, I am dear Judge O'Hagan, yours truly – Jerome Vaughan OSB.[27]

Lord O'Hagan was Thomas O'Hagan (1812-1885), the first Catholic Lord Chancellor of Ireland since 1688.[28] He had supported Newman's attempts to establish the Catholic University of Ireland.[29] Perhaps Cassidy decided Cullen was no longer an appropriate recipient of the books, and knowing Thomas O'Hagan as a great and learned establishment defender of Catholicism, decided to transfer the books to him and his family instead. (O'Hagan, indeed, seems to have fallen out with Cullen).[30] There were connections between the O'Hagan family and the Poor Clares; Thomas O'Hagan's sister Mary entered the order in

---

[27]   SCA, FA 59/29.4.
[28]   For O'Hagan, see John F. McEldowney, 'Thomas O'Hagan' in *ODNB* available at < http://www.oxforddnb.com > [accessed 13 January 2010]. See also the information provided by the Public Record Office of Northern Ireland available at < http:// www.proni.gov.uk/introduction__o_hagan_papers_d2777.pdf > [accessed 13 January 2010]. The extensive papers of O'Hagan are at Belfast, Public Record Office of Northern Ireland, D/2777 and Dublin, National Library of Ireland, MSS 17864-74.
[29]   John Henry Newman, *My Campaign in Ireland* (Aberdeen, 1896), pp. 300, 418.
[30]   See PRONI introduction to O'Hagan papers, p. 4.

1843 in Newry, becoming Abbess in 1855.[31] Could Cassidy and O'Hagan have known each other? In any case, it seems that Thomas O'Hagan had possession of the books, and wanted them transferred to Fort Augustus where he had stayed, and been impressed by the liturgy.[32] One further connection between Thomas O'Hagan and the Abbey was his nephew, George Teeling. Teeling had been educated at Fort Augustus and later returned as a priest. Subsequently, he also edited a collection of O'Hagan's speeches.[33]

When O'Hagan died on 1 February 1885, the rights to the books passed to his daughter Frances Mary who had married her cousin John O'Hagan (1822-90) in 1865. He was another devout Catholic who wrote for the Catholic Truth Society and, it seems, took responsibility for the collection. He replied to Jerome Vaughan on 8 November 1885:

> I delayed writing finally about Father Cassidy's books until I had an opportunity of seeing Mr Charles Teeling whose consent I thought right to obtain both because he is the surviving executor of Father Cassidy and is entitled under the will to the books for his life after the life estate of my wife. He was anxious that if possible the books should be confided to an Irish institution but on my representation of the almost insuperable difficulty in effecting this he fully assented to their being entrusted to you. So I will give directions that the books should be sent to Fort Augustus. There are however two conditions which I think it right to require. First, that two full catalogues of the books be made out – one to be kept by you, the other to be sent to me. Secondly that in each of the books, there be imprinted a declaration that it belongs to the library of the Revd Thomas Cassidy entrusted for safe keeping to the Abbey of Fort Augustus.[34]

---

[31]   Mrs. Thomas Concannon, *The Poor Clares in Ireland* (Dublin, 1929), pp. 142-3.

[32]   Fort Augustus was one of only three places in Britain in the late nineteenth and early twentieth centuries that performed the complete Catholic liturgy, (John Martin Robinson, "Selling up", *The Spectator*, 28 August 1999, p.42).

[33]   *Selected Speeches and Arguments of the Right Hon. Thomas, Baron O'Hagan*, ed. by George Teeling (London, 1885).

[34]   SCA, FA 59/29.2. Charles Hamilton Teeling (1778–1850) was the younger brother of the Irish nationalist Bartholomew Teeling (1774–98). Charles's eldest daughter, Mary, married Thomas O'Hagan in 1836; she died in 1868. The Charles Teeling who was Cassidy's executor may have been her brother. So it seems that Cassidy had left the collection to the O'Hagans, appointing members of the Teeling family as executors.

Prior Vaughan replied on 13 November 1885 consenting to 'have two catalogues made of the books', and 'a label pasted in each volume stating that the book belongs to the library of the Rev F. Cassidy entrusted for safe keeping to the Abbey of Fort Augustus.'[35] It would be nice to know what became of these 'catalogues', if they were ever produced.

The arrival of 'several tons of books' necessitated some re-organization at the Abbey.[36] David Hunter Blair O. S. B., the Abbey librarian, wrote on 12 September 1885 that 'plans are being concerted for fitting up the calefactory as a library'.[37] On 2 December 1885, Blair wrote, 'The first instalment of the "Cassidy Library" arrived – some sixteen large boxes: a lot of rubbish, but some good theology with it.'[38] On 9 December 1885, he added: 'The rest of the "Cassidy" books came – eighteen more boxes.'[39] They were stored 'in the big ground-floor chambers of the monastery (the former workshops of the old Fort) which, connected by lofty arches, made an admirable library'.[40] By the early twentieth century the monastery had 40,000 volumes.[41]

The collection was deposited in the National Library of Scotland (hereafter NLS) in 1992 along with other early books owned by the Abbey. In 1999 the Fort Augustus community was dissolved, and most of the non-Cassidy books deposited in NLS were sold by Bernard Quaritch of London. There were various sales and dispersals of the bulk of the library which had remained at Fort Augustus; the auction at Fort Augustus on 22 May 1999 was by McTear's of Glasgow, who

---

There may have been family connections between Cassidy and the O'Hagans and Teelings, which would make the arrangements seem less idiosyncratic. George Teeling, O'Hagan's nephew, may have been the son of the second Charles Teeling.

[35] SCA, FA 59/29.3.

[36] George Hume claims inaccurately that this took place at the start of the 20th century in 'A Whole New Shelf Life', *Herald*, 14 March 1996. Available online at < http://www.heraldscotland.com/sport/spl/aberdeen/a-whole-new-shelf-life-1.462185. > [accessed 2 July 2010].

[37] David Hunter Blair, 'Journal of a Scottish Benedictine', SCA FA 210/57, p. 41.

[38] Ibid., p. 48.

[39] Ibid., p. 49.

[40] David Hunter Blair, *A Medley of Memories: Fifty Years' Recollections of a Benedictine Monk* (London, 1919), p. 160.

[41] David Hunter Blair, *St. Benedict's Abbey, Fort Augustus: Past and Present* (Fort Augustus, n.d.), pp. 22-23.

listed 685 lots in their catalogue.[42] The University of the Highlands and Islands purchased some books; the Theology Collection went to the Highland Theological College, and the Celtica Collection to Sabhal Mòr Ostaig on Skye. The NLS purchased 759 volumes in 2000 which are now a separate special collection. The Cassidy Collection, however, was not the Abbey's to sell, and it remains in NLS on deposit, under the custodianship of the English Benedictine Congregation Trust. A few Cassidy books may be found in other locations, which is hardly surprising given the collection's history. There is at least one manuscript with a Cassidy bookplate among the other Fort Augustus papers now in the Scottish Catholic Archives (FA 61/6). The Getty Library has a copy of a 1583 Paris *Missale Romanum* with his bookplate. However, it seems reasonable to assert that the vast majority of Cassidy's books are indeed in the collection at the National Library of Scotland.

What of the books themselves? While cataloguing the books is still ongoing, it would be rash to make too many assertions. However, it does seem to be a coherent collection; it is the library of a Catholic gentleman, with a focus on scholarly and controversial works, especially those printed in the sixteenth and seventeenth centuries for English-speaking recusants. Although religious books are dominant, there are also editions of the classics, pamphlets, poetry, maps and scientific works. Many books are in fine bindings and have interesting marks of former ownership, such as bookplates, marginalia, inscriptions and library stamps. It could be argued that Cassidy was ahead of his time in being particularly interested in copy-specific information such as provenance, as he acquired significant numbers of duplicate texts. An example is Mumford's, *The Catholic Scripturist* of which there are five copies with different dates of acquisition.[43] The presence of so many duplicates may indicate that Cassidy was acquiring whole libraries, perhaps from Irish country houses during the Famine (although the Irish gentry would have been more likely to have collections that were primarily Protestant). Generally, the condition of the books is very good, particularly for a collection of this period;

---

[42]   Robert McTear & Co., *The Library, Fort Augustus Abbey: Auction Date Saturday 22nd May, 1999* (Glasgow, 1999).

[43]   J. Mumford, *The Catholic Scripturist*, 4th edn, corrected, ([London?], 1767), shelf-mark Cassidy.908-11.

nevertheless, Cassidy seems to have been happy to acquire imperfect books – sometimes there are several imperfect copies of the same book. These apparently contradictory tendencies may either indicate absent-mindedness or a vision of the collection which included sensitivity to copy-specific information.

Amongst the ten incunabula, which have all been reported to the Incunabula Short-Title Catalogue (ISTC), there is nothing of extreme rarity, but there are some very fine examples of early Continental printing. For example, the copy of Robertus Caracciolus, *Sermones quadragesimales de poenitentia* has some fine hand-colouring.[44] Cassidy dated it 13 February 1845, and paid £18 6s. 0d.; the bookplate is of Prince Augustus Frederick, the Duke of Sussex, whose extensive library was sold in 1844-45. Another notable item is Albertus Magnus, *Sermones de eucharistiæ sacramento*.[45] Dated by Cassidy 1863, it has numerous early annotations and a binding made from a manuscript on vellum.

The sixteenth-century items include several key works in English religious history. There is a fine copy of the folio edition of St John Fisher, *De veritate corporis et sanguinis Christi* (Coloniae: [Petrum Quentel], 1527), dated by Cassidy 15 October 1843.[46] More important still is a copy of the original setting of Stephen Gardiner, *An Explication and Assertion of the True Catholique Fayth* (Figure 2).[47] This black-letter work by the Bishop of Winchester was written while he was in prison in the Tower of London. Like the vast majority of the early English books in the collection, this copy has not been recorded in Pollard and Redgrave's *Short-Title Catalogue* (hereafter *STC*) nor in the English Short-Title Catalogue (hereafter ESTC). This copy is dated December 1843, and has notes which indicate that Cassidy purchased it for £3 16s. 0d. from a catalogue issued by the London bookseller Charles Dolman from whom he bought books on numerous occasions (Figure 3).

---

[44] Robertus Caracciolus, *Sermones quadragesimales de poenitentia* (Venice, 1472), shelf-mark Inc.119.7*.

[45] Albertus Magnus, *Sermones de eucharistiæ sacramento* (Cologne, 1498), shelfmark Inc.46.8.

[46] St John Fisher, *De veritate corporis et sanguinis Christi* (Cologne, 1527), not yet shelfmarked.

[47] Stephen Gardiner, *An Explication and Assertion of the True Catholique Fayth* ([Rouen], 1551), shelfmark Cassidy.402; ESTC S102829.

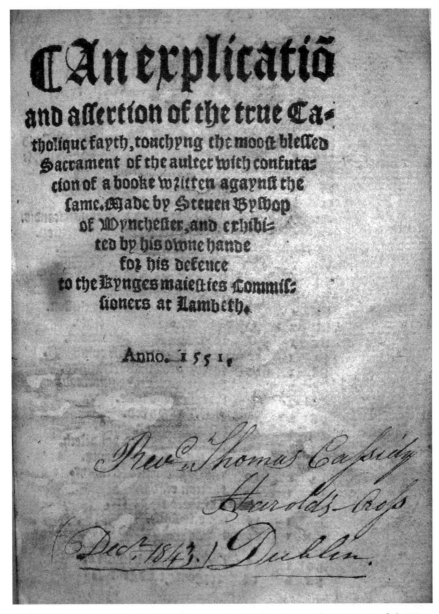

Fig. 2 Title-page of Stephen Gardiner, *An Explication and Assertion of the True Catholique Fayth* ([Rouen], 1551), (*STC* 11592, ESTC S102829). The Cassidy Collection under the custodianship of the English Benedictine Congregation, on deposit in the National Library of Scotland, with thanks to the Scottish Catholic Archives

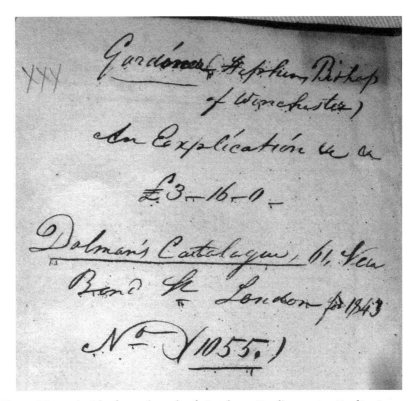

Fig. 3 Notes inside front board of Stephen Gardiner, *An Explication and Assertion of the True Catholique Fayth* ([Rouen], 1551). The Cassidy Collection under the custodianship of the English Benedictine Congregation, on deposit in the National Library of Scotland, with thanks to the Scottish Catholic Archives

There are a number of extremely rare *STC* books in the collection including the only copy listed in *STC* of *The Art to Dye Well*.[48] This copy was dated by Cassidy twice – 1834 and 1845. Allison and Rogers' bibliography of English Catholic books, which includes several books formerly at Fort Augustus, lists a second copy in private hands.[49] Even rarer, however, is the unique copy of a re-issue of the Rheims New Testament. This copy was dated by Cassidy 29 March 1839.[50]

---

[48] R. P., *The Art to Dye Well* ([St. Omer, 1626]), shelfmark Cassidy.67; ESTC S94822.
[49] A. F. Allison and D. M. Rogers, *The Contemporary Printed Literature of the English Counter-Reformation between 1558 and 1640: An Annotated Catalogue* (Aldershot, 1989), no. 665.
[50] *The New Testament* (Antwerp, 1630), shelfmark Cassidy.724; ESTC S91010.

The seventeenth-century books are more diverse than those of the earlier period. No item from the collection was recorded in Donald Wing's *Short-Title Catalogue* or Clancy's *English Catholic Books 1641-1700* and it is possible that there are unique items still to be identified.[51] An example of a non-religious work is the folio edition of *Ovids Metamorphosis Englished*.[52] This work, which contains numerous fine engravings, was acquired from a Dublin bookseller, T. Connolly (6 Chancery Place) but was not dated by Cassidy. There is a significant amount of pamphlet literature, including Civil War and Commonwealth tracts, such as the anonymous *The Worcester-shire Petition to the Parliament for the Ministry of England*.[53] There are also some surprising inclusions such as Job Ludolphus, *A New History of Ethiopia*.[54]

The eighteenth-century items seem to be completely unreported, and there are some rare and interesting examples. Wetenhall Wilkes, *An Essay on the Existence of a God* is an early Belfast imprint.[55] This copy, in a fine Irish binding, was dated by Cassidy 1859. There are also some particularly rare books such as the copy of Thomas Myles Burke, *A Catechism Moral and Controversial* which is not recorded in ESTC, although its existence is noted by *English Catholic Books 1701-1800*.[56] This copy was dated by Cassidy 23 January 1840. One apparently unique item is *The Old Fashioned Farmer's Motives* (Figure 4).[57] Cassidy acquired this early Manchester imprint, not listed in ESTC or COPAC, in 1837. When the collection is fully brought to light, there will certainly be many more discoveries and surprises.[58]

---

[51]   Donald R. Wing, *Short-Title Catalogue of Books Printed in England* [...] *1641-1700*, 2nd edn, 3 vols (New York, 1972-88); Thomas H. Clancy, *English Catholic Books 1641-1700: A Bibliography*, 2nd edn, (Aldershot, 1996).

[52]   Ovid, [trans. by George Sandys] *Ovids Metamorphosis Englished* (London, 1640).

[53]   Anonymous, *The Worcester-shire Petition to the Parliament for the Ministry of England* (London, 1653).

[54]   Job Ludolphus, *A New History of Ethiopia* (London, 1684).

[55]   Wetenhall Wilkes, *An Essay on the Existence of a God* (Belfast, 1730), shelfmark Cassidy.2067.

[56]   Thomas Myles Burke, *A Catechism Moral and Controversial* (Lisbon, 1753), shelfmark Cassidy.438. F. Blom, *English Catholic Books 1701-1800: A Bibliography* (Aldershot, 1996).

[57]   Anonymous, *The Old Fashioned Farmer's Motives* (No place; 1778; repr. Manchester, 1778), shelfmark Cassidy.161.

[58]   Anyone interested in the collection is welcome to contact the National Library of Scotland. Although NLS cannot yet provide access to the books in the normal way,

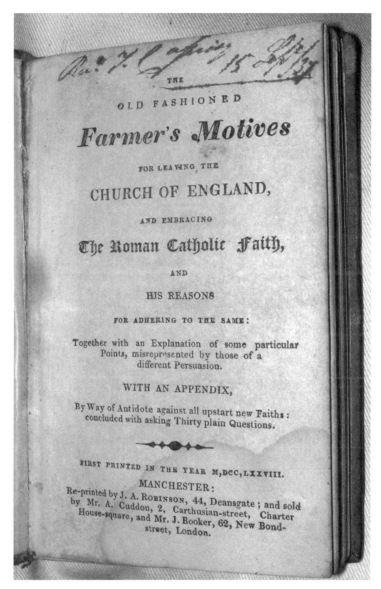

Fig. 4 Title-page of *The Old Fashioned Farmer's Motives*, (No place, 1778; repr. Manchester, 1778). The Cassidy Collection under the custodianship of the English Benedictine Congregation, on deposit in the National Library of Scotland, with thanks to the Scottish Catholic Archives

staff will try to help with specific queries and make arrangements to see books where possible.

Love, Blood, and Teddy Bears:
Twopenny Libraries, Parliament, and the Law of Retail Trade in the 1930s

K. A. MANLEY

One of the few occasions when the subject of libraries has been discussed by parliament involved a collision between culture and commerce. Public librarians were pitted against commercial librarians and the entrenched positions of the book trade against enterprising tradesmen who provided books to the paying public – but were not themselves booksellers. As for the teddy bears, they were unwitting pawns, but their role was crucial.

On 25 July 1935 the third Earl of Iddesleigh rose to his feet in the House of Lords and addressed his noble peers:

> My Lords, no doubt many of your Lordships have observed the very great growth in the last few years of popular lending libraries [...]. They do not require any subscription or any deposit, and any member of the public who likes to pay twopence can take a book out and keep it for a week. The books in which they deal are admirable from the point of view of the entertainment of the public, but no one would claim they have any particular educational value. They consist, in chief, of fiction, and I am informed that the books most in demand are those which deal with the subjects of love and blood – both excellent things in their places.[1]

The noble earl must be left in suspense so that the type of library which was exercising his mind can be considered. Twopenny libraries were a phenomenon of the 1930s. Lord Healey recalled how as a boy in that decade he read

> *The Boy's Magazine* [...] followed by *The Wizard*, *The Rover* and *Modern Boy*, with its tin cut-outs of racing cars and aeroplanes. Then I turned to the twopenny library for Bulldog Drummond and the Saint, and became hooked for life on thrillers.[2]

---

[1] *Hansard Parliamentary Debates: House of Lords*, 5th ser., 98 (25 July 1935), col. 865; reprinted in *The Times*, 26 July 1935, p. 7.
[2] Denis Healey, *The Time of My Life* (London, 1989), p. 16.

Twopenny libraries belonged at the bottom of the pile. Professor Raymond Irwin used to refer to the classical concept of the 'golden chain', by which written knowledge was transmitted down the ages through links of books and libraries – a 'conquest of space and time', as he wrote.[3] Twopenny libraries were part of that 'golden chain', but not at the summit; they were definitely in the bargain basement.

Their origins lay in the circulating libraries of previous centuries. The majority, found on most high streets, could amount to several thousands of volumes, ranging from cheap fiction to weighty tomes of science. At the bottom of the heap were corner shops, such as stationers, haberdashers, and tobacconists, who furnished a shelf or two of books for customers who might want to borrow a book for a night and had no interest in taking out a subscription. These shops were where the providers of cultural goods collided with retail trade. Shopkeepers could buy complete libraries off the shelf. By 1784, William Lane, proprietor of the famous Minerva Library in London, could supply ready-made collections for people wishing to run their own 'Minerva' libraries, comprising novels and romances published by his Minerva Press. He advertised that running a circulating library was 'an undertaking advantageous as well as genteel'.[4] This business continued well into the nineteenth century under his successors.[5]

Small circulating libraries made up entirely of novels spread like fleas. By 1900, corner-shop libraries still existed, but many of those on the high street had succumbed to the monoliths Charles Mudie and W. H. Smith. Mudie's warehouses in London – his main building was a landmark in New Oxford Street – lent books all over the country, thanks to improved postal services and the iron horse, which made feasible next-day delivery of goods, while W. H. Smith was lending from newsagents' stalls in railway stations and from high street shops. They were joined by Boot's, the chemists, Booklovers' Library, the Times Book Club, Harrods, and others. These outlets provided the latest books, because they could afford multiple copies in vast numbers and sell them off cheaply when demand died down.

---

[3]   Raymond Irwin, *The Heritage of the English Library* (London, 1964), p. 26.
[4]   *The World*, 25 March 1788, p. 1.
[5]   For Lane and his business, see Dorothy Blakey, *Minerva Press, 1790-1820* (London, 1939).

The tide changed against the monoliths because of two events in 1928: the launch by Victor Gollancz of his famous 'yellow-jacket' novels, with their distinctive eye-blinding yellow covers; and the re-launch of Mills & Boon. The latter had published books on a variety of topics up to 1928, when Mr Mills died. Mr Boon decided to concentrate on slushy romantic fiction making the reputations of Ethel M. Dell, Denise Black, Barbara Cartland, and many more. Gollancz and Mills & Boon achieved virtually instant popularity and, to the dismay of municipal public libraries, a new readership appeared, demanding what can best be described as lowbrow novels.

To satisfy this new demand, a plethora of cheap libraries arose, unconnected with bookshops: twopenny libraries. Initiated in Harlesden in 1930 by Ray Smith Ltd., a firm of printers in the city of London, such libraries were immensely popular. Mr Maurice Millem was appointed general manager, and when he expired in 1935, his obituary stated that the company then owned eleven libraries throughout the metropolis, employing a staff of 280 with a circulation of 100,000 volumes.[6] Kelly's trade directories for 1930 – before twopeny libraries had appeared – show that local circulating libraries were run on the one hand by W. H. Smith and Boot's, and on the other by individuals who were almost invariably booksellers. By 1934 the directories were dominated by libraries organized as limited companies unconnected to any bookshop. Many were chains; the biggest had perhaps twenty-five to thirty libraries, often with catchy names: Novel Library of Hastings and St Leonards; Dragon Libraries of Brighton; Good Companions Library of Hove; The Lounge Library of Chichester; Readwell Libraries of Burgess Hill; the Sunshine Library of Bournemouth; Eureka Lending Library of Landport, Hampshire (which also boasted an Imperial Library); the Non-Stop Library of Kilburn High Road; and Chain Libraries of Haywards Heath, Horsham, East Grinstead, Basingstoke, Swindon, Dorchester, Trowbridge, Grantham, Lincoln, Grimsby, and other salubrious places. Another chain which clearly eyed a particular clientele was On the Square Libraries Ltd. of Retford, Holbeach, Stamford, and Spalding. Anyone wishing to borrow a book from the Ideal Book Club on the North Acton Road, only had to send a telegram to 'Wellbound, Harlesden'.

---

6   *The Times*, 25 July 1935, p. 16.

The book trade regarded twopenny libraries with horror, because they took business away from libraries run by booksellers. Twopenny libraries did not sell books. In 1928 the Publishers Association had decreed that book borrowing was not conducive to book buying and regarded with unease the growing number of twopenny libraries which applied to join the Association as 'other traders'. This was the only way to acquire a trade discount for dealing in new books. Sixteen such libraries had been permitted to join by the end of 1932, another forty-two in 1933, seventy-seven in 1934, and ninety-one in 1935.[7] These figures give a more accurate idea than directories of how twopenny libraries increased.

As twopenny libraries spread, a growing resentment arose over a practice known as 'partial remaindering', whereby some booksellers offered novels to twopenny and public libraries for 2s. 9d., although the published price, paid by the rest of the trade, was 7s. 6d. The Publishers Association expressed unhappiness but did nothing; one of the chief booksellers who favoured the arrangement sat on their Council. The Association also objected to a practice whereby some booksellers sold books to libraries below the net price, claiming they were soiled, when really they were review copies.[8]

Public libraries treated twopenny libraries with horror – because these usurpers were seducing their natural constituency – and bewilderment, because many public librarians were glad to see the back of people who wanted purely the lower forms of fiction. Their dilemma was that they felt their mission was to raise reading standards by offering the chaff as well as the wheat. The effect of the competition was immense; in 1934 Bermondsey Public Libraries complained that their fiction issues had declined by 20,000, while Fulham Public Libraries reported an all-round decrease of 82,512.[9]

In 1933, T. E. Callander, public librarian of Fulham, drew attention to the increasing demand for books from people who read for amusement only, quoting Mrs Leavis's comment that the 'reading man is not now necessarily a cultured man'. (He might have quoted Mrs Leavis's description of twopenny libraries as 'tupenny dram-

---

[7] R. J. L. Kingsford, *The Publishers Association 1896-1946* (Cambridge, 1970), p. 149.

[8] Kingsford, *Publishers Association*, pp. 149, 151, 198-99.

[9] 'Municipal Library Notes', *Library Association Record*, 4th ser., 1 (1934), 237; *The Times*, 1 September 1934, p. 7.

shops'.[10]) Callander examined a twopenny library catalogue, finding it predominantly lowbrow: titles by Edgar Wallace alone amounted to 100, forty-one were by Warwick Deeping, thirty-eight by E. P. Oppenheim, thirty-two by P. G. Wodehouse, and so on. Middlebrow writers were headed by Arnold Bennett with twenty-five titles, while others had far less: J. B. Priestley was represented by five, Hugh Walpole by nine, though there were thirteen titles by D. H. Lawrence and five by Radclyffe Hall; but William Faulkner, E. M. Forster, Virginia Woolf, and T. F. Powys did not feature at all. Callander's conclusion was that twopenny libraries provided the kind of literature which public library users could only obtain by hanging around book-return counters in strategic positions. He argued that public libraries should not compete directly with private enterprise.[11]

One year later, James D. Stewart, public librarian of Bermondsey and nephew of the pioneer of open access in public libraries, James Duff Brown, welcomed twopenny libraries as tapping into a new reading public; but he damned them with faint praise:

> They catered directly for the people who did not require any books in particular, but merely something amusing or exciting to read – the people who liked their daily dose of imaginative dope. They were prepared to pay handsomely for their intermittent amnesia, their periodical escapes from wives or husbands or other worries.[12]

Stewart pointed out that repeated tuppences added up to more than the rate levied for a public library; but he welcomed twopenny libraries in the hope that they would relieve the public library of the burden of providing the lowest fiction.

Colin Watson, in his classic study of the detective novel, *Snobbery with Violence*, provides basic statistics. At its peak in the 1930s Boot's Booklovers' Library had branches in 450 of its chemists' shops, serving up-to half a million customers. In 1933 W. H. Smith and Son had library services operating from 300 shops and 375 bookstalls; its largest branches comprised over 1000 subscribers while 160 branches contained over 1000 volumes each. Medium-sized shops would offer 400 to

---

[10]   Q. D. Leavis, *Fiction and the Reading Public* (London, 1932), p. 8.
[11]   T. E. Callander, 'The Twopenny Library', *Library Association Record*, 3rd ser., 3 (1933), 88-90.
[12]   *The Times*, 14 September 1934, p. 6.

900 volumes. Smaller and more remote shops were supplied from a central depot in London. Smith and Son also lent books to groups such as staff associations, clubs, Civil Service clerks, and local government officials.

As for the competing chain libraries, one reported in 1933 that its Poole branch was issuing 6000 books per week, and that seventy-five per cent of the readers were lower middle-class women. Furthermore, each book was forced to last for 180 issues, while 'non-returns' – stolen books – only accounted for one in eight thousand.[13] Thomas Joy, formerly manager of Harrods Library before establishing the lending library of the Army and Navy Stores (he began his career at the Bodleian Library), wrote a handbook for twopenny librarians in 1949 in which he stated that thefts were rare because it was hardly worthwhile stealing a book worth only a few shillings. As for books not returned, Joy recommended employing an 'ex-policeman with tact and a bicycle'.[14]

The classic description of a twopenny library is fictional. George Orwell's novel, *Keep the Aspidistra Flying*, was published by Victor Gollancz in 1936 but set in 1934. Orwell's hero, or rather anti-hero, Gordon Comstock, wants to be a poet and believes that he must spurn capitalism and live in poverty in a filthy garret. He throws up his job as an advertising copywriter to work in a second-hand bookshop, with twopenny library attached.

The bookshop contained a mixture of second-hand books and, near the door, new books to catch the eye:

> Novels fresh from the press – still unravished brides, pining for the paperknife to deflower them – and review copies, like youthful widows, blooming still though virgin no longer, and here and there, in sets of half a dozen, those pathetic spinster-things, 'remainders', still guarding hopefully their long preserv'd virginity.[15]

The library was in a separate room and was lined with novels:

> Eight hundred strong, the novels lined the room on three sides ceiling-high, row upon row of gaudy oblong backs, as though the walls had been built of many-coloured bricks laid upright. They were arranged alpha-

---

[13]   Colin Watson, *Snobbery with Violence* (London, 1971), pp. 30-32.
[14]   Thomas Joy, *The Right Way to Run a Library Business* (London, [1949]), p. 39, 41 n.
[15]   George Orwell, *Keep the Aspidistra Flying* (London, 1954), pp. 12-13.

betically. Arlen, Burroughs, Deeping, Dell, Frankau, Galsworthy, Gibbs, Priestley, Sapper, Walpole. Gordon eyed them with inert hatred. [...] Horrible to think of all that soggy, half-baked trash massed together in one place. Pudding, suet pudding. Eight hundred slabs of pudding, walling him in – a vault of puddingstone. The thought was oppressive.[16]

When customers finally appear, Comstock adopts 'the homey, family-doctor geniality reserved for library-subscribers'. Two women arrive, one 'carrying under her arm a copy of *The Forsyte Saga* – title outwards, so that passers-by could spot her for a highbrow'.[17] The other is returning an Ethel M. Dell, at which the *Forsyte Saga* woman smiles at Comstock as if to say, highbrow to highbrow: 'Dell! [...] The books these lower classes read!' Later a chemist's shop assistant arrives, and Comstock has to change his manner again:

'What kind of book would you like this time, Miss Weeks?'
'[...] Well, what I'd *really* like's a good hot-stuff love story. You know – something *modern*'.
'Something modern? Something by Barbara Bedworthy, for instance? Have you read *Almost a Virgin*?'
'Oh no, not her. She's too Deep. I can't bear Deep books. But I want something – well, you *know* – modern. Sex-problems and divorce and all that. *You* know.'
'Modern, but not Deep', said Gordon, as lowbrow to lowbrow.[18]

Of course, Gordon did know what she meant and soon found something suitable. However, Gordon falls on hard times and accepts work in a twopenny library:

one of those cheap and evil little libraries ('mushroom libraries', they are called) which are springing up all over London and are deliberately aimed at the uneducated. In libraries like these there is not a single book that is ever mentioned in the reviews or that any civilized person has ever heard of. The books are published by special low-class firms and turned out by wretched hacks at the rate of four a year, as mechanically as sausages and with much less skill. In effect they are merely fourpenny novelettes dis-

---

[16]   Ibid., p. 9.
[17]   Ibid., pp. 15-16.
[18]   Ibid., p. 25.

guised as novels, and they only cost the library-proprietor one and eight-pence a volume.[19]

Gordon might have been describing 'Minerva'-type novels of the late eighteenth century. As Gordon's fortunes wilt, so does his aspidistra. In Orwell's view, the poorer the library in which Gordon works, the worse his social and economic circumstances become. Gordon only achieves salvation when he gives up working in a twopenny library and returns to life as an advertising copywriter.

Like Gordon, the users of twopenny libraries were perceived as belonging to the lower classes of society. The libraries were frequented by those who were easy to please and unaccustomed to frequenting more formal premises. F. R. Richardson, chief librarian of Boot's Booklovers' Library, wrote in 1935 that twopenny library users 'will hesitate to enter one of the better-class bookshops or libraries because they would feel mentally and socially ill at ease in its unaccustomed atmosphere'.[20]   This enormous preamble returns the story to the Earl of Iddesleigh's speech to the Lords in 1935: Iddesleigh – alias Henry Stafford Northcote (1901-70) – had literary connections; his mother-in-law was a well-known novelist, Mrs Belloc Lowndes, whose brother was Hilaire Belloc. He was also a Conservative peer (his grandfather had served as a minister under Disraeli) who believed that the Lords' prime job was to act as an amending chamber while the Commons was busy initiating legislation.

Iddesleigh had discovered that twopenny libraries considered themselves exempt from the provisions of the Shops Act of 1912 on the grounds that they did not sell anything. Under this Act, shop assistants could only work eight hours a day and only until eight o'clock in the evening, nine o'clock on Saturdays; and they were entitled to a half-day holiday each week. Twopenny libraries, on the other hand, regularly opened for an additional hour each night and on Sundays; and employees did not enjoy half-days off.

One chain of libraries had twenty-five branches between Liverpool and Worthing, most opening at 8.30 a.m. and not closing until 10 p.m.; some were open from 8 a.m. until 11 p.m., or fifteen hours. Iddesleigh's view was that assistants in twopenny libraries were being made

---

[19] Ibid., p. 247.
[20] F. R. Richardson, 'The Circulating Library', in *The Book World*, ed. by John Hampden (London, 1935), p. 197.

to work excessive hours, offering unfair competition to W. H. Smith's and Boot's, the sort of libraries, as he pointed out, with which their lordships were familiar. Smith's and Boot's libraries closed when their shops closed. Twopenny libraries were also undercutting tradesmen who ran small libraries as add-ons to their main businesses, as many stationers, tobacconists, newsvendors, and booksellers did. This was unfair competition.

Iddesleigh moved that lending libraries be included in the definition of retail trade in the Shops Act. Labour MPs had already raised the subject after interested trade unions complained of exploitation of staff. In April 1934 the Home Office had issued advice that hiring out bicycles was not a retail trade, and that twopenny libraries were in the same position. In April 1935 the Ministry of Labour drew to the Home Office's attention the Novel Circulating Library of Southampton which employed library assistants under the age of eighteen to work fifty-four and a half hours per week. Old books and jigsaws were sold elsewhere in the shop, but that business stopped trading at 8 p.m., and 1 p.m. on Wednesdays; the library assistants continued working. The Government's advice, however, was that a library was not part of a shop. Pressure was building, though, and on 22 July 1935, three days before Iddesleigh spoke in the Lords, the National Federation of Retail Newsagents wrote to the Home Office enclosing a resolution from their annual conference, moved by a Mr W. Shakespeare from Warwickshire, that lending libraries be included in the Shops Act.[21]

Iddesleigh's argument was based on a recent court case involving a twopenny library proprietor. One morning in May 1934 Police Constable Whitton entered the premises of 8 Chariot St., Hull. He observed a man take a book down from a shelf, go to a girl sitting at a pay-desk, and deposit a few coppers. Whitton queried the manager, Mr Ralph Lee, as to whether he was running a library and charged him with contravening the Sunday Observance Act of 1677.[22] Lee was found guilty and fined five shillings. He appealed. In the following year, the case of Lee *vs.* Craven (Craven being the Hull police chief) came before the High Court, King's Bench Division, in front of the Lord Chief Justice, Lord Hewart, and Justices Avory and Humphreys. Mr Lee contended that he was not a tradesman because he was hiring

---

[21]   National Archives, HO45/16666, 22 July 1935; cf. *The Times*, 18 June 1935, p. 18.

[22]   *The Times*, 2 April 1935, p. 4.

out, not selling, goods, citing the case of Palmer *vs.* Snow (1900) where it was held that a barber was not a tradesman. The Lord Chief Justice replied: 'I thought a tradesman meant a man who has mastered the art or mystery of his craft'. Lee's solicitor argued that the Postmaster General provided telephones on Sundays, just as the gas companies provided gas. 'But they don't keep a shop', snapped the Lord Chief Justice. 'No, but they buy and sell' was the unavailing response. The appeal was dismissed, with the Lord Chief Justice's opinion that Lee was 'trafficking in goods'.

The Government minister responding to Iddesleigh was Lord Feversham, and the civil servants had advised him not to alter the Government's position, unless the High Court specifically found against it, but suggested that he might express a little doubt. Feversham's view was that Lee *vs.* Craven did not change matters, because the prosecution had not been brought under the Shops Act. Furthermore, the legal basis of what constituted retail trade had been decided in a previous test case which was of fundamental importance in underpinning the entire legal foundation of shopping in this country: Dennis *vs.* Hutchinson. Mr George Dennis was the occupier of a stall, or 'pitch', on Skegness beach, which he rented from Lord Scarborough. On 18 July 1921 a police sergeant observed Mr Dennis at his 'pitch'. His business was teddy bears which he did not sell but stuck to a metal pole attached to handles. Customers paid threepence to turn the handles and get their bears to the top of their poles first. They were known as the 'slippery bears', and the winners could choose from sweets or cigarettes. The policeman took the names of everyone in sight.

Mr Dennis appeared before the magistrates, along with the proprietor of the neighbouring pitch, both accused under the Early Closing Act of 1920 – those teddy bears should have been tucked up in bed. Dennis and neighbour were fined ten shillings for each offence. They appealed to the High Court, King's Bench Division, and in 1922 came before the Lord Chief Justice and Justices Avory and Roche. Dennis contended that he was not running a shop, merely a place of amusement, while the prosecution argued that a trade or business did not have to involve a sale to fall under the Shops Act. At which the Lord Chief Justice asked: 'Is the Casino at Monte Carlo a shop?' The prosecutor replied: 'It might be for the purpose of the Act'.[23]

---

[23] *The Times*, 19 January 1922, p. 4.

The prosecution case was that Dennis and neighbour were carrying on the business of 'amusement caterers'. 'What did they retail?' asked the Lord Chief Justice. 'Amusement', was the answer, at which Mr Justice Roche asked: 'How do you distinguish between retail and wholesale amusement? By the *encores*?' – (laughter in court). The upshot was that they decided that the judges at the original trial were wrong to categorize as a shop a stall where teddy bears had a metal pole stuck to their backsides for the amusement of punters. 'An amusement caterer was not a shopkeeper'; there was no distinction between a teddy-bear stall and a London theatre. By analogy, librarians were clearly 'amusement caterers', and so the law did not consider twopenny libraries to be shops.

Lord Feversham expressed sympathy to the noble Earl, but was not going to overturn that High Court decision. Iddesleigh asked whether the Government would afford time in the Commons for a bill on the subject, but Feversham could not 'commit another place on that point'. Iddesleigh prepared a draft bill himself to include libraries 'lending for reward' in the Shops Act, excluding public or charitable libraries such as those of Sunday schools. It was introduced into the House of Lords on 5 February 1936, with its second reading on 13 February.[24]

The civil servants consulted interested departments such as the Board of Trade, who were concerned over public libraries, the Board of Education, and the Ministry of Health, and organizations such as the Library Association and the Charity Commissioners. The Library Association wanted to draw attention to how happy public library assistants were with their working conditions, while the Charity Commissioners, who were responsible for John Rylands Library, the Cripplegate Institute, various village libraries, and many others, were not particularly interested. One civil servant wanted to define twopenny libraries as 'recreational', 'though', he added, 'I am not sure that this word has any established place in the English language'. Indeed, it did not appear in the *Oxford English Dictionary* and therefore could not be used in an act of Parliament. Iddesleigh raised the problem of exempting Sunday school libraries, but wrote to Feversham that he would not pursue that particular hare.

---

[24] National Archives, HO45/16666, House of Lords Bill, 26 Geo. 5 & 1 Edw. 8; *Hansard Parliamentary Debates: House of Lords*, 5th ser., 99 (5 & 13 February 1936), cols 425 & 611-14.

Iddesleigh's bill passed on 25 February, but the Government insisted on amendments, worked out by the civil servants. The sticking-point was how to distinguish between different kinds of libraries. In the event, the wording referred to exempting libraries 'from which no private profit is derived' from the Shops Act, as well as libraries founded under the Public Libraries Acts or for charitable purposes. This was amended by Lord Lucan to include libraries at which no other retail business was carried on at the same premises.[25]

Iddesleigh's bill eventually passed muster and was sent to the Commons. The second reading took place on 8 May 1936, and the bill was referred to Commons Standing Committee B.[26] This large committee gave rise to renewed amendment and argument. Discussion centred on the best phraseology to include twopenny but exclude other kinds of libraries. The Government's spokesman was Geoffrey Lloyd, Under-Secretary of State in the Home Office. His speech was prepared by the civil servants along the lines of their previous discussions about definitions. He also brought up the question of club and Sunday school libraries, which might turn a small profit for charitable purposes. Were they operating for gain?

Rhys Davies (Labour, West Houghton), raised a point much beloved of Labour MPs. What about brass bands? Suppose an emporium employed a brass band to march down the High Street advertising its wares: would the members of the band be regarded as employees, and therefore as shop assistants? By analogy, he argued, what if a lending library was acting as an incentive to a business of which it was not actually part? J. R. Leslie (Labour, Sedgfield) claimed that shop assistants in tobacconists worked longer hours where there was a lending library. 'We know', he said, 'that this book-lending is a subterfuge to enable people to enter the building and buy other things'.[27] In other words, without a library, tobacconists would have to close earlier, to the obvious advantage of shop assistants.

---

[25] *Hansard Parliamentary Debates: House of Lords*, 5th ser., 99 (25 February 1936), cols 743-45; (3 March 1936), cols 862-63.

[26] *Hansard Parliamentary Debates: House of Lords*, 5th ser., 99 (10 March 1936), col. 954; *Hansard Parliamentary Debates: House of Commons*, 5th ser., 308 (7 & 21 February 1936), cols 505, 2150. National Archives, HO45/16666, Standing Committee B, *Report on Shops Bill*, 21 May 1936.

[27] National Archives, HO45/16666, Standing Committee B, *Report on Shops Bill*, 21 May 1936.

R. C. Morrison (Labour MP for Tottenham) was concerned about Co-operative Society libraries. A few still existed in Lancashire and Yorkshire and traditionally operated above shops, such as grocers'; their librarians tended to be volunteers. Morrison was anxious they should not be regarded as operating for gain. Geoffrey Lloyd's advice from civil servants was to lie low and say nothing, because it was tricky. One pointed out that Bolton Co-operative Society Library employed paid staff; another regarded Morrison's amendments as meaningless, and scrawled 'otiose' on a memo; either a library was run for gain or not. Ministers were urged not to give in to Morrison, who wanted an exemption for 'free libraries attached to clubs'. The Government's argument was that any retail business might establish a free library for 'educational purposes', claim exemption from the Shops Act and stay open all hours. However, another member threatened to wreck the bill and accused the Government of adopting 'a typically Civil Service attitude'. Tempers rose, though a personal meeting between the Home Office and interested MPs was minuted as 'quite amicable'.

In the event the Government changed the wording to exempt libraries which were not carried on for the purposes of gain other than that of making a profit for some philanthropic or charitable object (including any religious or educational object) or for any club or institution which is not itself carried on for purposes of gain – 'gain' now replaced 'reward'. An exemption to the Shops Acts was inserted for co-operative societies registered under the Industrial and Provident Societies Acts, provided that 'no pecuniary profit is directly derived from the lending of books', and that no person employed in any shop occupied by a co-operative society should be engaged in library work as well. These amendments were made in the Commons on 6 July and agreed in the Lords on 7 July. Royal Assent was given on 14 July 1936.[28]

The Home Office sent circulars to local authorities, while some libraries did not believe that their opening hours had to fall in line with shops. In December 1936 Peerless Libraries of Liverpool, whose director was a Mr Fagin, complained to the Home Secretary of the hardship of closing their libraries earlier, because seventy per cent of

---

[28] *Hansard Parliamentary Debates: House of Commons*, 5th ser., 314 (6 & 7 July 1936), cols 991-92, 1403; *Hansard Parliamentary Debates: House of Lords*, 5th ser., 101 (9 & 14 July 1936), cols 594-95, 793.

their business was conducted in the evenings. Many customers were shop-workers who would now find the libraries closed when they went home. The Home Office answered that twopenny libraries had to close at 8 p.m., 9 p.m. on Saturdays, and have a half-day holiday but that *selling* books was exempted from the provision for a half-day holiday.[29]

Iddesleigh's amendment to the Shops Act came into operation on 1 January 1937. On Saturday 12 July Mudie's suddenly closed by order of the courts after ninety-five years in business. Wyndham Lewis recalled Mudie's as a relic from a lost age,

> a superbly Forsyte institution, solid as roast beef. [...] It was about the only place in London where you could still find muttonchop whiskers, lorgnettes, tall hats from late-Victorian blocks, feathered and flowered toques, [...] and that atmosphere of unhurried, fastidious leisure which has quite gone.[30]

Blame for its demise was attributed to the twopenny libraries, though William Foyle, the bookshop owner, pointed out that W. H. Smith and Boot's, with their local outlets, were the real competitors to the centralized Mudie's.[31] Twopenny and public libraries together were, perhaps, the final death blow.

Twopenny libraries were not left triumphant. They had jumped onto a bandwagon and many fell off. Blue Triangle Libraries of Walthamstow, for instance, was registered in 1933 as a limited company. The directors were Bella Guyster, of Stamford Hill, and Bernard Guyster, a medical practitioner and director of Walthamstow's Picture Theatre and Homerton Amusements. Shares were also owned by Red Triangle Libraries of Holloway. The library dissolved only six years later, having ceased trading 'a long time ago'. Clearly, these 'amusement caterers' had failed to satisfy Walthamstow.[32]

The case of Herbert Odell, formerly Mayor of Ilford, who opened twenty-three twopenny libraries, was more unusual. His libraries failed to show a profit, and in 1936 he received summonses for failing to pay rates in Sheffield, Eastbourne, Bradford, Worthing, and Hastings.

---

[29]   National Archives, HO45/17142.
[30]   Guinevere L. Griest, *Mudie's Circulating Library and the Victorian Novel* (Newton Abbot, 1970), p. 27.
[31]   *The Times*, 12 July 1937, p. 13; 19 July 1937, p. 10, letter by Foyle.
[32]   National Archives, BT31/33406/272710; *London Gazette*, 14 March 1939, p. 1776.

Odell petitioned for bankruptcy but set up a new company to protect his estate agency, which, too, went bankrupt. He blamed various international crises and the economic situation, while the Official Receiver blamed Odell's gross mismanagement, the fact that he collected rent for landlords which was not paid into their accounts, and, because of the failure of his library business, deemed he had broken the law by starting up another business while an undischarged bankrupt. He was not discharged until 1952.[33]

Iddesleigh's bill did not affect libraries kept as an adjunct to another business. Many stationers and tobacconists rented small ready-made libraries, like William Lane's 'Minerva' libraries of the eighteenth century. A number of suppliers existed to serve them; Foyle's advertised in 1938 that they supplied 3000 retail outlets around the country. They were partly why the ire of the Publishers Association had been directed towards twopenny libraries; most disappeared in the 1960s. Argosy & Sundial Libraries Ltd. ceased in 1962. Their local agencies in the north were acquired by Allied Libraries of Manchester, in the midlands by Wholesale Libraries of Leicester, and in the south by South Country Libraries of Croydon.[34] Allied Libraries had 1489 agents, mostly newsagents, in 1961, but closed in 1975. In about 1969 South Country Libraries Ltd. had almost 1200 agents, mostly newsagents but also post offices, general stores, and hairdressers; less than 150 were left by 1978. The impetus to closure often came when shops were taken over by younger people or immigrants. The latter company managed to survive into the 1980s, but W. H. Smith's and Boot's libraries had closed in 1961 and 1966 respectively.[35]

Public libraries debated the fiction question for years but became the chief purveyors of Denise Black and Barbara Cartland. Writing in 1956, Audrey Donne-Smith of Countryside Libraries Ltd. of Hitchin argued that twopenny libraries 'provided any reader worth his salt with ample opportunity to broaden his literary horizon, passing him on to the public library if and when he outgrew "escapist" reading'. She continued that public libraries had 'flattened out these brave little shops', whose proprietors paid towards their own extinction whenever

---

[33] *The Times*, 18 June 1936, p. 4; National Archives, J13/16345; *London Gazette*, 21 July 1936, p. 4716; 24 October 1952, p. 5637; 19 May 1967, p. 5699.
[34] *Bookseller*, 20 January 1962.
[35] Patricia M. Long, 'The Commercial Circulating Library in the 1970s', *Library History*, 5 (1981), 185-93.

they paid their rates. Yet, she queried, what was the point of spending 'vast sums of public money', when three out of four books issued in public libraries were still novels: 'What should we say of the National Health Service if (on the principle that one must have jam to hide the powder in) it had spent most of its money on barley sugar and bull-seyes [...]?'[36]

Twopenny libraries failed in the long term but succeeded in bringing about a reading revolution. They created a general increase in the level of readership of fiction, even though public libraries proved to be the main beneficiaries.

---

[36] *The Times*, 4 September 1956, p. 9.

'My Own Small Private Library': USA Armed Services Editions and the Culture of Collecting

HELEN SMITH

On 1 December 1942, Franklin D. Roosevelt wrote to William Warder Norton, Director of the newly established Council on Books in Wartime (hereafter CBW), commenting: 'a war of ideas can no more be won without books than a naval war can be won without ships. Books, like ships, have the toughest armor, the longest cruising range, and mount the most powerful guns'.[1] A year later, the CBW launched its most ambitious project: the production and distribution of paperback Armed Services Editions (hereafter ASEs). Between 1943 and 1947, nearly 123 million copies of 1322 titles were sent out from Army and Navy warehouses to military personnel in Overseas Theatres of Operation, hospitals, and Prisoner of War camps.[2] Their contents ranged from poetry and literary classics to foreign policy, westerns, historical novels, occasional cartoons, mysteries, humour, and self-help texts.

The ASEs were different from many of the books circulated to soldiers, not only in the range and volume of titles, but also in the fact that they were designed to be expendable. The books were printed on cheap paper and enclosed in flimsy cardboard covers. This design not only kept costs to a minimum but enabled the ASEs to circumvent army property regulations and move freely among troops. As John Jamieson notes, for military purposes 'expendability' referred to objects which were 'lawfully subject to be consumed in use'.[3] In a 1945 article, Jamieson explained: 'unlike cloth-bound books, [the ASEs]

---

[1] Reprinted as the frontispiece to Robert Ballou, *A History of the Council on Books in Wartime, 1942-1946* (New York, 1946).

[2] A full list of titles is published in *Books in Action: The Armed Services Editions*, ed. by John Y. Cole (Washington, 1984), pp. 33-78. For an engaging overview see Daniel J. Miller, *Books Go to War: Armed Services Editions in World War II* (Charlottesville, Va., 1996).

[3] *Editions for Armed Services, Inc.: A History together with the Complete List of 1324 Books Published for American Armed Forces Overseas* (New York, 1948).

were not kept under guard, so to speak, on library and dayroom bookshelves. Soldiers did not have to sign for them and bring them back to the library after using them'.[4] The books' flimsy construction was also intended to assuage fears that they might endanger existing war markets. Early publicity materials stressed that the books'

> very physical nature will make it impossible to include them in libraries or to keep them on any permanent basis, and this is a part of our arrangement with the armed services which contemplate no change in plans for purchasing hard-bound books for library stocks.[5]

There is evidence to suggest that many ASEs were literally read to pieces. In June 1945, Major Merrill Moore reported:

> Your books are distributed every month through military channels in our hospitals and I have never seen one that was wasted, for each copy is read and re-read until the cover falls off or the book comes apart from excessive and continuous use.[6]

In letters to the CBW, and fan letters to authors, servicemen recounted sharing and swapping books. Director of the Army Library Service, Colonel Ray Trautman, returned from an overseas tour to inform the Council: 'It is not unusual for a man to tear off the portion of a book he has finished to give it to the next man who doesn't have a book to read, saying, "I'll save my pages for you"'.[7] Despite their ephemeral form, and distribution outside usual channels, however, the ASEs frequently were collected together, whether to supplement existing library stocks, create makeshift or informal libraries, or form the basis of private collections. In this chapter, I will explore the ways in which the ASEs were gathered together and argue that these collections expose two conceptions of the status and function of a library. Recent critics have noted 'the disjunction between book as object and book as

---

[4]   John Jamieson, 'Books and the Soldier', *Public Opinion Quarterly*, 9 (1945), 320-32 (pp. 322-23). The Navy policy was different: on 3 April 1944, Isabel Du Bois, Head of the Navy Library Section wrote to Philip Van Doren Stern to note: 'They are issued for use but not to the individual'. Princeton, Princeton University Library, Council on Books in Wartime (hereafter CBW) Archives, Box 26. Used by permission of Princeton University Library.

[5]   CBW, 'Armed Services Editions Plan', 5 May 1943, p. 2. CBW Archives, Box 6.

[6]   Letter to Spencer Scott, 23 June 1945. CBW Archives, Box 26.

[7]   Proceedings of the third Annual Meeting of the Council on Books in Wartime, 1945, pp. 10-11. CBW Archives, Box 1.

idea', and Valerie Holman's recognition that 'all books have a dual personality: as repositories of knowledge [... and] as physical objects' can be extended to the collection.[8] The institution of the library, whether as a place to house books or as a space for the circulation of ideas, is the product of more than one system of values. Collections of ASEs reveal a fault-line between one tradition which located democracy in the free movement of ideas epitomized by the public library, and another that sought to establish the exercise of consumer choice as the full expression of the democratic ideal.

I open this chapter by exploring the home-front rhetoric of the Council on Books in Wartime, which presented the library as an 'arsenal of ideas' within a liberal democracy. I move on to show that the supposedly expendable ASEs were brought together to form improvised libraries which functioned to create or support military identity, as well as to establish relationships among servicemen, even across national boundaries. Finally, I chart the mechanisms by which these flimsy, pocket-sized texts functioned for some soldiers as consumer objects and for others as the potential foundation for a personal collection.

An analysis of book collecting offers a challenge to the expanding literature on collecting more generally, as libraries sit uneasily within dominant paradigms of the collector as fetishist, or as one driven to preserve and re-articulate the past.[9] It is true of book collecting, as of other modes of formalised gathering, that much research 'has concentrated upon the meaning of individual items or groups of collected material rather than upon the significance of the collecting process'.[10] In this chapter, I chart the understandings and socioeconomic import

---

[8]   Susan Stewart, *On Longing: Narratives of the Miniature, the Gigantic, the Souvenir, the Collection* (Durham, 1993), p. xi; Valerie Holman, *Print for Victory: Book Publishing in England, 1939-1945* (London, 2008), p. 247.

[9]   Russell Belk, for example, suggests that if books are 'freely [...] read, or act as mementoes of family and experiences, these ordinary uses would disqualify them as part of a collection. If instead they are valued for their contribution to a set using either aesthetic or "scientific" criteria, then they are indeed a collection' ('Collectors and Collecting', in *Handbook of Material Culture*, ed. by Chris Tilley and others (Los Angeles, 2006), pp. 534-45 (p. 535)). Belk's taxonomy does little to account for the ways in which books may move between the categories of use and value, or the possibility that they may occupy both simultaneously.

[10]   Susan M. Pearce, *On Collecting: An Investigation Into Collecting in the European Tradition* (London, 1995), p. 6.

of the library that drove servicemen's and others' impulses towards acquisition and display. In doing so, I accept Baudrillard's claim that objects are 'profoundly related to subjectivity' but not, as he suggests, that objects constitute 'a mental realm over which I hold sway, a thing whose meaning is governed by myself alone'.[11] Rather, as Susan Pearce argues, the collection works not only to express but to produce the collector, forming 'part of the poetic through which individuals define themselves'.[12] The cultural meaning of particular objects is the product of numerous social, economic, and political transactions, many of which exist prior to their encounters with a given individual; collections help to define the proper place of their owners as much as owners attempt to place and organize their collections.

'A free library for a free people'

The Council on Books in Wartime was initially conceived of as a home-front operation, using books 'in the building and maintenance of the will to win', to 'expose the true nature of the enemy', provide 'technical information', 'sustain morale through relaxation and inspiration' and 'clarify our war aims and the problems of the peace'.[13] These activities cohered, in 1943, around the tenth anniversary of the Nazi book burnings. In speeches, bookstore display materials, cartoons, editorials, and reading lists, the Council and its associates contrasted the free circulation of knowledge in the USA with the censorship and alleged cultural brutality of the Nazi regime. Norton reminded attendees at the Boston Book Fair that 'a totalitarian and militarized nation has no place for the individual expression of the writer of books, nor for the individual interest of their readers', while J. J. Kavanagh informed Radio WHAS listeners that they were 'representatives of "a free library for a free people"'.[14] A July Fourth speech penned by the Writer's War Board reminded its hearers:

---

[11] Jean Baudrillard, 'The System of Collecting', trans. by Roger Cardinal, in *The Cultures of Collecting*, ed. by John Elsner and Roger Cardinal (London, 1994), pp. 7-24 (p. 7).
[12] Pearce, *On Collecting*, p. 28.
[13] 'Aims', n.d.. CBW Archives, Box 1.
[14] William Warder Norton, 'Opening Remarks', Boston Book Fair, 22 October 1943. CBW Archives, Box 13, p. 1; J. J. Kavanagh, 'They Burned the Books', Radio WHAS, 10 May 1943, p. 1. CBW Archives, Box 6.

we are fighting today lest this very spot be desecrated by a fire fed by the books within these walls, flung from their shelves where they have been available to all of us, and turned to smouldering ashes by the haters of freedom.[15]

As Paul Fussell notes, this rhetoric contributed to an 'anti-totalitarian, anti-uniformitarian stance, a way of honoring the pluralism and exuberance of the "democratic" Allied cause'.[16] At the same time, Trysh Travis suggests, for members of the publishing industry, the war 'provided a set of images and discourses that linked books and reading to a high political purpose, thus dignifying the project of outreach'.[17]

Thomas Augst argues that the great American public libraries valued books 'not as *goods* – private property that enforced educational and social distinctions – but a public good, whose benefit to community required popular circulation and use'.[18] The July Fourth speech is telling, however, in its revelation that the 'public good' of knowledge was anchored in a series of physical 'goods'. Having hailed the library as 'an arsenal of ideas', the writer paused to assess the term's utility: 'because the word "arsenal" suggests that this building is impregnable [...] that the thousands of volumes it contains will always be here, to pass on the ideas of the world's great thinkers to our children and to their children'.[19] Though the speech argues that the USA is not 'fighting for material things [...] but for the preservation and the continued existence of the truths and ideals housed in this very library', its insistence on the imperilled status of those truths is couched in terms that reveal the vulnerability of the physical book and the material location of ideals. While, on the one hand, the library operated as the physical and ideological home of the ideas contained in

---

[15]   Writers' War Board, 'July Fourth Speech', n.d., pp. 5-6. CBW Archives, Box 6.

[16]   Paul Fussell, *Wartime: Understanding and Behaviour in the Second World War* (Oxford, 1989), p. 245. See also Christopher P. Loss, 'Reading Between Enemy Lines: Armed Services Editions and World War II', *The Journal of Military History*, 67 (2003), 811-34.

[17]   Trysh Travis, 'Books as Weapons and "The Smart Man's Peace": The Work of the Council on Books in Wartime', *Princeton University Library Chronicle*, 1999 (60), 353-99 (p. 362).

[18]   Thomas Augst, 'Introduction', in *Institutions of Reading: The Social Life of Libraries in the United States*, ed. by Thomas Augst and Kenneth Carpenter (Amherst, 2007), pp. 1-23 (p. 11).

[19]   Writers' War Board, 'July Fourth Speech', n.d., p. 6. CBW Archives, Box 6.

books, it was only the circulation and reading of those books which would ensure the preservation of their contents.

Members of the CBW and ASE Selection Committee were committed to the powerful ideological connection between 'public access to books and education' and 'the onward march of democracy in the United States'.[20] In this, they paralleled innovations such as the creation of the Special Services Division, with its recreational, educational and welfare remit, and the foundation of the Armed Forces Institute three weeks after the attack on Pearl Harbor.[21] An anonymised letter from a former associate of the Council, however, reveals a tension between education as a hallmark of democracy and publishers' awareness that increasing literacy was linked to growing sales. Describing the ship he was on as 'a floating library', he continued: 'I bet dollars to G. I. Spam that half the men on it never cracked a book before'. The sight, the writer noted, 'would touch your salesman's heart [...]. [I]t is easy to guess that book sales should really boom in our post war world'.[22]

'Welcome to the Stork Club'

For troops stationed on USA soil, the United Services Organisation (hereafter USO) provided library facilities which depended largely on donations, leading, as Holman notes of the British experience, to the problem that 'the reading tastes of soldiers did not always coincide with those of the bodies responsible for collecting and sorting the books'.[23] Speaking to a home-front audience, Lieutenant J. C. Kennan noted:

> U.S.O. libraries [...] are generally scant in quantity as well as in quality. This is the natural result when collections are made as the result of voluntary gifts of well-meaning persons. One chap told me that as he explored the shelves of a local U.S.O. library he found such stuff as WHOM GOD HATH SUNDERED, A FIRST COURSE IN EMBALMING, HOW

---

[20]   Augst, 'Introduction', p. 2.

[21]   For contemporary commentary on both organizations, see Fred K. Hoehler, 'Services for Men in the Armed Forces', *The Social Service Review*, 16 (1942), 389-400 and Spencer D. Benbow, 'University of the Armed Forces', *Journal of Educational Sociology*, 16 (1943), 577-90.

[22]   Anonymous Letter, Somewhere at Sea, n.d.. CBW Archives, Box 32.

[23]   Holman, *Print for Victory*, p. 45.

TO BE A MOTHER'S HELPER, and GIVE PROHIBITION A CHANCE.[24]

Kennan acknowledged that 'In happy contrast, many of the older camps have well-established and well-supervised libraries'. These were run by the Army Library Service; in 1945, Captain John Jamieson, Assistant Executive Officer of the Library Branch, reported that in the Hawaiian and Marianas Islands alone 'there are over two thousand portable libraries of forty volumes each in operation, and thirty field libraries of five hundred to one thousand volumes each'.[25]

In some battalions and camps, ASEs were used to supplement existing library provision. John Cuddeback recalled the moment when his jeep carrier's 'small ship's crew library' produced a box of ASEs and 'we grabbed them up like children with a box of chocolates'.[26] At Pearl Harbor the ASEs were 'exceptionally valuable [...] because most of the inmates of such places are transit trade [...] and the regular library will not loan books out to us'. As Cuddeback continued his journey 'our collection [of ASEs] again augmented the library of the ship we took to Guam', where they discovered 'a complete library of your books in a Quansit hut, for us transits'. While celebrating the ability of the ASEs to circulate outside the usual library channels, Cuddeback also revealed an impulse to integrate them conceptually with existing library provision. He was able to fulfil that urge when he got a job in a navy library: 'with it's [sic] four thousands or so standard bound books, and with two complete shelves of your pocket books, we have a well rounded establishment'.[27]

Another service librarian, Corporal Max Schaffner, wrote to William Sloane, of Henry Holt & Co., asking:

> May I bid you welcome to the STORK CLUB, the smartest community center and library for the GI's in the jungles of New Guinea. The library consists of seven cases, five of which contain cloth bounds, one of Council books, and one of Pocket Book detectives. The walls are adorned with

---

[24] J. C. Keenan, 'Books for the Armed Services', delivered at the Books in Wartime Institute, Minneapolis, n.d., p. 3. CBW Archives, Box 19.
[25] Jamieson, 'Books and the Soldier', p. 321.
[26] Letter to Editions for the Armed Services, Inc., n.d.. CBW Archives, Box 32.
[27] Ibid.

maps of the world, a Picasso, two Dega's [*sic*], a Van Gogh, and this week's exhibit of colored photographs of Arizona wildflowers.[28]

The address at the top of Shaffner's letter is 'THE STORK CLUB, New Guinea's Smartest Nite Spot operated by the fourth platoon of the twelfth special service company'. Transplanting the nightclub from the fashionable streets of New York to the jungles of South-East Asia, Schaffner at once emphasized the platoon's distance from literate USA society, and established their continuing status as consumers of contemporary cultural goods. At the same time, the Stork Club participated in a project which mirrored the missionary functions of early American libraries. Colonial foundations established the library as 'an outstation of civilization in the wilderness' and demonstrated that 'civilization was transportable and sustainable'.[29] Though the ironic and playful tone of the Stork Club project is apparent, it nonetheless allowed its membership 'not only to solidify their own aspirations and status, but to convert the personally anxious, socially fragile colonial enterprise into the permanent structure and impersonal offices of "culture"'.[30] The club showcased a delicately achieved balance between the maintenance of civilized culture away from home, and an ironic sense of the performativity of that enterprise which reinforced military camaraderie.

Some libraries were considerably less sophisticated than the Stork Club, with its revolving programme of exhibitions. The Readers' Adviser at the Tompkins Square Branch of the New York Public Library reported a conversation with 'one of the boys on furlough from the Italian battlefront' who was 'made librarian for his unit. The books were all collected and brought up to a position to which the boys could crawl from their fox holes.'[31] This soldier's appointment as 'librarian' was clearly informal, yet books which were circulating along the unofficial channels of sharing and swapping were nonetheless brought together to order and manage the unit's scarce literary resources.

---

[28] Letter, n.d.. CBW Archives, Box 32.

[29] James Raven, 'Social Libraries and Library Societies in Eighteenth-Century North America', in *Institutions of Reading*, ed. by Augst and Carpenter, pp. 24-52 (pp. 41, 37).

[30] Augst, 'Introduction', p. 7.

[31] Extract from a report from the Readers' Adviser at Tompkins Square Branch, NYPL, 1944. CBW Archives, Box 26.

Makeshift service libraries were not a new phenomenon. Writing about British troops in the First World War, Mary Hammond and Shafquat Towheed note that 'impromptu lending libraries sprang up in all theatres'.[32] A former civilian librarian whose unit was posted to England shortly before the Normandy Landings in 1944 recalled that:

> the dearth of reading matter inspired my buying an armful of English novels with which I set up a miniscule lending library within my company. [...] Then we received our first set of Council Books. They were so much more attractive (in content, that is) than the English novels that I went quickly out of business, cheerfully pocketed my loss, and joined the enthusiastic audience.[33]

Libraries might be as informal as 'an armful of English novels' or on as small a scale as the box witnessed by a Corporal in New Guinea, which was built to hold three or four ASEs and fastened to the wall of the engine compartment of a landing boat.[34] Some attest to considerable ingenuity. Lieutenant Tom Casner informed the Council:

> We were on a British troop transport for a while, and we gave the British fellows access to our library – a crate of A.S.E.'s mounted on two oil drums on "B" Deck. [...] One of the English officers described your work as "Smashing" [...]. Many of the English fellows shook their heads and marvelled at how well taken care of the American soldier is.[35]

In the cramped conditions of a British transport ship, USA servicemen created a secure social and cultural location through the makeshift reproduction of the library as a communal space as well as a symbol of American culture and comfort. The ASEs appear here as an object of display which helped to negotiate national boundaries and the local politics of Anglo-American wartime cooperation.

Several other soldiers used the ASEs to forge links with Allied troops. Private Connor of RAF Thame wrote that he had occasionally been stationed alongside USA troops and that: 'At such times I have been able to share some of their literature, published & distributed by

---

[32] Mary Hammond and Shafquat Towheed, 'Introduction', in *Publishing in the First World War: Essays in Book History*, ed. by M. Hammond and S. Towheed (Basingstoke, 2007), pp. 1-8 (p. 5).

[33] Cited in Jamieson, *Editions for the Armed Services*, pp. 30-31.

[34] Ballou, *History*, p. 82.

[35] Letter to CBW, n.d.. CBW Archives, Box 31.

your council, and have thoroughly enjoyed it.'[36] Connor's letter
moves quickly from these recollections to his real purpose: attempting
to attain books he had begun to read as ASEs but been unable to finish.
The Council received numerous requests for particular titles. Corporal
Al Adlen, for example, asked the Council 'if you can mail me the
Book "A Tree Grows in Brooklyn" by Betty Smith listed as number
D-117, I've heard a lot about this book, and would like to read it'.[37]
Where Adlen phrased his request in terms of the desire to read, others
were explicit about the urge to possess, and ownership marks and
signatures are evident on a number of surviving copies (see Figure 1).
Some requested books on behalf of a company or group, like the thirty
men who signed a letter suggesting the publication of 'a good dictionary'. The joint composition and subscription of the letter suggests the
extent to which conversation around the books could be used to
confirm group, as well as personal, identity. These men saw the ASEs
as circulating, social objects, commenting: 'we ourselves would like
copies to reread and pass among friends as has been our pleasure with
other titles in the series'.[38] David Weisman, in contrast, wrote to the
Council, asking:

> Could you lend or give me copies of The Making of Modern Britain,
> George Washington Carver, Three Times I Bow, and others which deal
> with current events and the post-war world, such as My Native Land? Of
> course, I should like to own them.[39]

'My own small private library'

The desire to own ASEs undermined the Council's assertion that the
books were inherently uncollectible, thanks to their expendable design.
Most remarkable to CBW members may have been some soldiers' desire
to use the ASEs as the basis for a personal library. Ensign Jerry Bick
wrote in businesslike terms to W. W. Norton, noting: 'I would like to
know if it is possible to obtain several of these editions for my own
postwar library.'[40] Sergeant Harry Brown admitted that he had shipped

36 Letter dated 1 March 1946. CBW Archives, Box 31.
37 Undated postcard. CBW Archives, Box 32.
38 Undated letter. CBW Archives, Box 32.
39 Letter dated 19 November 1944. CBW Archives, Box 32.
40 Letter to W. W. Norton, 4 January 1945. CBW Archives, Box 32.

Fig. 1 Alexandre Pernikoff, *"Bushido": The Anatomy of Terror* (CBW, 1943), showing the ownership mark of 'P. R. Kynaston', and Robert Fontaine, *The Happy Time* (CBW, 1945) marked 'JEM'. From the author's collection

home 'a large number' of ASEs 'which particularly interested me and which I wanted in my library', but showed an awareness of the Council's determination to see the books circulate, writing: 'I have realized since then that sending these books home, and thus removing them circulation [*sic*] among the soldiers, was not right.'[41] Private Alfred J. Fallot explained that the books would allow him to fulfil the long-term aspiration of 'having my own small private library'.[42]

---

41 Letter dated 24 March 1945. CBW Archives, Box 32.
42 Letter, n.d. CBW Archives, Box 31.

Private Irvin Furgus was explicit: 'All my life I've wanted a library of good books but financial considerations have made it an impossibility. Your "Armed Forces Library" may make that goal be realized.'[43]

What is perhaps most telling about Furgus's request is his re-christening of the disparate ASE texts as the 'Armed Forces Library', and his desire to know 'how I might obtain the complete library as my own'.[44] The packaging of a small collection of books as a domestic library goes back to at least the late nineteenth century when the pages of the Sears, Roebuck catalogue offered purchasers 'a complete library', including the oak veneer shelf.[45] As Janice Radway notes, schemes like the 'Little Leather Library' in the 1910s established the idea of the off-the-shelf library as an object that could 'endow its owner with the status and legitimacy associated with learning and the school'.[46] The desire to own a collection of books was in part prompted by what Thomas Augst describes as the late nineteenth- and early twentieth-century 'institutionalization of leisure as moral education, where individuals acquired the capacity for self-government requisite to the circumstances of a mobile and heterogeneous society'.[47] Sergeant David Bradley expressed something of this sentiment when he wrote to Editions for the Armed Services, stating: 'I can't tell you how they make otherwise wasteful time into that of learning, and knowledge, and a broadening in one's education'.[48] Books provided a means to acquire the education necessary to those who aspired to become members of the white-collar economy, and at the same time marked their owner as possessing the cultural capital needed to participate in social and political life.

Radway argues that the success of the Little Leather Library depended upon its combination of cheapness and the aura of quality produced by the binding material, which offered consumers 'in addition to a series of individual and ephemeral books to read [...] a

---

43   Letter dated 20 February 1945. CBW Archives, Box 31.
44   Corporal Richard C. Johnson, for example, asked to receive 'a book listed in your Fighting Forces Series' (letter to Macmillan Co., 11 March 1945). CBW Archives, Box 32.
45   See Augst, 'Introduction', p. 13.
46   Janice Radway, *A Feeling for Books: The Book-of-the-Month Club, Literary Taste, and Middle-Class Desire* (Chapel Hill, 1997), p. 137.
47   Thomas Augst, 'Faith in Reading: Public Libraries, Liberalism, and the Civil Religion', in *Institutions of Reading*, ed. by Augst and Carpenter, pp. 148-83 (p. 154).
48   Letter dated 8 July 1945. CBW Archives, Box 32.

collection of potentially permanent, respected, almost sacred objects – a set of things to own'.[49] The ASEs, however, followed in the footsteps of a newer trend which showed that paperback books too could be appropriated as libraries. Series including Pocket Books (launched 1939), Avon Books (1941), and most particularly the Popular Library (1942) and the launch of the Viking Portable Library with Alexander Woollcott's anthology *As You Were: A Portable Library of American Prose and Poetry Assembled For Members of the Armed Forces and the Merchant Marine* (1943), created a sense of serial publications, and even individual anthologies, as coherent library collections which could be used to shape reading practice and direct acquisition. Paul Fussell reports that: 'Before shipping out, [one] ensign had checked off in a catalogue of the Modern Library the titles he wanted to read [...] and every month his father sent him four books.'[50]

The CBW was aware that readers saw contemporary books as objects to own as well as to read, noting, in their advertisement for *A Bell for Adano*, selected as a home-front wartime 'Imperative', that it should be 'part of your permanent library'.[51] That servicemen saw the ASEs – those cheaply-produced, expendable books which Council members assumed would resist retention or collection – as a library in their own right demonstrates how prevalent the desire for a domestic library had become by the 1940s. The cheerful, uniform covers of the books contributed to the perception that they constituted a coherent collection, as did their serialization: servicemen frequently requested the books by number as well as title. Each ASE contained, inside its back cover, a list of other available titles, perpetuating the sense that the books shared some intrinsic connection. *Yank, the Army Weekly* published a list of each month's ASE publications until Mess Sergeant Joe McCarthy, the magazine's managing editor, wrote to Philip Van Doren Stern, Director of Editions for the Armed Services, Inc., explaining:

---

[49]   Radway, *A Feeling for Books*, p. 160.
[50]   Fussell, *Wartime*, p. 237. Michael Hackenberg charts the long history of cheap paperback publishing: 'The Tauchnitz editions of the 1840s were tied to the opening of the Leipzig-Dresden railroad line and the need for railway reading. During the same period, vast numbers of cheaply manufactured "dime novels" of the Beadles and their imitators poured forth in thousands of titles in the paper-wrapped "library" series of cheap fiction' (Michael Hackenberg, 'The Armed Services Editions in Publishing History', in *Books in Action*, ed. by Cole, pp. 15-21 (p. 15)).
[51]   *A Bell for Adano*, 'Imperative' flyer. CBW Archives, Box 8.

> In the opinion of our overseas editors and correspondents, the average
> soldier in a foreign theater makes no use of the YANK listings in the se-
> lection of Armed Services Editions for his own use. He isn't able to read
> in YANK about a particularly issued book and then go out and obtain it.
> He makes his choice from whatever books happen to be available in his
> unit. If the book he wants happens to be there, he takes it. If it isn't, he
> merely takes whatever else is available.[52]

McCarthy suggests that in listing available titles, Editions for the
Armed Services created an illusion of choice that was not borne out by
soldiers' experience. In writing to the CBW to request particular titles,
however, servicemen reasserted their selective agency, establishing at
once their ability to discriminate between the 'goods' on offer (Sergeant David Bradley complained of being 'swamped by your merchan-
dise') and their familiarity with a language of rights predicated upon
consumer choice.[53]

As T. H. Breen notes, in charting the pre-revolutionary emergence
of USA consumer culture, the perception of '*choice* as a *right* [...]
indicated that the daily experience of making selections from among
competing goods and of spending one's money however one desired
[had acquired] an ideological voice'.[54] Private Bernie Abramson's June
1945 letter to Editions for the Armed Services, Inc., captures this voice
in striking terms. Protesting that sixteen pages were missing from his
ASE copy of William Ben Ames's *Strange Woman*, Abramson explained:

> I appreciate the fact that these books are sent to us gratis, but even so, in
> such condition they aren't worth anything. I, for one, feel that I would
> prefer to pay the full price, as accustomed, and get a book in perfect con-
> dition.[55]

In this demand for the right to pay, and hence control the processes of
selection, we witness the tension between the cheap production and
unrestrained circulation of the ASEs, based on an ideal of democracy

---

[52] Letter dated 7 March 1945. CBW Archives, Box 21.
[53] Letter dated 4 August 1945. CBW Archives, Box 32.
[54] T. H. Breen, *The Marketplace of Revolution: How Consumer Politics Shaped American Independence* (Oxford, 2004), p. 184. On early colonial libraries and the 'ideal of learned reading' as constitutive of 'a purported democracy of understanding and egalitarian improvement' see Raven, 'Social Libraries and Library Societies', pp. 49-50.
[55] Letter dated 26 June 1945. CBW Archives, Box 32.

rooted in the free dissemination of knowledge, and an alternative mode of democracy embedded in the practice of circulation and exchange.

Alongside the impulse towards opening culture to the 'general reader' even while attempting to delimit and improve that reader's tastes, the domestic library speaks to an enduring association between book ownership and economic as well as cultural capital. The possession of a library, even in the unlikely form of a collection of pocket-size paperbacks, expressed soldiers' aspirations towards 'the larger privileges and power that came with owning property'.[56] Where Susan Stewart suggests that the collection functions as a way of bringing the past into contact with the present, marking 'the place where history is transformed into space, into property', servicemen seeking to form a library of ASEs looked not for souvenirs but for ways of constructing the future.[57] The anticipated library did transform the books into property, but it did so by creating an imagined domestic space. The physical form of the books inevitably establishes their link to the material context of wartime experience, but unlike Stewart's souvenir, which 'reaches only "behind"', the form of the ASEs as items in a potentially complete collection rendered them the object of future ambitions rather than of memory.[58]

Corporal Irving Dropkin, who read ASEs whilst recuperating in an English hospital, wrote to the Council to explain that: 'Upon discharge from the Armed Force [sic], I would like to build up a library of these books.'[59] Graham L. Johnson, who wrote from China to request an unabridged copy of *The Moonstone*, claimed: 'I won't be able to rest in peace until I know that book is at my home waiting for me until I get back there.'[60] These letters establish the book collection not only as a set of texts but as a future space within the home. In this, they illustrate Joanna Bourke's contention that for most serving men 'home remained the touchstone for all their actions'.[61] As Radway notes, from as early as the 1920s, articles in magazines like *Good Housekeeping* and *House Beautiful* not only established the book as furniture, but

---

[56]   Augst, 'Introduction', p. 4.
[57]   Stewart, *On Longing*, p. xii.
[58]   Ibid., p. 135.
[59]   Letter dated 17 March 1945. CBW Archives, Box 31.
[60]   Letter dated 20 March 1945. CBW Archives, Box 32.
[61]   Joanna Bourke, *Dismembering the Male: Men's Bodies, Britain, and the Great War* (London, 1996), p. 22.

endowed books 'with a halo of meaning and an attendant affect' which could imbue a house with 'sentiment and feeling'.[62] The imagined ASE 'library' was predicated upon the book as item of display: in a domestic collection books are 'seen, by family, friends and visitors, and so they have a role which is, as it were, public in a private setting. [...] And, as part of doing this, they help to define the functions of rooms, and separate one from another'.[63] Just such a library is conjured in the bookplate of Shirlee and Murray Berger (see Figure 2) which survives in copies of *The Fireside Book of Verse* (a 'made' book compiled by Louis Untermeyer) and William March's *Some Like Them Short*.

Fig. 2 The Fireside Book of Verse, ed. by Louis Untermeyer (CBW, 1945), showing the bookplate of Shirlee and Murray Berger. From the author's collection

Through its title *The Fireside Book of Verse* invites the serviceman to imagine precisely the domestic scene depicted in the Berger's bookplate, in which the library and the hearth become one. The format of the ASEs, however, adds a particular charge to their potential display as the locus of culture: where *Good Housekeeping* and *House Beautiful* attempted to establish the correct display of books as the domain of the housewife, moving away from the masculinity of a study stocked with leather-bound volumes, the ASEs suggest a decisively male-oriented domestic space, one that remains bound to the materiality of wartime experience.

---

[62] Radway, *A Feeling for Books*, p. 148.
[63] Pearce, *On Collecting*, p. 258. As Pearce notes, in a perhaps defensive aside, we must distinguish the spatially ambitious displays of collectors of first editions from 'those who buy books to read, and who put them on visible shelving because they like to feel them close' (p. 259).

'An interesting momento [*sic*] of World War II'

In 1944, Lt. Col. Wendell Davis wrote to Margaret Lesser at Double-day and Doran to explain that he found it difficult to secure ASEs

> through Army channels and it occurred to me that I might, with your assistance, be able to make a personal investment which would not only assist me in my work here but would also give me an interesting momento [*sic*] of World War II.[64]

Davis worked at the Army Air Forces Redistribution Center in Atlantic City, and his request is markedly different from those put forward by men on active service. For Davis, the books were neither necessary reading matter nor the foundation of a personal library. Instead, they occupied the nostalgic ground of the souvenir, working to move the present realities of war into the realm of the remembered past. The ASEs trajectory towards the collection or souvenir and away from the library or reading text has continued. Roy Meador, writing for *Book Source Magazine*, complained:

> When I recall their ready availability during wartime, I regret my collecting antennae weren't focused on saving more of these unique volumes from extinction. The general practice was to treat them as expendables, handle them freely, and pass them along to others. [...] Now the unexpected discovery of an ASE in a secondhand bookstore can awaken memories and provide another rare memento of mid-20th century wars.[65]

Meador, while recalling fondly the camaraderie of exchange created by the books' expendable format, nonetheless regrets his earlier lack of an acquisitive impulse, though such an urge would have altered the structures and memories the books are now perceived to preserve.

Thirty-nine years after the cessation of hostilities, Matthew J. Bruccoli reflected upon his memories of the ASEs, stressing that his recollections were wholly divorced from the books' wartime context: 'I wasn't there when they were passing out the Armed Services Editions. I'm not certain when I first saw one; but it was around 1955 while I was a graduate student at the University of Virginia.' Bruccoli, who now possesses an almost complete collection of ASEs, notes that

---

[64]   Letter dated 11 May 1944. CBW Archives, Box 31.
[65]   Roy Meador, 'Books, Wars, and the ASEs', *Book Source Magazine*, <http://www.booksourcemagazine.com/story.php?sid=17> [Accessed 4 February 2010].

his interest was piqued by ASEs of Fitzgerald's *The Great Gatsby* and *The Diamond as Big as the Ritz and Other Stories*, and comments that a number of 'made' books (those published only as ASEs) 'qualify as first-and-only editions and are mandatory items in an author collection', incorporating the books within the terms of a broader, author-centred bibliophilia.[66] Bruccoli self-deprecatingly admits:

> I was slow to understand that the ASE provided a collecting situation with necessary elements for the long haul: There were many titles; they were cheap; they were hard to find (many of them were left behind in Europe and the Pacific). But these characteristics also apply to bottle caps. The key element was literary or cultural value, and I belatedly recognized that the ASE possessed such value as a series in addition to the desirability of individual titles.[67]

The ASEs, whose 'very physical nature' was supposed to make it 'impossible to include them in libraries or to keep them on any permanent basis' have become not potential libraries (though several libraries hold complete or almost complete sets) but collections. It is ironic that it is, in part, the characteristic, and supposedly expendable, design of the books that now marks them out as an enduring part of the USA's cultural heritage, and a compelling memento of wartime experience: an experience that the first ASE collectors sought to reframe or escape, whether through the excitement offered by reading or the imagined security of a post-war, domestic library.

---

[66] Matthew J. Bruccoli, 'Recollections of an ASE Collector', in *Books in Action*, ed. by Cole, pp. 25-28 (p.25).
[67] Bruccoli, 'Recollections', p. 26.

Index